Irish Theatre in the Twenty-First Century

Irish Theatre in the Twenty-First Century

NICHOLAS GRENE

OXFORD
UNIVERSITY PRESS

OXFORD
UNIVERSITY PRESS

Great Clarendon Street, Oxford, OX2 6DP,
United Kingdom

Oxford University Press is a department of the University of Oxford.
It furthers the University's objective of excellence in research, scholarship,
and education by publishing worldwide. Oxford is a registered trade mark of
Oxford University Press in the UK and in certain other countries

© Nicholas Grene 2024

The moral rights of the author have been asserted

All rights reserved. No part of this publication may be reproduced, stored in
a retrieval system, or transmitted, in any form or by any means, without the
prior permission in writing of Oxford University Press, or as expressly permitted
by law, by licence or under terms agreed with the appropriate reprographics
rights organization. Enquiries concerning reproduction outside the scope of the
above should be sent to the Rights Department, Oxford University Press, at the
address above

You must not circulate this work in any other form
and you must impose this same condition on any acquirer

Published in the United States of America by Oxford University Press
198 Madison Avenue, New York, NY 10016, United States of America

British Library Cataloguing in Publication Data

Data available

Library of Congress Control Number: 2024940106

ISBN 9780198893073

DOI: 10.1093/oso/9780198893073.001.0001

Printed and bound by
CPI Group (UK) Ltd, Croydon, CR0 4YY

Links to third party websites are provided by Oxford in good faith and
for information only. Oxford disclaims any responsibility for the materials
contained in any third party website referenced in this work.

For Anna, Ella, Gerry, Lorelei, Maureen, Sinéad, and Tanya

Acknowledgements

Some of the materials in this book appeared first elsewhere and I am grateful to the editors of the books and journals who gave me the opportunity to publish them as follows:

Chapter 1: 'Against Eloquence: Irish Drama in Century's End' [in Polish], *Acta Universitatis Lodziensis: Folia Litteraria Polonica*, 24.2 (2014), 7–27.

'Contemporary Irish Theatre: The Way We Live Now?', in Werner Huber, Margarete Rubik, and Julia Novak (eds.), *Contemporary Drama in English: Staging Interculturality* (Trier: Wissenschlaftliker Verlag Trier, 2010).

State of Play 1: 'Snapshots: A Year in the Life of a Theatre Judge', in Donald E. Morse (ed.), *Irish Theatre in Transition* (Basingstoke: Palgrave Macmillan, 2015).

State of Play 2: 'Re-Running the Rising: Centenary Stagings', *Hungarian Journal of English and American Studies*, 25.2 (2019), 325-39.

I have benefited enormously from interviews kindly granted me by Lian Bell, Selina Cartmell, Anne Clarke, Sarah Durcan, Niall Henry, Garry Hynes, Raymond Keane, Louise Lowe, Caitríona McLaughlin, Gavin Quinn, Lynne Parker, and Annie Ryan.

For access to archival material, I gratefully acknowledge the help of Mairead Delaney (Abbey Theatre), Barry Houlihan (Hardiman Library, University of Galway), and Gemma Reeves (Rough Magic).

My grateful thanks to Julie Bates, who read an initial outline of this project and gave me much needed encouragement, and to Adrian Frazier who offered very helpful criticism on drafts of two of the chapters.

One of the privileges of working in the School of English, Trinity College Dublin, has been the opportunity to offer specialist courses to advanced undergraduates. I have benefited from workshopping the ideas in the book with several groups of students who took my course on contemporary Irish theatre over the years.

The book is dedicated to Ella Daly, Gerry Godley, Lorelei Harris, Maureen Kennelly, Sinéad Mac Aodha, Tanya Dean, and Anna Walsh, my fellow judges on the *Irish Times* Irish Theatre Awards, as an affectionate tribute to their companionship on the road. We did not invariably agree in our judgements, but the discussions were always friendly and decisions on nominees and winners made by consensus. However, they bear no responsibility for the views expressed in the book which are all my own.

Contents

List of Figures	viii
Introduction	1

PART I. MAKING IT NEW

1. Changing Generations, Changing Styles: Irish Theatre in the 1990s	7
2. Belated Avant-Garde	23
3. Re-Imagining Synge	44
State of Play 1: 2006	58

PART II. PAST AND PRESENT

4. Live History	77
5. After the Troubles	96
6. Strategies of Adaptation	119
State of Play 2: 2016	137

PART III. THE POLITICS OF GENDER

7. Waking the Feminists: Women's Voices	155
8. Masculinity and Its Discontents	165
9. Women Writing Women	185
State of Play 3: 2020–2	205
Conclusion	220
Bibliography	223
Index	232

List of Figures

1. Michael Gambon as Joe in Gate Theatre production of *Eh Joe*. Photographer Anthony Woods. Courtesy of Gate Theatre and James Hardiman Library, University of Galway.   62
2. Tadgh Murphy, Rory Nolan, Rory Keenan, Peter Daly, and Barry McGovern in Rough Magic production of *The Taming of the Shrew*. Photographer Patrick Redmond. Courtesy of Rough Magic.   64
3. Andrew Bennett, Louise Lewis, Tom Murphy, Janet Moran, Derbhle Crotty, Mark O'Halloran, and Simon Rice in the Corn Exchange production of *Everyday* by Michael West in collaboration with the company as part of Dublin Theatre Festival 2006. Photographer Paul McCarthy. Courtesy of the Corn Exchange.   71
4. Sandra O'Malley, Barry Cullen, Brian F. Devaney, and John Carty in Blue Raincoat production of *Shackleton*. Photographer Peter Martin. Courtesy of Blue Raincoat.   139
5. Manus Halligan and Liz Fitzgerald with audience members in the Fishamble production of *Inside the GPO*. Photographer Patrick Redmond. Courtesy of Fishamble.   140
6. Jonathan Gunning and Zita Monaghan in Branar's production of *Maloney's Dream / Brionglóid Maloney*. Photographer Anita Murphy. Courtesy Branar.   144
7. Mahnoor Saad in the Abbey Theatre production of *The Plough and the Stars*. Photographer Ros Kavanagh. Courtesy of Abbey Theatre.   147
8. Jack Gleeson with virtual audience member in the Dead Centre production of *To Be a Machine (Version 1.0)*. Photographer Ste Murray. Courtesy of Dead Centre.   208
9. Will Thompson and Luke Murphy with audience member in the Luke Murphy Attic Projects production of *Volcano*. Photographer Emilija Jefremova. Courtesy of Luke Murphy Attic Projects.   210
10. Matthew Malone in the Gate Theatre production of *Once before I Go*. Photographer Ros Kavanagh. Courtesy of Gate Theatre.   213
11. Maeve O'Mahony, Patrick Martins, Jolly Abraham, and Mara Allen in the Abbey Theatre production of *An Octoroon*. Photographer Ros Kavanagh. Courtesy of Abbey Theatre.   218

Introduction

For three different periods, 2006, 2016, and 2020-2, I served as a judge for the *Irish Times* Irish Theatre Awards. The brief of the three-person panel was, as far as possible, to attend all new Irish productions of plays and operas across the island of Ireland for a full calendar year, and put forward nominations for outstanding achievement in a number of different categories: Best Actor, Best Actress, and so on.[1] My practice was to write up one or two pages of notes immediately after seeing a show and to file these along with the programmes. Without those fresh impressions, it would have been impossible for me to remember the details of what I had seen. Each year—with the exception of the 2020-1 Covid lockdown period—I saw between 120 and 150 performances, and over time I accumulated nineteen fat ring-bound folders full of these records. What if anything could be done with such an archive? Theatre is by definition an ephemeral art; if you miss seeing a production, it is gone. Very few of the plays I saw have been revived—some were not even intended to be capable of revival.[2] I decided that it might be worth offering a sample for each period as an overview of what the experience had been like. That is the basis for the three sections of the book which I have called 'State of Play', and which I have set apart from the numbered chapters by way of reports on Irish theatre for the years 2006, 2016, and 2020-2.

While I wanted to provide this sense of specific moments in contemporary Irish theatre, the book was also conceived in some part as a sequel to *The Politics of Irish Drama* which I published in 1999. I looked to consider how Irish theatre has changed and developed in the new millennium. In the earlier book I had been largely concerned with plays and playwrights, as the subtitle 'From Boucicault to Friel' indicated. But my concern here is with the broader business of theatre rather than just play texts and their impact. My design is to look at the proliferation of theatre companies and styles in the contemporary period, and the emergence of a changed theatrical landscape.

---

[1] For full details, see https://irishtheatre.ie/resources-page.aspx?contentid=148#:~:text=Categories%3A%20Best%20Actor%2C%20Best%20Actress,Special%20Award%2C%20Special%20Tribute%20Award (accessed 26 December 2023).

[2] For plays that have not been published, the Irish Playography is an invaluable resource: https://www.irishplayography.com/

Part I is focused on the impulse to make it new. Already in the 1990s there was a revolt against the association of Irish drama with lyrical language, challenged by playwrights such as Martin McDonagh, Billy Roche, Conor McPherson, Enda Walsh, and Mark O'Rowe working instead with broken, ungainly, inarticulate speech (Chapter 1). At the same time, there came a determination to break free of text-centred drama altogether, and to make use of all the resources of theatre: stylized movement and image, shows generated by an ensemble rather than authored by a single playwright. Companies looked at in Chapter 2, Barabbas, Blue Raincoat, The Corn Exchange, and Pan Pan, introduced avant-garde styles that were well established elsewhere in Britain, continental Europe, and the US, but were radically experimental in Ireland. For all the movement away from text, one dimension of the work of these companies was to revisit and re-imagine Irish canonical plays. Chapter 3 is devoted to the case of Synge, first major playwright of the national theatre movement, and the ways in which twenty-first-century directors sought alternative methods to make his plays available to contemporary audiences: Garry Hynes with her marathon DruidSynge; versions of *The Playboy* from Niall Henry's physical theatre interpretation in the Peacock, through Gavin Quinn's Chinese-language production for Pan Pan, and the Abbey's updated version by Bisi Adigun and Roddy Doyle which made the Mahons Nigerian immigrants in gangland Dublin.

Modern Ireland has changed rapidly, arguably more in the last thirty years than at any time in the previous century and a half, going from a poor, largely agricultural country, on the edge of the developed modern world, to the point where it was rated as one of the most globalized countries in the world. Irish theatre reflected this modernized, secularized society, going from the frenzy of its new Celtic Tiger riches to the trauma of its collapse. But it continued also to have to deal with the legacies of what went before. Part II of the book deals with the relationship of past and present as shown in the period. In the theatre of the twentieth century, preoccupied as it was with the representation of national identity, Irish history figured prominently. I analyse in Chapter 4 the ways in which received historical narratives were deconstructed by the playfulness of Donal O'Kelly's one-man show *Catalpa* (Red Kettle) and the spoof musical *Improbable Frequency* by Arthur Riordan and Bell Helicopter (Rough Magic), but also the exposure of the suppressed histories of inner-city Dublin by Louise Lowe in ANU's Monto Cycle. Nothing showed more dramatically the continuing impact of Ireland's past colonial history in the modern period than the thirty years of political violence in the North of Ireland. Though the Good Friday Agreement of 1998 brought a measure of peace, playwrights Owen McCafferty, David Ireland, Stacey Gregg, Michael Patrick, and Oisin Kearney have represented in their plays the unfinished business of northern society after the Troubles (Chapter 5). Adaptations of Greek classical tragedy, versions of Chekhov's plays, featured from near the beginning of the national theatre movement and proliferated in the late twentieth century. In

Chapter 6 I am concerned with the strategies of adaptation of Marina Carr with her relocation of *Medea* to the Irish Midlands in *By the Bog of Cats*, her technique of third-person narration in *Hecuba*; how Hilary Fannin, working with the composer Ellen Cranitch in *Phaedra*, looked to music to reproduce the elevated style of Racine; and the effects of Lucy Caldwell's relocation of *Three Sisters* to 1990s Belfast.

The centenary of the Easter Rising, 2016, was always going to be a crucially important year in what the Irish government had planned as a Decade of Centenaries for the revolutionary period 1912–23. However, the announcement of the programme for that year by the Abbey, Ireland's national theatre, produced a quite unexpected revolt. The notable underrepresentation of women in that programme provoked the #WakingTheFeminists movement. In Part III of the book, concerned with the politics of gender, I devote Chapter 7 to #WakingTheFeminists, with a collage of material from interviews I undertook with those who spearheaded the movement, and retrospectives from the women directors and producers who by 2022 had come to provide the main leadership of the industry. Toxic masculinity is dramatized in extreme forms in plays by Conor McPherson, Enda Walsh, and Mark O'Rowe, and in Chapter 8 I consider the effects of the male psychopathologies they represent. Chapter 9 is focused on the twenty-first-century women playwrights—Marina Carr, Stacey Gregg, Deirdre Kinahan, Sonya Kelly, Margaret McAuliffe, Sarah Hanly, Nancy Harris—who have staged women's experience of sexual violence, their defiance of stereotyping in performance, and their exploration of the fluidity of sexual and gender roles.

Irish Theatre in the Twenty-First Century does not attempt a systematic or comprehensive history. It is necessarily selective. In my 'State of Play' reports I can only comment on relatively few of the productions I saw, picking out those that seemed to me most significant, including some of the highlights but some shows that were less successful as well. (The worst cases I have left to oblivion in those ring-bound folders.) My approach is necessarily selective, and necessarily also subjective. As an awards judge, I was in the business of judging, and could not therefore avoid evaluating plays, performances, and production values. Outside the 'State of Play' sections, however, I have tried not to colour the discussion with my own personal responses but to present as analytically as possible the major features of Irish theatre in the twenty-first century. How far I have succeeded will be up to readers to decide.

PART I
MAKING IT NEW

1
Changing Generations, Changing Styles
Irish Theatre in the 1990s

Periodization is always open to question, all the more so in relation to recent periods, where full historical perspective is necessarily missing. Contemporary Irish theatre has been said to begin from the 1950s, with Beckett its absent founding father.[1] 1964, the year of Brian Friel's breakthrough play *Philadelphia Here I Come!* is also often picked out as a start date. Patrick Lonergan focuses on the Dublin Theatre Festival programme of that year as a 'coming of age' moment, not only for the production of *Philadelphia* but of Eugene McCabe's *King of the Castle*, which drew more attention at the time, and Máiréad Ní Ghráda's *An Triail*.[2] A new generation of Irish playwrights certainly came to prominence in the 1960s: Tom Murphy, whose first full-length play *A Whistle in the Dark* produced in 1961 is another landmark date; Hugh Leonard, who had been writing since the 1950s, but who brought what was felt to be a new dramaturgy to Irish theatre with *Stephen D* (1962); John B. Keane with his enormous popular success *The Field* (1965); Thomas Kilroy who is credited as the first Irish playwright to feature a gay central character in *The Death and Resurrection of Mr Roche* (1968).

The explicit treatment of previously taboo sexual matters was one of the features of this second dramatic revival of the 1960s. McCabe's *King of the Castle* was controversial because of its plot which involved an ageing and impotent farmer who bargains with a young man to have sex with his wife and thus provide him with an heir. *An Triail* challenged social attitudes towards extra-marital pregnancy with its tragic story which ends with the unmarried mother killing her child and herself; in the trial of the title, the audience is formally the jury, but as complicit members of the society of the time they are also on trial. Kilroy's play dramatized the vicious homophobia of the all-male group who persecute Mr Roche. The plays of the time broke new ground in their form as well as their content. While *A Whistle in the Dark* was a conventionally naturalistic tragedy, the plays that Murphy wrote immediately after it experimented with expressionism (*A Crucial Week in the Life of a Grocer's Assistant*), dystopian fairy tale (*The Morning After*

---

[1] See, for example, Patrick Lonergan, *Irish Drama and Theatre since 1950* (London: Methuen Drama, 2019) and Anthony Roche, *Contemporary Irish Drama*, 2nd ed. (London: Palgrave Macmillan, 2009).

[2] Patrick Lonergan, '"Feast and Celebration": The Theatre Festival and Modern Irish Theatre', in Nicholas Grene and Chris Morash (eds.), *The Oxford Handbook of Modern Irish Theatre* (Oxford: Oxford University Press, 2016), 637–53 [646] .

Optimism), and Brechtian alienation techniques (*Famine*). Brecht was an influence also on Ní Ghráda whose work was partly shaped by the director Tomás Mac Anna.[3] Friel's treatment of the very traditional subject of enforced emigration was transformed by the theatrical device of Private Gar voicing the unspoken thoughts of his tongue-tied alter ego Public. Though Irish theatrical dramaturgy remained sufficiently conservative that the theatrically fluid storytelling of Leonard's *Stephen D* was considered revolutionary, international styles of staging, often seen in the Dublin Theatre Festival from 1957 on, made its impact in the Irish theatre of the 1960s.

This generation of playwrights, Friel, Murphy, Kilroy, and Leonard in particular, were to dominate Irish theatre for much of the remainder of the twentieth century. However, in the 1990s they were to be succeeded by another new wave of Irish playwrights. Marina Carr's *The Mai*, commissioned by the Abbey, was staged there in 1994, which was also the year of Marie Jones's *A Night in November*. In 1996 Martin McDonagh had a sensational success with *The Beauty Queen of Leenane*, the first part of what was to become *The Leenane Trilogy*, while in 1996 also Enda Walsh was to make his name with *Disco Pigs*. If the precocity of McDonagh, aged just 25 when his first play was produced, was partly what made the event so remarkable, it was also a talking point with Conor McPherson (born 1971) when *The Weir* was staged in 1997, though by then McPherson had already had several other plays to his credit. Mark O'Rowe established his reputation with the production of *Howie the Rookie* in 1999. It is of course too neatly prescriptive to frame this theatrical generation exactly within the decade of the 1990s. Frank McGuinness was an important presence from 1985 when *Observe the Sons of Ulster Marching Towards the Somme* was produced. Billy Roche, a somewhat older playwright, had two of his 'Wexford Trilogy', *A Handful of Stars* and *Poor Beast in the Rain* staged in 1988 and 1989. *Boss Grady's Boys* was premiered by the Abbey in 1988, well before *The Steward of Christendom* (1995) gave Sebastian Barry an international hit. Nevertheless, there was reason to think of the 1990s as representing another generational shift in Irish theatre making.

There was certainly an awareness of this flowering of Irish theatrical talent in London. 'If you're a young Irish playwright, come to London', was the exultant headline for a *New Statesman* interview with Conor McPherson in 1998.[4] *The Weir* was commissioned by the Royal Court after the success of his play *St Nicholas* at the Bush Theatre. The Bush was an important outlet for Irish playwrights at this time. It was there that all three of Roche's Wexford plays were staged between 1988 and 1991, and it was the Bush again that produced O'Rowe's

---

[3] See Brian Ó Conchubhair, 'Twisting in the Wind: Irish-Language Stage Theatre 1884–2014', in Grene and Morash, *Oxford Handbook of Modern Irish Theatre*, 251–68 [260].

[4] Conor McPherson, 'If You're a Young Irish Playwright, Come to London', *New Statesman*, 20 February 1998.

Howie the Rookie. The Royal Court was the other major theatre showcasing Irish drama. They staged Barry's *The Steward of Christendom* and were co-producers with Druid Theatre Company of McDonagh's *Leenane Trilogy*. In the same year as *The Beauty Queen of Leenane*, McDonagh had *The Cripple of Inishmaan* staged at the National Theatre.[5] Transfers to London or New York were always the aspiration of Irish dramatists as the route to international recognition; it was the Broadway success of *Philadelphia Here I Come!* that was the making of Friel's career. What was distinctive about the 1990s was the fact that Irish plays were actually being premiered in London before being produced in Ireland.

The plays of the 1990s looked like earlier Irish plays but with significant differences. The country cottage kitchen or village pub had been the setting for countless Abbey plays right back to the time of the Revival; in the *Leenane Trilogy* McDonagh gave a lampoon version of that rural scene. Synge's Mayo people might have got excited about the story of Christy Mahon's supposed parricide, but in Leenane violence is everywhere, and everywhere casually accepted as the norm. In *The Mai* and Carr's plays that succeeded it, *Portia Coughlan* (1996) and *By the Bog of Cats* (1998), there is a use of myth and folklore that aligns them with traditional Irish drama. But with their suicidal female protagonists they challenged standard patriarchal norms of the family. *The Weir* features ageing bachelors telling ghost stories in a rural pub, traditional-seeming subject. However, with its quiet country setting the play was not typical of McPherson's earlier—or later—work, which dramatized a Dublin urban underworld of bombed-out alcoholic men. Equally, *Howie the Rookie* staked out new territory for Irish drama in its representation of a suburban badlands of violence and crime.

In formal terms, also, there was continuity with difference in the plays of the 1990s. Friel, who had a special liking for narrators, had set a precedent with *Faith Healer* (1978) with its four interlocked but entirely separate monologues by the three characters who never appear on stage together. Because of Ireland's storytelling tradition, the monologue seemed particularly appropriate as a theatrical form for Irish playwrights. But it was also a way of highlighting the special skills of the live theatre performer in an entertainment industry increasingly dominated by other media, indeed a way of fighting back. So, for example, Donal O'Kelly, as a would-be screenwriter in his one-man show *Catalpa* (1995), single-handedly created all the parts and the sound effects of the imagined epic film he was never going to be able to produce. Jones in *Stones in His Pockets* (1996) had two extras on an Irish movie set play all the actors and crew to highlight the meretricious misrepresentations of the filmmaking process. For O'Kelly and Jones, as for McPherson and O'Rowe, narrating monologues were a means of drawing an audience into

---

[5] James Moran highlights the importance of the theatrical agent Nick Marston in bringing Irish theatre to London stages: 'Irish Theatre in Britain', in Grene and Morash, *Oxford Handbook of Modern Irish Theatre*, 607–22 [612–13].

engagement with the performers in imagining whole scenes outside the theatre. The monologue was a flexible and effective theatrical medium that dispensed altogether with the naturalistic conventions of representation so long normative in Irish drama.

Irish plays in the 1990s gave a harsher view of rural society, and showed violently abusive families, culminating in the incestuous rape of Carr's *On Raftery's Hill* (2000). Beyond the traditional country setting, some playwrights extended the scope of Irish drama into the scabrous reaches of modern Dublin. Storytelling monologues broke with the need for box sets and cottage kitchens. But perhaps the most significant change in the drama of this period came in the use of language.

Kenneth Tynan, in his often-quoted review of Brendan Behan's *The Quare Fellow*, expressed a common, stereotypical view of the distinctive quality of Irish drama:

> The English hoard words like misers; the Irish spend them like sailors; and in Brendan Behan's tremendous new play language is out on a spree, ribald, dauntless and spoiling for a fight. [...] It is Ireland's sacred duty to send over, every few years, a playwright to save the English drama from inarticulate glumness.[6]

In the 1990s, Ireland sent over not one but a whole squad of Irish playwrights to London. However, their work did not reflect this reputation for extravagant eloquence in Irish drama that went back to Synge's dictum that '[i]n a good play, every speech should be as fully flavoured as a nut or apple'.[7] There were some plays of the time that did exactly fulfil these expectations. So, for example, Barry's *Steward of Christendom* was much admired for its poetic style. 'What takes one's breath away is the sheer beauty of Barry's writing. I venture to suggest that not even O'Casey or Synge wrote better than this'.[8] In most cases, however, the 1990s Irish dramatists seemed deliberately to subvert the preconceptions established by Syngean poetic lyricism and O'Casey's ornate Dublin demotic speech. McDonagh's language represents a deliberate 'uglification' of the forms of Synge's dialect, its distortions designed to kill any poetic effect. Roche's dialogue is written in a low-key realism far from O'Casey's or Behan's high colour; this provides the template also for McPherson in the theatrical uses of the hesitancies, the clichés and vulgarisms of colloquial speech. Walsh and O'Rowe both have idiolects of their own, strange specialized languages overstepping the bounds of traditional dramatic speech. The five playwrights each in their own way helped to create a new Irish drama resistant to fluency and eloquence.

---

[6] Quoted in Michael O'Sullivan, *Brendan Behan: A Life* (Dublin: Blackwater Press, 1997), 208.
[7] J. M. Synge, *Collected Works*, Vol. IV: *Plays, Book II*, ed. Ann Saddlemyer (London: Oxford University Press, 1968), 54.
[8] Quotation from *The Guardian* review of the play on the back cover of Sebastian Barry, *Plays 1* (London: Methuen Drama, 1997).

Uglification: Martin McDonagh, *The Beauty Queen of Leenane*

Martin McDonagh claimed not to have known *The Playboy of the Western World* when he wrote *The Beauty Queen of Leenane*.[9] Whatever the literal truth of that claim, there does appear to be an intertextual dialogue between the two plays. *Playboy* represents a remote, socially and psychologically impoverished western Irish community galvanized by the appearance of a young man who claims to have killed his father. *Beauty Queen* provides a latter-day equivalent of just such a community with matricide instead of patricide. Synge created a scandal by his representation of his Mayo people hero-worshipping the supposed father-killer, but at least the Mayo men did turn against Christy Mahon when he seemed to have repeated the action in their own backyard. In McDonagh's Leenane it would appear that no-one bothers to question Maureen's dubiously convincing account of the murder of her mother: such violence, to judge by the other two plays in McDonagh's trilogy, is all in the Leenane day's work. If Synge's story of the idolized father-killer played games with decolonizing Ireland's need to rebel against the authority of the colonizer, *Beauty Queen* can be read as some sort of ultimate revenge against Ireland herself, as the Joycean old sow who smothers if not eats her own farrow.

From the opening moments of the two plays, the language is significantly different. Pegeen, interrupted by Shawn Keogh in the ordering of her trousseau, pays scant attention to him, while he awkwardly explains his visit:

> I stood a while outside wondering would I have a right to pass on or to walk in and see you, Pegeen Mike ... and I could hear the cows breathing, and sighing in the stillness of the air, and not a step moving any place from this gate to the bridge.[10]

Shawn is no poet, but Synge's words enable him to conjure up vividly the desolately empty landscape that lies outside the lonely shebeen. Contrast the introductory exchange of the *Beauty Queen*:

MAG. Wet, Maureen?
MAUREEN. Of course wet.
MAG. Oh-h.[11]

---

[9] See Fintan O'Toole, 'Nowhere Man', *Irish Times*, 26 April 1997, cited by Shaun Richards in '"The Outpouring of a Morbid Unhealthy Mind": The Critical Condition of Synge and McDonagh', *Irish University Review*, 33.1 (2003), 201–14 [202].
[10] Synge, *Collected Works*, Vol. IV, 57.
[11] Martin McDonagh, *Plays: 1* (London: Methuen, 1999), 1. All further quotations from the play are taken from this edition, cited parenthetically in the text.

With these economical monosyllables, we are introduced to a whole world. There is the absurd unnecessariness of Mag's question asked of the soaked Maureen coming in out of the rain. There is also the sardonic implication of Maureen's snorted response: when is it ever anything but wet in Leenane? And what more is there to say about the place? Remarks about the weather are generally synonymous with boringly banal conversational interchange. Here they are reduced still further to a laconic six words brought to a dead end by Mag's utterly vacant 'Oh-h'. McDonagh is beginning as he means to go on.

McDonagh's language is a self-consciously adopted style as he himself made clear: 'In Connemara and Galway, the natural dialogue style is to invert sentences and use strange inflections. Of course, my stuff is a heightening of that, but there is a core strangeness of speech, especially in Galway'.[12] Synge too of course worked with this 'core strangeness of speech' derived from Irish language syntax, but to different ends from McDonagh. Two features of Irish are particularly striking in Synge's Hiberno-English, the use of the copula to advance an important word or phrase to the head of a sentence, and the substitution of paratactic phrases for what in standard English would be subordinate clauses. One sentence from *Playboy* may be used to illustrate the effect. It is in act II when Pegeen has been frightening Christy with the prospect of hanging, and at last reassures him he is safe. This is his relieved response: 'It's making game of me you were [...], and I can stay so, working at your side, and I not lonesome from this mortal day'.[13] The copula formation—'It's making game of me you were'—allows for inversion of normal word order, while the paratactic 'and I not lonesome' makes for a smooth flowing full sentence running on to Synge's favourite resolving rhythmic chord 'this mortal day'.

Contrast with that some examples from McDonagh. Mag sidles into one of her endless demands on Maureen early in the first scene: 'Me porridge, Maureen, I haven't had, will you be getting?' (McDonagh, *Plays: 1*, 3). This is a weirdly contorted version of 'I haven't had my porridge: will you get it for me, Maureen?', so contorted it almost sounds like pidgin. McDonagh, like Synge, is using Irish-derived inversion but increasing the strangeness. The effect is to catch Mag's simultaneous insistence on the foregrounded 'Me porridge', and her whining pseudo-tentativeness. But against the fluency of the Synge line, McDonagh contrives a halting ungainliness. It is even more striking in extended passages. This is the start of Maureen's confession to Pato of the circumstances that led to her mental breakdown:

In England I was, this happened. Cleaning work. When I was twenty-five. Me first time over. Me only time over. Me sister had just got married, me other sister

---

[12] Quoted in Joseph Feeny SJ, 'Martin McDonagh: Dramatist of the West', *Studies*, 87 (1998), 28.
[13] Synge, *Collected Works*, Vol. IV, 113.

just about to. Over in Leeds I was, cleaning offices. Bogs. A whole group of us, only them were all English. 'Ya oul backward Paddy fecking … The fecking pig's-backside face on ya.' The first time out of Connemara this was I'd been. 'Get back to that backward fecking pigsty of yours or whatever hole it was you drug yourself out of'. (McDonagh, *Plays: 1*, 31)

Again, McDonagh repeatedly uses the inverted word order—'In England I was, this happened', 'Over in Leeds I was, cleaning offices'. The racist abuse flung at Maureen by her English fellow workers is translated into crude Irish sounding abuse: 'The fecking pig's-backside face on ya'. Insults in Synge's Hiberno-English can be as colourful as his lyricism: not here. The pathos and pain of what Maureen suffered is rendered in staccato bursts of speech, distorted grammar and syntax, scraps of language as if torn from memory.

I have written elsewhere about McDonagh's work as an example of what I called 'black pastoral', that deliberately savage subversion in the 1990s of Ireland's iconic image as green idyll.[14] Cathleen ni Houlihan is no longer a mythical old woman about to be transformed into a young girl with the walk of a queen, but a grasping, parasitical old mother locked in a battle to the death with her sex-starved daughter. McDonagh's reworking of Syngean stage speech is a part of that iconoclastic strategy. The well-wrought poetic periods that Synge created out of the Hiberno-English dialect are wrenched out of frame; the defamiliarization that Synge put to poetic uses, McDonagh employs to create a deliberately ugly and dissonant idiom. The style feels like an aggressive attack on anyone coming to the theatre looking for lilting Irish lyricism—if they have, they have come to the wrong shop.

Low-Key Realism: Billy Roche, *Poor Beast in the Rain*, and Conor McPherson, *The Weir*

Roche sets almost all his plays in his own home town of Wexford. There is nothing unusual in a small-town setting for Irish plays—for most of the twentieth century it was the norm rather than the exception. But in most cases the town or village is generic rather than specific, as in the case of Friel's hallmark location of Ballybeg where the very name, which means 'small town', signals its representative status. Roche instead grounds his plays in a detailed local actuality and, in place of the standard family home or pub, places the action in a snooker hall, a betting shop, the belfry and vestry of a church. Those confined spaces act as specimen sections of the Wexford social organism. So, for instance, the betting shop of *Poor Beast in the Rain* is the regular hangout for the older man Joe and his younger counterpart

---

[14] See Nicholas Grene, 'Black Pastoral: 1990s Images of Ireland', in Martin Prochazka (ed.), *After History* (Prague: Litteraria Pragensia, 2006), 243–55.

Georgie. The innocent Georgie is adoringly in love with Eileen, the daughter of the sad and laconic Steven, the betting-shop owner. Snatches of the radio broadcast of the races provide a routine backdrop, but the real source of excitement is the All-Ireland Senior Hurling Final in which Wexford are playing on the weekend of the action. Counterpointed to the fervent anticipation before the match and the celebrations after is a sad little human drama being played out at the same time. Danger Doyle, once the local young tearaway, who ran off to London with Steven's wife ten years before, returns to town to ask Eileen to come back with him to visit her depressed mother. At the end of the play, Eileen agrees, and the miserable deserted father Steven acquiesces. That is all there is to the plot of the play. The real drama stems from the tension between the stay-at-home values of the townspeople—'A man without a hometown is nothing' declares Steven[15]—and the attractively wild Doyle whom they all variously admire, fear, or love. This is a play of atmosphere rather than plot.

There is no fine flow of language in Roche, just the convincingly colloquial speech of local people. As a sample, this is the infatuated Georgie trying to persuade Eileen to join the crowd on the bus going up to Dublin for the match: 'sure you won't be the only girl there yeh know. Some of the women out of the factory are comin' too. Anyway Eileen you'll be browned off hangin' around here because this place is goin' to be deserted over the weekend. Dogs and cats and all'll be gone boy' (Roche, *Wexford Trilogy*, 70). No colourful phrasing here, but none of McDonagh's estranging inversions of word order either. Instead, the localism of the speech is rendered in features such as the oral tag 'boy' used indifferently at the end of a sentence, whether the person addressed is young or old, male or (as in this case) female. The accent is caught in the spelling—'yeh' for 'you', the dropped terminal 'g's and the run of the voice suggested by the missing punctuation.

The men's language has a routinely reductive coarseness about women. The sour-tempered cleaning woman Molly, Joe tells Georgie, 'was a fine hoult in her day boy' (Roche, *Wexford Trilogy*, 76). 'Hoult', from 'hold', according to a dictionary of Irish slang, is used of a woman 'with desirable sexual attributes, hence [also an] act of sexual intimacy'.[16] It is a synonym for 'court', also used of Molly. The men affect a conventionally macho attitude towards women less sports-mad than themselves: Joe, again on Molly, 'Sure that one wouldn't know her arse from her elbow now regardin' hurlin'' (Roche, *Wexford Trilogy*, 108). But Molly can give back as good as she gets: 'Ah go and fuck off Joe will yeh' (Roche, *Wexford Trilogy*, 109).

---

[15] Billy Roche, *The Wexford Trilogy* (London: Nick Hern Books, 1992), 108. All further quotations from the play are from this edition.

[16] Bernard Share, *Slanguage—A Dictionary of Slang and Colloquial English in Ireland* (Dublin: Gill and Macmillan, 1997), 141.

And it is Molly who is given the climactic speech of the play, when she tells Danger how it felt when he left her to go off with Eileen's mother:

> Aw Danger … Doyle if you only knew! Yeh know when you ran away with her like that I kept tellin' meself that it wouldn't last, that it wouldn't be long until yeh came back again to me. I'd picture yeh strollin' into town, kickin' up the leaves, your hair fallin' down into your eyes the way it used to and I'd be smilin' away to meself at the very idea of it—in spite of the fact that there was a great big knot screwin' and twistin' inside of me all the time. After a while of course it all turned kind of sour so that in the end, I'm not coddin' yeh, I felt like some poor beast that had been left out too long in the rain. (Roche, *Wexford Trilogy*, 121)

Of course, this is dramatic eloquence of a sort too, but one achieved with the minimum of lyricism and only that one final homely image of the poor beast in the rain to express the desolation of frustrated love.

Roche takes on what had become a stock situation of Irish drama from *The Playboy* on, the stagnant small Irish town with all its repressions and its idolization of the stranger within its gates. Danger Doyle is heroized in town memory for his daring defiance of law and custom, the 'danger' of his sexual allure. This returned hero demythologizes himself not least by the stumbling way he expresses his sense of alienation: 'I'll tell yeh lads, today I found myself snakin' through the streets of me own hometown like a whatdoyoucall it … Ah I can't think of the word now'. It is Joe that has to supply him with the lost word 'A fugitive, Danger. Like a fugitive' (Roche, *Wexford Trilogy*, 94–5). This is a play without heroes and without heroic language; no-one like Christy Mahon finds himself capable of 'saying words would raise the topknot on a poet in a merchant's town'.[17] But Roche's style of homely realism equally denies to no-one a measure of sympathy and dignity: the 'lads' with their vicarious fantasy life lived out in their sports heroes; Eileen, aching for her mother who has left her at the age of 10; Molly with her thwarted sexuality and love; the cuckolded Steven; the fugitive Doyle all too aware of the consequences of his own mistakes. It is a play that is both funny and poignant, never one at the expense of the other.

The Weir does not evoke a comparably specific local world. In fact, it is anomalous among McPherson's work as the only one of his plays with the conventional setting of a rural pub in the west of Ireland. McPherson is a Dublin man and virtually all his drama makes use of the setting and the style of north Dublin. But McPherson, like Roche, takes over the standard formula of the group of celibate men stirred by the appearance of a sexualized stranger, in this case Valerie, the young woman from Dublin who has rented a cottage in the neighbourhood.

---

[17] Synge, *Collected Works*, Vol. IV, 165.

The two ageing bachelors Jack and Jim are sufficiently excited at the prospect of meeting her that they have spruced themselves up before their nightly visit to the local pub, and they are uneasily jealous of Finbar, the successful married hotelier who is showing Valerie around. The play opens slowly with an establishing dialogue between Jack and the barman Brendan in what Patrick Kavanagh called the 'half-talk code', the 'wink-and-elbow language' of male intimates.[18]

JACK. Were you in Carrick today?
BRENDAN. I wasn't, no. I had the sisters doing their rounds. Checking up on me.
JACK. Checking their investments.
BRENDAN. Oh yeah. 'Course, they don't have a fucking clue what they're looking for, d'you know? They're just vaguely ... you know.
JACK. Keeping the pressure on you.
BRENDAN. This is it.[19]

The Weir was commissioned by the Royal Court, apparently on the condition that it should not be a monologue play like McPherson's earlier works. The playwright cleverly met that condition by inserting into his dialogue a series of stories, told by the men in part as a competitive attempt to impress the visitor Valerie. In this, he was drawing on the Irish reputation for storytelling in general, and stories of the supernatural in particular. Finbar first introduces the topic as one of the tourist attractions of the neighbourhood. 'There's all this around here, Valerie, the area's steeped in old folklore, and that, you know' (McPherson, *Weir*, 19). But when he realizes that the story about the fairy road he is prompting Jack to tell took place in the very house he has just rented to Valerie, he backs off: 'You hear all old shit around here, it doesn't mean anything' (McPherson, *Weir*. 20). And the style in which Jack introduces the story naturalizes it, domesticates it into the local setting:

JACK. [...] Maura ... Nealon used to come in here in the evening, sit over there at the fire. How old was she, Jim? When she died?
JIM. Oh Jays, she would have been nearly ninety.
JACK. But she was grand, you know spritely kind of woman 'til the end. And had all her ... She was on the ball, like, you know? And she swore that this happened. When she was only a girl. (McPherson, *Weir*, 20)

This is not the stylized shanachie style used by Mommo in Tom Murphy's *Bailegangaire*, for instance. It reproduces all the vagueness, hesitancies, and *non sequitur*s of colloquial speech.

---

[18] Patrick Kavanagh, 'Inniskeen Road: July Evening', *Collected Poems*, ed. Antoinette Quinn (London: Penguin, 2004), 15.
[19] Conor McPherson, *The Weir* (London: Nick Hern Books, 1998), 4. All further quotations are from this edition, cited parenthetically in the text.

The strategy of the play, in fact, is to bring the stories steadily closer to the characters and by extension to the audience. Jack's story of the fairy road is an inherited part of local folklore, though told by someone actually remembered by the teller and set in the house where Valerie now lives. Finbar's story of a ghostly appearance is something he himself experienced, and which made enough of an impact on him to force a change in his life: giving up smoking and moving to the town. Jim's story, of an apparent encounter with a dead paedophile, is the more convincing because Jim (unlike the other two storytellers) is evidently not out to impress, and he tells it with a characteristic circumstantial literalism. All of this paves the way for the turnaround when Valerie tells her own story of getting a phone call from her dead young daughter from beyond the grave. The experience of the supernatural and the language in which it is expressed do not belong in some quaint, remote region of rural folklore; they speak out of the extremities of the human psyche surrounding death, bereavement, and change.

The last monologue of the play, Jack's retrospect on his lost opportunity for love and marriage moves the audience away from ghosts and fairies. Storytelling and by extension theatre stand revealed as a way of creating a community of teller, tale, and listeners that banishes temporarily the permanent condition of loneliness and isolation. The play is managed as a single uninterrupted act within the naturalizing conditions of a night's drinking and talking in the pub. The style is casually demotic, rich in offhand obscenity. Even Jack realizes that he has gone too far when he jokes to Brendan and Valerie, last lingerers in the pub, about the way her presence will draw in one customer at least:

JACK. [...] Sure you'll have Finbar in here sniffing around Valerie every night anyway.
VALERIE. Ah now stop.
  They laugh a little.
JACK. He'll be like a fly on a big pile of shite, so he will. Jesus. That came out all wrong, didn't it? (McPherson, *Weir*, 50)

Authentically colloquial, but hardly in Syngean terms, '[a]s fully flavoured as a nut or apple'.

Idiolects: Enda Walsh, *Disco Pigs*, and Mark O'Rowe, *Howie the Rookie*

Synge first made dialect an established medium for Irish drama rather than an occasional marker for comic characters. Since then, more or less local speech has been a hallmark of Irish drama: O'Casey's slum Dublinese, Behan's prison argot, Friel's modified Donegal, Carr's Midlands dialogue, the Wexford idiom of Billy Roche analysed above. But in *Disco Pigs*, Enda Walsh did something different: he virtually invented a language. Walsh, coming from Dublin to live in Cork in the 1990s, has said that one stimulus for his writing was the sheer difference of Cork speech. What he created in the play, however, was not merely a version of Cork dialect. It was Cork mixed with baby talk combined with a layering of puns and onomatopoeia recalling the Joyce of *Finnegans Wake*. When it was first performed by Corcodorca, the theatre company he was working with in 1996, Walsh reckoned the audience could not have understood more than half of what was said. But the effect was extraordinary, taking the play on to huge international success: there were apparently no less than forty-two different productions of the play in German in one three-year period alone.[20]

This is the play's opening sequence, which needs to be quoted at length in order to appreciate its texture. The stage direction establishes the basic convention.

> *Lights flick on.* PIG *(male) and* RUNT *(female). They mimic the sound of an ambulance like a child would, 'bee baa bee baa bee baa!!'. They also mimic the sound a pregnant woman in labour makes. They say things like 'is all righ, miss', 'ya doin fine, luv', 'dis da furs is it?', 'is a very fast bee baa, al righ. Have a class a water!' Sound of door slamming. Sound of heartbeats throughout.*

Then we get the scene of the two expectant mothers being rushed into the labour ward.

RUNT. Out of the way!! Jesus out of the way!
PIG. Scream da fat nurse wid da gloopy face!
RUNT. Da two mams squealin on da trollies dat go speedin down da ward. Oud da fookin way!
PIG. My mam she own a liddle ting, look, an did da furs liddle baba! She heave an rip all insie!! Hol on Mam!!
RUNT. My mam she hol in da pain! She noel her pain too well! She been ta hell an bac my mam!
PIG. Day trips an all!
RUNT. Da stupid cow!!
PIG. Holy Jesus help me!!
RUNT. Scream da Pig Mam! Her face like a christmas pud all sweaty and steamy! Da two trollies like a big choo choo it clear all infron! Oudda da fooking way cant jaaaaa!!
PIG. Da two das dey run the fast race speedin behine!

Then the point of view shifts to the father and the emerging baby:

RUNT. Holy Jesus keep her safe. Holy Jesus keep her safe!

---

[20] See Werner Huber, "'What's the News from Kilcrobally?' Notes on the Reception of Contemporary Irish Theatre in German-Speaking Countries', in Nicholas Grene and Patrick Lonergan (eds.), *Irish Theatre Local and Global* (Dublin: Carysfort Press, 2012), 81–91 [84].

PIG. Mamble my dad wid a liddle mammy tear in da eye! I'm da liddle baba cummin oud, Dada, I'm yer liddle baba racer!!!

And back to the trolleys and the mothers in labour:

RUNT. Da trollie dey go on
PIG. an on
RUNT. an on
PIG. an on
RUNT. an on
PIG. an on
RUNT. an on
PIG. an on!
RUNT. My mam she suck in da pain, grobble it up an sweat it oud til da liddle skimpy nighty idgo,
PIG. black wet black.
RUNT. Two gold fishys oudda da bowl!!!
PIG. A gasp gaspin! I'm ja liddle baba commin out! Open up ja big fanny!

They are about to be delivered, even while on the trolleys, with outside encouragement from the fathers:

RUNT. Trollie stop!
PIG. An leg open!
RUNT. Da fatty nurse schlap on with the rubbery glubs! Stop! An leg open! Da two fat sous pooshhh and pooshh ta spit da babas oud!!
PIG. Push girls push!!
RUNT. Scream da das oudsize!
PIG. Scream da das oudsize!
RUNT. My da he was fur his din dins real fas, yeah!
PIG. Take your time love!
RUNT. He say, stopwadch in han! Da fannys dey look like donna kebabs!
PIG. Bud looka da liddle baba heads!
RUNT. Pooosh da baba poosh da head!!
PIG. Pooshh Mam poosh!! Poosh da Pig
RUNT. An Poosh da Runt! She wan oud Mama!
PIG. And he wan oud, ta dada!
RUNT. Pooosh sous pooosh!!
PIG. We da liddle born babas!
PIG *and* RUNT. Pooosshhhhhh!
   Silence. We then hear the sounds of babies crying. Music.[21]

---

[21] Enda Walsh, *Plays: One* (London: Nick Hern Books, 2011), 45–7.

Some of this is easy enough to understand when you know the forms. So, for instance, initial 'th' consistently becomes 'd': 'da' for 'the', 'dis' for 'this', 'dat' for 'that'. This is no more than an orthographic rendering of common Irish pronunciation. So too is the erosion of terminal 'd'—'hol' for 'hold', 'behine' for 'behind'. There are whole phrases that look odd on the page, but are clear enough on the ear: 'Oudda fookin' way cant jaaaaa!!' = 'Out of the fucking way, can't you?' There are bits of standard baby talk like 'big choo choo' for 'train' or 'din dins' for dinner. Some of the deformations of standard English write action sounds into the words: 'Da fatty nurse schlap on with the rubbery glubs'. But some of the most expressive words one would be hard pressed to translate. What does 'gloopy' mean in 'da fat nurse wid da gloopy face'? Or what about 'grobble' in 'My mum she suck in da pain, grobble it up and sweat it oud'—perhaps a portmanteau combination of 'gobble' and 'groan' and 'grovel'? What is so striking is the way the two voices do the whole scene between them, the different speakers and the narration in a collage of sound and rhythm beyond any literal denotation. And built into the play's language is the ferociously satiric tone of the two teenagers with their gleeful mockery of everyone and everything outside their own shared space.

In a 2001 interview Walsh spoke movingly about one source for his writing style:

> I have this serious hang-up about being inarticulate. I went through years of speech therapy. I had a stammer. That has largely impacted on everything I have done: the sort of characters, the structure of my writing and the style of my writing. It is the poetry of being inarticulate.[22]

This idea of a 'poetry of being inarticulate' is a telling description of Walsh's language, and indeed of all the playwrights considered here. His aim is to come at forms of language below, beyond, or outside standard articulate speech. A key element within this strategy is ventriloquism. The first of Walsh's plays to be performed, the year before *Disco Pigs*, was *The Ginger Ale Boy* about a ventriloquist suffering a nervous breakdown. The strange, shared idiolect of Pig and Runt is designed to include all the different voices that constitute their mental landscape. As a result, the only world that exists in *Disco Pigs* is the one they create through language, into which we as audience are necessarily drawn, a distorted and (in the case of Pig) ultimately a psychotic world.

Mark O'Rowe's *Howie the Rookie* consists of just two monologues, the story as told first by the Howie Lee and then by the (unrelated) Rookie Lee. They use a very similar language, a specialized idiom of underworld Dublin that is another distinctively strange theatrical idiolect. The opening of the Howie Lee's speech gives a sense of its style of cinematic self-narration.

---

[22] Quoted in Patrick Lonergan, *Theatre and Globalization: Irish Drama in the Celtic Tiger Era* (London: Palgrave Macmillan, 2009), 179.

Smoke.
Black smoke ahead there, north end of the field.
Thick, billowin', curlin' up.
Somethin' burnin'.
Me, The Howie, south end, amblin'.
Approachin'.
A figure.
A man ahead, some fuck standin' there, stick in his hand, proddin' whatever's burnin'. Makin' sure it all goes up.
Me, The Howie Lee, gettin' closer now.
Passin' through the field, me way home.
Field, the back of the flats there, back of Ollie's flat, me mate Ollie's an', Jesus it *is* Ollie, little fire built, he's standin' there, watchin' it, one hand in his pocket, now an' again, stick prods the burnin' ... whatsit?
What *is* it?
Come close. All right, Ollie?
All right, The Howie?
Stop, stand, cock me tush.
The fuck're you burnin'?
Me mat, he says.
Ollie's flat befits a messy cunt like him.
Kip the night, you kip on the guest mat under an oul' slumberdown. You're a bloke and you're game, you can kip in the bed *with* him. Game meaning gay, neither of which I am, furthest thing from, so I go the mat. Or did.
On the mat I kip.
Did! Kipped!
It's gone now. That's it he's burnin'.[23]

Little pointillist fragments of speech conjure up the successive sense impressions. It is written in a sort of telegraphese, with many words left out. So, for example, 'The fuck you're burnin'?' can be reconstructed as 'What the fuck are you burning?' This can yield quite odd sounding syntax: 'Kip the night, you kip on the guest mat under an oul' slumberdown' = 'If you sleep the night, you sleep on the guest mat'. But this is not the sort of contorted word order of McDonagh's dialect. It takes over from hard man movies the convention that the fewer words you use, the tougher you are. There are unfamiliar words that more or less explain themselves—'tush' for 'head' in 'cock me tush'—or are actually explained in the text: 'You're a bloke

---

[23] Mark O'Rowe, *Howie the Rookie* (London: Nick Hern Books, 1999), 7–8.

and you're game, you can kip *with* him. Game meaning gay, neither of which I am, furthest from it'.

If *Disco Pigs* forces us to share the unique mindscape of Pig and Runt, *Howie the Rookie* takes us into a half-world of Irish urban grunge, of casual violence and sordid sex. It is different from what I have called the 'black pastoral' mode of McDonagh where the effect is to lampoon the image of the organic rural community of traditional pastoral. But it does also involve playing off a received idea of Ireland. So, for example, in the country which only finally decriminalized homosexuality in 1993, the fact that some of the characters are 'game', that is gay, is casually accepted. Any notion of a characteristically Irish sexual repression is sent up by scenes such as that where the Howie Lee is propositioned in the pub lavatory by the aptly nicknamed Avalanche, the monstrous adolescent sister of his friend the Peaches. This is British 'in-yer-face' theatre, Irish style: Ireland at the end of the twentieth century is modern enough to have its own urban criminal culture. To enter that milieu, you have to learn its language as you go along, a language as far as possible from Synge's 'popular imagination that is fiery, and magnificent and tender'.

The playwrights considered here developed forms of theatrical language that actively challenged expectations that the characters of Irish drama should be lyrically poetic, fluently expressive, eloquent in their distinctive use of dialect. By this means, they created a range of different versions of Ireland none of them corresponding to standard models of the past. Five of the dramatists who emerged in the 1990s—Carr, McDonagh, McPherson, Walsh, and O'Rowe—went on to become dominant figures in the twenty-first century, consolidating international reputations, their new work eagerly anticipated in Ireland, produced across the world. But Irish theatre itself has changed radically in this contemporary period, not least in a shift of focus away from individual playwrights and play texts. New forms of collective theatre making, postmodern and postdramatic styles, have emphasized process rather than product. Site-specific work has taken theatre outside the box of traditional venues. There has been a proliferation of independent theatre companies each with its distinctive house style, though often with a short lifespan due to the precariousness of funding. Where ambitious projects have been realized, it has been at least in part because of access to theatre festivals at home and abroad. National politics is still a concern in the era since the Good Friday Agreement of 1998, where legacy issues continue to trouble northern communities. But other forms of politics have become equally if not more important: the politics of gender; economic and cultural concern in a diversifying and rapidly modernizing society; the excavation of Ireland's long occluded history of social abuses. These are among the issues to be addressed in the rest of this book.

2
Belated Avant-Garde

For much of the twentieth century, Irish theatre remained dramaturgically conservative, the norm being a representational drama of modified naturalism. There were a number of reasons for this. The national theatre movement placed the emphasis on representing the nation, its country cottages and pubs standing as metonyms for the emergent society as a whole. 'Express a life that has never found expression', Yeats urged Synge when recommending that he mine his experience of the Aran Islands for creative purposes.[1] To give voice to the previously unvoiced remained an objective from O'Casey's Dublin plays through to Behan's urban sub-world of prisoners and prostitutes. This was the hidden Ireland, and to stage it required a belief in its authenticity—hence a more or less realist mode. Yeats, of course, revolted against the 'people's theatre' he had created with Lady Gregory, declaring for 'an unpopular theatre and an audience like a secret society where admission is by favour and never to many'.[2] And, as far as his own work was concerned, that was more or less what he got. Although, as Chris Morash has shown, his ideas on theatre relate to some of the major theatrical movements of the modern period, his plays never really took hold in the Abbey and he has had few Irish followers.[3] Denis Johnston's expressionist *The Old Lady Says No!* provided the Gate Theatre with its opening production, and the Gate, with the innovative direction of Hilton Edwards and the designs of Micheál Mac Liammóir, did much to bring to Dublin the contemporary theatrical styles of continental Europe. But Johnston's second play, *The Moon in the Yellow River*, reverted to a Shavian comedy of ideas, and was staged by the Abbey in realist mode. Over the decades, the Gate tended to relapse into a repertoire of stylish classical revivals.

Up until late in the twentieth century there was little opportunity for formal training that might have allowed actors to experiment with different styles. Intermittently, there was an Abbey School of Acting, but most actors learned on the job. Originally, the Abbey company was formed of part-time semi-professionals, key figures such as Barry Fitzgerald and F. J. McCormick continuing with day jobs until launched well into their careers. In later years, young actors were taken on and served what amounted to an apprenticeship to their more experienced seniors,

---

[1] J. M. Synge, *Collected Works*, Vol. III: *Plays, Book 1*, ed. Ann Saddlemyer (London: Oxford University Press, 1968), 63.
[2] W. B. Yeats, 'A People's Theatre: Letter to Lady Gregory', *Explorations* (London: Macmillan, 1962), 254.
[3] Chris Morash, *Yeats on Theatre* (Cambridge: Cambridge University Press, 2022).

eventually moving up into the lead roles. This created a continuity, an inheritance of performance, within which the opportunities for experimentation and innovation were limited. The Gaiety School of Acting was set up in 1986, but it was not until 2011, with the establishment of The Lir, that Ireland acquired a full academy for all forms of professional theatre training equivalent to Britain's RADA, founded over a hundred years before.

Irish drama was well known internationally from the time of Synge on, but it was to some extent a niche market. The expected product was a well-made play with the Irishness of the characters marked by their mellifluous or highly coloured local dialect. The corollary of that, though, was that there was little appreciation of theatrical work from Ireland that did not conform to this model. International reviewers tended to be particularly unforgiving towards experimental work. Mel Gussow's *New York Times* review of *The Great Hunger*, Tom McIntyre's adaptation of Patrick Kavanagh's long poem, was headlined 'A Dearth of Words'. In Ireland the collaboration between McIntyre, director Patrick Mason, and lead actor Tom Hickey to produce a physical image-based show had been acclaimed as excitingly cutting edge. For Gussow it was a throw-back to a previous era: 'the play is an artifact of the 1960s. It is as if the Open Theater and Jerzy Grotowski's Polish Lab had never existed and other theaters had not interpreted and expanded on their innovations'.[4] Twenty years later *Silver Stars*, a song cycle show about the experience of older gay men by the politically committed Irish company Brokentalkers, had a similar American reaction: 'seeing "Silver Stars" is like taking a very short trip in a time machine'. It 'sounds like something you might have heard in New York a generation ago'.[5] Belatedly avant-garde Irish theatre can seem old hat abroad. In the mainstream international centres what still sells is text-based, playwright-centred Irish drama.

In the first chapter, I looked at playwrights in the 1990s who rejected the Irish theatrical tradition of lyrical eloquence for broken forms of language. But in that same decade, there were many theatre makers and companies who wanted to introduce more radical modes of performance in which text and playwright were no longer paramount. They looked in particular to Europe for liberation from the Irish inheritance of literary drama. Within a few years, a series of companies were set up to produce alternative forms of theatre: Blue Raincoat (1991); Barabbas, Bedrock, and Pan Pan, all in 1993; The Corn Exchange (1995); Loose Canon (1996); Fabulous Beast Dance Theatre (1997). They were to be followed in the twenty-first century by Brokentalkers (2001); ANU (2009): and Dead Centre

---

[4] Mel Gussow, 'Review/Theater; "The Great Hunger," A Dearth of Words', *New York Times*, 18 March 1988, https://www.nytimes.com/1988/03/18/theater/review-theater-great-hunger-a-dearth-of-words.html (accessed 12 June 2023).

[5] Quoted from the *New York Times* review of 13 January 2010 by Peter Crawley, 'Viewed from Afar: Contemporary Irish Theatre on the World's Stages', in Fintan Walsh, '*That Was Us*': *Contemporary Irish Theatre and Performance* (London: Oberon, 2013), 211–28 [221].

(2012). All of these had their distinctively different artistic objectives, but they shared an emphasis on performance-based theatricality, language as secondary to movement, a focus on space and visual image. I will be considering the work of ANU in a later chapter. Here, for the purpose of illustrating this turn against text, I will be looking specifically at four of the 1990s companies: Barabbas, Blue Raincoat, The Corn Exchange, and Pan Pan.

European Styles: Barabbas and Blue Raincoat

'Physical theatre' is a term that covers a whole variety of performance, but there is one particular tradition in France starting with Jacques Copeau in the early twentieth century, through Etienne Decroux and Jacques Lecoq, down to the internationally celebrated mime Marcel Marceau.[6] It was France that provided training and inspiration for some of the key figures in 1990s Ireland who wanted to move away from literary theatre. Niall Henry and Mikel Murfi had set up their own Black Box Mime Theatre Company while still at school in Sligo.[7] Henry was so dedicated to training in mime that he auditioned no less than three times before finally being admitted to Marcel Marceau's school in Paris.[8] Raymond Keane's story is no less remarkable. Keane, originally from Waterford, but working as a hairdresser in Amsterdam, was so struck by mime performances on a visit to Paris that, with no previous background in theatre, he decided that was what he wanted to do.[9] Henry returned to Sligo to set up the Blue Raincoat theatre company with the playwright Malcolm Hamilton. Keane, with Mikel Murfi who had trained at the Jacques Lecoq school in Paris, and Veronica Coburn, founded what was officially called Barabbas ... the Company.

Coburn had started working as a clown, and in their first application to the Arts Council Barabbas styled themselves as 'an Irish company influenced by European traditions [...] clown, *bouffon*, and *commedia del'arte*'. Red-nose clowning was the dominant style of their first all but wordless show, *Come Down from the Mountain, John Clown, John Clown* (1994). Nothing if not ambitious, they staged this in a festival of three shows together. *Half Eight Mass of a Tuesday*, another devised piece, was a satirical rendering of Irish small-town life 'with a mixture of shadow play, puppetry, and the reality of the performers' bodies'.[10] The centrepiece of the trilogy,

---

[6] For a detailed account of the field, see Simon Murray and John Keefe, *Physical Theatres* (London: Routledge, 2007).
[7] See Rhona Trench, *Blue Raincoat Theatre Company* (Dublin: Carysfort Press, 2015), 9.
[8] Niall Henry, interview with the author, 19 April 2023. I am very grateful to Niall Henry for the generous use of his time; all information about Blue Raincoat, not otherwise attributed, is taken from this interview.
[9] Raymond Keane, interview with the author, 24 April 2023. All information on Barabbas, not otherwise attributed, is taken from this interview for which I am extremely grateful to Raymond Keane.
[10] Carmel Szabo, *The Story of Barabbas, the Company* (Dublin: Carysfort Press, 2012), 54.

however, was a five-hand version of *Macbeth*, in which the three company members, with blue painted faces and shaved heads, played both the witches and all the other characters except the Macbeths. The design featured a climbing frame as the inside of Macbeth's head, a cage from which he could never escape. The director and designer for the show was Gerry Stembridge, and it was he who directed the company in their greatest success, the production of Lennox Robinson's *The Whiteheaded Boy* (1997).

Stembridge chaired the Barabbas board, and it was the board that suggested taking on a popular play by way of extending the audience for the company. *The Whiteheaded Boy*, also Stembridge's choice, was a particularly suitable case for treatment. First performed in 1916, it became one of the Abbey's most popular pieces, and in fact ran for nine months in wartime London.[11] It was a typical comedy of the time, turning on the trope of the ne'er-do-well favoured son, the 'whiteheaded boy' of the title, for whom the interests of all the other family members are sacrificed. What made it such an excellent vehicle for Barabbas were the metatheatrical stage directions, written in the *faux naif* style of a local observer, looking on. The introduction of Mrs Geoghegan, the doting mother of the whiteheaded boy, may stand as sample:

> A great manager she is, and, indeed, she'd need to be with three unmarried daughters under her feet all day and two big men of sons. [...] she's not what I'd call a clever woman, I mean to say she's not got the book knowledge, the 'notions' her husband had or her sister Ellen. But maybe she's better without them, sure what good is book knowledge to the mother of a family? She's a simple decent woman, and what more do you want?[12]

This is an ironically distanced mimicry of local village language, local attitudes by Robinson, the Protestant son of a country rectory that he was. As such, it proved perfect for Barabbas sending up the style of the Abbey 'well-made play' from all but a century before.[13]

The play's stage directions were spoken in turn by Keane, Coburn, and Murfi, and the production emphasized the metatheatrical dimension. Costumed alike in monochrome outfits of grey, white, and black, they started the play looking down into a small model of the set, pointing out the various features mentioned in the stage directions. Though there was a beautifully realized period backdrop

---

[11] Hugh Hunt, *The Abbey: Ireland's National Theatre 1904-1978* (New York: Columbia University Press, 1979), 110.

[12] Lennox Robinson, *Selected Plays*, ed. Christopher Murray (Gerrards Cross: Colin Smythe, 1982), 65.

[13] In introducing the performance, the company gave it their own added subtitle 'A Well-Made Play' by way of underlining the point. My comments on the production are based on a recording made in the Project at the Mint in September 1997, kindly made available to me by Raymond Keane, as well as my memories of the original staging.

of a village street, designed by the photographer Sean Hillen, the playing area was restricted to a forestage with just a few items of furniture—a tea table and chairs, a settee, a piano. Intermittently, one of the performers would duck behind a chair to emerge as another character. *The Whiteheaded Boy* has a cast of twelve; in the Barabbas production, all the parts but Denis were shared between the three company members. It was a perfect showcase for their talents as physical actors, with each character sharply enough etched as to be immediately recognizable to the audience: the solid older brother George, head of the family, burdened with the business, was played by Murfi with a clunky walk, constantly wiping his mouth and smoothing his hair, transformed when he turned into one or other of his sisters, the independent-minded Baby with her hopes of training as a secretary, or the simpering young Jane. Keane as Mrs Geoghegan, head to one side, clenching and unclenching 'her' hands in anxiety, could become her own put-upon son Peter or, then again, the aggressive neighbour Duffy, father to Delia, the fiancée of Denis. Coburn, who appeared first as the eldest Geoghegan daughter Kate, also had the plum part of rich Aunt Ellen, spectacles on nose, but then bent herself double and acquired a zimmer frame to play the ancient servant Hannah. There were scenes in which the ramifications of the plot required the one actor to play two people in dialogue with one another. Keane was simultaneously the gruff Duffy drinking from a tumbler, and Mrs Geoghegan sipping from a sherry glass. The broad social comedy of the original was turned into a virtuoso clowning display.

Robinson prepares for the entrance of Denis through much of act I, where we hear about his extravagant life as a medical student in Dublin, and it transpires that he has once again failed his exams. In the Barabbas production, there was a double-take when it looked as if Murfi would play Denis also—he appears briefly swaggering with a cigar in his mouth. This, however, only made more sensational Denis's actual entrance, played by Louis Lovett in immaculate white suit and tartan waistcoat, spectacularly different from the other monochrome costumed actors. The difference in appearance and in playing style accentuated Denis's role as the unmoved mover. He sat at the table through the first act, nonchalantly at ease, munching through his large meal, unconcerned as the rest of the family flapped around him. Disgraced after his repeated exam failures, he is to be banished to Canada, forced to break off his engagement to Delia—it is all one to him. He contrives always to appear the injured party, the victim of his overbearing family. And of course, the switchback plot will always turn in his favour: he gets to marry Delia after all, falls in for the management of the newly opened co-operative shop in the village—originally intended for his brother Peter—will become Aunt Ellen's heir, frustrating all the hopes of his other siblings. He takes it all as no less than his due.

The discrepancy between the costuming and playing of Lovett as Denis and the others served the purposes of the play as the star of the show, the whiteheaded boy whose complete lack of deserts wins him everything. But it also served the strategic aims of the company, as Keane made clear at the time.

We've established ourselves as storytellers, but the new performer is from the old play, from the world of the theater [...] Through our performance style, we're saying, 'Here's a great play that we're going to act out for you now'. But then someone appears who is a real actor. That clash of theatre traditions is one of the things the production is about.[14]

A strategic point was made in a final costume change in the last act. The plot required Denis to appear in workman's clothes—one of his ploys is to take a navvy's job digging the roads, a loss of status that horrifies the class-conscious Geoghegans into accepting all his demands. But in the Barabbas production, this workman's outfit was changed once again and he was kitted out with the very same costume as the other three actors, made one of them. The change of costume, like the rest of the production, was a take-over claim by Barabbas. *The Whiteheaded Boy* was a classic example of the early national theatre movement. So, this was Barabbas, the alternative clown company invading the pitch of canonical text-based drama. It was a showcase of what they could do with a 'well-made play', guying all the conventions of the genre. Denis, the 'real actor' strayed in from the original play, as it were, is re-dressed to become one with the other three actors by the end. It was to be a repeated strategy with Irish theatre companies taking on classic texts to demonstrate the difference of their theatrical approach.

Though Barabbas continued to work through the first decade of the twenty-first century it was with diminishing resources, as first Murfi and then Coburn left the company to pursue independent careers. In 2010, in the wake of the economic collapse, it lost all its Arts Council funding, along with ten other independent companies (including Bedrock and Loose Canon). As a freelance performer since, Keane has used his mime skills in an internationally toured production of Beckett's *Act Without Words II*, directed by Sarah-Jane Scaife with whom he has become a regular collaborator. He appeared in *Laethanta Sona*, Scaife's Irish language production of *Happy Days*, and with her co-directed an outstanding staging of Thornton Wilder's *The Long Christmas Dinner* at the Peacock in 2021. The physical acting styles, which Barabbas and Blue Raincoat pioneered in the 1990s, have now been absorbed into the contemporary Irish theatre landscape.

Blue Raincoat, founded two years before Barabbas, survived the 2010 Arts Council cuts, though with diminished funding, and continues to operate in 2024 as 'a venue-based professional theatre ensemble' in Sligo.[15] Finding a venue, according to Henry, was relatively easy because Sligo was an 'old Protestant merchant town' with a large number of derelict buildings suitable for conversion. It was therefore possible to secure a long lease at relatively low rent on what had been

---

[14] Karen Fricker, 'Theater: An Energetic Irish Troupe That Keeps on the Move', *New York Times*, 3 October 1999, https://www.nytimes.com/1999/10/03/theater/theater-an-energetic-irish-troupe-that-keeps-on-the-move.html (accessed 14 June 2023).

[15] See https://www.blueraincoat.com/about (accessed 15 June 2023).

a bacon factory, and became the Factory Space, a seventy-eight-seat theatre on the Sligo quays. Having a theatre ensemble of regular actors has provided continuity and made it possible for the company to take longer over the development of productions with exploratory workshops well before the start of rehearsals.[16] They have also established close working relations with the internationally successful designer Jamie Vartan, who has designed most of their major shows since 2001, and with the dramaturg Jocelyn Clarke who has adapted texts for several of their productions.

In the initial phase of their work, they staged existing text-based plays: Thomas Kilroy's *Double Cross*, Tom Murphy's *A Whistle in the Dark*, Peter Shaffer's *Equus*, along with new plays by Malcolm Hamilton, co-founder of the company. This was a time when Henry was learning how to direct rather than making use of the physical acting skills he had been taught under Marceau. A breakthrough production was Clarke's adaptation of *Alice in Wonderland* in 1999. This, what Henry called a 'poor text, rich in idea but poor in text', allowed the actors to physicalize their performance, the dream-based script suitable for a more fluid dramaturgy and a conceptual design. Several other adaptations by Clarke of works by Flann O'Brien—*The Third Policeman* (2007), *At Swim Two Birds* (2009), and *The Poor Mouth* (2011)—reflected this same interest in the absurd. The preference for the surreal can be seen in their choice of original plays also, with stagings of Beckett—*Play*, *Krapp's Last Tape*, *Rough for Theatre II* (2002), *Endgame* (2013)— and (more unusually for an Irish company) Ionesco. They produced *The Bald Soprano* in 2005 and *Rhinoceros* in 2010 but the production that best illustrates their characteristic style and approach is *The Chairs* (2006).

The play itself, first produced in Paris in 1952, just a year before *Waiting for Godot*, has many of the features of the early so-called 'theatre of the absurd': the nonagenarian caretaker with his wife Semiramis, seventy-five years married, awaiting the arrival of the Orator whose speech will reveal the 'message' the frustrated caretaker has never been able to express; their ridiculous games-playing; the conflicting stories they tell; their climactic joint suicide and the anticlimax of the Orator's meaningless 'speech'. The Blue Raincoat staging stayed close to the original script and Jamie Vartan brilliantly realized the design of the empty space, its semi-circular series of doors framing the double entrance at the centre, the grey backdrop contrasted with the warmth of the natural wood chairs, the golden light that flooded the dim atmosphere with the arrival of the Emperor. Above all, the production showcased the talents of the performers.[17]

Mikel Murfi and Ruth Lehane, playing the old couple, both trained at the Jacques Lecoq school in Paris in the tradition of corporeal mime. A key skill in this

---

[16] On the details of the company, see Trench, *Blue Raincoat Theatre Company*, 30–1.
[17] For details of the staging, I am relying on a recording of the show kindly made available to me by Niall Henry, together with my memory of seeing the original production.

style is the manipulation of imaginary objects, and in *The Chairs* this involved the greeting and seating of invisible guests come to hear the Orator's speech. They conjured up in turn, among these guests, a pretty young lady, the Colonel who makes advances to her, an old woman, once the love object of the caretaker. The comedy of the interactions was sketched in entirely through the expressiveness of the actors on stage. As the guests proliferated, the ancient Semiramis had to fetch more and more chairs, always disappearing through a door on one side of the stage to reappear from the other. As the pace of the action became ever more frenetic, Murfi's gestures of welcome were reduced to ever quicker movements of hands and head, while Lehane set up a complete room full of chairs, without ever abandoning her old woman's shuffle. The deference towards the guests culminated in the positively grovelling welcome for the Emperor, an apogee of satisfaction that precipitated the couple's jump to their deaths from windows at opposite sides of the stage, with a last comic gag the impossibly long gap in time before the splash of their bodies was heard hitting the water. *The Chairs* may now seem somewhat dated in its tendentious insistence on the absurdity of the human search for meaning, but the Blue Raincoat production managed to bring it alive theatrically.

As a Sligo-based company Blue Raincoat has a specific local interest in the plays of Yeats, with *At the Hawk's Well*, *On Baile's Strand*, and *The Cat and the Moon* in their repertory from early on and repeatedly revived. The stylized movement of Yeats's Noh-influenced aesthetic is well suited to their approach. More recently, however, they have moved into a phase of largely devised performances, relying more on visual effect than on text. A key production here was *Shackleton* in 2016. Henry says that he has no interest in 'stories about white men that do derring-do from Victorian England'. The inspiration for the show came from the photographs taken by Frank Hurley on Ernest Shackleton's abortive trans-Antarctic voyage of 1914–17. Some of these original images were shown on a hoisted white sail at the back of the stage, counterpointing the play's action. The photos spoke to Henry of 'people in this beautiful place that was evidently horrendous, on the one hand, and extraordinarily beautiful on the other'. And that was the effect which the play worked to capture.

It was not Henry's original intention to make the show completely wordless. He was apparently at first aghast when Jocelyn Clarke, his dramaturg, looking at a ten-minute piece of devised work without words, said that this should be the mode of the play as a whole. But it proved strikingly successful, with a very flexible and inventive technique combining sound and image. At times the four performers, Sandra O'Malley and John Carty (long-term members of the Blue Raincoat company), Brian F. Devaney and Brian Cullen, dressed in seamen's outfits, manipulated props and puppets by hand or on poles. So, for example, in an arresting first sequence, a finely miniaturized model of Shackleton's expedition ship, the *Endurance* (designed like the show as a whole by Jamie Vartan), was moved slowly along the black floor of the stage, while the other actors pushed white bundles of cloth around it simulating the ice-floes of the Weddell Sea. By degrees these moved in closer and closer until the ship was completely lodged in the 'ice' to the accompanying grinding sound of the icebergs, achieved, according to sound designer Joe Hunt, by recording the creak of a woodbasket.

After the ship was abandoned—the model lit up aloft before it sank—the white cloths were spread out for the snowfields on which the men made camp on the ice. Silhouettes of their figures were seen inside a white sheet tent, while the sound and music conveyed the desolation of the scene. Three smaller more basic models were used for the three lifeboats, when it was decided to cross the sea to Elephant Island. The desperate conditions of that crossing were suggested by the models being moved at speed by two of the actors up and down a narrow strip of cloth held at each end by the other two, an action repeated for the single boat that sailed from Elephant Island to South Georgia. For the crossing of South Georgia, after the party of three, Shackleton, Henry Worsley, and Tom Crean, had landed on the wrong side of the island, there were black cloths in place of white, simulating the uncharted mountain peaks they had to traverse. The final rescue of the crew left on Elephant Island was represented by the four performers standing still, as if dazed, against the projected original photo of the triumphant men on their return.

Shackleton has proved to be the first of a number of devised pieces by Blue Raincoat, including *Hunting Darwin* (2021) and *The Last Pearl* (2022), which have used puppetry and projections to pursue themes of humans in the natural world with a strong ecological dimension. Although Henry remains unclear as to whether this is the direction in which the company will continue, these shows are in some sense the logical conclusion of the rejection of text, the emphasis on image and movement which first developed in the 1990s. 'Less words', suggested Veronica Coburn, Raymond Keane's co-founder of Barabbas, 'can we do theatre with less words?' Though both Barabbas and Blue Raincoat were to use text—very effectively in the case of the productions of *The Whiteheaded Boy* and *The Chairs*—their shared aim was to give a new centrality to physical performance within the visual field of design. A key event in this development was a workshop led by Mikel Murfi and Veronica Coburn, before the setting up of Barabbas, bringing together other people with similar interests. Among those were Annie Ryan and Michael West, who were to collaborate in the work of The Corn Exchange, the company established in 1995.

American Cousin to the French: The Corn Exchange

When she first came to Dublin in 1989, Annie Ryan said that she knew that in Ireland she 'would get a certain amount of respect as a practitioner of what I did, for bringing *commedia* and so forth, whereas people with my training were a dime a dozen in Chicago'.[18] It was a measure of how far Ireland was behind the curve, that someone with Ryan's background should feel that it offered her an opportunity for new and innovative work. When she first encountered Irish theatre, Ryan said 'I was so struck by the stillness and by the lack of embodiment and by the feeling of a lack of empowerment among the cast'.[19] This stood out by contrast with the tradition in which she had been trained, that of theatre games and improvisation. She had worked with the Piven Theatre Workshop, originally founded by Byrne and Joyce Piven, with its origins in the University of Chicago in the 1950s.[20] As Ryan described their technique, 'impulsive games' were used 'to allow the actors to come into fully embodied play on the floor through different structures. And the main principle behind almost all the games is around what I would call transformational theatre or ensemble-based theatre'. Such theatre games were applied, using 'third person past tense narration', in the animation and embodiment of stories, prose texts, or poems.

Commedia was not part of the original training but came later as a development led by Jeremy Piven, son to the founding couple, in association with Georges Bigot, who had worked with Ariane Mnouchkine's company Théâtre du Soleil. This, and the concentration on movement, is what leads Ryan to describe her work as 'American cousin to the French'. This rough version of *commedia* used white face paint rather than more elaborate forms of mask. In establishing Corn Exchange, Ryan set out to combine the techniques of theatre games and story theatre with *commedia*. Their early work involved adaptations, using *commedia* style, of classic texts such as Tennessee Williams, *A Streetcar Named Desire* (1996), Chekhov's *The Seagull* (1999), and Nabokov's screenplay for *Lolita* (2002)—which featured Ruth Negga in her first professional role—as well as original plays by Michael West, the movement-based *A Play on Two Chairs* (1997) and the one-man monologue *Foley* (2000). (Ryan and West, who came together over their shared tastes in theatre, are a married couple.) However, the play that probably best represents this first phase of the company's work and their collaboration with West is *Dublin by Lamplight* (2004).

The play had its origins in the awareness of two centenaries being commemorated in 2004, the opening of the Abbey as Ireland's National Theatre, and the imaginary date of the action of *Ulysses*, latterly celebrated as Bloomsday. Though it began as a show devised in workshop before there was a script, the ingenious play with the 1904 materials may be attributed to West, Ryan saying that she had

---

[18] Annie Ryan and Michael West, 'Annie Ryan and Michael West in Conversation with Luke Clancy', in Lilian Chambers, Ger FitzGibbon, and Eamonn Jordan (eds.), *Theatre Talk: Voices of Irish Theatre Practitioners* (Dublin: Carysfort Press, 2001), 424–31 [424].
[19] Interview with the author, 3 May 2023. All quotations not otherwise attributed are taken from this interview for which I am very grateful to Annie Ryan.
[20] For the background to Piven and their ongoing work, see https://www.piventheatre.org/our-story/our-history/ (accessed 20 June 2023).

'no real interest' in the founding of the Abbey. The names of the brothers Willy and Frank Hayes derive from the Fay brothers, William and Frank, who formed the Abbey's acting company, though in the play Willy, as the author of the mythological drama *The Wooing of Emer*, is a stand-in for Yeats. As such, he is entirely dependent on the goodwill of Eva St John, a malicious composite of A. E. Horniman, the English benefactress of the Abbey, and the militant nationalist Maud Gonne—how they would both have hated being merged together! The first name of Martyn Wallace, actor and entrepreneur in the play, is a nod to Edward Martyn, co-founder of the Irish Literary Theatre, while the character has aspects of Oscar Wilde and also resembles Yeats. The title of the play is taken from the short story 'Clay' in Joyce's *Dubliners*, where the character Maria works in the Dublin by Lamplight Laundry. The third act of the play is set in 'Nighttown', the red-light district of Dublin that provides the setting for the 'Circe' episode of *Ulysses*, and the ending rewrites the conclusion of the *Dubliners* story 'Eveline'.

The play was intended, according to Ryan, as a 'celebration of theatre', and at its centre is the production of *The Wooing of Emer*, as the inaugural performance of the 'Irish National Theatre of Ireland', the absurd title a reminder of the numerous groups vying for national theatre status at the time.[21] Staged as a play within a play in the second act, it is a hilarious send-up of early Abbey verse drama, with Maggie, the lowly amateur costume mistress, coming forward to play Emer (in place of Eva St John who is in police custody), opposite her real-life lover Frank playing Cuchulain. But *Dublin by Lamplight* also represented a bravura showcase for the Corn Exchange company style. The six performers in fixed *commedia* white face make-up, accentuated by heavy black lines, all played multiple parts. But, unlike the actors in the Barabbas *Whiteheaded Boy*, they had split-second changes of costume to mark each different character. They followed the *commedia* conventions of presentation, with extremely stylized movement and posture, when speaking their lines face out to the audience, standing still in profile when listening. This boldly caricatured playing style, however, was offset by the self-narration of Ryan's story theatre training, as in the opening line spoken by Martyn: 'Martyn Wallace awoke in his boarding house and held his aching head. His room was brown and dirty and bare. He called it Reading Gaol' (West, *Dublin by Lamplight*, 9). This slowed the frenetic pace of the *commedia* into an (at times) lyrical mode, while allowing the actors to realize the spaces around them in a largely bare stage.

In its combination of *commedia* and story theatre styles, the production was militantly anti-naturalistic. But it was politically subversive also. It was not only

---

[21] All quotations from the play are taken from Michael West in association with the Corn Exchange, *Dublin by Lamplight* (London: Bloomsbury Methuen Drama, 2017), the text revised for the revival of the play in the Abbey Theatre in 2017. I am indebted to Annie Ryan for access to a recording of the original staging. On the various theatre groupings of the time, see Mary Trotter, *Ireland's National Theaters: Political Performance and the Origins of the Irish Dramatic Movement* (Syracuse: Syracuse University Press, 2001).

the irreverence with which the story of 'Our Irish Theatre' was re-imagined.[22] The filthy physical conditions of 1904 Dublin were emphasized with the scene of the Dung Dodgers, carting away the night soil from the tenements. And the streets are in fact only being cleaned up because of the visit of King Edward VII (which West moved forward from the historical date of 1903 for the purposes of the play). Two early juxtaposed scenes point the class contrast between Eva St John, waited on by her maid, and the tenement dweller Maggie, who we see later working as a cleaner in the Nassau Hotel, where Yeats and Gregory stayed when in Dublin. The high cultural nationalist aspirations of the national theatre are undercut in the play by the active revolutionary movement. Frank Hayes, when not playing the part of Cuchulain, inspirational figure for the Easter 1916 Rising, is a rogue member of the Irish Republican Brotherhood (IRB) who sets off a bomb, killing one man and injuring many others. While the innocent Willy is the perpetual fall guy of the action—mugged by the IRB, renounced by his patron Eva, stripped by the Nighttown whores, finally shot dead by British soldiers—Frank survives and escapes.

The cost of that escape is underlined in the rewriting of the ending of 'Eveline'. In Joyce's story, it is Eveline who is paralysed into inaction on the quayside while her lover Frank calls for her to join him on the ship. The Frank of *Dublin by Lamplight* grabs the ticket for the Liverpool boat from Maggie, leaving her pregnant to face the consequences, already spelled out in her earlier thoughts: 'If she stayed here without him, she'd end up in the laundry or somewhere in disgrace' (West, *Dublin by Lamplight*, 70). The actual Dublin by Lamplight Laundry was one of the Magdalene homes for unmarried mothers, notorious by 2004. The last lines of the play, as a result, were deeply affecting: 'She stepped back from the rails, into the shadows, the better to think. The darkness swallowed her up' (West, *Dublin by Lamplight*, 76). *Dublin by Lamplight* was a high fantastical extravaganza, playing witty games with the foundational national theatre narrative. At the same time, it brought home to its audiences the brutal social and political realities of 1904.

Everyday (2006) resembled *Ulysses* in creating a day in the life of the city with multiple characters criss-crossing through its streets. But this was not Joyce's stagnant Edwardian Dublin; it was contemporary Dublin at the height of the economic boom, when house prices were doubling within months and Ireland had, for the first time, a cohort of the super-rich. *Freefall* (2009), by contrast, emerged out of the collapse of the Celtic Tiger, its title speaking to the freefalling economy in the wake of the global crisis of 2008. As the play was in development, the Ryan Report on the abuse of children in industrial schools was published, and this further exposure of what had gone on inside Church-run institutions also made an impact. As Ryan puts it in her 'maker's note' to the published text: 'Our play isn't overtly about the collapse of the Celtic Tiger or the Catholic Church, but it is our

---

[22] Lady Gregory, *Our Irish Theatre* (New York: G. P. Putnam's Sons, 1913).

setting—Ireland 2009'.[23] There were earlier versions in which the economic conditions were much more directly foregrounded. In the archives of the company, there is a detailed scenario in which a married couple are faking a divorce and burning down their house for the insurance money.[24] In the event, the play only figures the economic collapse in the metaphor of the dry rot in the basement of A and B's house, diagnosed by the head-shaking expert Fungal Man: 'You should have called me a long time ago. People always leave these things until it's too late' (West, *Freefall*, 16). The Ryan Report is even more tangentially implied, with A's haunted sense of his orphaned baby sister, lost without trace when he himself was adopted by his aunt and uncle, a reminder of the many children who went missing in the Ireland of an earlier time.

Everyday was performed with *commedia* white face masks, but in *Freefall* Ryan was looking for something else. In one of her notebooks, she commented that her aim for the play was '[t]o find a style that uses the best of the Commedia work but also exposes itself as a style that is of itself'. This notebook has jottings in which she uses *commedia* stock characters to provide a breakdown of contemporary social types:

Dottore—artists, scientists, journaliists, academic
Capitano—teachers, principles [sic], managers, civil servants, dole office, politicians.[25]

Accordingly, masking was abandoned for *Freefall*, but the four performers, only identified in the text as B, C, D, and G all played different parts which tended to conform to one or another set typology. The style was anti-illusionist throughout. The actors appeared at the beginning to arrange the minimalist set: a couple of hospital trolleys, one of which became a dinner table by the addition of a cloth, some plastic stacking chairs, a large screen behind, and curtains that could be pulled across mid-stage. With the exception of a few specific items (identified in the script), all the physical props were imaginary, and the sound effects—vomiting, tooth-brushing, toilet flushing—were visibly generated by the actors at microphones at the sides of the stage.[26]

All of this fast-moving, flexible theatricality surrounded the central figure of A, as he experiences a stroke. A major influence here, as acknowledged by Ryan, was the testimony of the neurologist Jill Bolte Taylor who 'suffered a catastrophic stroke yet recovered to tell her story' (Ryan, 'Maker's Note', West, *Freefall*). This allowed

---

[23] Michael West in association with the Corn Exchange, *Freefall* (London: Methuen Drama, 2010), n.p.
[24] Corn Exchange archives, Hardiman Library, University of Galway. I am most grateful to Barry Houlihan for access to these (as yet uncatalogued) papers.
[25] Corn Exchange archives, Galway.
[26] Comments on the performance here are derived from a recording of the 2009 production (to which Annie Ryan kindly gave me access) and my own memories of that production.

for the non-linear associative shape of the action as fragments of A's past life appear in flashback in the midst of the live drama. A, memorably played by Andrew Bennett, stands as Everyman figure always in his pyjamas, while all the other characters shape-change around him. Interviewed for a video project by his son Jack—a character only present as voiceover—A declares that he has 'had a completely normal life [...] I've been very lucky' (West, *Freefall*, 6). The play examines this statement: how normal is it to lose your mother at age 7, to be reluctantly adopted by an aunt and uncle who do not take in your baby sister; how lucky are you to be bullied right through your life by a predatory egotist, your obnoxious cousin Denis; to be married to a demanding wife who is on the point of leaving you?

Through much of the action, A seems to be a put-upon loser. Yet the remorseful address by his wife Louise to A, as he lies dying, appears true too: 'You've been such a good man. [...] Such a good husband and father' (West, *Freefall*, 61). This was the more moving in production because addressed by Janet Moran through a microphone to an empty trolley, while Bennett stood helpless at the other side of the stage, her face appearing on-screen as his point of view. These black and white videos, created by Jack Phelan, showing A's muzzy awareness of doctors and nurses peering down at him, were one of the most powerful features of the play in performance. Ryan said that, as *Freefall* developed, 'it became very clear that it was a play about grief'. The loss of all sense of security brought about by the collapse of the economy, the sense of shock at the revelations of the Ryan Report, were part of this 'grief'. But this collective experience was figured in the feeling of loss in the embodied bewilderment of a single man suffering the trauma of stroke and dying.

At the very point of the triumph of *Freefall*—Best Play of 2009 in the *Irish Times* Theatre Awards, with Ryan winning Best Director—Arts Council funding for Corn Exchange was cut in half. Ironically, in view of the play's theme, this was part of the drastic reduction in support for theatre that saw so many companies (including Barabbas) brought to an end. Corn Exchange continued to produce work for a further decade: the one-man show *Man of Valour* (2011), a large-scale adaptation of *Dubliners* (2012), an immensely successful stage reworking of Eimear McBride's novel *A Girl Is a Half-Formed Thing* (2015), a second version of *The Seagull* (2016). What turned out to be their final fully resourced production was the ambitious political satire, West's *The Fall of the Second Republic*, staged at the Abbey in 2020, with a run cut short by the Covid lockdown. The next year their Arts Council support was withdrawn altogether, making impossible the collaborative practice which distinguished Corn Exchange. Well in advance of the production of a play, Ryan led workshops with a group of actors, often the same performers that appeared in many of their shows: Andrew Bennett, Janet Moran, Louis Lovett, Mark O'Halloran, and Paul Reid. Drafts of a script, mostly written by West, were then pulled apart in development and rehearsal, scenes often cut or changed right up until close to opening night and beyond. Though West is a fine playwright, his dialogue witty and incisive, the shows he scripted have been rightly credited to him 'in association with the company'. As the policy of the Arts Council has moved towards supporting only individual projects, rather than the core funding of a company, it meant the loss to Irish theatre of the work of Corn Exchange which required a longer term process with a stable group of collaborators.

Deconstructing Theatre: Pan Pan

Both director Gavin Quinn and designer Aedín Cosgrove, co-founders of Pan Pan, studied drama at Trinity College Dublin and were much influenced by John McCormick who had first set up an academic degree programme in the subject. McCormick had a major interest in modern European directors and, according to Quinn, 'got us thinking about essentially European theatre aesthetics'.[27] Cosgrove said that from the beginning, they 'had a very clear aim to be different, to be very distinct from what was happening in the other theatres, in the Gate, in the Abbey'.[28] This was a conceptual idea of theatre, according to Quinn, 'where you could use the kind of visual arts principles of line, form and colour'.[29] Quinn's first play, *Negative Act*, written when he was still an undergraduate, toured to the Lyon International Student Festival, and made him very aware of how different French audiences were from Irish. From then on, the work of Pan Pan was made with a sense of this potential international dimension. They performed in avant-garde festivals in Poland and Germany, and later staged productions in China—I will be returning to their Chinese-language version of *The Playboy of the Western World* in the next chapter. By way of increasing the exposure of Irish theatre to work from abroad they hosted an annual Dublin International Theatre Symposium from 1997 to 2003. As well as achieving success in Ireland, they have what is probably the most widespread international reputation of any Irish company.

Quinn dismisses the term 'postdramatic theatre' when applied to the work of Pan Pan: 'such an old-fashioned phrase at this stage', 'incredibly narrow'. He prefers to style their productions as 'deconstructionist, contemporary, experimental'. Nevertheless, many features of Pan Pan's work do relate to the characteristics of postdramatic theatre as set out in the influential book by Hans-Thies Lehmann, first published in German in 1999. Within dramatic theatre, as Lehmann defines it, '[w]holeness, illusion and world representation are inherent'; postdramatic theatre begins 'when these elements are no longer the regulatory principle but merely one possible variant of theatrical art'. 'In postdramatic forms of theatre', Lehmann

---

[27] Interview with the author, 6 June 2023. All further information about Pan Pan, not otherwise attributed, is taken from this interview, for which I am very grateful to Gavin Quinn.
[28] Quoted in Noelia Ruiz, 'Scenic Transitions: From Drama to Experimental Practices in Irish Theatre', in Eamonn Jordan and Eric Weitz (eds.), *The Palgrave Handbook of Contemporary Irish Theatre and Performance* (London: Palgrave Macmillan, 2018), 293–308 [300].
[29] Ruiz, 'Scenic Transitions', 300.

claims, as against 'drama', 'staged text (if text is staged) is merely a component with equal rights in a gestic, musical, visual etc. total composition'.[30] This sort of dethroning of the sovereign text, its deconstruction within a multi-dimensional work no longer dependent on a conventional narrative shape, is fundamental to Pan Pan productions. *Oedipus Loves You* (2006) may be taken to illustrate their approach.

The play was written as a full collaboration between Gavin Quinn and playwright Simon Doyle. They began with Sophocles's Theban 'trilogy'—*Antigone*, *Oedipus Rex*, and *Oedipus at Colonus*—though the play covers mainly the events of *Oedipus Rex*: the plague, with Creon dispatched to Delphi to discover its source; Tiresias reluctantly revealing Oedipus as the murderer of Laius, and the gradual emergence of the truth; Jocasta's suicide and Oedipus's self-blinding. Much of this was recognizable as Sophocles's play rendered into modern colloquial prose. However, before Quinn and Doyle wrote the script, they wrote an album of ten rock songs to be used in the show, and the classical legend was given a jokey contemporary face-lift, set in a suburban house and garden. Jocasta (Gina Moxley) was not really bothered by the plague, it helped her sleep better. When Oedipus (Bush Moukarzel, later co-founder of Dead Centre) boasted of having vanquished the Sphinx, the ultra-cool Jocasta questioned whether she needed vanquishing. A motorcycle-helmeted Creon (Dylan Tighe) has all too obvious incestuous designs on Antigone (Ruth Negga again) who is a sullen teenager—'I just want to be left alone'. Tiresias (Ned Dennehy) is an ageing ex-percussionist turned psychotherapist, who wants to join the garage band set up by Creon and Antigone. He doubles as the Sphinx at the play's opening, singing naked with no apparent genitals, a nod to Tiresias's hermaphroditic status. The play ended with a posthumous family barbecue in which all joined in, including the mutilated Oedipus with bloodied eye-sockets, Jocasta with rope end round her neck: 'I'm dead. I'll be fine. It's the children I worry about'.[31]

All the performers sang and played the rock songs, singly and together, accompanied by a keyboard player at the side of the stage.[32] Loud sound, high visibility created an all-out assault on the audience's senses. The attenuated forestage featured a diminutive paddling-pool, a barbecue, some loungers, microphones as needed, imposing on the players a deliberately cramped playing area. But behind them was a skeleton model of a house showing the marital bedroom of Oedipus and Jocasta with suggestively red décor on one side, Antigone's bedroom on the

---

[30] Hans-Thies Lehmann, *Postdramatic Theatre*, trans. Karen Jürs-Munby (London: Routledge, 2006), 22, 46.

[31] *Oedipus Loves You*, rehearsal draft, 18 August 2006, Pan Pan Archives, James Hardiman Library, University of Galway, T27/1/15.

[32] All details of the performance are based on a partial recording in the Pan Pan archives, Hardiman Library, and my own memory of the original production.

other, a kitchen area between. When any of the five performers were not required on stage, they were to be seen in one or other of these rooms, a characteristic Pan Pan strategy. For Quinn it's a matter of 'trying to keep the energy there, not having actors go into the wings or turn off or become watchers themselves so they become observers of their own work'. Equally typical was the use of two screens mounted above the 'house'. One of these showed camera shots of the onstage or offstage actors, but the other had projections of what the director Quinn, visible in a radio sound booth in the wings, scribbled on paper: text of the dialogue, lyrics of the songs, stick-figure illustrations. The multiple simultaneous sights and sound disrupted any attempt of an audience at concentrated attention on what in *Oedipus Rex* is the single brilliantly constructed tragic narrative.

The play was highly successful both when premiered in Dublin, and touring across the world in Britain, Germany, China, the US, and Australia. There was some sales resistance to what was felt to be the modishness, or indeed outmodishness, of the dramaturgy. Several reviewers mentioned the American experimental Wooster Group as an obvious predecessor: according to one London reviewer, it had 'an earnestness that turns you against it. Quinn directs a Wooster Group-style deconstruction [...] but one that feels rougher and less playful'.[33] The first reaction of another was 'Been there. Seen that. Wooster Group'.[34] But most reviewers overcame that sense of distrust of the company's tricks and manners. So, for example, Ben Brantley, writing in the *New York Times*, commented that the staging was 'of a piece with the sort of standard-issue, detached parody you might expect from a company that considers itself postmodern and post-theater'. But he remarked that, though 'loud and obvious in its presentation', it was 'surprisingly subtle in its cumulative effect' as 'a dialogue between an ancient mighty myth and its adulterated forms in the present'.[35] The energy, the edginess, and the sheer attack of the show came to win out over the sense of predictable avant-garde stage effects. The success of the play and the production was to reroot the Oedipus myth in its modern Freudian interpretation, even as that Freudian framework had descended into cliché.

The iconoclastic deconstruction of canonical texts has been a key part of Pan Pan's repertoire, from *Macbeth 7* (2004)—so called because Quinn had seen six other productions of the play—through *A Doll House* (2012) to *The Seagull and Other Birds* (2016). The best known of these is probably *The Rehearsal: Playing the Dane* (2010), their version of *Hamlet*, which, after its opening in Dublin in

---

[33] Ian Shuttleworth, 'Oedipus Loves You / Oedipus', *Financial Times*, 18 February 2008, https://www.ft.com/content/e31fc274-de4a-11dc-9de3-0000779fd2ac (accessed 27 December 2023).
[34] Review by Timothy Ramsden of London Riverside Studio production, 14 February 2008, https://reviewsgate.com/oedipus-loves-you-to-23-february/ (accessed 28 June 2023).
[35] Ben Brantley, 'From Thebes to Suburbia: In Dire Need of Therapy', *New York Times*, 24 May 2008.

2010, was to play all round the world.[36] In the title, the colon marks the interval of the show. The first half had scenes of the play rehearsed before Quinn the director and his crew, who were on stage auditioning three actors for the part of Hamlet. The audience were then invited to stand behind the actor they chose to cast for the hero, and the elected performer then acted the role through the second half which was a (sort of) production of the play. But before any of that began, there was a warm-up by the actors, and a lecture on the play by an academic (Amanda Piesse in the Irish performances). The main burden of the lecture was the instability of the text, the differences between the unauthorized first quarto (generally thought to be a reconstruction of the play from memory by actors), the second quarto (put out by Shakespeare's acting company to correct the first), and the collected folio printing, with the many undecidable variants between the different versions. This emphasis on the variability of the play's text suited a production bent on creating its own wildly uncanonical *Hamlet*. And what was otherwise a sober academic lecture was rendered bizarre because Piesse held a Great Dane on a leash throughout, ending her talk by playing 'Greensleeves' on the recorder: 'Greensleeves', the hackneyed go-to music for any Tudor period piece, the recorder Hamlet's metaphorical instrument used against the spying Rosencrantz and Guildenstern, the dog a punning reminder of the hero's dramatic act IV re-appearance, 'This is I,/ Hamlet the Dane'. Teasing in-jokes, bizarre juxtapositions—this was the style of *Playing the Dane* from the start.

The aim throughout was to overcome that sense of here-we-go-again overfamiliarity with the text. When the chosen Hamlet finally got to speak the 'To be or not to be' speech, it was repeated in a fugue-like set of echoes by all the rest of the cast: everyone knows these lines—Hamlet meditates on suicide for all of us.[37] Calling an audience member up on stage to speak a line, having them literally vote with their feet for the casting of Hamlet, was a way of inhibiting any sort of fourth wall separation from the performance. A metatheatrical awareness of production history was added, for example, by Daniel Reardon, the veteran actor playing Polonius, originally American but long based in Ireland, reminiscing (Polonius-like) about his actual experience of seeing Burton play Hamlet in New York in 1964. Having school-age children play the Players, and then Hamlet and Laertes in the graveyard scene, riffed off the 'war of the theatres', Shakespeare's contemporary reference in the text to the competition between the adult actors and the boy companies. All this pitched the show somewhere between knowing iconoclasm and scholarly allusiveness.

It was not merely a matter of defamiliarizing the canonical text; the production never allowed the audience to settle, shifting abruptly from mode to mode.

---

[36] For details, see https://www.panpantheatre.com/shows/the-rehearsal-playing-the-dane (accessed 29 June 2023).
[37] I am relying here on the recording of the performance on 1 December 2011 in the Black Box Theatre, Galway, which is held in the Pan Pan archive, Hardiman Library.

So, for example, the bare set, designed by Aedín Cosgrove, seemed at first to figure a rehearsal space: long strip of red carpet, table for the auditioning team, a miscellany of props lying about. But it could be blacked out to show Andrew Bennett, holding up a table lamp, delivering the unaltered lines of the Ghost with moving intensity, or again, at the opening of the second act, transformed into a powerful chiaroscuro, with all the actors carrying candles in the darkness. One of the recurring intertexts through the play was Beckett's *Endgame*: Hamlet pushed on in a wheelchair by Gertrude (Gina Moxley) at one point—Gertrude who actually recited Clov's lines 'It's finished ...' later on. The bins in which Nagg and Nell are stored in *Endgame* proliferated in *Playing the Dane* and were used for multiple effects: Rosencrantz and Guildenstern appeared with them on their heads; the court audience in the play scene stood in them; the skulls for the graveyard were tipped out of one of them. Ophelia's appearances were concentrated into a single scene, in which instead of flowers she distributed crisp packets and discarded cigarette packets to the audience. Quinn insists that even with his unorthodox version '[o]nce you have the lines of *Hamlet*, it's still *Hamlet*'. Perhaps, but *Playing the Dane* was *Hamlet* overlaid with its own history, rescued from its canonical status by self-conscious playfulness and immersion in the heterogeneous modernity of its audiences.

One of the features of postdramatic theatre, according to Lehmann, is play with the 'density of signs'. This may take the form of an overstimulating 'plethora' or a low density which 'aims to provoke the spectator's own imagination to become active on the basis of the little raw material to work on.'[38] Pan Pan's versions of *Oedipus the King* and *Hamlet* went for the plethoric approach, breaking apart the texts, multiplying to the point of distraction competing and conflicting images that animated the stage. By contrast their productions of what amounts to a trilogy of Beckett's radio plays have adopted a low-density approach. This was the effect of *All That Fall*, for instance (premiered in 2011), evoked by an Australian reviewer in 2014:

> Pan Pan Theatre's production invites us to return to stopping still as we listen. We walk onto Aedín Cosgrove's design, the floor covered in a children's play carpet dotted with simple rocking chairs. On each seat a black cushion with a print of a skull, in front of us a large, tall bank of yellow lights, above our heads hundreds of yellow globes.[39]

The result, Patrick Lonergan claimed, was 'to create a space that is almost entirely free of sensory distractions, allowing us to listen to the play with a profound

---

[38] Lehmann, *Postdramatic Theatre*, 90.
[39] Jane Howard, 'All That Fall Pan Pan Theatre—Review', *The Guardian* 15 January 2014, https://www.theguardian.com/culture/australia-culture-blog/2014/jan/15/all-that-fall-pan-pan-theatre-review (accessed 29 June 2023).

concentration'.[40] The centrepiece of their *Embers* (2013) was a 'four metre high wooden sculpture of a human skull' (created by Andrew Clancy).[41] It was from microphones within this skull that the audience heard the meditations of Henry (Andrew Bennett). In *Cascando* (2016) the audience listened to the text on individual headphones, while wandering through a labyrinthine maze dressed in all-enveloping hooded black gowns. Pan Pan do not want spectators to sit back, relax, and enjoy the show. They are to be self-aware participants, whether trying to make sense of the welter of signs with which they are assailed, or invited into a Zen-like mode of listening and contemplation.

Of the four companies discussed in this chapter, two are no longer functioning, two are still in operation. All four, however, reflect the specific conditions necessary for their sort of theatre. To build a new show in these styles, something more is needed than a finished script put into rehearsal four to five weeks before opening. That standard model requires a set more or less fully designed in advance, and, according to Niall Henry, makes for the casting of actors according to type. The director needs already to have a detailed plan for the staging of the text. That renders impossible the exploratory techniques all these companies consider essential: workshopping, preliminary development, joint discovery between actors, director, designer, and dramaturg—the European model of theatre. If not a permanent ensemble, a group of performers used to playing together is a major advantage. Like Barabbas, Blue Raincoat, and Corn Exchange, Pan Pan has relied on a number of actors cast in many of their shows: Andrew Bennett, Gina Moxley, Daniel Reardon. One major bonus of international touring for Quinn is the opportunity to employ actors for some twenty-five weeks in the year instead of just five. And those extended periods of working together helps the coherence of the work.

Freehouse (2022) is Pan Pan's most determinedly non-linear, non-narrative show to date. In what was more like an art installation than theatre, audience members were free to wander at will through a variety of objects and events on display across several spaces in the Samuel Beckett Theatre, Trinity College. Billed as 'a happening', like a throwback to the 1960s, it was glossed as 'The attempted suicide of representational theatre'.[42] 'Attempted' is interesting here. The movement considered in this chapter can be seen as part of a resistance to standard text-based theatre. But, though much of the work of all four companies has been devised, text has had a way of creeping back in. The greatest success of Barabbas came with *The Whiteheaded Boy*, while Blue Raincoat found a congenial idiom in *The Chairs*. Both Barabbas and Pan Pan produced a *Macbeth*; Corn Exchange and Pan

---

[40] Patrick Lonergan, review of *All That Fall*, *Irish Theatre Magazine*, https://aran.library.nuigalway.ie/bitstream/handle/10379/6663/All_That_Fall_Irish_Theatre_Magazine_%7c_Reviews_%7c_Current_%7c_All_That_Fall.pdf?sequence=1&isAllowed=y (accessed 29 June 2023).

[41] Ian R. Walsh, 'Embers', *Irish Theatre Magazine*, 12 August 2011, http://itmarchive.ie/web/Reviews/Current/Embers.aspx.html (accessed 29 June 2023).

[42] For details, see https://www.panpantheatre.com/shows/freehouse (accessed 30 June 2023).

Pan each had its version of *The Seagull*. Text, representational theatre, appears to be dead but refuses to lie down. My next chapter is concerned with twenty-first-century efforts to revive and re-imagine the work of Synge, the playwright who did so much to establish the tradition of Irish literary theatre, against which these companies rebelled.

3
Re-Imagining Synge

J. M. Synge, the first major playwright of the Irish national theatre movement, over the twentieth century developed into that dustiest of things, a modern classic; his best-known play, *The Playboy of the Western World*, was prescribed on school exam syllabuses and appeared as a staple of the amateur drama circuit. After its first riotous reception and controversial reputation, it became a mainstay of the Abbey repertoire. The principal parts of Christy Mahon, Pegeen Mike, and the Widow Quin were played in turn by successive generations of the leading Abbey actors, with performance business handed down from one to another. The dialect of the plays, archaic sounding English vocabulary built upon a substratum of Irish-language syntax, had been resisted as inauthentic from the beginning: St John Ervine, another early Abbey playwright, had denounced Synge as 'a faker of peasant speech'.[1] It came to be heard as a predictable stage 'Synge-song', much mocked, easily parodied.

The Playboy at least continued to be revived, at home and abroad. The rest of Synge's work more or less disappeared from the stage. Dying in 1909, after a writing life of less than seven years, Synge left just six stageable plays, including the unfinished *Deirdre of the Sorrows*. The one-act *Riders to the Sea* (1904) made an enormous impact originally, hailed internationally as a tragic masterpiece, used as the template for plays by D. H. Lawrence (*The Widowing of Mrs Holroyd*) and Bertolt Brecht (*Señora Carrar's Rifles*), the text set to music as an opera by Ralph Vaughan Williams (1937). In the playing conditions of the early Abbey, one-act plays such as *Riders* and *The Shadow of the Glen* (1903) were welcome as curtain-raisers or parts of programmes of short plays. Though lunch-time shows do still provide an opportunity for one-act shows, curtain-raisers have disappeared from modern theatre and composite programmes are a rarity.[2] *The Well of the Saints* (1905) was Synge's first three-act play but is not long enough to fill a full evening show and, when staged by the Abbey, has often been eked out by an added forepiece. The two-act *The Tinker's Wedding*, never performed in Synge's lifetime, had to wait until the centenary of his birth in 1971 to get a first production at the Abbey. What if anything, could twenty-first-century companies do to bring Synge back upon the stage in forms that would work for contemporary audiences?

---

[1] St John Ervine, *Some Impressions of My Elders* (London: Allen and Unwin, 1922), 201.
[2] *Shadows*, billed as 'A Trinity of Plays by J. M. Synge and W. B. Yeats', staged by the Royal Shakespeare Company in 1998, is one exception. J. M. Synge and W. B. Yeats, *Shadows: A Trinity of Plays by J.M. Synge and W.B. Yeats. Riders to the Sea, The Shadow of the Glen, Purgatory* (London: Oberon, 1998).

Druid Theatre Company dealt with the problem by staging all of the plays together. Their long-planned project, realized in 2005 as DruidSynge, allowed audiences to see the six plays in a single day, offering a vision of Synge's theatrical imagination as an organic whole. For the most part, however, the reworking of Synge has been concentrated on *Playboy*. So, for example, Niall Henry, directing it in the Peacock in 2001, provided a very different version of the play by a nonnaturalistic production, casting Mikel Murfi as Christy Mahon. Pan Pan's *Playboy*, directed by Gavin Quinn in 2006, translated into Mandarin and staged in Beijing, transposed the action of the play to contemporary China. Bisi Adigun and Roddy Doyle adapted a new version of the play for the Abbey in 2007, setting it in modern west Dublin, with Christy and his father Nigerian immigrants. In my first two chapters, I looked at playwrights who created new sorts of language without the lyrical eloquence that began with Synge, companies that turned against the dominance of text in the sort of literary drama that he initiated. Here I want to consider the ways in which Synge's own work has been renewed theatrically in the twenty-first century.

Re-Creating: DruidSynge (2005)

At the end of *Riders to the Sea*, the first play in the 2005 DruidSynge cycle production, the director Garry Hynes chose to alter Synge's prescribed scene.[3] The original stage directions call for a group of women mourners in the background 'keening softly and swaying themselves with a slow movement'.[4] The keen was designed to continue as a choric background to the solo voice of Maurya's last great threnody: just before her final lines 'the keen rises a little more loudly from the women, then sinks away' (Synge, *Collected Works*, Vol. III, 27). Instead of this Hynes had the women, black petticoats over their heads in lieu of shawls, turn their faces to the wall of the cottage and noiselessly beat their hands against it. It was an inspired decision. It is difficult theatrically to manage the sound of the keen so as not to distract from Maurya's words; the traditional keen was itself a sort of sung elegy for the dead, though often rendered as a wordless lament.[5] In Hynes's version, the women with their heads covered, backs to the audience, recalled images of the

---

[3] The full cycle of plays was first produced at the Galway Town Hall Theatre on 16 July 2005: for details, see http://www.druidsynge.com/ Comments on the production here are based on my memories of this premiere and the later performance of the plays on Inis Meain in the Aran Islands, supplemented by the film recording *DruidSynge*, three-DVD set (RTÉ, Wildfire Films/Druid, 2007).

[4] J. M. Synge, *Collected Works*, Vol. III: *Plays, Book I*, ed. Ann Saddlemyer (London: Oxford University Press, 1968), 23. All quotations from Synge, except where otherwise noted, are taken from this four-volume edition and will be cited parenthetically in the text.

[5] See Angela Bourke, 'Keening as Theatre', in Nicholas Grene (ed.), *Interpreting Synge: Essays from the Synge Summer School 1991–2000* (Dublin: Lilliput Press, 2000), 67–79.

Wailing Wall.[6] It was characteristic of the DruidSynge project as a whole: innovative in its staging of the six Synge plays, and at the same time the culmination of Druid's long-term investment in the playwright.

The Playboy was in fact one of the first plays staged by the newly established company, founded in 1975 by recent University College Galway graduates Garry Hynes and Marie Mullen, along with their slightly older colleague Mick Lally. Initially chosen as a well-known text to draw in summer visitors, Synge's work was felt to have special resonance for them with their shared west of Ireland background. As Hynes put it, they were convinced that '*we* could speak this writer's language in a way that other people couldn't and that we had an authentic connection with the work that had long been lost to Dublin and the Abbey by the mid-70s'.[7] Their highly successful 1982 revival of *The Playboy* had the effect of removing the accretions of Synge-song picturesque, and returning it to an earthed authenticity. The Mayo shebeen of that production was in gritty period style, with an ad for Gold Flake cigarettes featuring the face of Edward VII juxtaposed with the icon of the Sacred Heart. Bríd Brennan, as a scarcely literate Pegeen Mike, penned her opening letter slowly, tongue between teeth, scratching her head the while.[8]

Having frequently directed other Synge plays, Hynes had a long-term plan of producing all six together. This project was given momentum by Druid's production of *The Leenane Trilogy* of Martin McDonagh in 1997, showing the rewards of such a large-scale theatrical enterprise. The problem was to find a style that could encompass such different works, tragedy, comedy, and tragicomedy. There was a sort of trial run for what was to become DruidSynge in 2004, with productions of the *Playboy*, and of *The Well of the Saints* and *The Tinker's Wedding* as a double bill. For *Playboy*, in this version, Hynes went in the opposite direction from her early realist stagings, with a caricatural mode almost reminiscent of nineteenth-century *Punch* cartoons. An eclectic *Well*, ranging in period from medieval to the 1920s, featured a solid stone wall that had to be raised and lowered for acts I and III. For the full-scale production of the six-play cycle in 2005, Hynes had to clear the stage of such theatrical encumbrances and establish a unified set sufficiently open and flexible to encompass the full range of the work.

This she did with the help of Francis O'Connor's single design. Though redressed for each of the plays, the rectangular box set remained essentially the same: three high walls painted a dirty blue-green, one door at the back, two other doors to right and left, windows at both sides, a high alcove in the back wall, with a

---

[6] The staging of this scene was devised by Hynes in collaboration with the choreographer David Bolger, with the mourning of Middle Eastern women in mind. They wanted something as strange to the audience as the keen would have been to Synge. Personal conversation with Garry Hynes, 29 September 2010.

[7] Interview with Garry Hynes, 3 July 2013. Parts of this were published as Nicholas Grene, 'An Interview with Garry Hynes', *Irish University Review*, 45.1 (2015), 117–25.

[8] For fuller details, see my 'Two London Playboys: Before and after Druid', in Adrian Frazier (ed.), *Playboys of the Western World* (Dublin: Carysfort Press, 2004), 80–2.

ladder to reach it, used to store a variety of objects needed for the different plays. A key design feature, however, was the stage covering of dark brown turf dust that allowed for the space to be alternatively interior or exterior. When an interior, it was the mud floor of a solid-appearing cottage or pub; when an exterior, it was the earth of a defined space of ground. So, the anxiously watched door through which the men carried the corpse of Bartley in *Riders* into the grief-stricken cottage, became the door of the church from which the Priest in *Tinker's Wedding* looked out at his disreputable potential clients in their roadside encampment.

But if the single set gave the production an organic unity, Kathy Strachan's eclectic costuming released the plays from a consistent period idiom. The Travellers of *Tinker's Wedding* in modern punk gear clashed with a Priest in full traditional black soutane. The timeless moral fable of *Well* was placed historically by 1960s costuming. The multiple casting of individual actors pointed thematic contrasts and similarities between the plays. Marie Mullen, who had no less than five roles through the cycle, appeared first in *Riders* as the agonized old mother by the hearth, lamenting the tragic fate of her sons on the sea. But she was next transformed into the scandalously anarchic Traveller Mary Byrne, mocking the orthodoxies of the settled life of marriage. *Shadow* opened the second half of the programme, with Catherine Walsh playing the melancholy Nora Burke trapped in the cottage-bound monotony of her miserable marriage to Dan Burke. In *Playboy*, which followed immediately after, she was Pegeen Mike, in an earlier version of that sort of situation; losing the only playboy of the western world, she was left with nothing but the prospect of life in the shebeen with the snivelling Shawn Keogh, a future as joyless as that of Nora.

The production cycle was bookended by the two tragedies, *Riders* at the start and *Deirde of the Sorrows* at the end. The plays were bound together by a single prop, the 'white boards' that feature so prominently in *Riders* as the prospective coffin for the older son Michael, ultimately to be used for Bartley the youngest. These remained on stage throughout the whole sequence to figure eventually at the scene of the mass deaths at the end of *Deirdre*. For that scene, Hynes also brought back the black-covered keening women to repeat their ritual action of beating on the walls of the set. But by this point, that set itself had been transformed. For in the last act of *Deirdre*, suddenly the previously solid-seeming walls were pulled back; the doors fell off their hinges, the window frame collapsed. A space appeared between the walls and the edge of the stage, and into that space the white boards descended. After the killing of the sons of Usna, their bloodied dead bodies appeared in this gap right beside the boards.

It was a way of enforcing the catastrophic ending—not only the death of Naisi and his brothers and the suicide of Deirdre, but the destruction of the High King Conchubor's palace at Emain Macha that follows. And yet the shattered set also had a multiple metatheatrical effect. It pointed to the unfinished state of the play itself. Synge died before he could complete *Deirdre* to his own satisfaction. The entropy of the set might be read as a gesture to Synge's only partially successful final experiment in the epic style. The other plays were complete theatrical spectacles, this one was a shell only of what might have been finally achieved. At the same time, it made manifest the performative status of all the plays in the constructed and deconstructable stage design. DruidSynge took the traditional box set, which in the Abbey tradition had always mimicked a real country cottage or pub with fourth wall removed, and turned it into an avowed performance space. The whole cycle re-created Synge's work as a theatrical vision moving at will between the sheltering, entrapping interiors of the house and an outside world that might represent a liberating affirmation of life but carried always with it the threat of death or an *unheimlich* uncanny.

Recasting: *Playboy* (Peacock, 2001)

For all the declared performativity of the collapsing set in *Deirdre*, the aim of DruidSynge was to realize the plays, to give them a believable social substance. With the production of *Playboy* staged in the Peacock in 2001, directed by Niall Henry, it was quite otherwise. Ben Barnes, artistic director of the Abbey, had been impressed by Henry's work on the Blue Raincoat production of *Alice in Wonderland*, and invited him to direct. The choice of play, however, was Henry's own. He felt that Synge had been 'mildly maligned' in Ireland, having been immensely impressed by a production of *Le baladin du monde occidentale* when he was living in Paris.[9] In his Peacock production, the stage was stripped bare of all the naturalizing features of previous versions. There were no visible doors or windows, no bar, no bottles. One bench did duty for whatever furniture was needed. There was a notional fire near the centre of the stage, but it bore no resemblance to the realistic hearth where in the DruidSynge *Riders*' soda bread was baked, in *Playboy* Pegeen plucked a reddened turf sod to burn Christy's shin. Props were picked up as needed—a blanket for Christy to sleep on at the end of act II, the inevitable loy as murder weapon—though often they were simply imagined: it was an invisible glass of porter that Pegeen offered Christy at first entrance. The play was staged in traverse in the small studio space of the Peacock, with black curtain 'hides' at the back of the audience at both sides, behind which performers could lurk and appear unseen and unheralded.

True to this placelessness, the play opened with Pegeen Mike walking in slow motion along a diagonal shaft of light to the bench where she knelt and read out the items she was ordering in her letter.[10] It was only with the entrance of

---

[9] For this and any other unattributed quotations, I am drawing on my interview with Niall Henry, 19 April 2023.
[10] I am here dependent largely on the recording of the play in the Abbey archives as well as my memories of the original staging.

Shawn Keogh that the whole rectangular stage space was seen. Again and again, the characters stood in choreographed tableaux expressive of the dynamics of the situation. When Michael James and the two other men try to force Shawn Keogh to stay the night with Pegeen, he was placed in diamond-shaped configuration with his persecutors; Michael James's efforts to hold Shawn back were played as a sort of circling dance. There was generally very little physical contact between the performers. The love duet between Christy and Pegeen in act III was for the most part acted out with them at opposite corners of the stage. The dialogue was spoken with convincing western accents, but often in what seemed deliberately unanimated tones. Lines were taken slowly, with pauses between the phrases, as though deliberately resisting the rhythmic flow of the Synge-song.

The costuming—by Jamie Vartan like the stage design—and the casting were also against type. The two barflies, Jimmy Farrell and Philly Cullen, are almost always played for laughs, often as an elderly Mutt and Jeff pair, one tall and one short. In this production, two younger actors, Michael Hayes and Conan Sweeny, were cast as an almost identikit pair. Like Michael James and Shawn Keogh, they were clothed in formal greys and blacks, figuring a uniform oppressively patriarchal community. By contrast Pegeen Mike and Widow Quin—like Christy—appeared barefoot. The most striking piece of countercasting, however, came about almost without design. Henry was sure that he wanted to cast Mikel Murfi as Christy but was doubtful about where to find a woman actor strong enough to play opposite him as Pegeen. He decided on Olwen Fouéré who, at the age of 47, already had a distinguished career as a theatre actor. So why couldn't Pegeen be in her 40s, Henry thought to himself, and cut the references to Pegeen's youthful age from the text. That, then, led to the casting of the younger Cathy Belton to play Widow Quin. The character of Widow Quin had traditionally been played as much older, a comically knowing, black-shawled widow woman. It was no contest between her and the youthful Pegeen for the love of Christy. Belton, in Henry's production, was sexily attractive, while the older Fouéré seemed more of the scolding termagant. The pathos of her loss of Christy became the tragedy of a last chance of happiness and fulfilment gone forever.

In casting the play, Henry used a number of actors he had worked with before in Blue Raincoat—Brendan Ellis as Michael James, Ciaran McAuley as Shawn Keogh—and were familiar with his movement-based style. However, it was the choice of his old school-fellow, the Lecoq-trained Mikel Murfi, for the lead that was central. If the opening scenes seemed conspicuously slow and still, it made the entrance of Christy the more dramatic. Murfi tumbled out from a previously unseen trapdoor high on one of the walls, suddenly lit up as if a window. He was the outsider who comes in from the void, as though born again into this new environment. His athleticism was again demonstrated when, at Old Mahon's appearance in act II, he scrambled up the wall to use the 'window' as hiding place, and it was from this perch that he addressed his lines to Widow Quin after the old man had left. The adoring girls who come at the beginning of act I with presents for Christy were all cut, and Murfi showed his clowning skills (honed in *The Whiteheaded Boy*) by playing out their lines as well as his own. In telling his story, he leaped histrionically about the stage reliving the 'murder' of his father. Overall, it was a performance to dazzle the audience in the theatre as it did the villagers on stage.

The window in the wall through which Christy entered was lit up at key moments: when he stands imagining his new life at the top of act II, and again when he re-enters in act III, having really killed his father this time, as he thinks, and imagining in his delirium that 'Pegeen'll be giving me praises the same as in the hours gone by' (Synge, *Collected Works*, Vol. IV, 165). If the window signalled the point from which he was delivered into this brave new world, it stood also for the Utopian future it seemed to offer him. But, of course, none of this was to be. When father and son exited at the end of act III, it was through a door in the opposite wall, also previously unnoticed and unopened. The Mahons were an apparition in the lives of the Mayo people. Though Christy himself might have been transformed by his time there, made 'a mighty man […] by the power of a lie' (Synge, *Collected Works*, Vol. IV, 165), nothing could be done to transform this deadened, inert community itself. This was a sombre *Playboy*, austerely beautiful in its balletic movement, illuminated by the sheer virtuosity of the lead performance, but enforcing the sense of a claustrophobic conformity that led to the final heartbreaking tragedy of Pegeen.

Translating: Pan Pan's *Playboy* (2006)

Niall Henry's staging of *Playboy* in the Peacock in 2001 challenged traditional versions of the play with its acting style and casting against type. But a transposed *Playboy*, translated into modern idiomatic Mandarin, was something else again. Even for the internationally disposed Pan Pan, this was a new adventure. It took four years and multiple visits to China by Gavin Quinn before their Chinese *Playboy* opened at the Oriental Pioneer Theatre in Beijing in March 2006, before being presented in the Project Arts Theatre in Dublin for a brief run in December of that year.[11] In Quinn's adaptation, translated by Yue Sun, the play was relocated to a 'whoredressers' in contemporary Beijing, the sort of hairdressing salon that offers 'foot massage' and other services behind the scenes. The idea was that this half-lit world of modern China, known but invisible to officialdom, containing oddments of folklore and traditional customs, was some sort of equivalent to Synge's west

---

[11] As in the previous chapter, I am here drawing on my interview with Gavin Quinn, 6 June 2023, as well as other sources referenced below.

of Ireland under late colonial rule.[12] Ma Shang, the Christy Mahon figure, as a rural Muslim from the distant province of Xinjiang, was an exotic stranger in this milieu. Where the locals invoked the Taoist god Lao Tianye or appealed to Tian Na (Heavens above), Ma Shang always deferred to Zhen Zhu (Allah).[13] The transposition made some changes in the text necessary. Zhao Yingiun was waiting for his mother's blessing rather than the papal dispensation Shawn Keogh needed to marry his cousin Pegeen Mike. Liu Ge (Michael James) and Zhang Xiaofei (Philly Cullen) went off for the night to a game of mahjong rather than Kate Cassidy's wake. It was a bicycle not a mule race that Ma Shang wins in act III. But the action of Synge's original text was followed fairly faithfully through most of the play.[14]

The hairdressing salon in the Beijing production (designed by Aedín Cosgrove) was a long narrow neon-lit strip with seats for the customers in front of a mirror which doubled the visual playing field.[15] Pegeen Mike's letter ordering her trousseau was cut; the play opened instead with a Chinese song playing over her entrance as Lala, who had charge of the salon, in pink coat, short skirt, and tall high-heeled white boots. The conformism of Zhao Yingiun (Shawn Keogh) was marked by the relative formality of his clothes against the hard man leather jackets of Liu Ge / Michael James, evidently the local gang boss, and his sidekick. When the Widow Quin figure, the very sexily dressed Kun Gaufu, appears, it was with a black eyepatch and a bandage on her leg, injuries sustained presumably in her final murderous battle with her late husband. The profession of the hero-worshipping girls, who work in the salon and come on in act II, was made very obvious in their costuming, and in their overtly seductive approaches to Ma Shang. His rural shy innocence was emphasized in this louche atmosphere. When he undressed at the end of act I to go to bed on the lilo that Lala had laid out for him on the floor of the shop, he turned away modestly from her frankly appraising gaze when he came to take off his trousers.

In socially conservative China, the overt eroticism provoked some negative reactions. There were complaints about the shortness of one of the girls' skirts and a glimpse of her underwear, provoking tabloid headlines in the Western press: 'Peking at Your Knickers'.[16] However, remarkably, though inspected by the

---

[12] For a detailed analysis of the contemporary Chinese context and the relationship between the Pan Pan production and Synge's original, see Antony Tatlow, 'The Chinese Playboy', *Dublin Review of Books*, June 2008, https://drb.ie/articles/the-chinese-playboy/ (accessed 21 July 2023).

[13] In the Chinese production, for political reasons, Xinjiang had to be changed to the province of Dongbei, but in the Irish staging they reverted to the original setting and Ma Shang wore a characteristic Muslim cap. See Clifford Coonan, 'Playboy Comes Home', *Irish Times*, 13 December 2006, https://www.proquest.com/docview/308913761/A868D81EAFB4EEAPQ/1?accountid=14404 (accessed 21 July 2023).

[14] There is an English-language text of Quinn's adaptation in the Pan Pan archives, Hardiman Library, University of Galway, T27/1/17, and the Chinese script (retranslated into English) figured in the surtitles of the Dublin staging.

[15] I am dependent here on a partial video recording of the original staging in the Galway Pan Pan archives, as well as my notes of watching the Dublin performance.

[16] *The Sun*, 24 March 2006.

Ministry of Propaganda, there were no political repercussions, given that the Muslim dimension of Ma Shang coming from Xinjiang, with its associations of dissent from Communist rule, had been suppressed. The audience very much enjoyed the production, assuming, in fact, that it was a Chinese play. Local detail helped. The action of the play was set on New Year's Eve, a time when it is considered bad luck to have your hair cut—hence presumably the relative lack of custom in the salon. The Beijing audience would have been amused by the difference between the rural Dongbei dialect of Ma Shang and his father—Dongbei being the province substituted for the politically unacceptable Xinjiang—and the slangy demotic of the urban characters. The Old Mahon character, Lao Ma, appeared like a veteran of the Long March, costumed in the uniform of the People's Liberation Army, invoking Lei Feng, discredited icon of Mao's Cultural Revolution.[17]

All such detail would of course have been lost on the Dublin audiences, where the production became something very different. In Beijing, it had been played 'straight', at least in so far as there was no metatheatrical dimension. For the Project performance, many of the characteristic elements of a Pan Pan show were added. So, for example, following Quinn's preference for making offstage performers visible to the audience, a screen showed the Chinese actors in their dressing-rooms. We saw Bao Shuo, playing the Widow Quin character, adjusting her make-up and putting on her black eyepatch. A microphone was introduced for the beginning of act III, with the original dialogue about skulls between Philly Cullen and Jimmy Farrell amplified, though spoken by the Philly character alone— Jimmy having been cut. And Liu Ge (Michael James) also used the microphone for his later blessing of Pegeen Mike and Christy Mahon. A second screen gave the surtitles, 'a retranslation of a translation', according to Quinn.[18] So, a slowly scrolling typescript, silently 'speaking' the lines of Pegeen and Christy's love duet in act III, was seen as Lala and Ma Shang began voicelessly to make love on stage.

For all its deliberately estranging dramaturgy and the impenetrability of the Chinese dialogue for the Irish audiences, this was felt as a re-invigorated version of Synge's original. Xia Zi Xin was wonderfully cast as Lala / Pegeen Mike, slim, tough as nails, with a sort of steely sexiness, genuinely thrown by the gaucherie of the rural Ma Shang / Christy (played in Dublin by Wang Zhuo). Zhang Wan Kun as Liu Ge / Michael James had a convincing aura of machismo gone to seed: in act III, when under threat from Ma Shang, who had grabbed a knife away from the cowardly Zhao Yingjun, he sighed resignedly: 'I myself scared the competition off with a knife 20 years ago'. Both Lao Ma / Old Mahon (played by Bao Gang) and Ma Shang were capable of rendering the pathos of their parts as well as the comedy. One had a sense of the availability in Chinese of a florid rhetoric that could

---

[17] See Tatlow, 'The Chinese Playboy'.
[18] Quoted in Coonan, 'Playboy Comes Home'.

provide a counterpart to Synge's ornate Hiberno-English. Where else in the world could director Quinn expect an actor to respond to one of his notes as Lao Wei (playing Zhao Yinguin / Shawn Keogh) did: 'Spotter of talent with peach blossom luck, thank you for pointing out my bad acting habits'?[19]

Though the performers came from different acting backgrounds, they were able to draw on the movement and musical styles of Chinese opera. This Beijing Michael James could throw Shawn Keogh around the stage with effortless kung-fu-like ease. The three girls entered in act II doing a masterfully syncopated dance routine. The tableaux were arranged and held with a stylized sense of posture that the Chinese actors could manage without any sense of self-consciousness, whether it was the girls in their individual hairdressers' chairs listening rapt to Christy's tale of his supposed parricide in act II, or the group standing completely still as spectators gathered to watch the fight between Christy and his father in act III. The final reconciliation and power struggle between father and son was completely convincing, Christy suddenly standing tall and firm beside his shorter but stockier opponent, who turns and goes off to magnificent peals of disbelieving laughter: 'Glory be to God! I am crazy again!' (Synge, *Collected Works*, Vol. IV, 175). And Xia Zi Xin had the emotional power to bring off Pegeen's famous last line, spot-lit alone stage centre, with the rest of the scene in darkness. This Asian fusion *Playboy* brought the play alive: its power, its violence, its strangeness, and its plangency, with the stylized poetry that is so hard to make credible in twenty-first-century Irish theatre.

Updating: *Playboy* (Abbey 2007)

The year 2007 was the centenary of the first production of Synge's *Playboy*. At the Abbey, it was decided to offer something more innovative than just one more revival of that much revived play. Instead, the theatre staged an updated adaptation by Bisi Adigun and Roddy Doyle. The play had originally been commissioned by Arambe Productions, founded by Nigerian immigrant Adigun in 2003, to produce 'classic and contemporary plays in the Irish canon' by members of Ireland's African communities.[20] In 2006 Arambe staged Jimmy Murphy's *The Kings of the Kilburn High Road* (2000), a play about long-term Irish immigrants in London, with impossible dreams of returning home. Acted with an African cast, the production pointed up the analogy between contemporary migrants and the diasporic Irish. Doyle, through years of teaching in the north Dublin suburb of Kilbarrack, had come to see *The Playboy* as one of the few texts prescribed for Leaving Certificate

---

[19] Quoted in Coonan, 'Playboy Comes Home'.
[20] Quoted by Christopher Murray, 'The Adigun-Doyle *Playboy* and Multiculturalism', in Nicholas Grene and Patrick Lonergan (eds.), *Irish Drama: Local and Global Perspectives* (Dublin: Carysfort Press, 2012), 109–20 [111].

really to interest and excite working-class teenagers, different as their lives were from Synge's remote rural characters.[21]

Like the Pan Pan Chinese *Playboy* of the year before, the Adigun-Doyle adaptation gave the play a contemporary urban setting. Instead of the Beijing whoredressers, Michael Flaherty's pub was in gangland West Dublin where he warred with other drug dealers for control of the territory. Christopher Malomo fetched up there as a Nigerian asylum seeker looking for a 'far out cousin' with an untraceable address somewhere in the area. The marriage between Pegeen and Sean (so spelled here) was planned as an alliance between two rival 'families', and Sean pulled back from love-making with his fiancée not only because of his pious faith, but because 'negotiations are at a delicate stage' between his 'ma' and her 'da'.[22] In looking for an equivalent to Synge's early-twentieth-century Mayo with its veneration for the lawbreaker, the authors targeted the modern cult of notoriety accorded to criminals. In their Widow Quin there were shades of Catherine Nevin, the much publicized 'Black Widow', convicted in 2000 of killing her husband, though in the Adigun-Doyle version Quin was innocent; her husband 'was shot down by Michael James's gang in a drugs dispute'.[23] Michael James's main rival is the Rattler, and the first half of the play ended with an attack on the pub by his heavies. It was in this fight, rather than in the local sports, that Christopher, hired as security man, won his glory. In a particularly clever substitution, in place of the triumphant mule race viewed through the window of the pub, the hero-worshipping girls played back the fight with the rival gang captured on their mobile phones.

The updating was reinforced by many topical references. The innocent Nigerian Christopher puzzled over a photo of Roy Keane, Manchester United star, the most famous Irish footballer of his day, on the wall with other pictures of Pegeen's family: 'What's he doing here? He cannot be related to her'. Jimmy, coming on at the start of act III, looked around in amazement: 'An empty pub? For fuck's sake. It must be the fucking smoking ban'. The 2004 ban on smoking in all enclosed workspaces, including pubs, had done much to deter drinkers; many publicans rapidly turned their outdoor yards into 'beer gardens'. The Chinese *Playboy* had been rendered in a demotic Mandarin, apparently known as 'cow's cunt'.[24] The lines of the Dubliners of the 2007 *Playboy* were written in the working-class argot that Doyle had popularized in *The Commitments* (1987), first of the Barrytown Trilogy. This made for a wholesale paraphrasing of the text. Where Synge's Widow Quin expressed amazement at Christy's unparricide-looking appearance—'and

---

[21] See Roddy Doyle, 'Wild and Perfect: Teaching *The Playboy of the Western World*', in Colm Toíbín (ed.), *Synge: A Celebration* (Dublin: Carysfort Press, 2005), 139–44.

[22] The text of the play has never been published. Besides my own experience of seeing the play, I am relying here on watching a recording of the 2007 production in the Abbey archives, quotations in the reviews, and the essay by Christopher Murray, who did have access to the script.

[23] Murray, 'The Adigun-Doyle *Playboy*', 113.

[24] See Tatlow, 'The Chinese Playboy'.

you fitter to be saying your catechism than slaying your da' (Synge, *Collected Works*, Vol. IV, 87)—her counterpart says '"I can see you playin' your Playstation or doin' your slam-dunkin', but killin' your da?"'[25] In place of 'a radiant lady with droves of bullocks on the plains of Meath, and herself bedizened in the diamond jewelleries of Pharaoh's ma' (Synge, *Collected Works*, Vol. IV, 155), Pegeen scornfully sends Sean off to look for: 'Paris Hilton or some rich bitch like that.'[26]

The audiences loved it. The play ran solidly for two months in 2007 and was revived as the Abbey's Christmas show in 2008. There was universal praise for the acting, the sensitive performance of Black British actor Giles Terrera in the lead, Eileen Walsh playing Pegeen in skin-tight jeans and enormous wedge heels, Angeline Ball (who had made her name in the film of *The Commitments* in 1991), a Widow Quin in slinky black velour tracksuit. The critical reception for the adaptation was more mixed. At one extreme, there was Mick Heaney's outright condemnation: 'the new Playboy fails even to live up to the modest aim of making [John Millington Synge]'s play more pertinent to modern audiences [...] Instead, it has presented its supposed national constituency with a version that substitutes poetry and violence with dumbed-down crassness'.[27] By contrast, Emer O'Kelly claimed that the adaptation 'travels, translates, and updates with the smoothness of a silk shift'.[28] For those who criticized the play, there were two areas of concern: the language and the treatment of the racial issue.

Peter Crawley opened his *Irish Times* review with the juxtaposition of a line from Synge's original text and its Adigun-Doyle equivalent: the latter's words 'fall with the dull thud of a literal translation'.[29] Where Synge's Christy imagined himself with Pegeen 'pacing Neifin in the dews of night' (Synge, *Collected Works*, Vol. IV, 147), Christopher had them 'walk[ing] hand in hand by the River Liffey ... and in Blanchardstown Shopping Centre'.[30] Ouch. In making Christy Mahon a Nigerian immigrant, some critics did not think the authors had engaged adequately with the issues that substitution raised. Karen Fricker thought that

> [t]he problem is the reimagining of Christy not as a desperate member of the social underclass, but an affluent, educated young Nigerian. The writers may be trying to counter the prevalent Irish representation of black people as oppressed refugees and asylum seekers, but the explanations needed to make this new twist work are far too convoluted.[31]

---

[25] Quoted by Alex Moffatt, 'Spruced-Up Playboy's Bursting with Comic Life', *Daily Mail*, 5 October 2007.
[26] Quoted by Mick Heaney, 'Cheap Talk from a Grubby Playboy', *Sunday Times*, 14 October 2007.
[27] Heaney, 'Cheap Talk'.
[28] Emer O'Kelly, 'Playboy of the Badlands: A Riot', *Sunday Independent*, 7 October 2007.
[29] Peter Crawley, 'Dublin Theatre Festival Review: *The Playboy of the Western World*', *Irish Times*, 5 October 2007.
[30] Quoted in Moffat, 'Spruced-Up Playboy'.
[31] Karen Fricker, 'The Playboy of the Western World', *Variety*, 15–21 October 2007.

Christopher in the Adigun-Doyle version had an MBA, his father Malomo was a well-to-do businessman who showed up as a dignified figure in traditional Nigerian robes; when invited for a drink in the pub he opted for a glass of Merlot. In spite of their face off over the father's highhanded treatment of his son as a mere subordinate in his business that led to the physical attack originally, they had the obvious makings of a good relationship, expressed in the tone of Christopher's last words as his father prepares to leave: 'Please, dad, don't mess up'.

Unlike the low-key *Playboy* in the small space of the Peacock, this was a main stage show aimed at a popular audience. The laughter at times threatened to drown out the dialogue and rounds of applause greeted high points of the farce. This was in part a conditioned reaction to the low-life Dublinese of Doyle (assuming he was responsible for this part of the writing, as seems likely). There may also have been an iconoclastic amusement at Synge's lyricism being sent up. When Christopher uses Synge's original phrase in talking of Pegeen's 'puckered lips', 'My what?' she responds. Her exclamation at the height of her love ecstasy—'The heart's a wonder' was followed by 'My granny used to say that'. There was a sort of comic pleasure at the reductiveness of her final 'Fuck off' to Michael James in place of the expected 'Oh my grief, I've lost him surely. I've lost the only playboy of the western world' (Synge, *Collected Works*, Vol. IV, 173). Instead of providing a renewed edge to the play by its contemporary setting and the switch to a Nigerian playboy, the play ran the risk of encouraging a sort of double complacency in the audience. They could laugh at the contrast between Synge's hackneyed rhetoric and the gritty slang of contemporary gangland Dublin. But they could also share in the superior values of the middle-class Nigerians so out of place in that world.

Synge's work is by now very remote for most audiences and readers. Already by the 1980s Doyle's Kilbarrack students had to go hunting to find out what Christy meant when he said that he had been walking 'since Tuesday was a week', or that he just 'riz the loy' over his father's head.[32] Teaching *The Playboy* in Trinity College Dublin in the year 2000, I realized that so much of the language, so many of the references were unintelligible, that I had more or less to translate the text for my class of millennials. In the US in 2006, DruidSynge had New York audiences 'queuing for earphones designed for the hard of hearing' at the end of the first play such was the obscurity of the language and the voices.[33] In Ireland, Synge comes weighed down with his performance history, all those years of Abbey revivals of *The Playboy* sounding more and more like their own sort of stage Irishry. Most of his plays are unstageable in modern theatre conditions. DruidSynge was only possible because of the exceptional dedication of Hynes to his work, and the willingness of audiences to take on the challenge of marathon performances for which

---

[32] See Doyle, 'Wild and Perfect', 142–3.
[33] Quoted in José Lanters, '"We'll be the Judges of That": The Critical Reception of *DruidSynge* in the USA', in Grene and Lonergan, *Irish Drama*, 35–47 [40].

there is an opening, particularly at theatre festivals. Tanya Dean comments on the effect of these sort of daylong productions: 'For both audience and actors, there is a sense of mutual achievement; everyone on stage and watching have committed to this extreme undertaking, and by the final curtain, they can all take pride in having participated in something extraordinary'.[34] Such an extraordinary event allowed spectators to feel that they were seeing Synge steadily and seeing him whole. *The Playboy* continues to attract Irish theatre directors to recover it from its overfamiliarity using new strategies. In the 2001 production in the Peacock, Henry applied his stylized dramaturgy to give the play a fresh intensity without the overlay of traditional stagings. Pan Pan went to the lengths of a Chinese version in Beijing to find again the force of the original play. However well intentioned the collaboration of Adigun and Doyle in their 2007 *Playboy*, its great popular success seems to have been achieved by easy laughter, failing to meet the potential of the updating it attempted. Synge is not easy to make over in twenty-first-century Irish theatre, but it can and has been done.

---

[34] Tanya Dean, 'Druid Cycles: the Rewards of Marathon Productions', in Fintan Walsh (ed.), *'That Was Us': Contemporary Irish Theatre and Performance* (London: Oberon, 2013), 181–95 [182].

State of Play 1

2006

Irish theatre in 2006 had undergone a radical transformation from its counterpart of thirty years before. To start with, it was no longer centred exclusively in the capital cities. 'Up until the 1970s', Chris Morash points out in his overview of 'places of performance' in Ireland,

> virtually all theatre funding on the island went to the three main theatres: the Abbey, the Lyric, and the Gate. However, policy changes in arts funding in both jurisdictions in the late 1970s initiated a new regional awareness, and this led to subsidies being given to companies outside Dublin and Belfast, which in turn led to calls for new theatre buildings that were equally geographically dispersed.[1]

From the establishment of Druid Theatre Company in Galway in 1975 and the Derry-based Field Day Theatre Company in 1980, the metropolitan basis for theatre was challenged. These were followed by Red Kettle in Waterford (1984), Galloglass in Clonmel (1990), Blue Raincoat in Sligo and Corcadorca in Cork (1991), Calipo in Drogheda (1994), and many more. From the 1980s, Dublin, also, was no longer dominated by the virtual duopoly of the Abbey and Gate. A flourishing independent theatre sector developed with the setting up of Rough Magic and Passion Machine (1984), Storytellers Theatre Company (1986), Pigsback (which became Fishamble), (1988), Calypso (1993), and Corn Exchange (1995). Each of these had a distinctive agenda and aesthetic, whether in the performance of contemporary British political theatre, the representation of Dublin working-class life, plays for younger audiences, or new Irish plays, agitprop, or *commedia dell'arte* style.

Regional companies were not only intended to serve their local communities. Field Day was designed from the start to tour its plays across both parts of the island. From 1982 Druid developed the URT (Unusual Rural Tours) to bring theatre to outlying areas, including the Aran Islands.[2] To house such touring shows, as well as to provide the home base of individual companies, a whole range of

---

[1] Chris Morash, 'Places of Performance', in Nicholas Grene and Chris Morash (eds.), *The Oxford Handbook of Modern Irish Theatre* (Oxford: Oxford University Press, 2016), 425–42 [441–2].

[2] See http://archive.druid.ie/websites/2009-2017/about/national-touring (accessed 7 February 2022).

arts centres were established. The Project Arts Centre, originally founded in 1969, with its own purpose-built premises from 2000, was the forerunner of many more such sites.[3] Some were buildings converted from other uses, like the Derry Playhouse, established in 1992 in what had been St Mary's Convent and St Joseph's School, or the Town Hall Theatre in Galway, which had gone from being a town hall to a cinema before being opened as a theatre in 1996. The Watergate Theatre in Kilkenny was another cinema conversion in 1993. Others were new buildings, designed for the purpose, like An Grianan, Letterkenny, set up in 1999, or the Solstice Arts Centre in Navan, newly opened in 2006. One of the most striking features of the changed landscape was the ring of suburban theatres round Dublin, generated in the peak years of Ireland's Celtic Tiger economy: the Civic, Tallaght (1999); axis, Ballymun, Draoicht, Blanchardstown, Pavilion Theatre, Dun Laoghaire (all in 2001); dlr Mill Theatre, Dundrum (2006). This diversification meant that, as an *Irish Times* Theatre Awards judge, I had regularly to travel to Sligo, Galway, Limerick, Tralee, Wexford, Kilkenny, Castleblayney (Co. Monaghan)—to Blanchardstown north of Dublin, Tallaght to the west, Dundrum, and Dun Laoghaire to the south.

Given the sheer multiplicity of variables in the choice and mounting of plays, it would be impossible to find a single pattern within a whole year's worth of theatre—all 121 shows that I saw. The aggregate appears as an unreadable miscellany. Still, there are some significant groupings that can be picked out within the 2006 repertoire. Apart from revivals of plays from the classical canon, of which there were quite a number, there was a new openness to staging work from outside the country. (All original productions of plays and operas from within Ireland are eligible for consideration for the Theatre Awards—they do not have to be Irish authored.) There were productions not only of work from the US and from British contemporary theatre, but also from continental Europe and from Australia. The delayed arrival of avant-garde modes of dramaturgy, considered in Chapter 2, brought with it also by 2006 a movement towards site-specific immersive theatre. The bulk of the plays staged were of course by Irish playwrights on Irish subjects. There were a number of efforts made to reflect contemporary society, state of the nation plays. But, following on what has been a longstanding tradition in Irish theatre, there were also many productions dealing with the impact of the past on the present. The aim of what follows is to draw upon the notes I kept of my experience of individual shows and, through samples and highlights, to give some sense of what it felt like to go to the theatre in Ireland in 2006, what was distinctively different about the experience, and how far it related to themes and trends discussed throughout this book as a whole.

---

[3] For the history of the Project, see Vic Merriman, '"As We Must": Growth and Diversification in Ireland's Theatre Culture 1977–2000', in Grene and Morash, *Oxford Handbook of Modern Irish Theatre*, 389–403 [393].

Classic Revivals

From the beginning of the national theatre movement there was an aspiration to stage classics of European theatre to provide models for the native Irish plays that it was the main aim of the movement to foster. That accounted for Lady Gregory's Hibernicized Molière comedies, for example, and Yeats's versions of *Oedipus the King* (1928) and *Oedipus at Colonus* (1931). Yeats's example had been followed by many Irish poets in the later twentieth century, Seamus Heaney among them, with his *The Cure at Troy* (1990), based on Sophocles' *Philoctetes*, and his *Antigone* staged as *The Burial at Thebes* (2004). While several of these had provided an Irish inflection to their re-imagining of the Greek tragedies—notably Tom Paulin with *The Riot Act* (1984), his version of *Antigone* in which Creon was an Ian Paisley lookalike—what was distinctive about the Abbey's *The Bacchae of Baghdad* was its relocation of Euripides' tragedy to the Green Zone of Baghdad in the wake of the 2002 invasion of Iraq.[4] You could see the basis of the director Conall Morrison's idea: Pentheus was seen to stand for an insistent, dogmatic belief in law and order, Western reason and logic, opposed to an alternative Eastern religion of faith and enthusiasm. But, as the *Guardian* reviewer put it, this was 'orientalism and occidentalism writ large: a didactic reduction of the original text and current political situation.'[5]

At the very simplest level, to play Pentheus as a thuggish, crew-cut, five-star American general was to belie the original in which he is the legitimate king of Thebes: it is after all Dionysus who is the invader, not Pentheus. It made nonsense also of the scene in which Dionysus mesmerizes his antagonist into dressing up in women's clothes to spy on the Bacchantes. The subtlety of Euripides here is to suggest the feminine within Pentheus that he has sought to repress, emerging in distorted form in the voyeuristic need to watch the Bacchic celebrations of the female worshippers. All this was rendered incomprehensible in Morrison's version. With a Dionysus (Christopher Simpson) who was an accomplished actor but burdened with a fake Middle Eastern accent, and the chorus (led by a young Ruth Negga) transforming into stereotypically sinister-looking suicide bombers, this was politically very uncomfortable, to say the least. Morrison is an extremely gifted director who has been responsible for some wonderfully imaginative productions; this is one for him to forget.

Anniversaries are occasions for celebration and, in the theatre, for revivals. The year 2006 was the centenary of the birth of Samuel Beckett and for some time in that year photos of his handsome head adorned every lamppost in his

---

[4] For details of this, and of other productions where there is not a published script, see the Irish Playography (https://www.irishplayography.com/).

[5] Karen Fricker, 'The Bacchae of Baghdad, *Guardian*, 15 March 2006, https://www.theguardian.com/stage/2006/mar/15/theatre2 (accessed 5 September 2022).

native city of Dublin. The great modern dramatist belonged peculiarly to us, and in 2006 there was a relatively rare opportunity to see one of the exceptional works in which he used a full-throated Irish English, his adaptation of Robert Pinget's *The Old Tune* (Watergate, Kilkenny). The stagings of his work that year, however, emphasized a paradox about the plays. *Waiting for Godot, Endgame, Krapp's Last Tape*, and *Happy Days* are repeatedly revived in Ireland, as around the globe. There was, indeed, a fine production of *Endgame* in the centenary year by the Belfast-based company Prime Cut. But it is much harder to find occasions to stage the later dramaticules that diminish almost to vanishing point. There was something distinctly contrived about *Beckett's Ghosts* (Bedrock), which brought together four shorts, *A Piece of Monologue, That Time, Breath*, and *Not I*. Beckett's later works, which approach the condition of art installation, are each unique and bringing them together in such a way felt like an artificial misrepresentation. The Gate Theatre had brilliantly solved the problem with the Beckett Festival in 1991, where all nineteen of the stage plays were produced together. For the April month of the author's birthday in 2006, the Gate mounted Beckett on Stage, a cut-down version of the original Festival, including just nine of his stage plays and one adaptation of a television play. There was a revival of the (by then much travelled) Walter Asmus staging of *Waiting for Godot*, but all the other plays were new productions. One of the great triumphs of Beckett on Stage was the transposition of the television drama, *Eh Joe* for the theatre by Atom Egoyan (staged with *Rockaby* and *Ohio Improptu*).

Joe's room was seen behind a scrim: a single narrow made-up bed, Joe (Michael Gambon) in his dressing-gown sitting on it with back to audience. The room, designed by Eileen Diss, was a square inset within the wider space of the stage, set at an angle to the proscenium, diamond shaped with curtained window on the right, curtained door on the left, curtained double doors to built-in cupboard upstage centre. Following Beckett's stage directions, Joe got up and in turn looked out from window and door and into cupboard before locking the doors, drawing the curtains, and finally looking under the bed for good measure. The only gesture not specified in the text came with the hands held upward, still for a moment as they reached for each set of curtains to draw them, a movement to return significantly at the end.

Joe sat on the bed, face in profile, lit from stage right. And then, as the voice in voiceover started to speak, a large video image of his head and shoulders appears facing out to the audience, occupying about a third of the scrim stage right. And behind it the shadow of the image was reprojected onto the curtained window wall that faced Joe. The effect was of a tripled, triangulated vision of Joe, the relatively diminutive live and motionless actor on stage, the projected face pitilessly exposed in front, and the ghost-like ashen version of the same haunting itself behind.

The amazing achievement was Gambon's face as it registered with the most minute changes the effect of Penelope Wilton's voice as the accusatory tone built steadily: the 'Eh Joe?' at first casual, not menacing, rising in tempo to an almost choking emotion in the evocation of her suicide. Just as Joe's eyes closed and the head tilted forward towards sleep, the voice would nudge it back into wakefulness. A tic started in one of the pouches beneath his eyes. The eyeballs rolled upward from time to time in anguish; when the voice referred to 'that lump in your bubo', the look was driven downwards. In place of the strategically placed successive close-ups of the face in the TV original, the image on the scrim steadily and imperceptibly grew in size. And finally, on the cue from the voice 'And the hands ... *Imagine the* hands', we saw Joe's hands come up into shot as the horror spreads over his face.[6] Echoing the raised hands on the curtains at the start, with the benefit of technology it turned the television play into compelling theatre (Figure 1).

Shakespeare remained a presence in Irish theatre throughout the twentieth century, but an uneasy one. There were necessarily productions for schools of plays on examination curricula—in 2006 a dutiful staging of *Macbeth* by Second Age.

Fig. 1 Michael Gambon as Joe in Gate Theatre production of *Eh Joe*. Photographer Anthony Woods. Courtesy of Gate Theatre and James Hardiman Library, University of Galway.

[6] Samuel Beckett, *Complete Dramatic Works* (London: Faber, 1986), 364, 366–7.

But there was also a sprightly *As You Like It* by Classic Stage Ireland, established in 2004 specifically to produce classics of world literature for Irish audiences, an acknowledgement that this was a missing element. Shakespeare, in particular, had felt a forbidding figure: the canonical playwright of the neighbouring island where actors were trained in verse speaking as they were not in Ireland. Lynne Parker, long-serving artistic director of Rough Magic, had a background as a literature student, and from the beginning of the company which she helped to found was committed to staging canonical English plays, though often with a distinctive twist. In the case of *The Taming of the Shrew*, which she directed in 2006, it was to give the play an Irish colouring.

This was a 1970s rural Irish *Shrew*, the setting Baptista Minola's pub in the Midlands, tacky, crude, tasteless, and graceless, provincial Ireland back then. The Project Upstairs space, where it was played in traverse, became a long bar-room with crumb-strewn, ashtrayed tables, black and green lino on the floor. The Irish setting gave a special coarseness to the men and their dealings over the marriage: the limping caricatured Gremio (Darragh Kelly), always with a cup of tea in his hand, while the other men drank whiskey; a strutting Hortensio (Rory Nolan) with the beginnings of a pot-belly, a toothpick in his stupid face; Barry McGovern's lurching walk suited to the publican father, brown-suited and bespectacled, only anxious to get his daughters well disposed of in a good bargain; Lucentio (Tadhg Murphy) fatuously in love with a fresh-faced Bianca (Simone Kirby). To them Petruchio (Owen Roe), purple-suited country wide-boy who affected a solemn tone when telling of his father's death only to break into peals of laughter at the thought of his inheritance. Sure, he was on for marrying a rich shrew, why the hell not? If she was rich enough, nothing else mattered.

It built splendidly to the first face-off between Petruchio and Katharina (Pauline McLynn). She was wiping down the tables, a Pegeen-Mike-like daughter of the pub, her nonchalant put-downs coming from one end of the space to another. He played the game well, though, drawing her into a waltz-like dance with glitterlight accompaniment at the climax of the wooing. But when the men came back, it was with Kate's arm half-twisted up her back that Petruchio assured the onlookers of their loving agreement to marry. Owen Roe was a big brutal Petruchio—not much hint of tenderness beneath the games-playing there. After the wedding, he drove his bride before him blackthorn in hand, while the group of wedding guests cowered at the buttery bar. Likewise, there was hardly a hint of playfulness in his breaking of her will with the deprivation of food and sleep. Only finally in the sun/moon scene, when Kate lay on the road in sunglasses, her head on a rolled-up towel, did she come back on level terms with him, casually humouring his whims. And the wager in the final scene was a put-up job between them: she had been tipped off ahead and performed her submission speech purely for the money. That speech itself was one of commanding authority as she fondled and playacted with both men and women, culminating in a lingering kiss for Tranio (Rory Keenan) that momentarily unsettled Petruchio. The final shot was of the happy couple in honeymoon farewell pose, both in their sunglasses.

Parker did not relocate the play—Padua was still Padua, Verona still Verona—and the language was completely unchanged, the verse spoken clearly and confidently by the actors. But at no point did the discrepancy between the Elizabethan language and the contemporary Irish setting seem a problem. Instead, the casual oaths and profanities that are part of the ordinary stuff of the characters' language—'Would to God', 'God be blessed', 'O mercy'—which sound merely inert and lifeless in most modern stagings of Shakespeare took on a new credibility as uttered by these Irish Midlands characters. For such people, as one suspects for Shakespeare's own contemporaries, these pious lardings of speech were testimony to an accepted faith that shaped popular discourse while not in any significant way informing their behaviour. The costuming (like the set by Monica Frawley) exactly caught the sleaze and styleless quality of the male-dominated group. The final scene had all the authentic tawdriness of a country wedding, with the men standing around in drunkenly dishevelled groups. This was a satiric version of not-so-long-ago Ireland with its sexist materialism and its awful lack of culture or refinement, a Shakespeare made our own (Figure 2).

Fig. 2 Tadgh Murphy, Rory Nolan, Rory Keenan, Peter Daly, and Barry McGovern in Rough Magic production of *The Taming of the Shrew*. Photographer Patrick Redmond. Courtesy of Rough Magic.

Opening Up to the World

When in the 1980s Rough Magic began to produce plays by contemporary British playwrights Howard Barker, Caryl Churchill, and Michael Hastings, they were responding to a gap in the market; these were plays that would not otherwise have been seen in Ireland. By 2006 Irish directors were well aware of the contemporary British theatre and the opportunities it offered. So, for example, b*spoke Theatre Company produced Terry Johnson's highly successful 1993 *Hysteria*, built around the encounter of Sigmund Freud and Salvador Dali. *Blue/Orange*, Joe Penhall's 2000 play about mental health and race, was staged in the Peacock, giving a then unusual opportunity for a Black actor on the Irish stage. *Mother Teresa is Dead*, Helen Edmundson's 2001 Royal Court play on Western guilt about the Third World, was adapted to an Irish setting in the Focus Theatre production. Two of the plays of the popular and prolific Scottish playwright David Greig were staged: *Outlying Islands* from 2002 by Island Theatre Company at the Beltable in Limerick, and *Pyrenees* (2005) by Hatch Theatre Company at the Project in Dublin.

Though most of the productions in 2006 were new plays by Irish playwrights, Ireland was by this time part of a globalized theatre market. Australian playwright Peta Murray's highly successful dance drama *Wallflowering* was staged by Tall Tales as the last in a season of Women Writing Worldwide. There had never been as much reluctance to stage American as British plays in Irish theatre; Eugene O'Neill, Arthur Miller, and Tennessee Williams had been fairly commonly produced, and the revival of Sam Shepard's *True West* at the Peacock in 2006 could be seen as part of this tradition of producing classic US drama. The production of John Patrick Shanley's Pulitzer prize-winning *Doubt* by the Abbey seemed merely a cash-in on its recent Broadway success. Still, it was enterprising of Prime Cut to stage *The Trestle at Pope Lick Creek*, the Depression-era coming-of-age play by the distinguished American playwright Naomi Wallace. And Glen Berger's very portable one-man show, *Underneath the Lintel*, produced everywhere across the United States from its premiere in 2001, fitted well into the Dublin Fringe Festival of 2006.

There is a long tradition of staging Chekhov, and to a lesser extent Ibsen, in Irish theatre but much less evidence of an interest in more recent European drama.[7] That too was changing in 2006. The production of Falk Richter's abstract and surreal *The System Parts I and II* by RAW Productions was right up to date, the German original only having been staged in 2005; the director Rachel West had been working in Germany for a number of years. Blue Raincoat staged Ionesco's *The Chairs*, but also leading Bulgarian playwright Stanislav Stratiev's *It's a Short Life*, a characteristically absurd satire on bureaucracy centred on a man's quest

---

[7] See Ros Dixon and Irina Ruppo Malone (eds.), *Ibsen and Chekhov on the Irish Stage* (Dublin: Carysfort Press, 2012).

to find a button to hold up his trousers. *A Dream of Autumn* was produced by Rough Magic, a sombre, lyrical play on love and death, by the then little-known Jan Fosse who was to win the Nobel Prize in 2023. The Holocaust is not a subject that has been much treated in Irish theatre.[8] It was all the more important to have the opportunity to see the Spanish playwright Juan Mayorga's *Way to Heaven*, about *Himmelweg*, the fake model concentration camp used to con 1944 Red Cross inspectors. The Galloglass touring production again closely followed the English-language premiere of the play in London in 2005. Irish theatre in 2006 was open to the world, alert to the world, in a way it had not been for much of the preceding century.

Festen, one of the outstanding productions of the year, reflected this new international awareness, based as it was on the original Danish film adapted for the stage by the British playwright David Eldridge; a Polish version had already been seen at an earlier Dublin Theatre Festival. But it made a particular impact in Dublin in 2006 as one of a number of plays about child sex abuse that year. The revelations about the abuse of children in Church-run institutions in the 1990s, of which the full evidence was to appear in the Ryan Report of 2009, had been a major scandal, and had led to a focus also on similar cases within the home. The silences around such subjects that had obtained through much of Ireland's modern history were being broken, and the plays that featured these themes resonated with a growing public awareness in 2006.

The immediate visual impact of the set design (Giles Cadle) of *Festen* was striking, with party streamers strung out from the back of the auditorium to a vanishing point at the back of the stage. Facing the audience, about one-third of the way upstage, was a blank wall of doors in dull Georgian green, picking out the detail of the Gate's own neoclassical pilasters. Heralded by a child clutching a red balloon, and piano music which was to sound hauntingly at intervals through the play, the family assembled: the mad, obnoxious younger brother Michael (Rory Keenan) quarrelling with his wife Mette (Cathy Belton), apparently overjoyed to meet up with his older—more successful—brother Christian (Ronan Leahy); Helene (Simone Kirby), the hippie dissenter sister in appropriately peasant-style dress, pleased also to see Christian but spitting at the sight of Michael who had not showed up for their dead sister Linda's funeral and was now gatecrashing their father's 60th birthday party.

When the doors in the wall opened, there were bedroom and bathroom spaces and, with a section of the wall removed, we saw the patriarch Helge (Owen Roe) already dinner-jacketed, savouring his glass of brandy, cheerily greeting Christian. The separate spaces made for a simultaneous narrative of the three siblings: Michael and Mette quarrelling, and then making love; Christian resisting the advances of a highly attractive and scantily clad maid; Helene in silent horror,

---

[8] A partial exception is Elizabeth Kuti's *Treehouses*, produced by the Abbey Theatre in 2000.

reading a hidden letter from Linda who had committed suicide. The scene was set for the opening out of the stage with a formally laid dinner table that trollied forward downstage, all nine guests already seated at it, with just one vacant place where Linda should have been.

The climax of the first act came with Christian's speech, in which he accuses his father of having repeatedly raped himself and Linda when they were children. The anarchy that follows, partly comic, partly emotional, seems to result in Helge regaining control of the situation. But in the second act, the party degenerates into further chaos with a second climax produced by Helene reading out her dead sister's heartbreaking letter, which confirms all of Christian's accusations. The most horrifying exchange of all comes between Christian and his father:

CHRISTIAN. Somehow, I've never understood why you did it.
pause.
        I've never understood why you did it.
pause.
HELGE. It was all you were good for.[9]

Michael's young daughter, the girl with the balloon from the start, playing around with her rag doll, in her innocence and vulnerability, was a stand-in for the absent Linda. In a final coda, there was a return to morning-after normality with the reappearance of the table set for family breakfast. But Helge, now alienated and ostracized, no longer occupied his central role, and was forced to exit through the auditorium, a broken and defeated man.

Outside the Box

Corcadorca was a pioneer of site-specific work, productions in 'unusual spaces', from the 1990s on. Their 2006 *The Tempest*, produced in Fitzgerald's Park in Cork, made good use of a lake and the surrounding green spaces for the shipwreck, Prospero's island, and the magical appearances and disappearances of the play, even if many of the elements of the staging, costuming, and voice production were not really well achieved. The sense of strangeness, of being removed from the familiar routines of purpose-built theatrical auditoria, is of the essence of such productions. There was the mysteriousness of not knowing where we were being taken as an audience for *The Waiting Room* by the company Kabosh, when we were ferried out by bus from the city centre to a warehouse in east Belfast to watch a whimsical fantasia about a French village in the wake of World War I. There seemed to be no discernible connection between the play and the surrounding streets, with

---

[9] David Eldridge, *Festen* (London: Methuen Drama, 2004), 60.

their hardline Unionist murals and posters encouraging people to vote for the Progressive Unionist Party. On the other hand, the extraordinary atmosphere of the Sick and Indigent Roomkeepers, the elegant eighteenth-century house right in the centre of Dublin next to the Castle, made for a most suggestive setting for *God's Grace*, Semper Fi's play by Paul Walker and Eugene O'Brien, about a hysterical young woman and the exorcism of her guilty terrors.

These were site-specific plays in that they were staged in locations outside purpose-built theatres, but neither of them had the particular connections of action to site seen in the work of ANU, which I will be looking at in Chapter 4. The same would be true of Tom Swift's *Drive-by* (Performance Corporation), a night show about boy-racers which was performed on the Cork docks to give room for the racing. And it was not immersive, in that the eleven of us in the audience sat in our individual cars watching and listening to the soundtrack on our car radios. Three performers (Tadgh Murphy, Aidan Turner, Ailish Symons), three cars: quick vignettes, the aggro of the young people directed against the audience in their parked cars, the erotics of the machine, the hypocrisy of two middle-class people deploring young people's speeding when one of them had been involved in a hit-and-run. The thrust of the piece was to attack the complicity of society as a whole in the boy-racing. It shifted finally into sombre documentary material: newsclippings from a fatal crash where young people had died, illustrated by Symons climbing out of the stationary car in a quite unexpected red dress—they were otherwise all in black and white—to the strains of the Queen of the Night's aria in *Zauberflöte*. And it ended with a heartbreaking real-life interview with a Derry man whose son and his girlfriend had been killed, while the actor who had driven the last car away at speed into the distance walked back slowly, unlit.

The most ambitious show in this mode was *Whereabouts* staged by Fishamble: the New Play Company. True to their name and mission they had commissioned eleven writers to contribute a total of fourteen playlets, and in the light of the inadequate representation of women in Irish theatre, to be publicized in 2015 by #WakingTheFeminists, it is to their credit that five of the playwrights were female. There was a 'daytime trail' and an 'evening trail', with the fifteen audience members guided round Temple Bar in Dublin's inner city to the various sites. Some of the plays were plotted actions indoors, like Colin Murphy's *Dublin Noir*, staged in the Amnesty International Café, where a nervous informant from the civil service was encouraged by a journalist to leak material showing government collusion with the CIA. The informant leaves, the 'journalist' gets on the phone to the authorities; sure enough, as we leave the café, we see the informant bundled into a car and driven away. This, though, was watched by a streetsweeper, who turned out to be the actor of Shane Carr's *Mean Sweeps I*—there was to be a sequel part *II* in the evening trail—who told us the story of how he crashed down into his present homeless state. Then on to a music shop, where we looked across a street at a woman sitting silent in a coffee house, while over a loudspeaker in the shop we heard her voiced thoughts in *My Brother Is Disappearing* by Anna Newell: the brother was disappearing into narcolepsy, his sister trying to tell him stories to keep him awake.

Ordinary-looking people turned into plays, like the cleaning woman smoking outside the Sin Theatre Bar in *The Other Woman* by Tom Swift. The 'other woman' turned out to be an eastern European lapdancer in the bar, apparently contrasted to the cleaner in her youth and sexy glamour, but as the action developed just as isolated and alone. Outside we met a desperate mother holding up a photo of her missing son, asking people had they seen him: this was *Lament for Joseph* by Jody O'Neill. *Drapes* by Belinda McKeon was much more elaborate, as we stood in a clothes shop with a disconsolate middle-aged man encumbered with packages waiting for his daughter to come out of the changing-room. The daughter's obsessive shopping related to the death of her mother, and when her father argued with her about her current purchase, she dramatically undressed and walked out into the street. The daytime trail ended with *Eclipsed I* by Louise Lowe, the case-history story of the junkie prostitute seen on the streets earlier, brilliantly performed by Aoife Duffin in this and its harrowing evening sequel.

Some of the same sites were revisited in the evening, the now lit up Sin Theatre for the grim drama of *Bernard Opens Up* by Jack Olohan, in which a sex bondage game goes wrong, ending with the death of one of the partners, whose body is bundled away as the nightclub prepares for a gala celebrity occasion. Sex figured strongly also in John Grogan's *Blind Spot* with its Genet- or Pinter-like choreography between a man and a woman where it was impossible to tell what was fantasy and what real. There was one comic piece, *Twenty-Two* by John Cronin with an absurd sequence involving two men as doubles for one another. And the night ended with the tour de force of Neil Watkins's performance as a florid drag queen in Jacqueline Strawbridge's *Eggshell*.

Living in the Present, Living with the Past

Whereabouts took the Dublin streets for its stage, a permissive, materialistic city with its bizarre urban contiguities, its dark corners and sad stories. The year 2006 represented some sort of peak for the so-called Celtic Tiger before it crashed and burned in the global financial crisis of 2008. From 2000 Ireland had been rated as one of the most globalized economies in the world.[10] The ongoing Mahon tribunal of enquiry into urban planning, which was finally to report in 2012, had already exposed widespread political corruption as the underbelly of this

---

[10] See Cliff Taylor, 'Ireland Ranked as the Most Globalised of 62 States Due to Exports', *Irish Times*, 8 January 2003, https://www.irishtimes.com/news/ireland-ranked-as-the-most-globalised-of-62-states-due-to-exports-1.344603 (accessed 1 September 2022).

economic success.[11] The expansion of the European Union in 2004 had brought a large number of immigrants to the country for the very first time. This was a very different Ireland from the largely homogeneous agrarian nation of much of the twentieth century: modernized, urbanized, increasingly secular, with a newly multi-ethnic population. And a number of the plays of the year sought to reflect that contemporary reality.

So, for example, Nicholas Kelly's *The Grown-Ups* (Peacock) tackled the subject directly. According to the blurb on the back cover of its published text, it 'casts a sharp eye on contemporary Dublin and the malaise of a generation seduced by money, status and self'.[12] The *Irish Times* reviewer took a dim view of the result: 'Kelly's play is so concerned with glumly mapping out "this splenetic city with its heart wrapped in ice" that it succumbs to a similar disorder, tracing its messy surface but unable to thaw any fresh insights from its cold centre'.[13] Paul Mercier, in *Homeland* (Abbey) used a parodic version of the myth of Oisín for his satiric indictment of modern Ireland. In the legend, Oisín, son of Fionn mac Cumhaill, was lured away by the fairy Niamh for 300 years in Tír na nOg and returns to Ireland to find the Fianna long dead and the country converted to Christianity by St Patrick. Mercier's equivalent was the political spin-doctor Gerry Newman (Liam Carney) who had to flee the country after having spilled the beans to one of the corruption tribunals on all the dirty tricks in which he was involved. He was back in Ireland for one day, but could not leave the airport terminal, his equivalent of Oisín's not being allowed to touch the soil of Ireland. The heroic Ireland he remembered, the Ireland of the Fianna—here Fianna Fáil, for long the default governing party and the one most implicated in the political scandals—turned out to have been the fakest of fake legends. The play exposed contemporary Ireland as a series of imagined solidities attached to the nothingness of spin-doctors, predatory capitalists, and crooks talking themselves into believing their own myths. The narrative played games in and out of the Oisín story. At one point on his *Walpurgisnacht* journey through derelict urban Dublin, Gerry fell into the hands of the Church of God's Gospel, led by Kenneth from the mainland—the equivalent of evangelizing St Patrick from Wales. Niamh, the fairy who led Oisin to Tír na nÓg, is the AIDS-afflicted junkie prostitute (Gabrielle Reidy), complete with green dress and blonde wig, whom he met at a party and who rolled him for his cash, wallet, and credit cards. A series of violent adventures follows, including Niamh's murder of her pimp and her own death, before Gerry returns to the airplane seat where we saw him at the start. The contrast of deeply corrupt modern Ireland with the romantic legend seemed heavy-handed and incoherent.

---

[11] See https://planningtribunal.ie/wp-content/uploads/2019/04/sitecontent_1257.pdf (accessed 1 September 2022).
[12] Nicholas Kelly, *The Grown-Ups* (London: Methuen Drama, 2006).
[13] Peter Crawley, 'The Grown-Ups', *Irish Times*, 16 February 2006, https://www.irishtimes.com/culture/review-1.1016232 (accessed 1 September 2022).

There was no such satiric thrust in *Everyday* (Corn Exchange) by Michael West and the company. Instead, what the play offered was a dawn to dusk cross-section of Dubliners whose lives touch through the day but do not necessarily intersect. Many of the narrative connections converged on Larry Brady, ruthless property developer, and his backer and about-to-be lover, the grotesque Madeline. Old Mr Delahunty was a tenant in one of Larry's properties, about to be evicted. Larry's two sons were contrasted, the one who worked in the business a go-getting womanizer, the other a moony wannabe singer; Cliff was a harried employee in a dead marriage—we saw his wife at home with kids screaming offstage—who was driven to attempt suicide. Representatives from across the social spectrum were included: a Ukrainian child-minder with little English, a brash Australian estate agent, a young teacher just up from the country, a working-class couple coming to terms with a new baby. The weakness of the play was indeed that very self-conscious need to get in all sorts and conditions, with the banality of some of the stories. But the skills of the seven performers who played all the parts, the distinctive Corn Exchange *commedia* style with white face and mannered movements, the delicacy of the changing lighting (Jane Cox), made for a beautiful and moving day in the life of the city (Figure 3).

Fig. 3 Andrew Bennett, Louise Lewis, Tom Murphy, Janet Moran, Derbhle Crotty, Mark O'Halloran, and Simon Rice in the Corn Exchange production of *Everyday* by Michael West in collaboration with the company as part of Dublin Theatre Festival 2006. Photographer Paul McCarthy. Courtesy of the Corn Exchange.

If some of the 2006 plays looked to render directly the contemporary state of society, more featured the interplay of present with past. Northern Irish works were particularly striking in this regard. The 1998 Good Friday Agreement had been designed to bring to an end the political violence of the Troubles that had begun in 1969. But the legacy from those years remained, and were highlighted by two plays about the Protestant Loyalist community. Gary Mitchell, the author of *Remnants of Fear* (Dubbeljoint), was himself from a Loyalist paramilitary background, and had been driven out of his Belfast home by threats to himself and his family because of his uncompromising representation of his ex-comrades. This play turned on the way in which teenagers were recruited for the violent UDA (Ulster Defense Authority), its climax the face-off between Charlie, the upright ex-UDA man, and his brother Geordie, the hard man drug-dealer, who is trying to persuade Tony, Charlie's son, to join his gang of thugs. Rosemary Jenkinson's *The Bonefire* (Rough Magic) was set on 11–12 July, when the enormous bonfires are built and set alight to celebrate the victory of Protestant King William at the Battle of the Boyne in 1690. It provided a scarifying, if at times blackly comic, view of the casually brutal Protestant underworld, ending with the revelation of how the central character Lorraine had been gang-raped by a group of men including her own brother.[14] Both plays dramatized the process by which the sectarian conflicts of the Troubles had mutated into local community violence and organized crime.

It was good to watch one play from Northern Ireland that was not about the Troubles or their aftermath. *Girls and Dolls* (Tinderbox) was written by Lisa McGee, subsequently to become very well known as the creator of the hugely popular TV series *Derry Girls*.[15] It involved the revisiting by two adult women of a terrible incident of their childhood in which they had been responsible for the death of a baby. There were four parts, all four women actors on stage all the time: the 10-year-old and the adult versions of Emma and Clare. They had not met since they were 10 and their meeting precipitates a return to the traumatic events of the summer of 1980. Adult Emma had been persuaded with great reluctance to meet with adult Clare; she had been told Clare is dead, she wanted no part in what took place all those years ago. But she was manoeuvred into rehearsing their childhood friendship and its consequences, with the scenes of the original summer intercut with the later encounter. Subtly and effectively, the play took us through the complex factors that led to the death of the baby, and the working through of the traumas left with the women involved.

Girls and Dolls was a psychological not a political study of the relationship between past and present. *The Townlands of Brazil* (axis, Ballymun) by Dermot

---

[14] Rosemary Jenkinson, *The Bonefire* (London: Methuen Drama, 2006).
[15] Lisa McGee, *Girls and Dolls* (London: Nick Hern Books, 2006).

Bolger was self-consciously historical in contrasting its two periods of action.[16] The Ballymun Flats had been Dublin's one (very unsuccessful) high-rise social housing project. Initiated in 1966, by 2006 they were in the process of demolition. Bolger set his play both in the present, when eastern European workers were employed in the task of demolishing the flats, and 1963 in the area before they were constructed: the part of north Dublin where they stood was the townland of Brazil. The play had a double parallel plot. The first section, set in Ballymun before it became Ballymun, had Eileen, left pregnant when her lover was killed in an accident in Liverpool, forced to emigrate rather than face incarceration with the nuns in the Magdalen homes that were to become so notorious. The second flashed us forward to 2006, focused on the Polish woman Monika, who had come to Ballymun for work as the tower blocks were being demolished. Her story duplicated Eileen's, in that she was four months pregnant when her lover was killed in an accident. She still mourned his loss, working to support her daughter being raised by her parents back in Poland. We heard the same lines, the same situations repeated from one story to the other. A resolution of sorts was achieved when Michael, the lost son of Eileen, encouraged Monika to bring her daughter over to Ireland, whatever the economic consequences. The somewhat sentimental and heavy-handed dramatic structure was designed to bring home to the audience the continuing suffering of an underclass of workers in spite of the enormous changes in Ireland over the fifty-year period of modernization.

Ireland in the twenty-first century has been radically transformed, economically, socially, and politically. But the long history of the preceding century has still to be worked through. The next part of this book is devoted to the various manifestations of that dialectic of past and present. The narrative of colonization and resistance long dominated Irish historiography and the partitioned island has meant that it remains a live issue in contemporary politics. Contemporary Irish theatre has felt free to play games with traditional versions of our history, parodying standard narratives. At the same time, the productions of ANU have taken audiences to some of the neglected sites of Irish history, bringing home to them occluded parts of past social experience. Playwrights from Northern Ireland have sought to confront the ongoing problems of their territory: legacy issues from the Troubles such as the 'disappeared', victims of paramilitary violence whose bodies have never been found; the sectarian divisions of the cities embodied in the so-called Peace Walls still very much in place in the twenty-first century; the embattled siege mentality of many in the Loyalist community. While adaptations of classic plays for the Irish theatre have been a standard part of the tradition, as we have seen, companies and directors have looked to make them more relevant to a contemporary society that is ethnically diverse for the first time. All of these elements that had begun to surface in 2006 are the subject of detailed study in the chapters that follow.

---

[16] Dermot Bolger, *The Townlands of Brazil* (Dublin: New Island, 2007).

PART II
PAST AND PRESENT

4
Live History

In *Northern Star*, Stewart Parker's dramatization of the life of Henry Joy McCracken, 1798 United Irishmen leader, McCracken responds to the declaration of his lover Mary Bodle: 'They forget nothing in this country, not ever'; 'No. It isn't true to say they forget nothing. It's far worse than that. They misremember everything'.[1] *Northern Star* was only one of many Irish history plays in the 1980s: Brian Friel, *Translations* (1980) and *Making History* (1988); Christina Reid, *Tea in a China Cup* (1983); Frank McGuinnness, *Observe the Sons of Ulster Marching Towards the Somme* (1985); Thomas Kilroy, *Double Cross* (1986).[2] All the dramatists wrote with a consciousness of the contemporary political violence in the North, explicitly so in the case of the plays staged by Field Day, *Translations*, *Double Cross*, and *Making History*. The company had been established in the 1980s by Brian Friel and Stephen Rea as a 'cultural and intellectual response to the political crisis in Northern Ireland'.[3] The plays explored how Irish history came to shape the present, the ways memories and misrememberings of the past helped to produce the deadly oppositions of Catholic and Protestant, nationalist and Unionist, offering alternative versions of those polarizing stories.

Friel in *Translations* went back to what he construed as a watershed period in the colonial relationship of England and Ireland. He represented the Ordnance Survey mapping operation and the establishment of the National Schools in the 1830s as part of a systematic Anglicization of Ireland. Through the play, there was the tragic awareness of the terrible mid-century Famine to come, which all but wiped out Irish as a living language. The theatrical convention by which the villagers of Ballybeg and the British soldiers, while both actually speaking English, were presumed to be mutually incomprehensible, worked as a powerful metaphor for the miscommunication between the two peoples. Though the play was widely read as an elegiac lament for a culture lost to colonization, it ends with the hedge-schoolmaster Hugh's declaration of the need to accept the changed landscape represented by the place names of the Ordnance Survey: 'We must learn those

---

[1] Stewart Parker, *Three Plays for Ireland: Northern Star, Heavenly Bodies, Pentecost* (London: Oberon Books, 1989), 64.
[2] *Northern Star* itself was the first of what Parker saw as a 'triptych' of history plays along with *Heavenly Bodies* (1986), framed around the playwright Dion Boucicault, and *Pentecost* (1987) about the 1974 Ulster Workers' strike that brought down the power-sharing executive: Parker, *Three Plays for Ireland*, 9.
[3] Field Day website, https://fieldday.ie/about/ (accessed 14 August 2023).

new names. [...] We must learn where we live. We must learn to make them our own. We must make them our new home.'[4]

Thomas Kilroy, in *Double Cross*, took another route towards challenging traditional antitheses of Irish and English nationality. 'The play', he maintained, 'tries to undermine the black and white divisions of all wars, to subvert the righteousness of all political causes and to see the political issues involved through the much more mysterious prism of individual human character'.[5] He juxtaposed the figures of Brendan Bracken, Churchill's Minister of Information during the Second World War, and William Joyce, the infamous Lord Haw Haw who broadcast propaganda for the Nazis. In the play, these arch-antagonists, Peter and Judas from an English wartime viewpoint, are imagined as something like doubles: each with an Irish past they are anxious to conceal, each self-invented, whether as blimpish British conservative or as fascist quisling, in both cases overcompensating for their own personal insecurities. Lord Beaverbrook, imperialist press baron, in a final interview with Joyce, seems to speak as an unlikely *raisonneur* for the author: 'I have always felt that there was something screwball about this emphasis on nationality'.[6] Irishness and Englishness are constructed fictions not ineluctable differences of national identity.

Service in the British armed services in both world wars has often been taken as a key constituent element in Northern loyalist feeling. McGuinness and Reid take this as a starting-point for *Sons of Ulster* and *China Cup*. The 'sons of Ulster' are a group of young men joining up in 1914, all but one of them committed Protestant Unionists, seeing their service as a continuation of the militant defence of their province against the threat of a Catholic takeover in an imposed Home Rule. The one exception is the upper-class Pyper, a dissident artist with a death-wish who seeks to undermine their unquestioning loyalty. In some ways he succeeds, but the paradox is that he himself is converted to their faith, and when he alone survives the Somme, he returns to Northern Ireland to take up his role as defender of the Unionist hegemony. The Elder Pyper, who dreams through the experience that leads up to the Somme in the flashback which is the main action of the play, is a figure tormented by survivor guilt. For all the sympathetic imagination of the serving soldiers in the play, the Elder Pyper stands for a dead-end isolationism, summed up in his own image: 'The house has grown cold. Ulster has grown lonely'.[7]

---

[4] Brian Friel, *Selected Plays* (London: Faber, 1984), 444.
[5] Thomas Kilroy, *Double Cross* (Oldcastle: The Gallery Press, 1994), 11.
[6] Kilroy, *Double Cross*, 84.
[7] Frank McGuinness, *Observe the Sons of Ulster Marching Towards the Somme* (London: Faber, 2016 [1986]), 21. Here McGuinness anticipated the image used by David Trimble in his Nobel Peace Prize address: 'Ulster Unionists, fearful of being isolated on the island, built a solid house, but it was a cold house for catholics': David Trimble, Nobel Lecture, https://www.nobelprize.org/prizes/peace/1998/trimble/lecture/ (accessed 14 August 2023).

Sons of Ulster has an all-male cast and McGuinness dramatizes a range of different sorts of masculinity within the play. Reid in *China Cup* focuses on a comparable working-class Protestant culture but from the perspective of the women. The action covers three generations of the one family in the period from 1939 to 1972. The men have all served in the army, the Grandfather in World War I, Samuel killed at Dunkirk, Sammy serving with the postwar forces abroad in Germany, their photographs displayed prominently in the home as a sort of patriotic shrine. But they are for the most part absent, and the other men in the family we hear about are irresponsible drunks and gamblers. The role of the stoical women is to sustain a cultural self-belief that rests on propriety and gentility—symbolized by the 'tea in a china cup' of the title—which differentiates them from their Catholic neighbours in their own view. The trajectory of the play follows the struggle of Beth as child and young woman to free herself from this ethos. As she confesses near the end, 'my head is full of other people's memories. I don't know who *I* am ... what *I* am'.[8] Both *Sons of Ulster* and *China Cup* work through the problematics of identity within a culturally conditioned social and political inheritance.

In *Northern Star*, Parker dramatized the last eight years of McCracken's life from his first heady debates with fellow Belfast Dissenters who were to become leaders of the United Irishmen to the disastrous failed revolution of 1798. McCracken looks back in disillusionment at his career, dividing it into a mocking 'seven ages of Harry. [...] Haven't we always been on a stage, in our own eyes? Playing to the gods. History, posterity'.[9] Each scene, from 'The Age of Idealism' on, is written in a pastiche of the style of successive Irish playwrights: Farquhar, Boucicault, Wilde, Shaw, Synge, O'Casey, ending with Behan and Beckett. McCracken regards his own claims to heroic status with scathing self-depreciation, and the shifting styles and the setting provide further irony. The 'safe house' where he shelters with his lover Mary Bodle and their baby is half-built, half-ruinous, a metaphor for the badly planned, calamitously failed revolution. In the final sentence, McCracken looks forward from his own present to that of the audience: 'So what if the English do bequeath us to one another some day? What then? When there's nobody else to blame except ourselves?'[10]

How to tell the story of Ireland's past leaders without indulging in the heroic misremembering that feeds historical mythology? That is the question canvassed in *Northern Star* and in *Making History*. *Translations*, Friel's first Field Day play, had won virtually universal popular acclaim, but among scholars there had been complaints about its factual inauthenticity and its nationalist tendentiousness.[11]

---

[8] Christina Reid, *Plays: 1* (London: Methuen Drama, 1997), 61.
[9] Parker, *Three Plays for Ireland*, 18.
[10] Parker, *Three Plays for Ireland*, 75.
[11] Of such critiques, one of the most telling was that by the historian Sean Connolly: 'Dreaming History', *Theatre Ireland*, 13 (1987), 42–4, which appeared at the time that Friel was writing *Making History*.

Although Friel defended himself against such charges, *Making History* could be read as an attempt to counter such accusations. The play is centrally concerned with how historical narratives are created and to what end. The history in question here is that of Hugh O'Neill, leader of the Irish in the Nine Years' War at the end of the sixteenth century, the last great revolt of Gaelic Ireland against English colonial control. In the play, we are shown the complexity of the figure of O'Neill, and his resistance to the hagiographical version of his story planned by Archbishop Lombard. Against Lombard's claim that history is 'a kind of storytelling', that 'art has precedence over accuracy', O'Neill demands that he 'record the *whole* life'—'[t]he schemer, the leader, the liar, the statesman, the lecher, the patriot, the drunk, the soured, bitter emigré'.[12] Friel actually played fast and loose with the facts of O'Neill's life in the play, most notably in making his third marriage to Mabel Bagenal, English Protestant sister to one of O'Neill's arch-enemies, the defining love of his life. The irony was not lost on Friel himself, noting in his preparatory work on the play that 'Lombard writing about ON is like Friel writing about Lombard & ON—fashioning events-facts into an acceptable fiction'.[13] Nonetheless, the play puts up to its audience the questionable nature of 'making history'.

Irish history plays continued to be produced through the 1990s and beyond. There were Sebastian Barry's 'family' plays, imagined lives of his own ancestors, including *Prayers of Sherkin* (1990), *The Steward of Christendom* (1995), and *Our Lady of Sligo* (1998). In *Good Evening, Mr Collins* (1995), Tom McIntyre created a version of the life and loves of Michael Collins. Elizabeth Kuti in *The Sugar Wife* (2005) linked the mid-nineteenth-century Irish situation with the American abolitionist movement. The plays I have chosen as the focus of this chapter share many of the aims of earlier works: connecting past to present; testing interpretations of history; recovering lost voices and forgotten narratives. In two of them there is a new spirit of comic playfulness. Donal O'Kelly in *Catalpa* (1995) recast the 1875–6 transoceanic voyage to rescue six Fenian prisoners from Australia as a Hollywood screenplay acted out as a solo performance by the screenwriter. *Improbable Frequency* (2004), by Arthur Riordan and Bell Helicopter, turned Ireland's experience of the 'Emergency', aka World War II, into a spoof spy thriller, a parodic musical comedy. These generic mediations distanced audiences from the history represented. The very opposite was true of the Monto Cycle, staged by ANU Productions, between 2010 and 2014. There, audiences of no more than four at a time were invited, like embedded war reporters, into conflict zones of the past. Yet these site-immersive productions were by no means intended as a literal re-creation of history; spectators had to negotiate spaces that were simultaneously past and

---

[12] Brian Friel, *Making History* (London: Faber, 1988), 8, 27. 63.
[13] Quoted by Marilynn Richtarik, *Getting to Good Friday* (Oxford: Oxford University Press, 2023), 25.

present, the lines between reality and fiction constantly blurred. Whether in the conventional theatres where *Catalpa* and *Improbable Frequency* were produced, or in the streets and buildings of the north Dublin inner-city area of the Monto, this was history in live performance.

Acting It Out: *Catalpa*

Donal O'Kelly is an actor, political activist, and playwright.[14] As a performer he is probably best known for his leading role opposite Colm Meaney in *The Van* (1996), Stephen Frears' film version of Roddy Doyle's novel. His play *Asylum! Asylum!* staged at the Peacock in 1994, centred on an African asylum seeker, highlighting issues of refugees and racism for the first time in the Irish theatre. He co-founded Calypso Theatre Company in 1993, which produced a number of his plays focused on national and international political subjects, including *Farawayan* (1997) which raised audience awareness of displaced people in the context of the Balkan wars. As a playwright he first came to prominence with *Bat the Father Rabbit the Son*, produced by Rough Magic in 1992, in which he played both Rabbit, the uptight, ruthless contemporary businessman, and his free-spirited, old-fashioned father Bat, who intermittently 'bubbled up' from within Rabbit's consciousness. It was when he toured *Bat the Father* to Australia that he learned of the Fenian prisoners in Fremantle, the starting-point for *Catalpa*.

The *Catalpa* was the ship used to rescue the group of Fenians who had been transported to Australia for their part in the abortive Irish rebellion against the British in 1867. Most of the Fenians involved had been amnestied by 1875, but those who had been Irish soldiers serving in the British army had not been included in the amnesty. Plans for the rescue of six of these imprisoned in Fremantle were organized by John Devoy, one of the leaders of the Irish-American Clan-na-Gael, who felt a special responsibility for them, as he had been the person responsible for recruiting for the Fenians in the army in Ireland; he himself had served a prison sentence and been released. It was a very elaborate and costly scheme by which the sailing ship the *Catalpa* was bought and kitted out as a whaler, using funds raised by Clan-na-Gael. It then sailed from New Bedford, Massachusetts, ostensibly on a whaling expedition in the North Atlantic, before heading south round the Cape of Good Hope and across the Indian and Pacific Oceans to western Australia. John Breslin, an agent of Clan-na-Gael, meantime, went the other way round the world, disguised as a rich American, to organize the prison breakout at the Australian end. The whole enterprise, conducted with maximum secrecy, took well over a year, from April 1875 to August 1876. The

---

[14] For fuller details, see Patrick Lonergan, 'Donal O'Kelly', in Martin Middeke and Peter Paul Schnierer (eds.), *Methuen Drama Guide to Contemporary Irish Playwrights* (London: Methuen Drama, 2010), 328–44.

prisoners and all those involved in the rescue were given a tumultuous heroes' welcome in New Bedford, the whole enterprise celebrated as a huge triumph and publicity coup for the Irish and Irish-Americans.

O'Kelly was very taken with the story, seeing it as a Hollywood blockbuster in the making, but decided to set himself the challenge of enacting it as a one-man performance. In the frame plot, Matthew Kidd appears as a screenwriter alone in his bedsit, having failed to sell his screenplay of the *Catalpa* expedition to two visiting movie producers. Sick of repeated rejections, he thinks to himself: 'Why didn't I just show them .../ The pictures in my head ....'[15] This is the cue for him to play out his potential epic movie. 'The theatrical challenge', O'Kelly writes in his note on 'Staging Catalpa' in the published text, 'is to flick the images into the audience's heads, to stimulate their imaginations so that they will see the Catalpa at sea, they will see and hear and smell the Atlantic swell, the whale blubber, the scorched Australian shore' (O'Kelly, *Catalpa*, 10). For *Bat the Father* he had already developed a special rhythmic, onomatopoeic prose. Here, for example, is a snatch of Bat's long climactic monologue in which he pictures all the various sorts of effluent of Dublin city making their way out to the sea: 'gulley gulley wash wash ging gang goo ging gang goo, gulley gulley wash wash ging gang goo ging gang goo, underneath the city in the dark'.[16] For *Catalpa* this was taken much further with verbal and aural sound effects created for each scene. These act as shorthand to 'flick images into the audience's heads'. A journey by pony and trap is sketched in: 'Pony-trappa clippa-cloppa clippa-cloppa'. The sails of the *Catalpa* are spread: 'Pulla rigga-ropey rigga-ropey rigga-ropey/ rigga-ropey oh!'. The flashback showing the arrival of the Fenians in Australia is conjured up with stereotypical cinematic associations:

> Whoa-woh-woh
> didgeridoo-de-didgeridoo-woowoh-woo ...
> Whoa-woh-woh
> didgeridoo-de-didgeridoo-woowoh-woo ...
> Fade into scorched Australian bush. (O'Kelly, *Catalpa*, 18, 30, 22)

O'Kelly's verbal score was supported by the changing mood and tempo of Trevor Knight's music performed live in the theatre.[17]

O'Kelly's two main sources for the play were *The Catalpa Expedition* by the journalist Zeph Pease, published in 1897, as the story of George Anthony, captain of the *Catalpa*, and Keith Amos's academically researched *The Fenians in Australia*

---

[15] Donal O'Kelly, *Catalpa* (Dublin: New Island Books, 1997), 12. All further quotations are from this text, cited in parentheses in the text. I have indicated rhythmic line breaks with a slash mark / as for poetry.
[16] Donal O'Kelly, *Bat the Father Rabbit the Son*, in John Fairleigh (ed.), *Far from the Land: New Irish Plays* (London: Methuen Drama, 1998), 229.
[17] A two-CD audio recording was made in 1999.

1865–1880.[18] Pease is enthusiastically pro-Fenian. The tone of his narrative is suggested by his introduction of the figure of Breslin: he 'was already a famous hero, and his burning love of country, his chivalry and his bravery, were written in the hearts of Erin's sons and daughters'.[19] Amos was conscious of this sort of partisanship and in the relevant section of his book he declares that a 'major purpose of this chapter is to reconcile Fenian accounts with an official viewpoint based on government, police and prison records'.[20] This he duly does but he is nonetheless broadly sympathetic to the Fenian cause. O'Kelly, whose aim in the play was 'to challenge the hero myth', was to tell the story very differently (O'Kelly, *Catalpa*, 8).

To start with, he had to simplify the narrative. There were, in fact, an astonishing number of different parties from various factions of the Irish republican movement who showed up in Fremantle wanting a share in the action, and O'Kelly had to clear away the conspiratorial clutter. The climactic confrontation of the steamer *Georgette* full of police threatening the *Catalpa* with the escaped prisoners aboard, as told in the sources, was a natural cinematic set-piece. All O'Kelly did to send it up was to set Anthony's recorded words of defiance to the tune of the Star-Spangled Banner:

> The American flag,
> I am on the high seas.
> Fire on this ship,
> and you fire on the American flag! (O'Kelly, *Catalpa*, 56)

A solo performer has to find means to differentiate his characters so the audience can immediately identify them. So, O'Kelly finding that 'Samuel Smith, first mate [on the *Catalpa*], was an American of Scots parentage' played him as Scottish throughout, and he Gallicized Mary Tondut, Breslin's lover in Fremantle, as Marie Tondut, with a strong French accent, on the basis of the information that she was the daughter of 'a French winegrower of South Perth'.[21]

These were necessary theatrical adaptations of the story. However, *Catalpa* is much more radical in the way in which it undermines the heroic Fenian narrative and the macho masculinity that underpins it. Hollywood movie tropes demand not only heroes but villains, and O'Kelly chose the Fenian leaders for his villains. Pease described the first meeting of Captain Anthony with John Devoy in the store of Anthony's father-in-law John Richardson, with all the

---

[18] Zeph W. Pease, *The Catalpa Expedition* (New Bedford, MA: George S. Anthony, 1897); Keith Amos, *The Fenians in Australia 1865–1880* (Kensington, NSW: New South Wales University Press, 1988).
[19] Pease, *Catalpa Expedition*, 110.
[20] Amos, *Fenians*, 227.
[21] Amos, *Fenians*, 216, 249.

lights out except one candle: 'It was an ideal conspiracy, you see, the plans being made under cover of darkness'.[22] O'Kelly transfers this to the cabin of the *Catalpa* and makes of the appearance of Devoy out of the darkness something distinctly sinister: 'Broad black brimmer, hollow cheeks, long black bushy beard, black cape, black eyes piercing in the dark, thin white hand extended to shake—crunch'. There are Mephistophelean associations to the self-introduction that follows, in which the words 'void' and 'apocalypse' are heard in the run of sound: 'Devoy devoy devoy apoc-a-lippa poc-a-lippa/ poc-a-lasha lippa-laddy-oh ...' (O'Kelly, *Catalpa*, 20). This then becomes the signature tune for Devoy every time he appears. The case of Breslin is equally striking. The 'famous hero' of the Fenians, as Pease has him, becomes in O'Kelly a '[b]ig thickset fellow with a grandee walrus moustache' with a coarse Dublin accent. He is a bluffer and a lecher; in the inn where he is introduced to Anthony, he '[k]eeps referring lasciviously to the proprietor's buxom wife, and even when not so referring, tracks her with his eyes shaded between his bushy eyebrows and his sprouting moustache' (O'Kelly, *Catalpa*, 26). O'Kelly is here preparing for what he regarded as a key revelation (uncovered in the police files examined by Amos) that Breslin deserted the Fremantle hotel servant Mary Tondut whom he had made pregnant.

Catalpa hollows out the nationalist rhetoric of the Fenians who are turned into self-interested deceivers. But it also challenges the gender dynamics of traditional heroic narratives. According to Pease, George Anthony's decision as to whether to take up the offer to captain the *Catalpa* was made the more difficult because he was just a year married with a young baby daughter. In the play this becomes a standard love versus honour dilemma, with the added corny motif of Anthony's mother-in-law who made him promise on her deathbed that he would never go to sea again on pain of her curse. An erotic sequence in which his wife Gretta invites George to '[c]ome into the dark sea' makes plain the implication of her threat when he decides to go with the *Catalpa*: 'You'll never sail these seas again' (O'Kelly, *Catalpa*, 24–5). So far, so Hollywood. But the whaling scene adds another dimension to the gender division. It is a mother and calf that the whalers go after, shown first below the surface of the water:

> Whale-momma pale-grey
> sailing in the smooth,
> nonchalantly pleasant in her awesome power,
> she strokes her flipper,
> soft like a momma's arm,
> ushering her calf-whale shy of the light,
> rising up from blackness to dark green sea

---

[22] Pease, *Catalpa Expedition*, 75.

This comes immediately after Anthony's memory, as a 'skinny boy' from the blubber deck of a whaler, of his first glimpse of Gretta as a girl in a pony and trap with her mother, her '[m]other's arm,/ warmly protective/ warding off the seamen predators' (O'Kelly, *Catalpa*, 33). Men are indeed predators in *Catalpa*, betraying the trust of women, like Breslin with Marie Tondut, with their whale-killing despoiling the natural world.

The play, then titled *Catalpa: The Movie*, was first staged by the Red Kettle Theatre Company in Waterford, directed by Bairbre Ní Chaoimh (O'Kelly's co-founder of Calypso). It was a huge success then, and subsequently when recast for production at the Gate in 1997. Enda Walsh, who saw the early version, called it 'the best performance I've ever seen':

> The stage was bare and he was only wearing grey trousers and a T-shirt. There was nothing special-looking about him but he had this incredible intelligence and power and precision. Donal's writing is almost Joycean: he can talk about the deep hell of everything in a way that's really funny and understandable. The play was all about the power of the actor on stage.[23]

As a one-man show, it is very portable, and O'Kelly has revived it many times over the years since. But in 2023 he took the principled decision that he would not perform it again. This was because he felt that the play 'risked reinforcing rather than challenging gender and racial stereotypes'. He went on to explain:

> I've found the 'dispensation' I gave myself—struggling screenwriter Mathew Kidd trying to fit his anti-epic into the Hollywood storytelling success formula [...] is too thin a bag to carry all that historical weight. While part of him is challenging the precepts of heroic narrative—he makes the stormy climax an imagined trial by the women his hero George Anthony feels deep down he has betrayed—part of him is also heavily influenced and excited, to an unwitting degree, by those ancient storytelling precepts.[24]

It's a very interesting authorial retrospect on the play. There is no doubt that the stereotypical representation of the sailors, like the dialect-speaking West Indian Mopsa playing on his concertina, can feel uncomfortable, even allowing for the Hollywood idiom which is being mocked. The strategy of *Catalpa* is to allow us to enjoy the absurdities of the filmic form—Kidd speculates on the then A-listers he would cast for Gretta; 'Winona could do it and Julia'd be fine/ but best of all would be Michelle, yes, Michelle' (O'Kelly, *Catalpa*, 14)—while rereading

---

[23] Enda Walsh, 'The Best Performance I've Ever Seen', *Guardian*, 22 August 2010, https://www.theguardian.com/stage/2010/aug/22/enda-walsh-penelope-traverse-hampstead (accessed 22 August 2023).
[24] Donal O'Kelly, personal email, 11 August 2023.

the conventional narratives that they represent. The virtuosity of the performance simultaneously distances us from the events narrated and brings them alive in a quite new way. For Irish audiences it is a deconstruction of inflated anti-colonial history as it has been handed down. For a wider public it makes the question, 'what is a hero?', which the play is designed to ask, unanswerably problematic. In spite of O'Kelly's current reservations about it, *Catalpa* remains an innovative and imaginative way of replaying the past.

Guying It: *Improbable Frequency*

Arthur Riordan was a founder member of Rough Magic, who appeared as an actor in many of their shows through the first twenty years of the company, as well as contributing a number of plays. *Improbable Frequency*, however, created with Conor Kelly and Simon Park, the musicians who composed under the name Bell Helicopter, was at the time his most ambitious show. Since then, he has worked extensively as a writer, producing a clever adaptation of *Peer Gynt* (2011), the book and lyrics for the musical *The Train* (2015), as well as several other musical collaborations. *Improbable Frequency* is set in 1941 and explores the condition of Ireland under the 'Emergency', the name given to the Second World War in Ireland derived from the Emergency Powers Act passed by the Irish legislature in September 1939.[25]

The neutrality, which that Act declared at the outset of the war, was historically inevitable; Ireland's neutral status in relation to conflict by the major international powers has been much cherished then and since. However, during World War II it was resented by supporters of the Allied cause in Ireland, many of whom joined the British forces. And the attitude of Winston Churchill can be gauged by his snorting reference in an official memo to 'the so-called neutrality of the so-called Eire'.[26] Éire was the official name for Ireland in the 1937 Constitution, and Churchill with his 'so-called neutrality' voiced a commonly held British view that it was pro-German. Ireland's neutral status certainly created a peculiar situation: a small, divided island where the North, as part of the United Kingdom, lived under wartime conditions, while the rest of the territory continued relatively unchanged. Visitors from a darkened, ration-dominated Britain were astonished at blackout-free Dublin where luxuries like milk and butter seemed readily available. For many it seemed a state of artificial cultural isolation, caught in Patrick Kavanagh's line, 'All Ireland that froze for want of Europe'.[27] And with legations from the several warring nations

---

[25] See Clair Wills, *That Neutral Island* (London: Faber, 2007), 2.
[26] Quoted in Eunan O'Halpin, *Spying in Ireland: British Intelligence and Irish Neutrality During the Second World War* (Oxford: Oxford University Press, 2008), 1.
[27] Patrick Kavanagh, *Collected Poems*, ed. Antoinette Quinn (London: Penguin, 2004), 103. The line is taken from 'Lough Derg', Kavanagh's wartime satire on the insularity of the pilgrims and pilgrimage.

present in Dublin, it was a natural home for espionage and counterespionage, real and imagined. This was the take-off point for Riordan's parodic spy thriller.

The template for *Improbable Frequency* must surely have been Tom Stoppard's *Travesties* (1974), a play which Lynne Parker directed when still a student in Trinity College. *Travesties* centred on three historical figures who happened to be living in Zurich at the same time in 1917: James Joyce, Vladimir Lenin, and Tristan Tzara, the pioneer of Dadaism. The observer of the interactions between these three is the Englishman Henry Carr, remembered only for a dispute with Joyce over a performance of *The Importance of Being Earnest*. Riordan's equivalent characters, all based in Dublin through World War II, are Flann O'Brien, John Betjeman, and the theoretical physicist Erwin Schrödinger. The observer figure here is the crossword puzzle enthusiast turned cryptographer Tristram Faraday—his first name might even have been suggested by that of Tzara.

Flann O'Brien, penname of Brian O'Nolan, who also wrote newspaper columns as Myles na gCopaleen, was a civil servant in the Department of Local Government. By 1941 he had already published his best-known novel *At-Swim-Two-Birds* (1939), the Irish language *An Beal Bocht* (1941), and written the as yet unpublished *The Third Policeman*. The poet John Betjeman, who had been declared 'mentally unfit for military service', joined the Ministry of Information, and in 1940 was posted to Dublin as press attaché to the Office of the United Kingdom Representative, Sir John Maffey.[28] Erwin Schrödinger, as an Austrian refugee, had been invited to Dublin in 1939 by Taoiseach Eamon de Valera to become one of the founding professors of the Dublin Institute of Advanced Studies, modelled on the Princeton Institute of Advanced Studies that had provided a base for Einstein.[29] Supposedly censorious Ireland did not seem to be bothered by his unconventional household of wife, mistress, and children, nor yet his subsequent affairs, 'bemusing Dublin with his sexual voracity and brilliance alike'.[30]

If *Travesties* represented a model for the plot of *Improbable Frequency*, the film *Cabaret* (1972), based on Christopher Isherwood's *Goodbye to Berlin* (1939), must have affected the performance style. The torch singing of Sally Bowles, with her ambiguous position in 1930s Nazi Germany, would have been a prompt for the equivalent figure of Agent Green (Cathy White) singing in the Red Bank Restaurant, notorious Dublin hangout for Nazi sympathizers. What is more, the Rough Magic production, originally in the O'Reilly Theatre of Belvedere School and subsequently in the Abbey, used a cabaret setting, with café tables set around the stage occupied by some audience members as well as cast. This dramaturgy gave both an

---

[28] Wills, *That Neutral Island*, 184.
[29] See Walter Moore, *Schrödinger: Life and Thought* (Cambridge: Cambridge University Press, 1989), 363–6.
[30] O'Halpin, *Spying in Ireland*, 60.

intimacy and a distancing effect to the fantastic show as it unrolled. One dimension to the estrangement was the use of *commedia* type make-up for almost all the characters. It was the style initiated in Ireland by Annie Ryan and the Corn Exchange, and remarkably, *Improbable Frequency* opened on 27 October 2004, just days before the premiere of *Dublin by Lamplight*. As in *Dublin by Lamplight*, the fixed make-up was counterpointed by quick costume changes, highlighting the virtuosity of actors such as Rory Nolan playing both the jauntily English Betjeman bouncing along in striped blazer and boater, and the red bewigged broadcaster Meehawl O'Dromedary—'don't mind me, I'm anti-British,/ That's my way'.[31] Only the part of Faraday (Peter Hanly) was not doubled and wore conventional costume and make-up.

The play takes on the touchy subject of English-Irish attitudes to one another in 'Be Careful Not to Patronise the Irish', the first choric number sung by the British office staff, which satirically illustrates what it warns against:

> A single mention, *en passant*
> Of drinking, fighting and maudlin song—
> Suddenly one is in the wrong
> And Paddy's up in arms.

But there is a sting in the tail of this song:

> Yes, be careful not to patronise the Irish,
> Though they don't object to patronising you.
> Is it smugness or insurgency
> That makes them say 'Emergency'?
> I feel it lacks the urgency
> Of World War Two. (Riordan, *Improbable Frequency*, 9–11)

There is a similar even-handedness in the satire throughout, in the outrageous 'Hymn to Drink' with the barman elevating a pint of Guinness as the communion chalice, or 'The Bedtime Jig' where the ingénue Philomena O'Shea (Lisa Lambe) exclaims in the middle of sex with Faraday, in every sense the climax of act one:

> I'm not looking forward to going to confession;
> God bless us, I wouldn't know where to begin.
> Infiltrated by British intelligence,
> Oxymoronic as well as a sin. (Riordan, *Improbable Frequency*, 54)

---

[31] Arthur Riordan and Bell Helicopter, *Improbable Frequency* (London: Nick Hern Book, 2005), 38. All further quotations are taken from this edition.

This is typical of Riordan's hit-and-run wit throughout the play. The parodic form of the musical, with the dialogue between the songs partly rhymed and underscored, allows for a light treatment of what would otherwise be serious enough. So, for example, the IRA man Muldoon (Darragh Kelly, who also played Myles na gCopaleen) is introduced with 'a rousing Republican ballad':

> I'm a wild Irish boy, I'm the pride of my town,
> In song and in story I'm widely renowned.
> And if my roguish grin doesn't win you around,
> Then I'll bury you where you won't ever be found. (Riordan, *Improbable Frequency*, 23)

The last line here refers glancingly to the 'disappeared', the IRA victims whose bodies had never been recovered, still, in 2004 at the time of the show's performance, an unresolved trauma of the Troubles. This reality, like the threat of a German invasion of Ireland backed by Republican activists which was thought a genuine possibility in 1941, is caught up in the tortuous swirls of the play's satire.

Faraday, true to his role as uncomprehending outsider, can break codes but fails to get the message. He misidentifies Philomena as the sinister figure of 'Molly Mayhem', whereas an audience can guess from the start that she will turn out to be the slinky (double) Agent Green. The denouement of the wildly unlikely plot comes in act II with the revelation of the Probability Adjustment Tank (PAT for short), a machine jointly devised by Schrödinger and Myles na gCopaleen, capable of creating improbable events by the influence of radio waves, as with the weather caused by the titles of broadcast songs. A spectacular scenic transformation in Alan Farquharson's set design signalled the build-up to this climax, as the pillars of the GPO, which stood behind the central bar for most of the action, 'rotate backwards becoming vast cannons pointing towards the audience and revealing a huge fantastical machine, with numerous flashing lights and pulsating tanks behind the portico' (Riordan, *Improbable Frequency*, 65). Predictably unpredictable twists and turns of the plot follow: Faraday and Schrödinger are captured, tied up, and about to be tortured by Muldoon and Agent Green; Green then shoots her lover and accomplice Muldoon, singing exultantly about the pleasures of 'betrayal', the machine runs out of control generating chaos in which Green and O'Dromedary are consumed; Faraday is rescued by Philomena.

It is difficult to do justice to the sheer comic inventiveness of *Improbable Frequency*, its by-play with Schrödinger's work on light waves and particles, O'Brien's mock atomic theory, its jesting literary allusiveness, as in the signature song 'We're all in the gutter,/ But some of us have an ear to the ground' (Riordan, *Improbable Frequency*, 21–2). It has proved to be Rough Magic's most successful show to date, winning awards when premiered in 2004, repeatedly revived at home in Ireland and across Europe and the US. It managed to deal parodically with controversial or uncomfortable topics. Irish neutrality has remained a sensitive subject, raised once again in 2022–3 by government support for Ukraine against Russia; more than one reviewer pointed to its topicality in 2004, when US planes were refuelling in Shannon Airport on their way to the Iraq war.[32] The whole history of Ireland's colonial relationship with Britain lay behind the vexed issue of Irish attitudes during the 'Emergency'. Sending it all up was a way of putting it in perspective. Peter Crawley concluded his *Irish Times* of the 2012 revival: 'the reason that Improbable Frequency is so richly worth revisiting is that Riordan and Rough Magic leave the peculiarities of Irish past and the present contentedly unsolved'.[33]

Living through It: The Monto Cycle

Nothing could be less like *Improbable Frequency*, or *Catalpa* for that matter, than the sequence of four plays mounted by ANU Productions from 2010 to 2014 as the Monto Cycle. The two earlier plays were staged in conventional auditoria with normal collective audiences, even if, in the case of some of the spectators at *Improbable Frequency*, given privileged access to the cabaret performance. No more than four audience members were admitted to any of the Monto Cycle, and these were then separated, so that no two ever saw quite the same sequence. They were taken from one building to another, into cars, out on the streets, never knowing what was going to happen next. The plays were shown in a continuous loop, restarting every hour or half-hour, rather than a standard matinée or evening performance. *Catalpa* and *Improbable Frequency* played theatrical games with generic forms, sending up the Hollywood blockbuster or the spy thriller. There were no jokes, no games-playing in the Monto Cycle; the plays were in deadly earnest throughout, simulating the immediacy of real life. ANU did not take one period for its setting, one episode from history as its subject; the Cycle explored the experience of one particular urban area as a lived continuum of past and present. It was a hugely ambitious project, all four of the plays planned together in advance as a sequence that would cover the time from the 1920s with *World's End Lane* (2010) through the later twentieth century in *Laundry* (2011), the 1970s of *The Boys of Foley Street* (2012), and *Vardo* (2014) set in the contemporary period.[34]

ANU Productions was co-founded by theatre director Louise Lowe and visual artist Owen Boss in 2009. They had met on a diploma course in youth arts at

---

[32] See, for example, Harvey O'Brien reviewing the 2012 revival in *irish theatre magazine*, 15 March 2012, http://itmarchive.ie/web/Reviews/Current/Improbable-Frequency.aspx.html (accessed 25 August 2023).

[33] Peter Crawley, 'Improbable Frequency', *Irish Times*, 22 March 2012, https://www.irishtimes.com/culture/music/classical/improbable-frequency-1.486463 (accessed 25 August 2012).

[34] Louise Lowe, interview with the author 15 August 2023. All other information, not otherwise cited, is taken from this interview for which I am very grateful.

Maynooth University, and had collaborated on *Tumbledowntown* (2005), about the demolition of the high-rise flats in Ballymun. Their work has been very much influenced by their own family history. Boss's grandfather was P. T. Daly, an early activist in Sinn Féin, a leading figure in the Irish labour movement. Four generations of Lowe's family came from the area of the Monto, the north inner-city of Dublin 'bounded by Gardiner Street, Talbot Street, Seán McDermott Street and Amiens Street'.[35] It took its name from Montgomery Street, subsequently Foley Street, notorious in the early twentieth century as a redlight district where Lowe's own grandmother had been a sex worker. In 2009 Lowe gave up her position as staff director at the Abbey, feeling disconnected from the work being presented there. As a working-class woman from an area so very close to the Abbey itself, she said, 'I only ever see myself on that stage as a trope or a joke'. For her the objective of the Monto Cycle was to make work reflecting the truth of that life which the national theatre so signally failed to represent.

The ANU plays could be seen as belonging to the genre of site-specific and immersive drama in so far as they were played outside ordinary theatre spaces and involved the audiences actively in the performance. But there was no effort to convince spectators that they were time-travelling back to the periods in which the plays were set. The actual buildings were gone for the most part; the tenements of Montgomery Street had been pulled down by 1938. On the corner of what became Foley Street and James Joyce Street (formerly Corporation Street) is the LAB, the Dublin gallery space for emerging artists, where much of *World's End Lane* was played. In most of the shows the actors wore contemporary clothes, not period costume; the one exception was *Laundry* where the women all wore the regulation Magdalene uniform, white shirt, black tunic, beige cardigan, and wellington boots. Audience members were able to interact with the performers; they were propositioned for help, were buttonholed by monologuing strangers, were shouted at angrily. The dialogue was often shapeless and repetitive, the sequence of events apparently bewilderingly random. But the illusion that the spectators were participating in a real-life situation was constantly disrupted. At times, precisely choreographed dance routines interspersed the dialogue; spectators were given headphones to listen to audio recordings or watched video projections. The collaboration between Lowe and Boss made for an interdisciplinary hybrid throughout.

World's End Lane, first in the sequence, took its name from what Montgomery Street was called before it was changed again to Foley Street. Such repeated name changes have been a feature of the area, repeatedly failing efforts to erase the

---

[35] Brian Singleton, 'ANU Productions and Site-Specific Performance: The Politics of Space and Place', in Fintan Walsh (ed.), *'That Was Us': Contemporary Irish Theatre and Performance* (London: Oberon Books, 2013), 21–36 [21].

bad reputation of the name before. From the nineteenth century on, Monto was notorious for its brothels that flourished due to the proximity of British army barracks and the docks. The situation only began to change in the 1920s with the crusade led by Frank Duff, founder of the Legion of Mary (1921). This was the notional period of *World's End Lane* which featured a number of actual historical figures from the time, the infamous madam, May Oblong, and two prostitutes, Honor Bright and Harriet Butler who were both murdered.[36] The individual spectator, only one of three audience members, was led through a series of intimate encounters, ordered about by the pimps who enforced discipline for the brothel owners: into a brothel-room set up in the LAB with religious icons and holy water fonts, witnessing violent confrontations, enacted in dance, between pimps and prostitutes, one of them Honor Bright (Una Kavanagh); led out along the streets by an actor who identified herself as Harriet Butler (Dee Burke) to a skipping game with local children; back in the LAB urged to fill the holy water fonts with methylated spirits, as a covert way of selling the cheap alcohol, this under the cold gaze of the actor playing May Oblong (Niamh Shaw).[37] It was a way of bringing the audience members into a disorienting secret history of the past that lived simultaneously with the present of performance.

Laundry was set in the St Mary Magdalene Asylum, one of the Magdalene homes for 'fallen women' established in Ireland originally in the eighteenth century. A vast building on Seán McDermott Street, now derelict, it was only closed in 1996, and operated a commercial laundry in which the incarcerated inmates—former sex workers, unmarried mothers, or otherwise socially unacceptable women—worked without pay. The scandal represented by the treatment of these women, including their separation from their babies often put up for adoption without the mothers' knowledge or consent, has now been much publicized, eventually producing an apology in the Dáil from the then Taoiseach Enda Kenny 'on behalf of the State, the Government and our citizens' for what had happened.[38] *Laundry* was designed to make audience members feel this experience from the inside: the prison-like atmosphere enforced by the opening image of the woman's face behind a grille in the outside door, the smell of carbolic soap used in the laundry, the institutionalization of the inmates—one woman who had been released and married, voluntarily returned after being widowed, another appeared

---

[36] See Maurice Curtis, *To Hell or Monto: The Story of Dublin's Most Notorious Districts* (Dublin: The History Press, 2015), 168, 178.

[37] As there are no published texts of the plays, apart from *The Boys of Foley Street*, analysis of the performances is dependent of the detailed accounts of audience members, here Brian Singleton, *ANU Productions: The Monto Cycle* (London: Palgrave Macmillan, 2016), 19–25. This has been supplemented by (partial) video recordings of the Cycle, to which Owen Boss very kindly gave me access.

[38] Quoted in Singleton, *Monto Cycle*, 38.

to escape only to come back every day. It involved the most intimate of encounters, an audience member asked to unbind one woman's breasts and help her into and out of a cold bath, or to hold the hand of another in the chapel. Most horrifying of all was the glimpse through peepholes of 'highchairs for babies, dozens of them in a disused room'.[39] Such metonyms exposed the spectators/participants to traces of the absent, asked to remember from a long list four of the names of the inmates, to look into a filing cabinet filled with bars of soap and clippings of hair. Sara Keating spoke for many of those who saw the play: '*Laundry* is shocking and difficult to watch without being remotely sensationalist. It is probably one of the most important, provocative works about institutional abuse in Ireland, and the social complicity that enabled it to permeate our culture for so long'.[40]

If *Laundry* was felt to be the most moving and beautiful of the Cycle, *The Boys of Foley Street* was the most violent. The initial starting-point was a 1975 radio documentary made by RTÉ hosted by Pat Kenny in which boys from the area were questioned about their lives of petty crime. One of those interviewed, Thomas Reilly, actually featured as a performer in the ANU play, so that when he listened in with the audience members to a recording of the programme, he was speaking the literal truth when scripted to say 'that was us! That was us'.[41] The action is set in the 1970s at the time of the heroin epidemic in the Monto area; the character called Tony in the play (Jed Murray), who is seen beating up a pusher who has welshed on his debts, and later weighing out drugs, may be a reference to the convicted criminal and infamous dealer Tony Felloni. Audience members got close up to this scene in a long sequence in a small flat, with the violent interactions of the characters including Maeve (Dee Burke), a rape victim, whose rape is seen on a mobile phone, and Kathleen (Caitríona Ennis), 'a young child in a school uniform' who lured Maeve to the flat and is seen already to be drinking and shooting up.[42] In tandem with the drug scenes, the 1974 bombing of Talbot Street, another terrible trauma of the area from that time, was played out in stylized but no less shocking forms of dance and monologue.

One of Lowe's prompts for the Monto Cycle was watching the American crime series *The Wire*, and admiring the way early episodes planted scenes and images that would only make sense in a later season. She wanted her four plays to be bound together in a similar way. So, for example, a spectator carried in a taxi away from the Magdalene Asylum in *Laundry* could spot Harriet, the sex worker from *World's*

---

[39] Singleton, *Monto Cycle*, 46.
[40] Sara Keating, '*Laundry*', irish theatre magazine, 29 September 2011, http://itmarchive.ie/web/Reviews/Ulster-Bank-Dublin-Theatre-Festival-2011/Laundry.aspx.html#:~:text=Laundry%20is%20shocking%20and%20difficult,our%20culture%20for%20so%20long (accessed 29 August 2023).
[41] Louise Lowe, 'The Boys of Foley Street', in Patrick Lonergan (ed.), *Contemporary Irish Plays* (London: Bloomsbury Methuen Drama, 2015), 351. Although Lowe is given as author in this collection, the credits page of the text states that it was 'Devised and created by the company'.
[42] Lowe, 'Boys of Foley Street', 362.

End Lane on the street. 'Eagle-eyed viewers at *World's End Lane* may have noticed tarot cards discreetly placed in a mirror, one of several intricate and teasing clues scattered throughout the tetralogy.'[43] This clue was to Terriss Lee, the fortune-teller at the centre of *Vardo*, the final part of the Cycle, known personally to Lowe as the grandmother of her best friend—'vardo' is the Romany word for caravan where Lee lived in the Monto in the 1930s. With her fortune-telling, she 'was in the business of hope', Lowe is quoted as saying. 'We wondered if that could underpin a lot of the work that we are looking at for this part of the cycle.'[44] If so, it does not greatly appear in *Vardo* which, set in the present of 2014, shows how the sex trade has moved off the streets to an online business, no longer supervised by the madam May Oblong but run equally ruthlessly on the phone by a woman in a car. In the bus station, audience members met Natasha (Rebecca Warner) a Russian woman trafficked into prostitution. The play came to its climactic conclusion in Lee's flat where she set out the Tarot cards and scenes from earlier episodes in the Cycle were replayed on a television screen. It was an aesthetically satisfying conclusion, binding together the four plays as the palimpsest of past and present they were designed to be. But the effect of such recycling was to suggest that any hope for the future of Monto could only be delusive hope.

Many audience members testified to the disturbing ethical choices they faced in their involvement with the performance. Should they give the name of the pusher seen in *The Boys of Foley Street* to the vigilante group Concerned Parents Against Drugs? What was their degree of complicity in watching a man being beaten up without intervening? 'The genius of Lowe's approach is that she tears your senses asunder. You know it's only a play. You've seen the other two in the series. Yet every part of you bucks in panic and loathing as you partake in activities you would never consider engaging in.'[45] This was Lowe's deliberate strategy leaving the spectator free to be participant or mere observer. But she too as theatre maker felt the force of comparable ethical choices. She was committed to representing the truth of the Monto area as she knew it, and to that end she enlisted the help of expert opinion, a local GP and an architect familiar with housing issues, as well as working with community groups, involving the people who lived in the district at every stage. And yet she found herself challenged by the situation in which the work was made. The flat rented for *Vardo* had been used as a working brothel; next door was one still in operation. Performances of the play were not scheduled for 3 o'clock because it was known that drug deals were done at that time. Such knowledge created the fear that she was 'making poverty porn [...] bringing people in to see this because they can afford a ticket for Dublin Theatre Festival'. The only defence against such

---

[43] Peter Crawley, 'Monto Is Back: The Sex Trade and the Business of Hope', *Irish Times*, 24 September 2014, https://www.irishtimes.com/culture/stage/monto-is-back-the-sex-trade-and-the-business-of-hope-1.1938979 (accessed 29 August 2023).
[44] Crawley, 'Monto Is Back'.
[45] Caomhan Keane, review of *The Boys of Foley Street*, quoted by Singleton, *Monto Cycle*, 71.

self-accusations of voyeurism and exploitation was the belief in the truthful telling of stories that needed to be heard and the aesthetic integrity of the work made.

The history of Monto, from Lowe's point of view, needed to be told because it had been forgotten, suppressed, written out of the nation's narrative. All the plays considered in this chapter, though, beginning with those in the 1980s, represented new ways of telling old stories. Some of them, like ANU's Monto Cycle, were concerned with erased parts of Ireland's history, like the women's experience within Ulster Protestant culture shown in Reid's *Tea in a China Cup*. Others tackled the 'misremembering' of the past, the partisan narratives of the heroes Henry Joy McCracken or Hugh O'Neill that fuelled the violent political and sectarian oppositions of the Troubles. What *Catalpa*, *Improbable Frequency*, and the Monto Cycle have in common, wildly different though they are, is the innovative ways they made history live in the audience's present. With its playing out of an imagined epic film, O'Kelly undermined the macho values of the genre, while demonstrating all that the solo performer could achieve theatrically. Riordan and Bell Helicopter created a satirical musical comedy, of a sort rarely seen in Irish theatre, for a slyly fantastical version of the 'Emergency', to be enjoyed as cabaret by the audience. No such collective enjoyment was allowed to those who watched/participated in the plays of the Monto Cycle; they experienced a (mostly) solitary journey through a past that was always also disquietingly present. In whatever form it took, this was Ireland's history as it had never been seen before.

5
After the Troubles

The Good Friday Agreement (GFA) in 1998 was hailed as a major breakthrough, and understandably so. After thirty years of political violence which had claimed more than 3,500 lives, it promised an end to the conflict. The arms used by paramilitaries on both sides were to be 'decommissioned', a tactful term that masked any suggestion of surrender. The issue of governance which had so plagued the state of Northern Ireland since its foundation in 1921 was to be solved. An inbuilt Protestant Unionist majority in charge of the state, protected by gerrymandering, with a biased police force and discrimination in housing and employment, had left the Catholic nationalist minority feeling oppressed and disenfranchised. Under the GFA, Northern Ireland, which had been directly ruled from Westminster since 1972, was to have a devolved government with a legislative assembly of delegates elected by proportional representation, and a power-sharing executive in which all the political parties would be involved. The agreement was a masterly example of 'constructive ambiguity' by which both sides could claim a victory.[1] David Trimble, leader of the Ulster Unionist Party declared: 'We rise from this table knowing that the Union is stronger than it was when we first sat down. We know that the fundamental act of union is there intact.'[2] On the other hand Republicans could portray the GFA 'not as a "settlement" but as a stop on the road towards a United Ireland'.[3] Though fiercely opposed by the Democratic Unionist Party, it was ratified by a large majority of voters in Northern Ireland, and an overwhelming majority in the Republic.

There were, however, problems with the implementation of the Agreement from the start, and difficulties that have continued ever since. Its very constructive ambiguity left unclear just when decommissioning should take place, the Unionists expecting arms to be put beyond use before Sinn Féin entered the power-sharing executive—'no guns, no government' was the slogan—while Sinn Féin acknowledged no such timeline.[4] This and other standoffs between the two main political groupings have resulted in prolonged periods when there was no Executive in

---

[1] See David Mitchell, 'Cooking the Fudge: Constructive Ambiguity and the Implementation of the Northern Ireland Agreement, 1998–2007', *Irish Political Studies*, 24.3 (2009), 321–36. I am very grateful to Roy Foster and Ian McBride for directing me to this article and other historical analyses of the period.
[2] *Irish Times*, 'Trimble Says Great "Opportunity" to Start Healing Process Promises Stable Future for All in Northern Ireland', 11 April 1998.
[3] Eamonn O'Kane, *The Northern Ireland Peace Process from Armed Conflict to Brexit* (Manchester: Manchester University Press, 2021), 104.
[4] See Mitchell, 'Cooking the Fudge', 331.

place.⁵ Apart from the specific controversies that have led to these suspensions of the governing institutions, the ongoing difficulties after the Troubles seem to have had a number of basic sources. One is the fact that terrorism and lawlessness are still very much there. Even though the main paramilitary organizations did decommission their weapons, fringe groups continue to be active, most terribly so with the Omagh bombing in 1998, the very year of the GFA. The armed robbery of the Northern Bank in 2004 and the murder of Robert McCartney in 2005 further showed that violence was not under control. Organized crime, long used to fund and enforce the paramilitaries, has remained a feature of post-GFA society.

One of the key issues for any state coming out of a prolonged period of conflict is how to deal with the legacies of the past. The Truth and Reconciliation Commission in South Africa, given the task of reporting on the history of the *apartheid* regime, represented one model. There have been a number of efforts to establish a similar process in Northern Ireland but '[s]o far it has proved impossible to devise a method of dealing with the past that commands widespread support'.⁶ The 'disappeared', victims of violence whose bodies have never been recovered, represent a particularly grievous part of these unresolved legacy issues. Another problem has been the sense of beleaguerement of the Protestant Unionist community; so long in a dominant position of power, Unionists have felt increasingly threatened in the period since GFA. This is illustrated again and again in Susan McKay's two books based on interviews with Northern Irish people from a Protestant background. Typical is the view of Dale Pankhurst, a Democratic Unionist Party (DUP) city councillor from north Belfast speaking in 2020: 'It's paranoia in the psyche. [...] Community relations are at an all-time low and loyalists especially, and unionists, feel the Good Friday Agreement and the peace process are geared against them.'⁷

The power-sharing principles of the GFA were intended to build bridges between the communities, but, in some respects, they have had the opposite effect. Because the political parties within the Assembly are identified as Unionist or nationalist, Eamonn O'Kane concludes, 'the sectarian basis of much of Northern Ireland's society and politics remains intact. [...] The result of the peace process in Northern Ireland has indeed been to entrench ethnonational divisions by making them the basis of the governing structure'.⁸ Symptomatic of this are the ironically named 'peace walls' of Belfast, established as far back as 1969 to separate the two often juxtaposed communities in working-class areas. The deadline set by the

---

⁵ See Eimear Flanagan, 'Stormont without NI Leadership for a Third of Its Lifespan', *BBC News*, 14 February 2022, https://www.bbc.com/news/uk-northern-ireland-60249249 (accessed 21 November 2022).

⁶ Ian McBride, 'The Truth about the Troubles', in Jim Smyth (ed.), *Remembering the Troubles* (Notre Dame: University of Notre Dame Press, 2017), 9–43 [14].

⁷ Susan McKay, *Northern Protestants on Shifting Ground* (Belfast: Blackstaff Press, 2021), 111. McKay's earlier book is *Northern Protestants: An Unsettled People* (Belfast: Blackstaff Press, 2021 [2000]).

⁸ O'Kane, *The Northern Ireland Peace Process*, 224–5.

Northern Ireland (NI) Executive in 2013 to have all the peace walls demolished by 2023 shows no sign of being met;[9] they have in fact been extended since then. The Brexit referendum of 2016, by which the United Kingdom decided to leave the European Union, has once again made the issue of borders of critical importance. While both the UK and the Republic were members of the EU, the nominal border between the two jurisdictions on the island of Ireland was not a real problem. Brexit, in potentially reinstalling a hard border, endangered that position which had helped to enable the North-South co-operation that was fundamental to the GFA. The Protocol to the Brexit agreement between the UK and the EU sought to solve this difficulty by an anomalous status for Northern Ireland whereby, for trading purposes, it remained a part of the EU single market, while still being within the UK. However, this created an effective border in the Irish Sea, something which is absolute anathema to Unionists. In the divided state of Northern Ireland, boundaries and borders at local and national level are fraught places of contention.

The Troubles generated a plethora of plays about the conflict, so that already by 1972 Frank Ormsby could guy the genre with his 'The Write-an-Ulster-Play Kit'.[10] Since 1998, playwrights have sought to dramatize the supposedly postconflict situation. Owen McCafferty's *Scenes from the Big Picture* (2003) is the most ambitious rendering of the city of Belfast as metonym for the society at large. The Troubles are no longer a central focus there, although one key thread running through the action is recovery of the body of one of the 'disappeared'. And in the intersecting lines that connect life to life across the urban environment, the violence generated originally by the paramilitaries is still a potent force. The failure of the state to deal with legacy issues from the past is highlighted in David Ireland's *Everything Between Us* (2010) in which an imaginary truth and reconciliation commission has been set up in Northern Ireland and gets off to a disastrous start. Much more low-key is McCafferty's *Quietly* (2012), where a local resolution is sought to a single horrific incident from the time of the Troubles in a face-to-face encounter between two of the people involved. Stacey Gregg's *Shibboleth* (2015) takes on intercommunal relations by dramatizing (and animating) the force of the continuing Belfast peace walls. *The Border Game* (2021), by Michael Patrick and Oisín Kearney, tracks the aftermath of an intersectarian love affair as a means of exploring Border lines. Ireland's *Cypress Avenue* (2016) takes us inside the head of one deranged Ulster Unionist, the ultimate example of the 'paranoia within the psyche'. The engagement of these dramatists with Northern Ireland after the Troubles brings alive a still very troubled place.

[9] See Gerry Moriarty, 'Robinson and McGuinness Want "Peace Walls" Down within Ten Years', *Irish Times*, 10 May 2013.
[10] Frank Ormsby, 'The Write-an-Ulster-Play Kit', *Honest Ulsterman*, 36 (1972), 2–3, cited in Mark Phelan, 'From Troubles to Post-Conflict Theatre in Northern Ireland', in Nicholas Grene and Chris Morash (eds.), *The Oxford Handbook to Modern Irish Theatre* (Oxford: Oxford University Press, 2016), 372–88 [372].

Belfast City: *Scenes from the Big Picture*

Sometimes the way people have talked about my work, it's as if they have this notion that I avoided what was going on here. I've never avoided what's gone on. I actually think I've attacked it head on, but I've attacked it from another point of view. I wasn't ever interested in the sabre-rattling of political attitudes: I was interested in how that affected people. I was also interested in the notion of saying that, regardless of what we're told, politics isn't the most important thing in our lives.[11]

This is a point Owen McCafferty has frequently made about his work and it reflects the reality of many of his plays. So, for example, much of his early monologue, *The Waiting List* (1994), is taken up with a nameless character detailing a life somewhat like McCafferty's own: growing up as a Catholic in the Ormeau Road, a mixed area of South Belfast; as a child learning about local prejudice the hard way; going to university; settling down with wife and children. But the 'waiting list' of the title is the hitlist of potential sectarian victims, on which his name may appear. *Mojo Mickeybo* (1998), still McCafferty's most popular and most revived play, features two young boys who strike up a friendship though one comes from 'up the road', the other from 'over the bridge', code for Protestant and Catholic parts of the Ormeau Road. For much of the play, they only register the ongoing violence as part of the everyday environment of the 1970s, 'watchin the soldiers stoppin cars', or hoarding the treasure of a rubber bullet—'the brits fired it down the street durin the riotin'.[12] The scene changes, however, and the friendship inevitably ends, when Mickeybo's father is killed, and Mojo re-aligns himself with the boys from his own area against Mickeybo.

One of McCafferty's initial aspirations was to 'bring the language spoken in Belfast to the stage'. He described the peculiar notation he developed to achieve this and its origins. After his first play appeared in print,

I was able to look at what was written and realise that there was something wrong with it. [...] It looked too like a prose. And I thought that because this is dialogue: it's different and it should look different. So I immediately thought that I should take out all the punctuation and capital letters, and use dashes. The dashes would be about beats or about breathing. The dashes work as punctuation. It just needs to look different.[13]

---

[11] Owen McCafferty, quoted in Connal Parr, 'Something Happening Quietly: Owen McCafferty's Theatre of Truth and Reconciliation', *Irish University Review*, 47 (2017), 531–48 [531–2].
[12] Owen McCafferty, *Plays: 1* (London: Faber, 2013), 112, 130. This is the text cited parenthetically for quotations throughout this part of the chapter.
[13] Fernanda Verçosa, 'Interview with Owen McCafferty Scenes from the Big Picture', *ABEI*, 15 (2013), 65–76 [68, 72].

This phonetic orthography causes considerable difficulty for a reader at first encounter; you have to get used to 'a' or 'i' for 'I', depending on where it comes in the sentence, 'the' for 'they', 'mon' for 'come on'. Many of the dialect words and the rhyming slang may be unfamiliar, but McCafferty risks obscurity in the interest of localizing authenticity of speech sounds and rhythms. To that extent, truth to the specific realities of Belfast is paramount for the playwright. At the same time, he rages against the insularity of the Northern Irish and their fixation on their own political obsessions, so petty on a global scale of things.

> They don't see the bigger picture, they just see the small thing. [...] Nobody outside of here cares about us and our issues. [...] 'X' amount of children die every day because they don't have enough food, whereas here we prefer to think about what flag we should hang, or who owns what street. All of it is ridiculous.[14]

As its title suggests, the strategy in *Scenes from the Big Picture* is to represent the small scenes of individuals within the aggregation of an urban life in ways that open out to some wider perspective.

'The play', we are told at the head of the published text, 'takes place over the course of a hot summer's day in an imagined area of present-day Belfast' (McCafferty, *Plays: 1*, 224). Four nodal sites are used, the small corner convenience shop, the abattoir (which seems more like a meat-processing plant from the description), the pub, and the hospital, with additional street and interior settings as required. In and around these places, we watch the characters criss-crossing, interacting, or failing to connect. This, no doubt is Belfast, but it could be almost any depressed postindustrial city. The ageing Sammy and Betty, who run the little shop, are under constant threat from robbery and vandalism by aimless young men, and from supermarket competition. There is a crisis in the factory as the owner is away trying to negotiate better priced supplies from the Republic, all dependent on the sterling-euro exchange rate, while there is a container load of meat waiting to be unloaded at the docks, and it is not clear there will be enough cash to pay the men their wages. The shop steward Joe Hynes inveighs against the factory owner and his 'big bucks'; Theresa Black, the office manager, is probably speaking nothing but the truth when she says 'there is no big bucks joe' (McCafferty, *Plays: 1*, 321). Certainly, there is no sign of the 'peace dividend' promised to Northern Ireland after the GFA. Repeatedly through the play we hear of the sense of powerlessness typical of urban alienation. Dave Black, husband of the harassed Theresa, complains: 'no control over anythin—that's what's wrong with us—no control' (McCafferty, *Plays: 1*, 238).

---

[14] Quoted in Parr, 'Something Happening Quietly', 544.

The dynamics of the individuals' lives and their relationships play out through the multiple short scenes of the action. We are aware of connecting contiguities, even when the characters themselves are not. Maeve, Joe's wife, is obsessed with her failure to conceive and haunts the maternity ward of the hospital, which is next door to oncology where the shopkeeper Betty has gone for a check-up. The marriage between Joe and Maeve finally fractures when it seems as if she has snatched a baby from the hospital—it is in fact only a practice doll used for expectant mothers. He blows up at her, she realizes he is having an affair and throws him out, by which time it appears his lover Helen no longer wants him either. The funeral of a former worker at the abattoir, mandatory social occasion, brings together several of the characters in the pub afterwards, including Bobbie Torbett—another separated husband—who is fending off a renewal of a relationship with the chronic drunk Sharon Lowther. There are some good outcomes in the play as well as downturns. Bop, son of Bobbie, will work with Helen in the pub rather getting a dead-end job in the factory like his father before him, and it is he, rather than the obnoxious lout Cooper, who finally gets together with the attractive teenage Maggie. Over the course of the day, individual lives take shape one way and another. Nothing is more horrifying in the whole play than the juxtaposition of two wordless scenes at the end of act 2, when we see Betty, confused after her cancer diagnosis, drop her handbag while trying to cross the street, and the addicted prostitute Connie Dean is savagely beaten up by her drug-dealer pimp Robbie Mullin.

This is one thread of the drama that takes us closer to the Troubles and their aftermath. At the start of the play, Robbie has defied his bosses in the dealing network, and tells Connie to pack up for them to leave, taking his drugs and cash with them. She is told to stay indoors and watch for any sort of surveillance of the house. When she lets in Bop and Swiz Murdoch, one of those involved in the burgling of the shop at the start of the play, it will lead to a tip-off to the gang on Robbie's plans—and the beating of Connie when he realizes what has happened. Prostitutes on drugs, and the drug-dealers who control them, no doubt exist in every modern city, but in Belfast this sort of crime has been long associated with the paramilitaries. There is some *schadenfreude* for an audience when the two hoods who break into Robbie's house and tie him up, unknowingly let Connie escape with the drugs and the money. But the revenge they inflict, shooting him in the knees and ankles, was a standard form of punishment by the paramilitaries on anyone they believed had betrayed them.

Of all the relationships in the play, the marriage between Dave and Theresa is under the most severe strain. Their son disappeared fifteen years before and his body has never been recovered. Dave has continued to obsess about the loss and on the day of the play's action is desperate because the authorities have decided to stop digging at the site where it is suspected that the body is buried. He will not go to work but tries to get on to a radio show to protest against the decision to call the excavation off. He is angry with Theresa who will not accompany him to the site of the dig. In a bitter standoff between them he asks what the people will think, when the mother of their son is not prepared to be there:

DAVE BLACK [...] what type of person are they goin to think you are
THERESA BLACK the type that's kept us goin all these years—the type that gets on with what the have to do in order to keep our lives together—do you know what it's like to have to look an listen to you this last fifteen years—all the time wimperin in my face—like ya were the only person ever felt any pain. (McCafferty, Plays: 1, 284)

How to deal with such grief, stoically as Theresa does, or in a constant state of mourning like Dave? Just how much Theresa does feel is revealed at the end of the poignant scene when Dave rings to say that at the last moment they have found the body of their son. As she is left alone, when he 'exits' after the call, '[h]er scream is silent then she howls with grief' (McCafferty, Plays: 1, 347).

This scene is followed immediately by the climax of another strand of the play. Following on the funeral, the two sons of the dead man, long bitterly estranged, have to meet and talk in the pub if only because they have been left a letter detailing the terms of his will. One of the oddities about the father is that he kept both the sons away from his allotment, telling each that he had been forced to sell it to pay the other's debts, but the allotment has remained his throughout. Enough rounds of drink in the pub bring the bitterly recriminating brothers to maudlin reconciliation. They end up digging in the allotment as some sort of memorial ritual to the father, where they discover, to their horror, buried guns. The question is what to do about them: turn them in to the police, risking their dead father's reputation, or bury them back where they found them. The latter is what they decide to do. The recovery of the body of the disappeared son in the previous scene, the reburial of the guns in this—these are the legacy issues of the Troubles. McCafferty was to focus on them more directly in *Quietly*, as David Ireland did in *Everything Between Us*, discussed in the next section.

Scenes, with its wide-angled lens view of Belfast, has been seldom revived because it needs the resources available to the London National Theatre that originally commissioned and staged it in 2003 with a cast of twenty-one (largely Irish) actors. For all its scale, however, McCafferty insists in his interview about *Scenes* that 'I'm not writing state of the nation plays'.[15] The big picture is for him much bigger than the tiny state that is Northern Ireland. There is a clue to what he means by the term in the response of Iggy, a character in McCafferty's earlier play *Closing Time*, when he is accused of doing 'nothin but talk': 'it touches me—everythin touches me—the world—the whole lot—the big picture—it touches me'

---

[15] Verçosa, 'Interview with Owen McCafferty', 70–1.

(McCafferty, *Plays: 1*, 184). It is within such a global big picture that the scenes of McCafferty's play are designed to be viewed. Frank Coin, the lone widower who wanders through the play, speaks of something he heard on the radio: 'there was another fella on—this programme was all about space—he said that when we talk—the sound we make travels up into space and goes on forever—it never goes away' (McCafferty, *Plays: 1*, 360). The play ends with a return of the miscellany of city sounds heard as a prologue, and Frank, Maggie, and Bop looking up at a meteorite storm in the sky. *Scenes* renders feelingly the full resonant range of Belfast voices that echo out into infinite spaces that put them and the Troubles into perspective.

Legacy Issues: *Everything Between Us* and *Quietly*

There have been numerous attempts to set in motion some sort of institutional process for dealing with legacy issues from the period of the Troubles, including the draft agreement drawn up under the Haass Report in 2013, but none of them have as yet been implemented.[16] That, though, has not stopped writers imagining versions of what a Northern Irish truth and reconciliation commission might look like. David Ireland in *Everything Between Us* establishes a Commission under the chairmanship of a veteran South African lawyer Dikeledi Mashiane, only to have it disrupted at its very opening by the obstreperous sister of one of its leading members. In *Quietly*, given the lack of any such formal institution, two of those involved in a terrible incident from thirty years before, perpetrator and victim, meet in a pub for a one-on-one confrontation. Both plays, in their very different ways, address the legacy of the past as the state has failed to do.

Ireland has made a name for himself as a playwright by the outrageousness of his breaches of decorum, his willingness to have his characters act and speak the unspeakable. This is most notably and successfully true of *Cyprus Avenue*, discussed later in the chapter. Already, in *Everything*, one of his earliest plays, he began as he meant to go on. It opens with the still offstage Teeni, screaming: 'FUCK *YOU*, YOU FUCKING BITCH, I'LL TEAR YOUR FUCKING *EYEBALLS* OUT YA *CUNT!*'[17] This is being addressed to the chair of the Commission, whom she has just assaulted. Within the opening minutes, she has added the 'n'-word to the

---

[16] For the Haass Report, see https://www.northernireland.gov.uk/publications/haass-report-proposed-agreement (accessed 5 December 2022).

[17] David Ireland, *Everything Between Us* (London: Bloomsbury Methuen Drama, 2017), 5. All further quotations from the play are cited parenthetically from this edition. The shock value of the actual words used here was lessened by the fact that they were not distinctly audible screamed as they were offstage; the violence with which Sandra has to control Teeni was much more striking. I am very grateful to Lynne Parker who made available to me a recording of the Rough Magic production of the play from February 2015; it was originally staged by Tinderbox Theatre Company in Philadelphia in 2010 co-produced with Solas Nua (Washington, DC).

four-letter obscenities yelled at the unfortunate Mashiani. The situation is made all the more devastating because it is her sister Sandra who has had to bundle her out of the tribunal, her sister who sits on the Truth and Reconciliation Commission as its lead representative of the Unionist community. Teeni and Sandra were raised in Ballybeen, the working-class housing estate in east Belfast where Ireland himself grew up, the daughters of a Protestant paramilitary father, killed by the IRA when the girls were young. Sandra, however, has developed into the very opposite of her psychotic sister: teetotaler, fundamentalist church-goer, Member of the Legislative Assembly, pillar of the establishment. Teeni has been missing, presumed dead by the family, for eleven years. On the last occasion when the two met, Teeni attacked Sandra's newborn baby with a knife. At the start of the play, Sandra has managed to hold off the security guards coming to arrest Teeni as a terrorist, saying that she would 'contain the problem', but this is a problem that is not going to be easily contained (Ireland, *Everything*, 12).

The Commission is established to take the testimony of those who have suffered during the Troubles. We hear of one of those 'waiting to speak', a Catholic woman whose husband was killed by the UVF (Ulster Volunteer Force) in the presence of herself and her 4-year-old son; she is to meet her husband's killer. There are those who 'lost people to the IRA', and the widows of British soldiers (Ireland, *Everything*, 63–5). This is what one would expect of a process chaired by 'the world's leading expert on conflict resolution' (Ireland, *Everything*, 10). But that is not the subject of the play in which the Commission itself never actually gets going. Instead, the conflict that requires resolution is between the two sisters; they are the 'us' of the title, their family history and antithetical temperaments the 'everything' that lies between them. With this shared heritage there can be no reconciliation and very little by way of certifiable truth.

Teeni is so unstable that it is hard to trust anything she says. Where has she been for the last eleven years? Most recently, it seems in Norway, building boats in Stavanger, but before that all over the place: 'England, Scotland, Germany, Canada, America' (Ireland, *Everything*, 13). She claims to have given up drinking, with a dramatic account of the degrading public incident that led to her joining Alcoholics Anonymous. Sandra believes that she has returned to take Step Nine in the AA recovery process, to 'make amends', seek forgiveness for those she has injured (Ireland, *Everything*, 46). But Teeni has no notion of making amends or looking for reconciliation with her sister. Her whole story of being a member of AA unravels as she admits that she is having an affair with the man who is supposedly her AA sponsor and that he is not in fact a reformed alcoholic, as she has claimed. But then there is the strangeness of Sandra saying that she too is a member of AA, even though she has never taken a drink, feeling the need to join, having left her original church in humiliating circumstances.

In the sisters' shared memory of their father's murder, which happened when Sandra was 9, Teeni 4, it might seem as if we are reaching the trauma that took them in different directions: Sandra to an uptight repressive conformism, Teeni to anarchic violence. But the 4-year-old Teeni had already dismembered her Barbie doll, suggesting that her aggressive tendencies were there from the start. Her volatility and iconoclastic willingness to break every sort of taboo is what makes for the play's comic effect. So, for example, when Sandra reminds her of her father's brutal behaviour as a wife-beater, Teeni maintains that this was quite understandable: 'I mean you have met our mother haven't you? Anyone who talks to her for more than five minutes wants to beat the shit out of her' (Ireland, *Everything*, 52). For the audience there is a shocked pleasure in hearing every sort of conventional piety blown sky high. The dialogue is indeed a minefield, with Teeni's outrageous speech and behaviour providing a continuous set of explosive eruptions. That, though, is one of the problems of the play. Sandra may stand in for a type of Northern Irish politician, but Teeni is too ungovernable to represent anything other than herself. As a consequence, it is difficult to see it as a serious and sustained analysis of the fissures within the Protestant Unionist mentality, something Ireland was to achieve in *Cyprus Avenue*.

For *Everything*, Ireland invented a Truth and Reconciliation Commission that the state had failed to set up, as starting-point for his extreme, violent confrontation of the two estranged sisters. In *Quietly*, McCafferty anchored his action in identifiable historical events. As the play opens, Robert, the Polish barman, is watching the World Cup qualifying match between Poland and Northern Ireland that took place on 28 March 2009. The actual facts match the details given in the play: Northern Ireland won the match 3-2, and there were disturbances in the city provoked by Polish supporters, as Robert suggests.[18] The protagonists, Jimmy and Ian, are enacting their own individual truth and reconciliation process, reliving the events of thirty-five years before in that same pub. This is based on the bombing of the Rose and Crown in the Lower Ormeau Road which happened on 3 May 1974 when, as in the play, six Catholic men were killed. McCafferty only changes the date to 3 July 1974 to have the men in his fictional pub watching the Poland v. Germany World Cup match played on that day. Jimmy recalls a Vanguard rally of 20,000 men marching at the top of his street. Vanguard was the political party led by William Craig which opposed the Sunningdale Agreement and helped to bring an end to that first Northern Irish power-sharing government in the Ulster Workers Council strike of May 1974. Though the central drama of *Quietly* is imagined, it is precisely contextualized in the Belfast realities of its two time periods.

Ian, who, at 16, threw the bomb into the pub on the orders of the UVF, asked for the meeting with Jimmy, son of one of those killed. But it is Jimmy who insists that the encounter should not be in private: 'i think it should be open—if this succeeds we will be seen as the first—we will be held up as a beacon—a fuckin nobel prize

---

[18] Henry McDonald, 'Belfast Pub Wrecked as Violence Flares before World Cup Qualifier', *The Observer*, 29 March 2009.

maybe—seeing our politicians have no bottle—robert will be our committee—our truth and reconciliation committee'.[19] Though the sardonic tone belongs to the character, the aim of the play is to imagine what this process might look and feel like. It begins unpromisingly with Ian headbutted by Jimmy the very moment he comes through the door. Right through the play, there are points when a fight seems imminent: 'Jimmy stands up, Ian stands up. They face each other. The moment lasts, then they sit down' (McCafferty, *Plays: 2*, 207). But the anger and guilt by degrees are channelled into memory, confession, contrition.

Ian is confused about his motives for proposing the meeting: 'i don't know why i'm here—i feel dislocated or something—i have to sort things out' (McCafferty, *Plays: 2*, 207). But it is Jimmy who is most profoundly damaged, continually haunted by the trauma of what happened, so that he can recall every detail: not only the ages and professions of every person in the bar, but everything about the football match they were watching down to the names of the individual players. So focused as he is on his own hurt, he is impatient with Ian's insistence that 'i have to tell this my own way' that 'it can help explain', brushing this aside: 'i don't need an explanation—i get it—we were—are fenian bastards—and our existence threatened the state—we were—are the enemy—you were at war with us—all of us' (McCafferty, *Plays: 2*, 213-14). He forces Ian to visualize the scene of the men watching the match, to name their names, to face the carnage of the bombing as he, Jimmy, experienced it. He cannot accept Ian's attempt at an apology: 'being sorry has no meaning—i don't know what sorry is'. But Ian's response has a crucial clarity and dignity: 'it means now as a man—ian gibson feels that what he did as a sixteen-year-old kid was wrong—and wasn't worth it' (McCafferty, *Plays: 2*, 220).

Through an intense exchange of stories, something like the truth of what took place does emerge. And if no full reconciliation is possible, a recognition of sorts is achieved. It begins with Jimmy's childhood memory of savagely beating up a local Protestant boy over a lost football: 'see when i was doin it too—i was screaming in his face—fuckin orange bastard—it came out o nowhere—fuckin orange bastard—fuckin orange bastard—fuckin—orange—bastard' (McCafferty, *Plays: 2*, 209). There is an acknowledgement here of the reciprocal demonization of 'fenian bastards' from the other side of the sectarian divide. Eventually, the two men can get past this sort of conditioned animus, but only just. There was real suspense in performance when Ian stood holding out his hand, while Jimmy slowly got to his feet and paused before joining in the handshake.[20] Still, Jimmy's last words to him were 'don't ever come back here' (McCafferty, *Plays: 2*, 229). Robert's suggestion that they might meet again, and that 'some good might come from it', is summarily

---

[19] Owen McCafferty, *Plays: 2* (London: Faber, 2016), 210, cited parenthetically in the text from here on.
[20] Recording of the Abbey production of 2012, viewed in the Hardiman Library, University of Galway, 6 December 2022. I am grateful to Barry Houlihan for making this available to me.

dismissed by Jimmy: 'you know nothing do you—some good did come from it—we met—we understood each other—that's enough' (McCafferty, *Plays: 2*, 231). After what happened, no more can be expected.

Jimmy comments on the changes in Northern Ireland since 1998: 'more money here—peace process—when i was a kid no one came here—only people in belfast were belfast people—an british soldiers—the only black men here had uniforms on them'. But he adds, 'we're not very good with foreigners' (McCafferty, *Plays: 2*, 198). So it would appear from the riots over the football, and the racist taunts at Robert coming from outside the bar at the end: 'fuckin polish bastard—dirty smelly fuckin bastard—go back to where you come from' (McCafferty, *Plays: 2*, 232-3). The abuse exactly reproduces that interchanged between Protestants and Catholics. The peace process and the increased prosperity had turned Northern Ireland into the beginnings of a multi-ethnic society. But the violence has not gone away; it has just been rechannelled into xenophobia.

McCafferty, true to his principles of inclusiveness, was evidently determined not to make Robert just a token outsider witness. We hear of his past life, child of alcoholic parents, abusive father, still living back in Poland. He is settled with a Northern Irish woman and has a young child with her, but he is also keeping on a string a Polish lover who has followed him to Belfast. We learn of this situation through a series of text messages projected up onto mirrors behind the bar. It is not a wholly satisfactory part of the play, but the two-timing barman does contribute to the indictment of toxic masculinity which is a feature of *Quietly*. One of the most horrific parts of the story is the licensed rape of a young girl by Ian, offered to him by the UVF men as a 'reward' for his part in the bombing. He meets her years afterwards to discover that this had resulted in a pregnancy, and she had travelled to Liverpool to have an abortion. Hers is just one more messed-up life in the aftershocks of the pub bombing. The climactic speech of the play is Jimmy's confession of remorse at his failure to give emotional support to his mother in the long years of her widowhood: 'she wanted me to notice her and i didn't' (McCafferty, *Plays: 2*, 228). Jimmy and Ian through the action of the play seek to go beyond their aggressive hostility conditioned by sectarian hatred; the failure to acknowledge the needs of women remains something endemic within the culture.

Walls and Border: *Shibboleth* and *The Border Game*

In 1921, with the establishment of a separate Northern Ireland, the island was partitioned. In 1969, a wall was built separating Catholic and Protestant communities in Belfast, the first of what were to become many 'peace walls'. The Border was one of the causes of the brutal 1922-3 Civil War when Republicans claimed that the compromise Treaty with Britain had betrayed the principle of a thirty-two-county Irish Republic for which they had fought. A recrudescent IRA in the 1950s led a

Border campaign attacking the Northern Irish administration. Throughout most of the twentieth century, the Border made for low-level criminal activity: smuggling, double social security, and agricultural subsidy claims in both jurisdictions. Common membership of the EU and the institution of the GFA, which provided some level of co-operation between governments north and south, helped to improve matters. But the Brexit vote which made the Border a land boundary between the UK and the EU made it a site of contention once again. Within Northern Ireland itself, the peace walls have proliferated and been made more permanent. And, though there have been repeated commitments to dismantle them since 1998, they have actually grown in number since the GFA. In 2019, fifty years after the first one was built, there were no less than ninety-seven such structures in Belfast alone.[21] *Shibboleth* and *The Border Game* dramatize walls and border as manifestations of a community and a nation still fundamentally divided in the period after the Troubles.

Stacey Gregg had one early play, *Lagan* (2011), which provided a composite picture of Belfast rather like McCafferty's *Scenes*. But much of her work has not been specifically concerned with Northern Ireland or the political issues there. Her focus has more often been on questions of gender and sexuality, paedophilia in *Perve* (2011), and in *Scorch* (2015) on 'gender fraud', a girl posing as a boy prosecuted for having sex with another girl (discussed in Chapter 9). *Shibboleth* was originally jointly commissioned by the Goethe Institute and the Abbey Theatre in 2008 as part of a Europe-wide response to the fall of the Berlin Wall.[22] It seems, though, to have been written mainly after 2013 and not staged until 2015. But the international comparative dimension is evident in the play's focus on the Belfast peace walls. One of the bricklayers at work on the wall makes little of them: 'It's hardly Berlin. Hardly Gaza' (Gregg, *Shibboleth*, 16). The analogies with other divided spaces were highlighted in the production in the Peacock where an LED display featured a sequence of signs in red from Israel/Palestine, Cyprus, and Kashmir, with President Kennedy's famous 1963 statement 'ich bin ein Berliner' also frequently flashed up on the screen.[23]

Shibboleth is very much about divided communities, but Gregg takes care never to use the words Protestant or Catholic. Instead, the characters only every speak of 'Usens' and 'Themens'. Gregg herself grew up in Dundonald, a Protestant working-class area of north Belfast, and it seems likely, if only from their names—Stuarty, Alan—that the brickies belong to the Protestant side of the division. But the coded Usens and Themens makes possible a series of different intersectional axes of othering. Like McCafferty in the earlier *Quietly*, Gregg represents the changed

---

[21] See https://www.peacewall-archive.net/peacewalls-50 (accessed 21 December 2022).
[22] Stacey Gregg, *Shibboleth* (London: Nick Hern Books, 2015), 88. This is the text used for quotation through what follows.
[23] Video recording of 2015 production viewed in the Abbey archive, 12 December 2022, by kind permission of the Abbey archivist, Mairead Delaney.

social make-up of Belfast of the period. Two of her central characters are Yuri and Agnieszka, the Polish father and daughter who are paired with the Northern Irish couple Alan and Ruby in the intercut morning domestic scenes that open the play. When Yuri appears at the building site, having been hired to replace an unsatisfactory local worker, he is the representative of the class of emigrants initially cast as Themens. There is a build-up of hostility that looks likely to turn to violence: 'Job thief, give him a slap'. The watchword 'Look out for the Lads' expresses the male bonding of opposition to the intruder (Gregg, *Shibboleth*, 32). But when Yuri wins favour with the group, the phrase will be reapplied to their determination to take revenge on the man who has hit his daughter, even though he is one of their own workmates. Equally, Usens and Themens can express the vertical power dynamics of labour and established authority. When no-one can tell who has ordered the building of the wall or why, Alan remarks: 'Sure they never bother telling Usens what's what' (Gregg, *Shibboleth*, 28).

The play centres on the building site and the psychology of the men who work on it. It is their sense of blocked and frustrated energy that fuels much of the action. One of the younger men, Corey, voices this in a passage expressive of underlying feeling rather than spoken words: 'What'm I to do with this adrenalin?' (Gregg, *Shibboleth*, 36). He and Mo, the other young man on the job, speak their shared sense of being born too late:

COREY [...] I haven't even had a scrap before, my fair share / of Trouble
MO. I was just a child when peace was signed, I haven't touched e'en a mouse.
    (Gregg, *Shibboleth*, 17)[24]

By contrast, there is the older man Stuarty who did see action as a paramilitary; he gave himself an education while in prison, and is now apparently a reformed character. Yet, he still revels nostalgically in the memory of violence: 'In my day slicin ears was all the rage—I'm not advocatin it, but Jesus Christ it gave ye a buzz' (Gregg, *Shibboleth*, 70). What we hear of Stuarty's past is terrifying, and his capacity for violence is only dormant. We can assume he leads the charge in the play's tragic climax when the men turn on Mo and beat him up so badly that he kills himself in despair. In fact, he is being scapegoated for the assault on Agnieszka, when it was actually her boyfriend Corey who hit her. The stored-up aggression of the men must find a target, someone classed as Themens, however mistakenly.

In the play's Prelude, the audience hears an extract from a speech by Barack Obama, given in Belfast in June 2013, in which the Northern Irish peace process is seen as exemplary. 'We need you to get this right. And what's more, you set an example for those who seek a peace of their own'. But the last line quoted rings out ironically: 'But the fact that so far we've only got a gate open and the wall is

---

[24] Gregg explains that she uses a slash, as here, to indicate an interruption (Gregg, *Shibboleth*, 5).

still up means there's more work to do' (Gregg, *Shibboleth*, 6).[25] Though intended metaphorically, in context this refers to the achievement of Groundwork NI, led by Sylvia Gordon, in having a gate opened for a limited number of hours a day in the wall dividing Alexandra Park. More work to do, indeed. The men in the play are in fact building a further extension to the existing wall. This is defended by the satirically observed figure of the Councillor who argues '[t]he only way to overcome divisions is to build *more* walls' (Gregg, *Shibboleth*, 61). When Alan actually cites the President—'Obama says the wall should come down', she replies, 'Obama doesn't appreciate the complexity of the situation' (Gregg, *Shibboleth*, 59–60). That 'complexity' is based on the vested interests of developers who want to ensure safe zones in which to build apartments, and the flourishing tourist trade of those who come to see the murals on the walls.

Gregg, like McCafferty, brings a Belfast working-class language to the stage, though without his idiosyncratic notation. Instead, below the surface dialogue she sketches in a gestural poetry of mood and feeling. So, for example, Corey's pleasure in his body and in his work is rendered thus: 'Muscles bulgy from the liftin, the gravysweatin, whiteringed weatherbeaten, manly manual labour, taut Adonis / muscles' (Gregg, *Shibboleth*, 16). Sometimes this language is given to individual characters, sometimes to a chorus of the 'Brickies' but often to the animated Wall itself. In the realization of the Wall, as in much of the staging, Gregg leaves theatrical decisions up to the director and designer. In her notes that preface the printed text she says: 'The staging of the wall is an invitation. [...] It may be that the wall is manifested in one being, or in all, or in none; that its growls and voices grow throughout; that it slouches towards Belfast to be born' (Gregg, *Shibboleth*, 5). The director of the original production, Hamish Pirie, chose to give the part to an individual woman singer in a sexy pink costume, crooning the Wall's lines. This has been read metaphorically 'as Capital in seductive guise, a force that feeds on [the men's] anger, binding the group to its interests through the promise of protection from the outside threats of migrants and "themens" over the wall'.[26] It might be hard for an audience to recognize such an explicitly political interpretation in production. What did seem clear was the contrast between the seductive eroticism of the Wall and the companionate love of Alan and Ruby, Yuri and Agnieszka.

In many ways, this is an imaginative study of working-class male group psychology, and their stranded state in a post-Troubles Belfast that has given them little or nothing. But there is a felt need by the playwright to set against that some alternative, some indication of another way forward. This is most often expressed

---

[25] The full speech, addressed by Obama to the young people of Northern Ireland in Waterfront Hall, Belfast, 17 June 2013, when he was visiting Northern Ireland as part of the G8 meeting in Fermanagh, can be heard at https://www.youtube.com/watch?v=sc9gupTbsIo (accessed 21 December 2022).

[26] Alexander Coupe, 'Defiantly Mercurial: An Interview with Stacey Gregg', *The Honest Ulsterman*, February 2021, https://humag.co/features/defiantly-mercurial (accessed 22 December 2022).

politically by Ruby and Alan, Ruby who is bent on sending their son Darren to an integrated school with both Catholic and Protestants, Alan who insists they should be taking down the walls, not building more. The caring father-daughter relationship of Yuri and Agnieszka and their concern for the cultural values of dance stands for another sort of exemplary contrast to the Philistine bullishness of the brickies. To offset the horror of Mo's suicide—he is eaten up and finally swallowed by the Wall as he recounts the events that led up to his death—there is a reconciliatory ending in which the initially recalcitrant Alan agrees to Darren going to the integrated school and proposes that their dance-mad 10-year-old son should take lessons from Agnieszka. In the published text this is all spelled out in a final scene. This last scene, however, was cut altogether in production, which showed instead a whole group of young children starting dance lessons with their Polish teacher, one of them casually taking the microphone away from the singer/Wall who exits voiceless. Point taken. The need to find some form of theatrical closure is matched by a rather too willed impulse towards an upbeat political message. It is again a feature of *The Border Game*.

Michael Patrick and Oisín Kearney work as a partnership, Patrick as writer/actor, Kearney as writer/director. Their first one-man theatre show, *My Left Nut* (2017), was later adapted as an award-winning BBC TV series (2020). *My Left Nut* was followed by a full-length play *The Alternative* (2019), a witty satire based on a counterfactual history of Ireland in which there had been no War of Independence, no Partition or Civil War, and the whole island had remained part of the United Kingdom with a Home Rule devolved administration. Riffing brilliantly on the Brexit campaign, the action, set in 2019, turns on a referendum for Ireland to leave the UK, with an Irish Prime Minister returning from Westminster to Dublin to campaign for Remain. *The Border Game* was less original in so far as it is centred on a conventional love across the barricades between Protestant shopkeeper Henry and Catholic farmer Sinead. It is, however, different from the standard trope in so far as the couple are already estranged at the start of the action, their long-term affair having broken up some years back. They pick their way back through their relationship, and the audience gradually learns how it developed and what brought about its bitter end.

The Border is literally at the centre of the action. The setting is a rubbish-strewn hill with 'an old manky portacabin', originally, it transpires, a customs border post, but also the hideout where the couple used to make love.[27] The Border runs right through Sinead's land, and she has come up (significantly) to repair a fence that has been broken down. This is the Border of the contemporary period, neglected but still very much there. The abandoned portacabin is a reminder of the Troubles when such customs posts were repeatedly blown up, on one occasion in 1971 no

---

[27] Michael Patrick and Oisín Kearney, *The Border Game* (London: Samuel French, 2021), 1. All other quotations are taken from this text.

less than eight at the one time.[28] References through the text make it clear that the play, first performed in 2021, is very much up to the minute. Early on Sinead is about to throw away a 'ragged fluffy lion doll', when Henry stops her: this is 'Frederick. He's Northern Ireland's new mascot. Celebrating the centenary'. One might imagine that this was a joke but, no, the Northern Irish administration did promote the centenary of its foundation in 1921 with just such a mascot. Even Henry's pun of the mascot's purpose, 'to show our wee country's been a "roaring" success' is taken from the strapline under the lion (Patrick and Kearney, *Border Game*, 10).[29] Henry expresses the widespread Unionist opposition of the time to the Protocol which required some border checks on goods coming to Northern Ireland from the rest of the UK: 'I'm not happy about that sea border. But we'll get rid of that' (Patrick and Kearney, *Border Game*, 32). At the time of writing late in 2022, this is still the resolution of the DUP.

In their 'Authors' Note', Patrick and Kearney describe a research trip they took along the whole length of the Border. They stress that the play is 'intentionally ambiguous as to where exactly on the border it takes place' (Patrick and Kearney, *Border Game*, n.p.), though occasional references suggest the eastern area between Dundalk and Newry.[30] For much of the action, the play affords a showcase for the two performers as they act out various absurd 'Border games', like the Southern Customs Man with his heavy Kerry accent interrogating the Old Lady smuggling contraband butter in her knickers. Smuggling in this part of the world was an occasion for pride: Sinead protests indignantly at the insinuation that her father was not successful at the business. 'My dad was a brilliant smuggler! [...] He swindled the tax man out of thousands!' (Patrick and Kearney, *Border Game*, 22). In a climactic set-piece they act as English Commentators watching the Border Collie dog run the full 300 kilometres of the boundary from Carlingford Lough up to the Foyle, the Irish names all mispronounced on the way.

But that comic animation of the Border turns into something very different later on when the customs hut turns into a snorting and snarling Black Pig. This draws on the association of the Border with the Black Pig's Dyke, mythologized as the dividing boundary of Ulster.[31] It is the inescapable borderland psychology that has wrecked the love between Henry and Sinead. Flashback sequences show their first meeting as participants in the Cross Border Choirs initiative in the Ulster Hall in

---

[28] See https://www.rte.ie/archives/2021/1021/1,255,124-border-customs-posts-bombed/ (accessed 23 December 2021).

[29] Very remarkably, all references to Frederick have disappeared from the internet, except for a single tweet: https://twitter.com/shanehoranpr1/status/1,356,249,383,625,494,532 (accessed 23 December 2022). It appears that Frederick and the centenary he was designed to celebrate were not such a roaring success.

[30] Sinead listens to 'The Newry Bird' by local singer Jinx Lennon, and it seems probable that when she talks of sending her daughter to an Irish-language 'Bunscoil' it would be Bunscoil an Iúir in Newry (Patrick and Kearney, *Border Game*, 14). Kearney comes from the nearby town of Warrenpoint.

[31] Vincent Woods's 1992 play *At the Black Pig's Dyke* already drew on this association for his borderland tragedy.

2004.[32] Henry's father insists on serving British army soldiers in his shop in spite of the warnings of the IRA who eventually murder him. The breakpoint in the relationship between Henry and Sinead comes when she insists on attending the funeral of his father's killer who has committed suicide. For her this was a matter of social obligation: 'I was there for the family' (Patrick and Kearney, *Border Game*, 70). For him it was a deliberate rejection of him and their love. Their situation and those of all the people caught up in the Troubles and its aftermath is summed up in one invented word: 'Borderfucked'. This is defined by Sinead as the 'condition of being fucked economically, socially, and psychologically due to the stroke of a pen. Common in Ireland, the Middle East, and all over the fucking world' (Patrick and Kearney, *Border Game*, 69).

'Something there is that doesn't love a wall'. Patrick and Kearney, like Gregg, want to give dramatic expression to that other force. They, too, vehemently deny the assertion of Frost's interlocutor in 'Mending Wall' that 'Good fences make good neighbours'.[33] In *The Border Game*, although Sinead and Henry have something of a *rapprochement*, there can be no question of them getting together again. He is with another partner, this time from his 'side of house', one of the many Northern Irish codes for religious affiliation (Patrick and Kearney, *Border Game*, 45); she has her 2-year-old daughter to bring up. Yet at the end he does go to help her with a calving cow. And in the final tableau, when the two have tidied away all the rubbish and re-erected the barbed wire fence, 'suddenly, the fence collapses' (Patrick and Kearney, *Border Game*, 86). This is a purely wishful theatrical gesture, rather like Gregg's Utopian dance class of Irish children led by the Polish teacher, politically admirable but unearned by anything in the play. By contrast, David Ireland's *Cyprus Avenue* remains true to its savage logic to the end.

Shifting Ground: *Cyprus Avenue*

Susan McKay called her second book surveying attitudes of Northern Irish people from a Protestant background *Northern Protestants on Shifting Ground*. The phrase was taken from an interview with the poet Jean Blakeney who said that she had voted DUP for the first time in 2017: 'I felt the ground shifting', she told McKay; Unionism was feeling 'aggrieved, isolated and anxious'.[34] There were evident reasons for this feeling. To start with, the demographic map was decisively changing. Where Protestants had at one point been in a two-thirds majority in the six counties of Northern Ireland, in the 2021 Census they were outnumbered by

---

[32] For details of Cross Border Orchestra of Ireland, the likely real-life counterpart, see https://web.archive.org/web/20,091,031,053,514/http://www.thecboi.org/about/ (accessed 23 December 2022).
[33] Robert Frost, *The Complete Poems* (London: Jonathan Cape, 1951), 55.
[34] McKay, *Shifting Ground*, 6.

Catholics for the first time.[35] In the 2022 elections, Sinn Féin became the largest party in the Assembly, and its leader Michelle O'Neill, First Minister designate.[36] Irish unification, long thought to be a mere fantasy projection of Republicans, is being seriously discussed, and even Peter Robinson, former leader of the DUP, has said that Northern Ireland needs to be prepared for it as a possibility.[37] It is no wonder that traditional Loyalists should feel threatened. Molly Carson, half-sister of hardline Unionist Willie Frazer, told McKay of his last days terminally ill with cancer: 'Whenever William was in hospital before he died, he was so full of morphine that he thought Gerry Adams was under his bed'.[38] Eric Miller, protagonist of *Cyprus Avenue*, takes paranoia one stage further and imagines his newborn granddaughter *is* Gerry Adams.

In the prologue to the play '[a] Muzak version of Van Morrison's "Cyprus Avenue" plays in the background'[39] For Morrison and for Ireland, both of whom came from Protestant working-class areas in east Belfast, prosperous leafy Cyprus Avenue was an idealized other place.[40] In the play this attitude is expressed by Slim, who lives in the playwright's own home territory, the proletarian Ballybeen housing estate, and who is overcome when he finds out that Eric lives in Cyprus Avenue: 'That's my favourite street in Belfast. My favourite street in the world' (Ireland, *Cyprus Avenue*, 49). The location is important because Eric is not like Slim, who is a caricature of the balaclava-wearing paramilitary. Eric is a respectable, middle-class professional from a solidly well-to-do neighbourhood. In the first production, Lizzie Clachan designed a set and costumes to reinforce the point, a pristine white wall-to-wall carpet, Eric in a formal blue suit. By the end of the play, the carpet was soiled all over and Eric, in a role-swap with Slim, had donned a balaclava and leather jacket.

In *Cyprus Avenue* Ireland adopts a softly, softly approach which is the exact opposite of his strategy in *Everything*. Instead of the in-your-face attack of screamingly abusive language from Teeni, we are introduced to the consulting room

---

[35] See https://theconversation.com/northern-ireland-census-shows-more-catholics-than-protestants-a-political-scientist-on-what-this-really-means-191,273 (accessed 27 December 2022).
[36] It was only belatedly in 2024 that O'Neill took up this position, after a period when the DUP blocked the formation of the Assembly and Executive.
[37] Conor Gallagher, 'North Should Prepare for United Ireland Possibility—Ex-DUP Leader', *Irish Times*, 28 July 2018, https://www.irishtimes.com/news/ireland/irish-news/north-should-prepare-for-united-ireland-possibility-ex-dup-leader-1.3578620 (accessed 27 December 2022).
[38] McKay, *Shifting Ground*, 261.
[39] David Ireland, *Cyprus Avenue* (London: Bloomsbury Methuen Drama, 2016), 5. All quotations from the play are taken from this edition.
[40] Morrison said that it's 'a place where there's a lot of wealth. It wasn't far from where I was brought up, and it was a very different scene. To me it was a very mystical place. It was a whole avenue lined with trees, and I found it a place where I could think', quoted in Finola Meredith, 'Van Morrison's Belfast: From Cyprus Avenue to Hyndford Street', *Irish Times*, 29 August 2015, https://www.irishtimes.com/culture/music/van/van-morrison-s-belfast-from-cyprus-avenue-to-hyndford-street-1.2332247 (accessed 27 December 2022). Ireland expressed similar views in talking about the play: https://www.youtube.com/watch?v=oeDidHSC7_A (accessed 27 December 2022).

where Eric is about to have a first session with his psychiatrist Bridget. She is at pains to reassure him: 'This is a safe space. A safe space for us to talk about you. To talk about anything you want to talk about' (Ireland, *Cyprus Avenue*, 6). She encourages him to ask questions even when what he says might be 'a bit of a stupid question'. It is all the more of a shock when he asks his Black British psychiatrist: 'Why are you a nigger?' (Ireland, *Cyprus Avenue*, 7). It was a line calculated to produce gasps from the audiences of the Abbey Theatre that commissioned the play, and the Royal Court, its co-producer, for whom the word would be unutterably unacceptable. But it also raises laughter in Eric's apparent lack of awareness of its offensiveness. 'Was it wrong for me to say that word?', he asks, adding by way of extenuation: 'If I can say in my defence, I *did* grow up in Belfast. I never met a black person until I was forty-seven' (Ireland, *Cyprus Avenue*, 7–8). However, when Bridget moves smoothly into the correct response, 'I accept and understand that being Irish you haven't been exposed to multiculturalism', she is stopped politely but firmly by Eric: 'The last thing I am is Irish. [...] I am British. I am exclusively and non-negotiably British. I am not nor never have been nor never will be Irish' (Ireland, *Cyprus Avenue*, 8–9). If for Eric the idea that Bridget is a Black British person is unimaginable, she hardly understands the nuances of Irish and Northern Irish identity.

Cyprus Avenue works on the basis of a destabilizing comedy—and, for a play about a man who murders his wife, daughter, and infant granddaughter, it is remarkably funny. As it takes us ever deeper into Eric's psychosis, it simultaneously calls in question our 'normal' attitudes and their expression. As Bernie coos over the newborn Mary-May: 'Aren't you the best baby in Belfast? Aren't you? The best wee baby in the whole of Belfast?', Eric comments 'Well we don't know that. [...] It's not very scientific' (Ireland, *Cyprus Avenue*, 11). Bridget gets a similar response when she asks Eric if he loves children: '*Love?*' he responds in puzzlement. She defines it further for him: 'Kindness. Affection. Respect'. Eric considers this: 'I don't see how one can respect children' (Ireland, *Cyprus Avenue*, 28). He proceeds to produce a series of figures that do earn his respect, significantly all adult men, and we can see that his inability to feel love for children is a part of his deeply repressed (and misogynistic) frame of mind. Still, his literal-minded logic comically subverts some of our most ordinary assumptions about feeling and behaviour.

Bridget, wife Bernie, and daughter Julie stand for the principles in which a liberal progressive audience would like to think they believe. When Julie is asked by Eric whether she will raise Mary-May as a 'Unionist or a Republican', she gives the right fair-minded response: 'I'll raise her as nothing. I'll raise her to respect all people and not judge a person on their religion or their race' (Ireland, *Cyprus Avenue*, 61). And it is for that admirable statement that she is shortly to be brutally murdered. But, though watching the play we can see this as the terrifying catastrophe it is, the play traps us within the abnormal mindscape of Eric to whom such a principle of political neutrality is an ultimate betrayal. Through the exposition of the play, the narration is shared between Bridget's questioning of Eric and the dramatized scenes of the past, as he recalls them: his first seeing the face of Gerry Adams in his granddaughter, his initial suspicion that Julie has slept with the President of Sinn Féin, his experiments with putting spectacles and a beard drawn on the baby, the outraged Bernie telling him to leave the house. But with scene six, we enter a quite different dramatic territory. As Eric sits on a park bench, '[h]e talks to the audience, through the audience. In his mind he is talking to Bridget' (Ireland, *Cyprus Avenue*, 34).

His extended monologue here is at the heart of the play. There is a hilarious account of his venturing into an Irish pub in London, with its displays 'of mischievous leprechauns drinking the black stuff and smoking the blarney. More Irish a pub than anything I'd ever seen in my own city' (Ireland, *Cyprus Avenue*, 36). In his encounter with an 'Irish' Englishman there, where he pretends to be interested in football about which he knows nothing, there may be a sly send-up of Marie Jones's *A Night in November* (1994) in which Unionist Kenneth McCallister runs away from his wife and family and finds his true Irish identity bonding with fans at the World Cup in New York. The speech plays throughout with the rhetoric of identity politics, so that we cannot be sure of the status of the insecurity displayed:

> And then I thought the most terrifying thought of all. Maybe I am Irish. [...] maybe I have always been Irish. Maybe I've been led to believe that I'm British by successive governments of the English crown to further their own nefarious purposes. And throughout the centuries, British governments, as we all know, have been nothing if not nefarious. Particularly if it furthers their own purposes. (Ireland, *Cyprus Avenue*, 36–7)

This is characteristic of the ironic topspin of Ireland's comedy: the ultra-Unionist borrowing the arguments of left-wing Irish nationalists wanting to wish away Unionism as an illusion, constructed by self-seeking British authorities.

And then there is the appearance of Slim, gun in hand, threatening to kill Eric because of the disturbing doubts he has been expressing overheard by a young boy: 'He's only ten and already he's beginning to question the validity of loyalist cultural identity' (Ireland, *Cyprus Avenue*, 45). It is not clear whether Slim is to be taken as an actual character, or if he is Eric's grotesque alter ego. (The social dimension to the contrast was well brought out in production by Chris Corrigan playing Slim with a thick working-class Belfast accent as against the refined gentility of Stephen Rea's extraordinary deadpan performance as Eric.) The twists and turns of the conversation with Slim pitch it somewhere between nightmare and high comedy. Slim, like the young men in *Shibboleth*, is frustrated by the lack of action for his generation: 'I joined the UVF after the peace process started. [...] Very bad time to become a terrorist' (Ireland, *Cyprus Avenue*, 46). The tense confrontation between the two men is continually shifting into absurd riffs on pop songs and bad Hollywood movies. When Eric confesses to his anguished doubts about his possible Irish identity, Slim casually acquiesces: 'Aye. Well we all worry about that. For what it's worth, I myself think there is an Irish dimension to loyalist identity' (Ireland, *Cyprus Avenue*, 45). Yet from this scene of absurd, track-switching comedy, develops the ghastly plot to murder Mary-May.

Ireland does nothing to mute the horror of that final scene in which the baby is killed, surely every bit as shocking as the stoning scene in Edward Bond's *Saved* (1968) which brought an end to theatrical censorship in Britain. Even as hardened a theatre critic as Michael Billington could wish that this had not been performed on stage. However, he ended his enthusiastic review of the play with a defence of its instructive value: 'Ireland is writing about the danger of living in the past and using murderous violence as a means of re-enacting battles long ago. In a world where sectarian divisions remain as potent as ever, I'd have thought that was a point well worth making.'[41] This makes the play more simply monitory, less disturbing than it actually is. Eric rejects all attempts to attribute his mania to post-traumatic stress disorder, or to a difficult childhood having lost his father in the Second World War. He also vehemently denies that he is a psychopath. He certainly is fully aware of the nature of his actions. 'I know what it is to take innocent life, and to grieve that life, to question the morality of one's actions. It's part of my Christian duty as a Protestant to do so' (Ireland, *Cyprus Avenue*, 67). Yet he remains unrepentant. In his final conversations with Bridget, when she asks him what he now feels about what he did, he replies '[p]roud' (Ireland, *Cyprus Avenue*, 80). In the very last moments he laughs: 'Why do you laugh?', asks Bridget. 'I'd forgotten how much I enjoy saying no' (Ireland, *Cyprus Avenue*, 83). 'Ulster Says No', the slogan of the 1985 campaign against the Anglo-Irish Agreement, is taken in *Cyprus Avenue* to its ultimate deranged level of intransigence. For all the changes brought about by the peace process and the GFA, *because* of those changes, it remains a point of bedrock resistance.

With the one exception of Owen McCafferty, all the playwrights in this chapter started work in the twenty-first century. They belong to the generation most of whose adulthood has been lived since 1998, and the Northern Ireland they represent in their plays is the society that has developed since the peace process. In many ways the emphasis in their work has been to show the failures of the GFA to deliver on its promise, the continuing fall-out from the Troubles, the dysfunctional features of their world. Violence has not gone away, even if it has turned to the organized crime of *Scenes*, or the inturned aggressions of the brickies in *Shibboleth*. There are very few signs of a 'peace dividend' for most of the characters who

---

[41] Michael Billington, 'Cyprus Avenue: The Most Shocking Play on the London Stage', *Guardian*, 11 April 2016, https://www.theguardian.com/stage/theatreblog/2016/apr/11/cyprus-avenue-david-ireland-belfast-play-royal-court-theatre-upstairs (accessed 28 December 2022).

feature in these plays. The beginnings of a multi-ethnic culture in Belfast have only given a new direction to the racism of traditional intersectarian conflict. The legacies of the Troubles have not been worked through and are still manifested in the peace walls and the Border. Yet most of these playwrights try to suggest some sort of resolution, some upturn in the action, that might point a way forward. This is no facile gesture towards optimism but a need to work through in the theatre what the society itself has left unresolved: the private 'peace and reconciliation' process of the two men in *Quietly*, the degree of *rapprochement* of the estranged lovers in *The Border Game*. Only Ireland, in the fierce sisters' unending war of *Everything*, with the irreconcilable Eric in *Cyprus Avenue*, leaves his audience to contemplate a violence which twenty-five years of peace have been unable to temper or change.

6
Strategies of Adaptation

In the late twentieth century it seemed that there was hardly an Irish writer who had not written their version of a Greek tragedy. In 1984 alone there were three *Antigone*s by Brendan Kennelly, Tom Paulin (retitled *The Riot Act*), and Aidan Carl Matthews. Kennelly went on to produce *Medea* (1991) and *The Trojan Women* (1993). Derek Mahon published a version of Euripides' *The Bacchae* (1991) and *King Oedipus*, a combination of Sophocles's two Oedipus plays in 2005, though neither of them has been produced as yet, while his *Phaedra*, based on Racine's play, was staged at the Gate Theatre in 1996. Seamus Heaney's *The Cure at Troy* (1990), an adaptation of Sophocles's *Philoctetes*, was his contribution to Field Day, and he was to follow it up with *The Burial at Thebes*, his version of *Antigone*, commissioned by the Abbey in 2004 for the theatre's centenary year.[1] Greek tragedy which stands at the very foundation of western European theatre is a common property, adapted and recycled in multiple languages from Seneca on. But Irish writers have been perceived to have a special affinity with Anton Chekhov.[2] Again there is a rollcall of Irish playwrights who have adapted his plays. Brian Friel had a special devotion to Chekhov, from his *Three Sisters* (1981) through *Uncle Vanya* (1998) and *The Yalta Game* (2001), loosely based on the short story 'The Lady with the Dog', to *Three Plays After* (2002) a composite of one-acts derived from Chekhov. Frank McGuinness also contributed an *Uncle Vanya* (1995), while both Thomas Kilroy and Michael West produced versions of *The Seagull* (1981, 1999). Tom Murphy's *The Cherry Orchard* followed in 2004.

In so far as none of these writers knew either Greek or Russian, their texts must be considered adaptations or versions rather than translations. However, the opposition of foreignization against domestication, popularized by translation theorist Lawrence Venuti may be applied to these Irish texts also.[3] Paulin thoroughly domesticated his *Antigone* in calling it *The Riot Act*, using an Ulster dialect vocabulary, and making plain the relevance of the play to the politics of Northern Ireland. Antigone became the equivalent of the civil rights activist

---

[1] For a full listing of versions of Greek tragedy in Ireland up to 2000, see Marianne McDonald, 'The Irish and Greek Tragedy', in Michael Walton and Marianne McDonald (eds.), *Amid Our Troubles: Irish Versions of Greek Tragedy* (London: Methuen, 2002) 37–82 [80–2].

[2] See Robert Tracy, 'Rehearsing the 1916 Rising: Theatre Politics and Political Theatre', and Nicholas Grene, 'Chekhov and the Irish Big House', both in Ros Dixon and Irina Ruppo Malone (eds.), *Ibsen and Chekhov on the Irish Stage* (Dublin: Carysfort, 2012), 127–38, 139–48.

[3] See Lawrence Venuti, *The Translator's Invisibility: A History of Translation* (London: Routledge, 2018 [1995]).

Bernadette Devlin (McAliskey), while referring to Creon as 'the big man' hinted at an identification of him with Ian Paisley.[4] Seamus Heaney made the Irish dimensions to *The Cure at Troy* less explicit, but introduced a much quoted final chorus giving equal valency to all the suffering victims of the Troubles:

> The innocent in gaols
> Beat on their bars together.
> A hunger-striker's father
> Stands in the graveyard dumb.
> The police widow in veils
> Faints at the funeral home.[5]

In Chekhov versions, the domesticators were led by Kilroy who relocated his *Seagull* to the west of Ireland in the late nineteenth century, his Konstantin a would-be Celtic Twilight playwright, while Arkadina became a conventional Victorian prima donna from London's West End. Friel in his *Three Sisters* did not go so far; he kept the original Russian setting and characters but heavily Hibernicized their dialogue, reclaiming Chekhov for Irish actors and Irish voices. There was no such self-conscious local familiarizing of the text in McGuinness's *Uncle Vanya* or Murphy's *Cherry Orchard*, though both felt free to give an Irish flavour to their characters' speech. The alternate strategies of adaptation for Irish playwrights were to make the originals their own, reaching out to Irish audiences, or to allow the cultural otherness of Greek tragedy or Chekhov to speak for itself.

All these earlier adaptations were by male writers, though with a definite feminist slant in the case of Kennelly. The three playwrights I have chosen to focus on in this chapter are all women. Marina Carr is much the most prolific in adaptations, producing no less than five plays based on Greek tragedy, a sequence beginning with *By the Bog of Cats …* (1998), a free adaptation of Euripides's *Medea*.[6] She has shown a particular concern with the *Oresteia* and the sacrifice of Iphigeneia from *Ariel* (2002) to *Girl on an Altar* (2022). Her *Phaedra Backwards* (2011) and *Hecuba* (2015) are based on myths and character configurations behind the Greek plays rather than providing adaptations of the originals as such. The other two plays looked at in this chapter are more one-off productions. Hilary Fannin's *Phaedra* (2010) was an experimental collaboration with composer Ellen Cranitch, which took off not only from Racine's play but Jean-Philippe Rameau's opera *Hippolyte et Aricie*. Lucy Caldwell set her *Three Sisters* (2016) in 1990s Belfast against the background of the Troubles, most provocatively reframing the action from the viewpoint of the character of Natasha, played as a Chinese immigrant.

---

[4] Tom Paulin, *The Riot Act* (London: Faber, 1985), 15.
[5] Seamus Heaney, *The Burial at Thebes* (London: Faber, 1990), 77.
[6] The Abbey is scheduled to produce *The Boy*, Carr's loose adaptation of the Theban plays, in the spring of 2024.

Taking these texts together, we can identify the contemporary perspectives three twenty-first-century Irish playwrights have brought to bear on European theatre of the past.

Midlands Medea: *By the Bog of Cats...*

Over the last twenty-five years, Marina Carr has produced as many adaptations as original plays. The Greek tragedies aside, she has written a stage adaptation of Tolstoy's *Anna Karenina* (2016) and of Woolf's *To the Lighthouse* (2021), as well as a version of Lorca's *Blood Wedding* (2019). There have also been riffs on the work of other writers: *The Cordelia Dream* (2008), a response to *King Lear*, and *16 Possible Glimpses* (2011), taking off from the life and death of Chekhov. In terms of the Venuti distinction, *By the Bog of Cats...* and *Ariel* represent full domestication. The stories of *Medea* and *The Oresteia* are very loosely adapted, relocated to contemporary Ireland, and written in a strong local dialect. *Phaedra Backwards* underpins the tragedy of Euripides' *Hippolytus* with Phaedra's mythological origins and her parents Minos and Pasiphae. Intercut scenes and images on film show Phaedra's sister Ariadne, one of Theseus's many abandoned lovers, and the Minotaur, product of Pasiphae's coupling with a bull. With *Hecuba* and *Girl on an Altar*, Carr developed a new technique of self-narration in which the characters involved in the fall of Troy and its aftermath speak their own actions and thoughts, retell their dialogue with others. I want to look here at the cycle of Carr's adapted Greek tragedies, beginning with *By the Bog of Cats...*

How might Euripides' *Medea* be adapted to a contemporary Irish setting for modern audiences? There would probably be sympathy for the woman rejected by her husband for a more advantageous marriage. An attractive feminist note is sounded in one of the Euripidean choral odes seeking a reversal of patriarchal narratives so that 'Women are paid their due./ No more shall evil-sounding fame be theirs'.[7] Still, the central character is a semi-divine mythological figure. She is an enchantress who invokes Hecate, goddess of magic and witchcraft, as her patron (395–7). She is the granddaughter of Helios, the sun god, who, at the end of the play, sends a dragon-drawn chariot to take her and the bodies of her dead children away from Corinth. She has been promised sanctuary in Athens where, in the legends, she goes on to have another life as the wife of King Aegeus. The issue for a playwright attempting a modern transposition is to make Medea's a human predicament without the superstructure of Greek mythological culture.

---

[7] Euripides, *The Medea*, ll. 419–20, trans Rex Warner, in David Grene and Richmond Lattimore (eds.), *The Complete Greek Tragedies*, Vol. III: *Euripides* (Chicago: University of Chicago Press, 1959), 73. Further citations from the play are to the line numbers in this edition.

One cue for Carr was Medea's situation as foreign outsider in Corinth. Jason, in one of his more egregiously obnoxious moments, points to the benefit she has gained by being brought to civilization:

> instead of living among barbarians
> You inhabit a Greek land and understand our ways,
> How to live by law instead of the sweet will of force. (536–8)

In making Hester Swane a Traveller woman, Carr sets up an equivalent opposition between her values and that of the settled community. She used to live in a caravan but has moved to a house 'though I've never felt at home in it'.[8] It is from this house that she is now being evicted, counterpart to the banishment of Medea by Creon. It seems that she signed a legal contract agreeing to yield the property, but she now refuses to accept the validity of that document: 'Bits of paper, writin', means nothin', can as aisy be unsigned' (Carr, *Plays: 1*, 283). It is for land that Carthage left Hester; his brutal prospective father-in-law Xavier Cassidy has promised to transfer ownership of the farm to him on his wedding day. Fields, stocked with cattle, secured by law, are the material goods that are all important to the settled community. By contrast, the Traveller women, Hester and her mother, the mysteriously absent Big Josie Swane, are tied to the shape-shifting unproductive bog.

Bog of Cats is one of the series of Midlands plays which started with *The Mai* (1994) and made Carr's name. There was an element of local partisanship in the Midlands setting, the area where Carr herself grew up. The flat centre of Ireland is often neglected for the more picturesque east and west coasts. After the success of the tourist branding of the Wild Atlantic Way and Ireland's Ancient East, the best that could be managed for the Midlands was Ireland's Hidden Heartlands.[9] Carr made its landscape of lakes and bogs central to her plays. Synge had given literary currency to an Irish English of the west; O'Casey and Behan had made vivid dramatic use of a highly coloured Dublin demotic. No-one before Carr had tried to stage the Midlands voice, apparently as thick and flat as its own plains. Beginning with *Portia Coughlan* (1996), as if defiantly, Carr's dialogue was cast in such a strongly accented dialect, rendered orthographically on the page, that she had to revise it for a later edition to make it more readable.[10] However, this was not designed, like the other 1990s plays considered in the opening chapter, as a challenge to the Irish tradition of theatrical eloquence initiated by Synge. On the contrary, it was a claim for just such eloquence for the Midlands dialect. 'It's a very rich language', she maintained in a 2000 interview. 'It's a language of metaphor and

---

[8] Marina Carr, *Plays: 1* (London: Faber, 1999), 266. All further quotations from the text are from this edition.
[9] See https://www.failteireland.ie/IrelandsHiddenHeartlands.aspx
[10] See Melissa Sihra, *Marina Carr: Pastures of the Unknown* (Cham: Palgrave Macmillan, 2018), 104. Sihra shows how *Bog of Cats* in its first draft was composed in a similar idiom: *Marina Carr*, 122.

story-telling'.[11] The language and the landscape of the Midlands provide the poetry of *Bog of Cats*.

Though there are no dated events to establish the period, the play is very clearly set in contemporary Ireland. The 40-year-old Hester spent long years of her childhood in one of the fearsome Industrial Schools, as any parentless child of her generation would have done. Ireland in 1998, after the scandalous revelations about the Church and Church-run institutions such as the Industrial Schools, was well on its way to being post-Christian. So, the grotesque wedding scene that figures in the play's second act shows just how little substance is left to the long-venerated traditions of Catholic Ireland. It is like a Renaissance *charivari*, or Hardy's 'skimmity-ride' in *The Mayor of Casterbridge*, in its travesty of the wedding ceremony. The senile Father Willow, in pyjamas under his dishevelled robes, dreaming of taking off on holiday with the Catwoman, could have walked straight out of the sitcom *Father Ted*. Mrs Kilbride, the grasping self-obsessed mother of the bride, appears in bridal white: 'How was I supposed to know the bride'd be wearin' white as well' (Carr, *Plays: 1*, 309). It only needs the entrance of a drunken Hester, kitted out in the dress Carthage had bought her years before for a wedding that never happened, to complete the mockery of the occasion.

In the absence of a functioning practice of conventional religion, the supernatural and the uncanny reappear on the margins of folkloric belief. The opening scene has Hester trailing the 'corpse of a black swan' over the winter landscape of ice and snow, the black swan whose life was prophesied to end on the same day as Hester's. Waiting there is the Ghost Fancier, semi-comic figure who has come for her soul, and who apologizes for having mistaken dawn for dusk.[12] The Catwoman, blind Tiresias-like character, who lives off mice and whiskey, can foretell the future and hear ghosts. Warned by a premonitory dream, she declares the disastrous ending of the day to come: 'Hester Swane, you'll bring this place down by evenin'' (Carr, *Plays: 1*, 273). Disreputable as she is, the Catwoman cannot be excluded from the community. Even the materialistic Xavier knows that 'it's bad luck not to invite the Catwoman' to a wedding (Carr, *Plays: 1*, 307). It is to her that the ghost of the murdered Joseph first manifests himself. Hester shares this psychic gift: 'Can she hear ghosts?', asks Joseph. 'Oh aye, though she lets on she can't' (Carr, *Plays: 1*, 301). This exchange, near the start of the largely comic act II, sets up the revelations of the encounter between Joseph and Hester in act III.

Medea in Euripides has a history of violence behind her. She murdered her brother Apsyrtus, to impede the pursuit of the Argo by her father; she had Jason's uncle Pelias killed by having him boiled alive. Both of these terrible acts are

---

[11] Quoted from Mike Murphy, *Reading the Future: Twelve Writers from Ireland*, in Sihra, *Marina Carr*, 103.
[12] Eamonn Jordan interestingly suggests the Button Moulder who comes for Peer Gynt's soul in the last scene of Ibsen's play as an antecedent: 'Unmasking the Myth: Marina Carr's *By the Bog of Cats ...* and *On Raftery's Hill*', in Walton and McDonald, *Amid Our Troubles*, 245–62 [247].

recalled by Euripides' Medea as reproachful testimony to all that she has done for love of Jason. Carr chose to focus only on the murder of the brother and make this the mainspring of Hester's guilt and remorse, and she changed the motives for the action altogether. Though Euripides has Jason say that Medea killed her brother 'at your own hearthside' (1334), there is another version of the story that has Apsyrtus killed when the couple are already on the Argo, his dismembered body cast into the sea so that the distraught father will stop to pick the pieces up. This seems to have been the version Carr uses, at least in so far as it is on a boat on Bergit's Lake that Joseph is murdered. Carthage has always assumed that Hester did it for the money, the money which ironically Joseph had been sent by his father to share with his long-lost sister, and which was used to give Carthage his start towards landed prosperity. But, no, Hester insists, it was jealousy of the ten years Joseph had with their mother after she had abandoned Hester herself. She accuses the ghost of Joseph of provoking her: 'ya just wouldn't shut up talkin' about her as if she wasn't my mother at all' (Carr, *Plays: 1*, 319).

Carr took elements of the plot of *Medea* and left others out altogether. In *Bog of Cats*, Hester does not murder Xavier and his daughter Caroline, as Medea does Creon and Glauce. The revenge she does take, burning down the house and sheds with the cows and calves shut up in them, seems almost as terrible. (There is a trace of the poisoning of Creon by contagion in the story of Xavier's son dying from strychnine when he digs up and embraces the beloved dog his father has poisoned.) In Euripides, as soon as Medea has secured herself a place of refuge in Athens, she announces openly her intention of killing her children, as her ultimate act of revenge: 'it is not bearable to be mocked by enemies' (797). Though the Chorus pleads with her not to go through with it, and she herself agonizes over the decision, an audience knows that this is what will happen.

That is absolutely not the case in *Bog of Cats*. Hester's own death is overdetermined: it is foredoomed by the death of Black Swan, predicted by the Catwoman, feared by Hester's more kindly friend Monica Murray (counterpart to Euripides' Nurse)—we know that the Ghost Fancier will be waiting for her at dusk. What we do not know, and she does not know, is that Josie will die too. It is only when Hester is trying to prepare Josie for the fact of her own coming death, and Josie pleads to be allowed to go with her, that she makes the decision. She cannot bear the idea of Josie waiting for her return, as she has waited for her own mother all her life. It is the prospect of that trauma repeating itself that drives her to cut 'Josie's throat in one savage movement' (Carr, *Plays: 1*, 39). It is thus a mercy killing rather than an act of revenge. The play ends with Hester in a final dance of death with the Ghost Fancier, a fitting conclusion to the tragedy. All that remains are unanswered questions about Big Josie: why did she leave her 7-year-old daughter and then her son? where did she go to? is she still alive or dead? We are left only with her song 'By the bog of cats' that repeatedly haunts the play and gives it its title.

Bog of Cats was acclaimed at its first production in the Abbey and by 2018 was still 'Carr's best known and most performed play'.[13] *Ariel*, her version of the *Oresteia*, did not achieve comparable success. Even reviewers sympathetic to her work felt that it did not altogether come off, and audiences stayed away.[14] It was hugely ambitious, trying to compact elements of Euripides' *Iphigenia in Aulis* with the three plays of Aeschylus's trilogy. It was hard to believe in the re-creation of the ancient Greek story in the very literal version of Carr's play where the Agamemnon character is Fermoy Fitzgerald, an ambitious Irish politician who kills his daughter Ariel on her 16th birthday in the belief that it will bring him success. It does, and by the second act he is about to become Taoiseach. But when his wife Frances discovers what he had done to their daughter, she stabs him to death, only herself to be killed at the end of the play by Elaine, the counterpart of Electra. There was none of the suggestive scenic atmosphere of *Bog of Cats*, and the use of a very strong Midlands dialect for almost all the characters did not help. Significantly, Carr declared her intention of 'going back to Standard English after this. Dialect has taken me somewhere else, but ... I can't wait to go back to English, I can't wait to obey those rules'.[15] Her next adaptation, *Phaedra Backwards*, was also felt to be flawed, when premiered in Princeton. It was an experiment in form, switching between past and present, myth and mundane reality, live action and filmed images. Yet, as one reviewer concluded, 'for a story steeped in lust and violence, this production ends up being disappointingly bloodless, both literally and figuratively. Every punch is pulled, each invective half-hearted'.[16] It took a quite new strategy in her later adaptations to release the full force of the tragedies adapted.

Tragedy Retold: *Hecuba*

The Greek tragedies come down to us with two and a half millennia of classical prestige. Although neither the Greek tragedians nor yet Homer from whom their stories derived glamorized the Trojan war and its aftermath, or minimized its human cost, this is an epic world of heroes and demi-gods. In *Hecuba*, Carr stripped out all the heroics, and told it like it was, or as she imagined it was. For the Greeks all non-Greeks were barbarians, as when the smug Jason tells Medea of the benefits of no longer 'living among the barbarians'. Carr turns this around in *Hecuba*—it is the Greeks who are the barbarians attacking the ancient, rich civilization of Troy. Hecuba, the Queen, proud even in devastated defeat, gives

---

[13] Sihra, *Marina Carr*, 117.
[14] See, for example, Marianne McDonald, 'Marina Carr's *Ariel*', *Didaskalia*, https://www.didaskalia.net/reviews/2002_10_02_01.html (accessed 16 September 2023).
[15] Ian Kilroy, 'Greek Tragedy, Midlands Style', *Irish Times*, 20 September 2002.
[16] Tanya Dean, 'Phaedra Backwards', *irish theatre magazine*, October 2011, http://itmarchive.ie/web/Reviews/Current/Phaedra-Backwards.aspx.html#:~:text=But%20the%20real%20loss%20in,is%20unfocussed%20and%20emotionally%20d (accessed 16 September 2023).

Agamemnon her view of the Greek invasion: 'You came [...] stinking of goat shit and mackerel and you came with malice in your hearts. You saw our beautiful city, our valleys, our fields, green and giving. You had never seen such abundance. You wanted it. You must have it. You came to plunder and destroy'.[17] When Odysseus enters and announces himself as 'King of Ithaca', Hecuba thinks: 'Another king and not one of them looks like one' (Carr, *Plays: 3*, 237). Even Agamemnon cuts the hero of the *Odyssey* down to the size of his tiny island 'kingdom', sardonically summing up his henchman as he leaves: 'he slinks off, sly islander that he is, bandy-legged mountain man, invisible, indispensable' (Carr, *Plays: 3*, 233). Agamemnon aspires to the sort of law-bound civil society for the Greeks that the Trojans have long achieved: 'I'm trying to start a country, bring all the warring factions together, the fiefdoms, the small fierce kingdoms, we need a system' (Carr, *Plays: 3*, 250). But the Greek army he actually commands is a barely controlled coalition of ignorant warring tribes.

Fermoy, the Agamemnon figure in *Ariel*, sincerely believed in the gods to whom he sacrificed his daughter; as Minister of Education he argued (most implausibly) for a new anti-Christian theology. Agamemnon in *Hecuba* has no such faith. When the Greeks are on their way home after the sack of Troy, Polyxena, young daughter of Hecuba and Priam, must be sacrificed to appease the ghost of Achilles and provide a favourable wind, exactly replicating the sacrifice of Iphignenia at the start of the war. Agamemnon reacts with impatience and disgust as he is robed for the ceremony: 'Get away from me with that fucking mask, I tell him, trying to smother me. [...] The word has gone out, Agamemnon is going to conjure the wind again. Do they actually believe this shit?' (Carr, *Plays: 3*, 241). It is only the ignorant foot-soldiers who believe in this sort of superstition; their elite leaders see through it all. Staged rituals are shams designed to cover up the reality of the underlying power politics.

'I always thought Hecuba got an extremely bad press', said Carr. 'Rightly or wrongly I never agreed with the verdict on her. This play is an attempt to reexamine and, in part, redeeem a great and tragic queen' (Carr, *Plays: 3*, x). Arguably, in Euripides' original *Hecuba* she is characterized quite sympathetically. Maddened by grief at the killing of her daughter Polyxena, discovering the dead body of her last son Polydorus, she takes revenge on her supposed friend and ally Polymestor who has had Polydorus killed, luring him into a trap where he is blinded and his young son killed—all this with the tacit connivance of Agamemnon. Carr changes the story so that it is Agamemnon who has Polydorus murdered, holding Polymestor's sons hostage to ensure he is delivered up, and it is subsequently the uncontrollable Greek tribes who blind Polymestor and kill his sons. In the closing speech of the play, Cassandra, with all the authority of the truth-telling prophet,

---

[17] Marina Carr, *Plays: 3* (London: Faber, 2013) 215–16. This is the text used for all further quotations from the play.

speaks for the playwright: 'They said many things about her after, that she killed those boys, blinded Polymestor, went mad, howled like a dog along this shore. The Achaeans wanted to get their stories down, their myths in stone, their version' (Carr, *Plays: 3*, 259).

Violent actions were never shown in Greek tragedy; they were literally 'obscene', offstage. Carr spares us nothing of the brutality of war in her plays. This is how *Hecuba* opens:

> So I'm in the throne room. Surrounded by the limbs, torsos, heads, corpses of my sons. My women trying to dress me, blood between my toes, my sons' blood, six of them, seven of them, eight? I've lost count, not that you can count anyway, they're not complete, more an assortment of legs, arms, chests, some with the armour still on, some stripped, hands in a pile, whose hands are they? (Carr, *Plays: 3*, 211).

The self-narration, however, is somewhat like the alienated acting style recommended by Brecht resembling a witness describing a road accident.[18] And yet at the same time it brings an audience into a terrifying intimacy with the characters and what they are evoking. This was the more strikingly the case with the 2019 Rough Magic production of *Hecuba* which was played in traverse on a virtually bare stage, with the actors remaining visible throughout.[19] There was no attempt made to realize the scene or the characters' actions. The set showed nothing but red-covered stacking chairs, a trestle table, Priam's 'throne' a black leather office swivel chair. A very limited number of props were brought on as needed and put to multiple uses. The characters rarely touched, much less enacted what they described: the words did it all. But this stripped back, understated dramaturgy made the action all the more viscerally present.

With the technique of self-narration, we are taken inside the thoughts and feelings of the characters as a continual underscoring of their actions. It is as if the subtext below the lines is actually voiced. So, for example, when the two antagonists meet in the opening scene, each is registered in the eyes of the other. Agamemnon on Hecuba:

> Fabled Queen, I say. She hears the mockery in my voice, though it's not complete mockery. I've been wanting to get a good look at her for a while. And there she is perched on her husband's throne, holding what? His head? The blood flowing down her arms. And what arms they are, long and powerful. What's that, I say? She doesn't answer, just looks at me as if I'm a goatherd, the snout cocked, the straight back, three thousand years of breeding in that pose.

---

[18] See Bertolt Brecht, 'The Street Scene: A Basic Model for an Epic Theatre', in John Willett (ed. and trans.), *Brecht on Theatre* (London: Methuen, 1964), 121–9.

[19] A filmed version of this staging was screened in 2022, and I am very grateful to Rough Magic and their general manager Gemma Reeves for making it available to me.

And the reciprocal view from the other side:

> They told me many things about him, this terror of the Aegean, this monster from Mycenae, but they forgot to tell me about the eyes. Sapphires. Transcendental eyes, fringed by lashes any girl would kill for. I pretend I don't know who he is. And you are? I say. You know damn well who I am he laughs. (Carr, *Plays: 3*, 212-13)

The mutual sexual attraction is obvious here. And yet is it shocking when they make love, the night after Agamemnon has slit the throat of Hecuba's daughter Polyxena. We might expect no other from the lustful Greek commander with his predatory promiscuity, but this is consensual sex, Hecuba herself making the first move. The key is in the comment of Agamemnon: 'she's all over me, starved for love, no shame in that, I am too. We go to it. We do what men and women do' (Carr, *Plays 3*, 254). The act of love brings a moment of release, however temporary, to the grief-stricken queen, the war-weary general.

The play was designed to rehabilitate Hecuba, rewrite the patriarchal narrative inherited from the victorious Greeks. Yet the effect of the play's distanced style of interior and exterior storytelling is to reveal a sort of helplessness in all the characters involved in the war, brutal conquering men as well as the women and children who are their victims. This is a very different strategy for rendering Greek tragedy accessible to a modern audience from the domesticating approach of *Bog of Cats* with its Irish setting. Carr remained true to her principle of abandoning dialect after *Ariel*. 'There's a formalism to the language I use', she wrote in a programme note for the play's first production by the Royal Shakespeare Company, 'that is maybe best described as Trojan English'.[20] It is a flexible, almost transparent, style that can move register easily from the crudely colloquial to highly patterned lyricism. It translates the remote, heroicized actions of Greek tragedy into a vision of war appallingly familiar in the modern period. Contemplating the massacre at Troy, Hecuba comments, 'this is not war. In war there are rules, laws, codes. This is genocide' (Carr, *Plays: 3*, 212). The twentieth century, from the Holocaust through to Rwanda and the Balkans, has made such genocidal war the history of our times. Carr's *Hecuba* rewrites Euripides' play without any of the inherited afflatus of the original so that it, terrifyingly, inescapably, belongs to us.

Racine Spoken and Sung: *Phaedra*

Greek tragedy is a common property with adaptations by many Irish writers in the later twentieth century. Racine is a different matter. For Greek tragedies, playwrights have to work out some way of dealing with the chorus and the gods,

[20] Quoted in Sihra, *Marina Carr*, 268.

neither of which are easily transposed onto the modern stage. But that is as nothing compared with the problems created by Racine. There is the high formality of the virtually untranslatable rhymed Alexandrine couplets. Derek Mahon, one of the few Irish dramatists to tackle Racine with his *Phaedra*, has to resort to half-rhyme, alternating rhymes, or assonance, for his fairly close adherence to the original French. (A famous version by Robert Lowell from 1961, which does use fully rhyming couplets, takes considerable liberties with the text.) The highly abstract and elevated French vocabulary of love and honour finds no easy equivalents in the Anglophone tradition of poetic drama dominated by Shakespeare's eclectically metaphoric language. Each of Racine's protagonists has a confidant so that they can express their feelings without resort to asides or extended soliloquies, both unacceptable according to the neoclassical rules. And those rules also mandated strict adherence to the three unities of time, place, and action. However implausibly, all the drama has to happen in one setting within a single twenty-four-hour period.

Carr in *Phaedra Backwards* started from Euripides' *Hippolytus* for her re-imagining of the story of the wife of Theseus who falls in love with her stepson, though she did borrow Aricia, Phaedra's rival, from Racine's play. As Hilary Fannin explains in the preface to the published text of the play, her collaboration with composer Ellen Cranitch was inspired both by Racine's *Phèdre* (1677) and by Jean-Pierre Rameau's operatic version *Hippolyte et Aricie* (1733). Fannin began her career as an actor and went on to write several plays, including *Doldrum Bay* (2004), a satire on the aimless lives of the Dublin middle classes in the Celtic Tiger years. Since then, she has become best known for her work as a columnist with the *Irish Times*, while also publishing a childhood memoir and a novel. Ellen Cranitch, though she trained as a classical flautist, has worked as a composer and broadcaster across the genres. Her contribution to *Phaedra* was based on a perceived affinity between the baroque style of Rameau and traditional Irish music.

In the wake of the financial crisis of 2009, the play was domesticated for an Irish audience by moving the action 'into the febrile atmosphere created by Ireland modern boom-to-bust. We decided to set the piece in the outskirts of Dublin on a small private estate by the sea, where Phaedra, Theseus and their precarious household are doing their loving and loathing in lush and perilous excess'.[21] The atmosphere of corrupt decadence, dominated by sex, money, and power, is suggested by the opening lines where Enone reads to Phaedra from a magazine advertising vaginal plastic surgery. Theseus is a predatory venture capitalist, who tells his family, '[t]he living ain't so easy on Easy Street no more. Oh no. No no

---

[21] Hilary Fannin, Preface to Hilary Fannin and Ellen Cranitch's, *Phaedra*, in Patrick Lonergan (ed.), *Rough Magic Theatre Company: New Irish Plays and Adaptations, 2010–2018* (London: Methuen Drama, 2020), 4. All quotations from the text are taken from this edition. The text varies quite often from the staged version; I am again grateful to Gemma Reeves for access to a recording of the show.

no no no. We are going to have to tighten our belts, curb our excesses' (Fannin and Cranitch, *Phaedra*, 37). Theseus's unexpected return from the dead after his journey to Hades in Racine is recast as a night spent 'in a failed investment of mine, a stinking nightclub in the crucified north' (Fannin and Cranitch, *Phaedra*, 28). Pirithous, Theseus's companion, who tried to steal Persephone out of Hades and was imprisoned there, is reduced to Perry, who is permanently incapacitated after a row in the nightclub. Theseus himself appears with bandaged head and blood-spattered shirt from the incident.

There are difficulties with some of these transpositions. In Racine there is a complex political situation in which Aricia, sister of failed rebels against Theseus's Athenian rule, lives in provincial Troezen under interdict not to marry. When Theseus is believed dead, and Aricia, Hippolytus, and Phaedra are all possible successors to the throne of Athens, Hippolytus renounces his claim in favour of Aricia. In the modern version, somewhat awkwardly, the estate of Theseus was taken from Aricia's father when he went bankrupt, and Aricia is allowed to live on in the summerhouse. Hippolytus declares to Phaedra, that with Theseus dead: 'This house belongs to Aricia' (Fannin and Cranitch, *Phaedra*, 25). The modern counterparts of Racine's confidants are more skilfully managed. Enone, assistant to Phaedra, is a cynical older woman always aware of the practical dangers of their shared situation. It is when physically threatened by the brutal Theseus that she gasps out the slander that Hippolytus has raped Phaedra. Ismene is a coke-snorting young companion to Aricia, urging on her love for Hippolytus. The confidant of Hippolytus, Theramenes, is turned into a psychotherapist hired to help Hippolytus recover from the trauma of his mother's suicide. There seems to be no prompt for this in Racine where Hippolyta is not even mentioned, but she is Phaedra's immediate predecessor, and in this version of the play his mother's death gives added animus to Hippolytus's resentment of her.

In the Fannin and Cranitch version, Hippolyta killed herself by driving her car into the sea, opening a window to allow Hippolytus to rise to the surface and survive. There is a trace of this death in an early line of Phaedra's: 'A woman washed up on the shore yesterday. I think she may have been a friend of mine' (Fannin and Cranitch, *Phaedra*, 9), though this also voices Phaedra's own death wish. The sea is everywhere in the play, associated with death and love, the destructive and the erotic. In Racine, Hippolytus is the athlete huntsman, identified with the woods and the horses that pull his chariot. Fannin makes him a swimmer, watched on the beach by Aricia and Ismene. For Ismene, it is a purely sexy spectacle, as she sees him '[s]licing open the water like it is a peach and he is a knife'. But a more troubled Aricia asks the question: 'Are those tears on his cheeks, Ismene, or is that salt water from the sea?' (Fannin and Cranitch, *Phaedra*, 16–18). It is on the beach that Enone falsely claims Hippolytus had sex with Phaedra; it is on the beach that Hippolytus and Aricia embrace, watched by the jealous Phaedra. And it is in the sea that Hippolytus dies, deliberately driving his car into it, as his mother did, his father having wished him dead and told him Hippolyta tried to drown him. No sea-monster here called up by Theseus to terrify Hippolytus's horses and drag him to his death, just the power of the sea itself as Eros and Thanatos.

In Euripides, the tragedy is framed by the appearance on stage of Aphrodite and Artemis, the human actors merely collateral damage in the war between the goddesses. Racine disposed of the gods, but Cranitch brings them back as singers. The play's updated setting gave what one reviewer called a 'mocking view of a meretricious, misogynist Ireland'.[22] The function of Cranitch's music was to provide a high style that could give back to the play something of the Racinian sublime. 'Plaisirs', for example, the opening song, takes its title ironically from a line by Love in the allegorical prologue to Rameau's opera: '*Plaisirs, doux vainquers, à qui tout rend les armes*'—'Pleasures, sweet conquerors, to whom all surrender'. In performance it is sung by Aphrodite, expressing the unbearable experience of Phaedra's passion:

> My eyes are burning,
> I can't breathe in here,
> Close the shutters, close the ...
> Leave the window ajar,
> Cursed love, raw love,
> I can't breathe ... breathe ... (Fannin and Cranitch, *Phaedra*, 7)

This matches the sense of exposed vulnerability in the first appearance of Racine's Phaedra as she comes out into the light from her darkened chamber. In the production, Aphrodite shadows Phaedra throughout, figuring the force of illicit desire, as Artemis sings for the innocent first love of Aricia and Hippolytus. In act II, when Theseus 'returns from the dead', they are joined by Poseidon (who in the production lay apparently asleep on one side of the stage through act I) to add the baritone voice of male domination to the trios that followed. The lyrics for all the songs were taken from the characters' own lines, shaped into arias, the singing supported by the onstage musicians playing traditional Irish instruments, percussion, accordion, flute, bass, and fiddle. What might otherwise have been a squalid love triangle played out among Ireland's corrupt elite took on the dignity of tragedy with the forces of human emotion externalized as unstoppable powers. It was a convincing demonstration, according to Michael Billington, that 'classical myth can be adapted to the modern world'.[23]

---

[22] Peter Crawley, 'Phaedra', *Irish Times*, 5 October 2010.
[23] Michael Billington, 'Dublin Theatre Festival Takes the Recession Seriously', *Guardian*, 11 October 2010.

Belfast Chekhov

'I think that I saw one too many productions that was too upper-middle-class English, all languid gentility and crumpled linen suits', said Lucy Caldwell, commenting in interview about her reaction against traditional productions of *Three Sisters*.[24] She wanted her version of the play to be different, and more radically different than Friel's version with its strong Donegal English. She moved the action from the 1890s provincial city in reactionary Russia to 1990s Belfast, where she had spent her own teenage years, herself the eldest of three sisters. Though best known as a fiction writer, Caldwell had written stage and radio plays before. However, writing her version of Chekhov for the Lyric Theatre was especially significant for her: 'My first major play in my home city, my first play in the theatre I first saw plays in'.[25] Where Chekhov's characters quote from Pushkin and Lermontov, Caldwell's sing snatches of 1990s popular songs. Caldwell grew up in east Belfast with a Catholic mother and Protestant father. In the play, Olga, Masha, and Irina become Orla, Marianne, and Erin, children of a mixed marriage between an English Catholic father and a Northern Irish Protestant mother.

The transposition involved some clever substitutions. So, for example, Masha's husband, the fatuous schoolteacher Kulygin, reappears as DJ Cool, the dreadfully facetious disc jockey whom Marianne married after doing work experience at the radio station when she thought him 'the coolest thing in town' (Caldwell, *Three Sisters*, 40). Chebutykin, the drunken doctor who is so devoted to the three sisters, turns into 'Uncle' Beattie, a hospital orderly, whose embarrassingly overgenerous birthday present to Erin is a set of Tyrone crystal rather than a silver samovar. The counterpart to Tusenbach goes by the nickname of Baron—it is not an actual title as in Chekhov. But he is upper class, and it is class difference that separates him from Solyony/Simon. Simon is one of Caldwell's most interesting and convincing pieces of recasting. Chekhov's gauche and angry Solyony models himself on the sub-Byronic heroes of Lermontov, his destructiveness a part of his affected role as 'superfluous man'. Simon is a lower class British soldier, suffering from post-traumatic stress disorder after three tours of duty in Northern Ireland, telling vicious misogynist jokes to cover up his besotted infatuation with Erin. When he finally kills his successful rival Baron, he is driven by class animus as well as sexual jealousy.

Tusenbach and Vershinin are typical of Chekhov's Utopians, dreaming of a future unlike the hopelessness of the present, though on different timescales. Tusenbach foresees a transformative event in twenty years' time, sometimes taken as a prophecy of the revolution, whereas Vershinin believes that in 'two or

---

[24] Joanne Sweeney, 'Sister Act—Lucy Caldwell Takes on Her Biggest Literary Challenge Yet', *Irish News*, 27 October 2016.
[25] Lucy Caldwell, 'Introduction', *Three Sisters* (London: Faber, 2016), 10. This is the edition used for all further quotations from the play.

three hundred years life on earth will be astonishingly, unimaginably beautiful'.[26] Vershinin argues that the high culture of the sisters, though apparently lost in the ignorant provincial life, will have contributed to this new world. In Caldwell, it is the sisters' background that will bring about this change. Marianne has complained: 'English Catholic Dad and Ulster Protestant Mum—who gave us Irish-sounding names—I mean how fucked-up is that?' But it is this very fact that is the occasion for a Northern Irish vision of the future:

> Just by living you will have shown that a different sort of life here is possible. And after you will come a few more, a few more, and so on, until in the end, people like you will be in the majority. In two, three hundred years life here will be beautiful. (Caldwell, *Three Sisters*, 36)

In 1990s Belfast, where sectarian violence, bombs, atrocities, and hovering army helicopters continued in spite of the hopes generated by the 1994 IRA ceasefire, it can only be to some sort of distant ecumenical era to which this can look forward. In the play, even the Good Friday Agreement, when it comes, does not bring peace. In place of the devastating fire that provides the crisis of Chekhov's act III, Caldwell writes in a counterfactual reaction to the Agreement with serious rioting in the streets. It is as though, looking back from 2016, the time of the play's composition, she is fully aware of all the disappointments that followed the Good Friday Agreement. A gloomy speech by Andy in the last act seems to speak out of that later disillusionment: 'This place will never change. [...] Underneath the treaties and beneath the handshakes the same hatreds will bubble and fester until finally they erupt again' (Caldwell, *Three Sisters*, 96). This is the situation in the post-Troubles plays explored in the previous chapter.

It is not of a return to Moscow that Caldwell's sisters dream, but of escape to America. This makes geographical and cultural sense. Chekhov's Prozorovs were marooned in a city such as Perm, 700 miles away from Moscow with no direct rail link; with their father the General dead, returning there was never going to be easy.[27] The 1990s Belfast sisters could have moved anywhere they wanted in Northern Ireland, or indeed the whole island of Ireland. Nowhere is more than a bus journey away. But in imagining a glamorized America, Caldwell was drawing on her own memories:

> In my teenage years, we talked incessantly about going to 'America'. We didn't know what we meant. It was partly the famous Hollywood sign, partly the yellow cabs in *Friends*; part *Sweet Valley High* and space rockets launching from Cape

---

[26] Anton Chekhov, *Plays*, trans. Michael Frayn (London: Methuen Drama, 1998), 206. For the different critical interpretations of these speeches, see Frayn's Introduction to this edition, lviii–lix.

[27] See Frayn, Introduction, Chekhov, *Plays*, lvii.

Canaveral and fast food and Disney World and MTV. [...] It wasn't a real place, but an idea, an idealisation.[28]

In Caldwell's text, Vershinin comes with all the aura of this imagined America. He is not an army officer as in Chekhov, but an American United Nations adviser posted to Northern Ireland, child of Lithuanian Jewish refugees, who had known the Prozorovs when he had met their father in Germany years before. With this change, Caldwell emphasizes a globalized modern world. Projecting forward to the people of his Utopian future, Vershinin imagines them looking back in horror 'on the twentieth century, on the First World War and the Second, on the Cold War, on Vietnam, on the Gulf War and the Bosnian War and the Troubles and Rwanda and the countless other conflicts and they're going to think how barbaric we were' (Caldwell, *Three Sisters*, 73). This sets the 'Troubles' in perspective as a relatively minor example of the violent atrocities that have disfigured modern history. Though in the final act of the play the British soldiers are pulling out in the wake of the 1998 Agreement, they will be moved to some other conflict zone across the world.

Caldwell's boldest revision of Chekhov was the creation of Siu Jing in place of Natasha. In performance, it was startling to hear her direct address to the audience as prologue to the play.

> These are my sisters and this is their story.
> It is also my story. It might not have my name on it, but it is my story too. (Caldwell, *Three Sisters*, 18)

This is writing strikingly against the grain. In Chekhov Natasha is a monster, taking advantage of Andrei's weakness and naivety, flagrantly unfaithful to him with Protopopov, chair of the local council, steadily dispossessing the sisters from their home. We are invited to share in the sisters' initial contempt for her taste in clothes, her provincial vulgarity. It is quite different with the racism of Caldwell's characters towards the girl their brother is obsessed with who 'works in the chinky' and is mocked for her '[o]ver-the-knee socks, hair in pigtails', whom they persist in calling Jenny because they claim not to be able to pronounce her Chinese name. Orla does rebuke Marianne for a crudely racist joke about Siu Jing: 'She should know better. She should think for half a minute about how hard it is to be any sort of different around here' (Caldwell, *Three Sisters*, 78). The sense of sympathy with Siu Jing is reinforced near the end of the play, as she remembers her own homeland, Hong Kong, where in 1997 power had been transferred from the British to the People's Republic of China. 'You leave a place ... and it leaves you too. It leaves

---

[28] Lucy Caldwell, 'On Writing *Three Sisters*', in Linda Anderson and Dawn Miranda Sherratt-Bado (eds.), *Female Lines: New Writing by Women from Northern Ireland* (Dublin: New Island, 2017), 117–18.

you behind. Look at Hong Kong. The place I was born ... no longer exists. [...] I can never go home' (Caldwell, *Three Sisters*, 101).

There are problems, however, with this re-imagining of Natasha as Hong Kong immigrant. Although Caldwell takes out some of Natasha's more reprehensible actions—there is no equivalent to her affair with Protopopov and we never see anything as vicious as Natasha's dismissal of the old servant Anfisa—her part in the plot remains the same. Siu Jing is still the baby-obsessed mother who steadily pushes out the three sisters, and looks forward to transforming their house: 'now that you're all gone there are going to be more changes around here. I'm going to cut down those trees, for a start' (Caldwell, *Three Sisters*, 100). That sounds like an echo of Lopakhin's destruction of the cherry orchard after the ousting of the owners of the estate. We can see the pathos of the immigrant having to assimilate into the new environment—Siu Jing's English becomes progressively less broken over the course of the play—but she is still the predatory intruder in the house. The dramatic focus remains on the heartbreaking failure of the expectations of the three sisters. The production had mixed reviews, with complaints that the adaptation was too far from Chekhov's original, that the relocation to 1990s Belfast did not work. Caldwell's intention was clear, however. She wanted to have audiences look again at the play in a modern context of multiple sorts of conflict, many different displaced peoples. From the viewpoint of 2016, when she was writing, 1990s Belfast leading up to the Good Friday Agreement looked like a period of false dawns, mirroring the lost hopes of the three sisters.

In her introduction to *Three Sisters*, Caldwell uses the acquisition and remodelling of an old house as a metaphor for adaptation:

> There is a certain house you walk past, every now and then, and when you do you dream about what it must be like to live there. [...]
> Then one day someone gives you a key and says, 'Go inside.'
> The structure is sound, carefully planned and built and tested by the years. You don't need to blaze in with bulldozers and start again entirely. But at the same time, too, you need to inhabit it utterly: you need to fill it with everything that's meaningful to you, to let yourself belong to it, or it to you. (Caldwell, *Three Sisters*, 9)

This appropriation can take a number of forms in stage adaptation, the most obvious being a relocation in time and place. Carr makes her Medea a Traveller woman living in the Irish Midlands, cast out by a land-hungry conformist community. In their version of *Phaedra*, Fannin and Cranitch set the story in the decadent milieu of 2009 Ireland, where the amoral rich are about to be not so rich. Caldwell updates Chekhov by a hundred years, moving the action from a provincial town in Russia to her own Belfast. All three women playwrights choose plays with female protagonists and further emphasize their gendered roles in a toxic male-dominated environment. But there is also the need to go out to the strangeness and difference of the original texts. It is particularly difficult to recreate the sense of inevitability in Greek tragedy created by the pantheon of gods and goddesses, or the mediating role of the Chorus. In *Bog of Cats*, Carr uses folklore motifs to provide an otherworldly dimension to the tragedy, and in *Hecuba*, the technique of self-narration yields something like a choric distance from the action. The singers and the music in *Phaedra* play above the sordid modern plot with a stylized beauty that stands in for Racine's high neoclassical style. In each of the plays, even in Caldwell's more representational *Three Sisters*, there is a sense always of the interplay between the modern adaptation and the original, the structure of the old building below the personalized reconstruction.

State of Play 2
2016

Irish theatre in 2016 was always going to be dominated by the Easter Rising. It was the hundredth anniversary of 1916, the foundational event in the history of the independent Irish state, the centrepiece of what the government had planned as the Decade of Centenaries.[1] And indeed there were no less than sixteen shows that featured the 1916 rebellion, its leaders or its latter-day consequences. Still, these represented only a small minority of the 151 shows which I saw through the year; elsewhere, it was business as usual. There were, in fact, an exceptionally large number of revivals. These included a range of classic plays—no less than three productions of *Hamlet*, an exam-prescribed text, and a major staging of *Othello* at the Abbey, Strindberg's *Creditors* in an adaptation by David Greig, Shaw's *Saint Joan* (irritatingly mistitled *St Joan*) by the Lyric Theatre, Belfast, a rediscovered *The Constant Wife* by Somerset Maugham at the Gate. One of the highlights of the year was Druid's production of *Waiting for Godot*, which won the Best Director prize for Garry Hynes in the *Irish Times* Theatre Awards.

Many more recent Irish plays were also revived: two by Tom Murphy, *The Wake* at the Abbey, *Bailegangaire* toured by the Nomad Theatre Network; two by Conor McPherson, *This Lime Tree Bower* at the Project, *The Weir* staged by Decadent Theatre Company; Martin McDonagh's *The Beauty Queen of Leenane* in a twentieth anniversary production by Druid; Jimmy Murphy's *Kings of the Kilburn High Road* by the Livin' Dred Company; Stewart Parker's *Northern Star* produced by Rough Magic; and in what was the centenary of the Battle of the Somme as well as of the Easter Rising, Frank McGuinness's *Observe the Sons of Ulster Marching Towards the Somme* at the Abbey. It seemed somewhat like a fallback on the tried and trusted with so much imaginative energy invested in the 1916 projects.

Not but what there were plenty of new plays from within Ireland. In fact, there were notably fewer works from Europe and the rest of the world relative to 2006. Many emerging playwrights and start-up companies staged individually scripted plays or devised work. In this there was a visible impact of The

---

[1] See https://www.decadeofcentenaries.com/ (accessed 8 August 2022).

Lir, founded in 2011 as an Irish national academy of dramatic art at Trinity College Dublin. This offered for the first time not only fully professional training in acting but also in directing, playwriting, stage design. The skillsets of Irish theatre makers were startlingly improved as a result. Additional opportunities for small-scale new work were created by the Show in a Bag project, established by Fishamble in association with the Dublin Fringe Festival and the Irish Theatre Institute. This allowed writers and performers to create low-budget one-act plays that could be easily taken on the road. As a result, two outstanding 2016 shows were produced both in the tiny Bewley's Café Theatre. *To Hell in a Handbag*, by Jonathan White and Helen Norton the author/performers, daringly riffed off *The Importance of Being Earnest*, creating a fantastic and hilarious offstage life for Miss Prism and Canon Chasuble. Margaret McAuliffe's *The Humours of Bandon* made a mini-drama out of traditional Irish dance competition, an astonishing one-woman show acted and danced by the author, discussed in a later chapter.

Some of the major new plays by established playwrights in 2016 showed the trend towards the integration of other forms within Irish drama. In Enda Walsh's *Arlington*, staged by Landmark as part of the Galway Arts Festival, a whole section of the play was performed by a dancer, while Frank McGuinness's *Donegal* at the Abbey was a musical, building on the Irish taste for country and western. CoisCéim (Irish for 'footstep'), the dance company founded and led by David Bolger, collaborated with the musical group Crash Ensemble and Fishamble on *Invitation to a Journey*, staged at the Galway Arts Festival as an exploration of the life and work of Eileen Gray the Irish designer; but the company was also a collaborator with ANU in *These Rooms*, the production discussed below. The dance drama *Swan Lake / Loch na hEala* was conceived and directed by the theatre choreographer Michael Keegan-Dolan with his company Teaċ Daṁsa. The vestiges of Tchaikovsky's original ballet were here fused with the Irish myth of the Children of Lir, who were magically transformed into swans, and anchored in a contemporary narrative of mental health within a socially desolate and politically corrupt contemporary rural Ireland. It won Best Production at the Theatre Awards and laudatory reviews when it transferred to Sadler's Wells. Equally original was *Shackleton* devised by the Blue Raincoat company, already discussed in Chapter 2, which was nominated for Best New Play in the Awards (Figure 4).

The trend within Irish theatre away from traditional text-based representational production was evident also in the 1916 shows—that and its opposite also. For many of these plays were absolutely conventional in their dramaturgy. The range of different theatrical styles, from the standard well-made play through to the most experimental, is one focus in the analysis that follows, reflecting as it does the state of the art and the tastes of audiences in 2016 Irish theatre. In the

Fig. 4 Sandra O'Malley, Barry Cullen, Brian F. Devaney, and John Carty in Blue Raincoat production of *Shackleton*. Photographer Peter Martin. Courtesy of Blue Raincoat.

representation of Easter 1916, however, there were not only dramaturgical issues but political and ideological ones as well. Debates in the 1990s had raged between contesting parties of Irish historians. Traditionally Irish history had centred on the national narrative and the anti-colonial struggle. Revisionists sought to bring other perspectives to the discipline and were accused of belittling the achievement of the nationalist independence movement. In this context, and given the continuing sensitivities of the political situation, the Irish government, in setting up the Decade of Centenaries, looked to acknowledge and commemorate equally the different traditions on the island of Ireland in the revolutionary period. So, it began in 2012, the anniversary of the Ulster Covenant, resisting Home Rule, continued with the Dublin lockout in 2013, a key date for the labour movement, while in 2014 the focus was on the role of Irishmen in the British armed forces in World War I. The Easter Rising was to be duly remembered in 2016 but so too was the Battle of the Somme in which so many men from the Ulster Division of the British army had lost their lives. The emphasis throughout was to be on 'parity of esteem'. How 1916 was remembered a hundred years on, how it was represented on stage, and how the retrospect bore upon the 2016 present—these were all questions that were to be manifested in the productions of the year. In what follows, I want to look first at those shows that dramatized the Rising itself, then at plays dealing with its consequences. In both cases, I will be considering the theatrical styles and the political interpretations and the extent to which the two are interrelated, drawing once again on my notes from seeing the productions as a Theatre Awards judge.[2]

Dramatizing the Rising

At the most literal end of the spectrum of representation was *Inside the GPO* by Colin Murphy (Fishamble), directed by Jim Culleton. Murphy has a background as a journalist and drew on original documents for his recreation of the scene in the headquarters of the Rising in Dublin's General Post Office (GPO). So that is where we found ourselves on an April evening, a hundred years on, sitting in the great entrance hall of the GPO, waiting for it all to begin (Figure 5).

The first time-travel signal was the command from the gallery above for us all to be upstanding for the National Anthem. But, of course, it was not 'The Soldier's Song', the Irish National Anthem, that was played; it was 'God Save the King', a startling reminder that in 1916 Ireland was still part of the British Empire. The first speech heard, in fact, was from Arthur Hamilton Norway, Secretary

Fig. 5 Manus Halligan and Liz Fitzgerald with audience members in the Fishamble production of *Inside the GPO*. Photographer Patrick Redmond. Courtesy of Fishamble.

---

[2] Most of these plays have not been published; for details of the productions, see https://www.irishplayography.com/

of the Post Office at the time; this was delivered again from the gallery, on the occasion a month before the Rising when a major refurbishment of the building had just been completed. Throughout the play Norway's wife Louisa (Karen Ardiff) provided an alternative point of view on the Rising: her speeches were based on the memoir she published in 1916.[3] Though she, like her husband, spoke from the gallery, suggestive of their hierarchical position as members of the governing class, above the rebels on the floor of the hall, her account brought out the personal destruction involved in the Rising. In particular, there was the sense of devastating loss of the mementoes of their dead son Frederick stored in the GPO, who had been killed at age 19 in the Western Front.

But obviously the main action was devoted to the excitement of the Rising in all its day-to-day urgency, with loud noises off a reminder of the artillery used by the British forces as the week went on. Much of the drama came from the tensions between the leaders: the idealistic Patrick Pearse (Ronan Leahy) as against the more practical James Connolly (Aidan Kelly) who was very much in charge of the military operation; the romantic figure of the O'Rahilly (Don Wycherley), who had tried to stop the Rising happening but then fought with the others in the GPO, as against the tough-minded activist Sean McDermott (Manus Halligan). For all such internal dissension, however, by the end of the show, the audience did have a sense of just what the Rising had achieved in inspiring the Irish people with a vision of independence voiced in the Proclamation of the Republic. While the show accorded some sympathy to the Norways and the catastrophe the event represented in their lives, the main effect was to stir an Irish audience with the daring achievement of the Rising.

Three of the 1916 plays focused on the individual leaders. *McKenna's Fort* was a one-man show written by Arnold Thomas Fanning about the life of Roger Casement staged in the Project (Fire and Ice Theatre Company). It took its title from the fort where, according to this version, Casement spent his one night in Kerry in April 1916; he had landed from a German submarine, bent on stopping the rebellion, knowing that he was not bringing the men and armaments he had hoped for. In the play, the night is given over to a retrospect on his life: his early background, his service in the British consular service in the Congo, meeting Joseph Conrad there, his exposure of the oppression of native peoples in South America, his conversion to Irish nationalism, and his doomed mission to Germany to recruit Irish prisoners of war to the Republican cause. There was also plenty about his sexual encounters with young men and his obsession with the size of their genitals: the author was not evidently one of those who subscribed to the theory that the so-called Black Diaries were forgeries.[4] It was deftly done, well performed

---

[3] Mrs Hamilton Norway, *The Sinn Fein Rebellion as I Saw It* (London: Smith Elder, 1916).
[4] After Casement had been convicted of treason for his part in the Easter Rising and sentenced to death, the British government privately circulated extracts from the so-called 'Black Diaries' recording his homosexual encounters with young men, as a means of discrediting him and resisting appeals for clemency. Many nationalists have claimed these diaries were forgeries, though it is now generally agreed

by the actor Michael Bates, giving a sense of Casement's loneliness and isolation, someone who, because of both his sexual orientation and his peculiar political trajectory, could fit in nowhere. But it showed the limitation of this sort of theatrical biopic. There is only so much that can be done to render a life story on stage—occasional minor changes of costume, lighting, and sound—while sticking more or less to the facts. One was no nearer to solving the mystery of what motivated Casement, the knighted British diplomat turned Irish rebel.

It was the men who signed the Proclamation, read out at the start of the Rising outside the GPO, who were the subject of *Signatories*, a play devised in University College Dublin (Verdant Productions).[5] The plan was to invite several contemporary Irish writers to create individual monologues for each of the seven signatories of the Proclamation. But here evidently another sort of politics came into the equation. All the seven signatories were men. One of the notable features of the many books published in and around 2016 was the focus on the occluded part women played in the rebellion. R. F. Foster's book *Vivid Faces* showed how the feminist strand, which was an important element in the political fervour inspiring the revolutionary generation, was suppressed in the largely conservative patriarchal state that emerged after Independence. Senia Pašeta's *Irish Nationalist Women* and Lucy McDiarmid's *At Home in the Revolution* provided analyses of the roles of women in the period.[6] And, of course, the #WakingTheFeminists movement, protesting the inadequate representation of women in Irish theatre, had been sparked originally in 2015 by the announcement of the Abbey's 2016 programme Waking the Nation. It was no doubt with that consciousness that four of the eight writers asked to contribute to *Signatories* were female: Marina Carr, Emma Donoghue, Éilís Ní Dhuibhne, Rachel Feehily. In addition, Elizabeth Farrell, the nurse who had been with the insurgents in the GPO through Easter Week and carried Pearse's flag of surrender to the British forces, was given a monologue of her own at the very start of the show.

This too, like *Inside the GPO*, was a site-specific play designed to be staged in Kilmainham prison where the seven signatories were executed in May 1916. It was a promenade performance in which the audience were moved from station to station standing to listen to each of the monologues. After what was effectively a prologue by Farrell, providing an overview of the Rising and the conflicted feelings it created in retrospect, the challenge for each of the writers was to come at the life and character of each of the leaders. Thomas Kilroy, for instance,

---

that they are genuine. For a full account, see Lucy McDiarmid, *The Irish Art of Controversy* (Dublin: Lilliput Press, 2005), 167–210.

[5] Emma Donoghue, Marina Carr, Joseph O'Connor, Frank McGuinness, Thomas Kilroy, Éilís Ní Duibhne, Hugo Hamilton, and Rachel Feehily, *Signatories* (Dublin: UCD Press, 2016).

[6] R. F. Foster, *Vivid Faces: The Revolutionary Generation in Ireland 1890–1923* (London: Allen Lane, 2014); Senia Pašeta, *Irish Nationalist Women, 1900–1918* (Cambridge: Cambridge University Press, 2013); Lucy McDiarmid, *At Home in the Revolution: What Women Said and Did in 1916* (Dublin: Royal Irish Academy, 2015).

suggested that Pearse's actions were an overcompensation for an inner sense of weakness fostered by a dominant father. Most playwrights had the signatory himself speak the monologue, but some came at their subject from another angle. So, for example, Hugo Hamilton testified to the power of James Connolly's personality by having a woman several generations later remember stories about him told her by her nursemaid. Éilís Ní Dhuibhne gave her monologue to Min Ryan, fiancée to Sean McDermott, remembering him with a surprisingly distant, at times satiric vision. Though the perspectives and styles of the eight writers were necessarily quite different, the collective effect was certainly not that of nationalist hagiography.

By contrast, nationalist hagiography was very much the genre of *Thomas Kent, 1916 Rebel* by Ferghal Dineen and Eoin Ó hAnnaracháin staged in Cork's Everyman Theatre (Lantern Productions). This was the good old story of the making of an Irish rebel, the battle between heroes and villains in the freedom struggle. Thomas Kent was one of four brothers from a family farm in Castlelyons, Co. Cork, and when the audience first met him in the play he was working in the US, promoting the Irish language as the owner of the Boston *Irish Echo*. Letters back and forth between Thomas at his Boston desk on one side of the stage, and his indomitable mother at the other in the family kitchen with its beautiful wooden dresser lined with shining crockery, ponderously built up the picture of the iniquities of the landlords and the sufferings of the imprisoned Land Leaguers of the 1880s. Thomas returned to join the fight with his brothers and all four went to jail for their boycotting activities. Their trials were narrated by two supposedly comic old fellows with heavy Cork accents who provided a choric commentary throughout. After an hour and twenty minutes, the 1890 Parnell divorce scandal ended this phase of the story, but at the interval there were still twenty-six years to cover.

Happily, the action fast-forwarded in the second act to one of the few truly comic moments in the play. Terence McSwiney, future Sinn Féin Lord Mayor of Cork, who was to die on hunger strike in Brixton Prison, appointed Thomas to command the local battalion of the Irish Volunteers. Thomas, as a special favour, asked that it should be a teetotal battalion: no consumption of alcohol. Terence agreed, suggesting, though, that it might not be the most attractive way to recruit men. However, true to his own pledge, when Thomas was in the condemned cell, he handed over to the priest his Pioneer pin, token of his lifelong abstention from drink. This, along with the last parting with his mother, left not a dry eye in the house. The Cork audience loved the play and were on their feet to give it a standing ovation. It was a very special occasion for them: it was exactly a hundred years since Kent had been executed and there had been a municipal commemoration in the city earlier on in the day. Thomas Kent was Cork's own hero, their railway station called after him, the only man executed in 1916 outside Dublin. For all the government strategy of political balance and parity of esteem, for all the growing sophistication of

Irish theatrical forms, there were still Irish communities, like that Cork audience, who were fully committed nationalists and liked their plays straight and irony-free.

Companies staging plays for children also had 1916 productions and, in both of these, the emphasis was on the cost of the Rising rather than its glories. So, for example, there was *Maloney's Dream / Brionglóid Maloney*, a bilingual show in English and Irish credited to Marc Mac Lochlainn, but created collectively by his company Branar, staged in the Town Hall Theatre, Galway. This figured a hotel keeper called Maloney (Jonathan Gunning) who returned to Ireland having inherited a hotel on Sackville Street (later to become O'Connell Street) determined to turn it into the best hotel in Europe. He found it extremely run down with a comically incompetent staff, but managed to turn it round, planning to have a grand opening on (needless to say) Easter Monday 1916. All the parts were played, with attractive brio and inventiveness, by the company of six actors who also doubled as musicians, using puppets and masks for variation in some scenes. What it brought out, however, was the devastation created by the Rising for the businesses in the neighbourhood, as first the Volunteers, then the British army commandeered all the hotel's resources and the place ended up a burnt-out ruin. Appropriately for a children's show there was an upbeat ending with Maloney vowing to rebuild his dream (Figure 6).

In *The Messenger*, written by Mike Kenny for Barnstorm Theatre Company, and staged in the Kilkenny Watergate Theatre, the Rising was seen from the viewpoint

Fig. 6 Jonathan Gunning and Zita Monaghan in Branar's production of *Maloney's Dream / Brionglóid Maloney*. Photographer Anita Murphy. Courtesy Branar.

of the working-class children of Dublin. Almost all of the children were played by adult actors with the exception of the central figure of the Bullet, Christy Brady (Conal O'Sheil), who aspires to be the fastest messenger in the city. Video projections of period Dublin streets behind Christy created the illusion of his running, while most of the set was completely non-realistic. This one, though, did not have a soft landing for the children, as in the final moment of the play we see Christy hit by a bullet as he attains his highest ever speed.

Rebel Rebel, created by Robbie O'Connor and Aisling O'Meara, was staged in Bewley's Café Theatre (Fishamble in association with ANU Productions). It featured two real life Abbey actors who were actually involved in the Rising, Helena Moloney (Aisling O'Meara) and Sean Connolly (Aonghus Og McAnally). The play intercut their real-life relationships and their actions in the rebellion, with a metatheatrical frame in which Moloney was offstage in the Abbey wings waiting to play Cathleen ni Houlihan in Yeats and Gregory's famously allegorical play about the earlier 1798 Rebellion, which had inspired so many nationalists. *Rebel Rebel* emphasized the performative element of the Rising with an ironic awareness of the mixed motives of the performers behind the scenes. Mixed motives, but also mixed forms, were equally a feature of *Wild Sky* by Deirdre Kinahan (David Teevan, Ten42 Productions in association with Meath County Council).[7] Kinahan brought out the tangle of different allegiances among young Irish people in 1916, some of whom were committed activists working for women's suffrage as well as Irish independence, some like the poet Francis Ledwidge, who joined the British army, and some who got involved in the Rising almost by accident. The central narrative here was a more or less standard love triangle but it was performed partly in dance, interspersed with the singing of ballads of the period.

ANU Productions, with their tradition of immersive re-creations of Ireland's past history, discussed in Chapter 4, were bound to invest heavily in the 1916 centenary. In fact, in 2016 they delivered a triptych of their hallmark site-specific shows to expose people to the experience of the Rising. All year long, several times a day, you could board a bus in O'Connell Street for *The 1916 Tour: Beyond the Barricades*; the time-travel tour had stops in Stephen's Green where you met both a runner for the rebels and an Irish soldier in the Dublin Fusiliers, and Dublin Castle where the daughter of James Connolly told of her last visit to him when he was under sentence of death. The second of the ANU shows, *Sunder*, emphasized the simultaneity of the past and present. A small group of audience members was assembled in Moore St, close to the GPO, where the rebels made their last stand. They were directed (by individual mobile phone) to urgent, secretive debates as to whether to surrender or not, in places which were now an Indian restaurant, or a Polonez foodstore selling eastern European groceries, testament to Ireland's contemporary globalization. ANU's most ambitious 1916 piece was

---

[7] Deirdre Kinahan, *Wild Sky* (Navan: Meath County Council Arts Office, 2016).

These Rooms, based on an event late in the Rising where residences in North King Street were attacked by British forces and fifteen civilians killed. ANU collaborated with CoisCéim on this production which was set in a disused bank at 85/86 Dorset St, on the site of the birthplace of Sean O'Casey. For this show, the bank was redesigned as a 1966 pub in which the audience of about a dozen watched the fiftieth anniversary celebrations on television, only to have the space erupt into a dance performance. This was followed by separate groups of two or three hustled through a labyrinth of rooms behind the bank/pub in which they participated in individual scenes from the North King St story in all its strangeness and terror. If *Inside the GPO* gave the central drama of the Rising, and *Signatories* insights into the minds of the leaders, the ANU site-specific shows were designed to make us feel what it was to live through these chaotic times.

It was inevitable that in 2016 the Abbey Theatre would have to stage *The Plough and the Stars*; and that in itself constituted a problem. After its controversial, iconoclastic premiere, *Plough* has become the Abbey's favourite play, more often revived than any other in its repertoire. Before 2016, it had been staged as recently as 2012. Many Irish theatregoers would have all but known it off by heart. For 2016 the Abbey promised a *Plough* production unlike any seen before, and that it certainly was. On the first night, the audience faced the blank safety curtain shutting off the stage, a stand microphone in front of it. After we had all stood to attention for the entrance of President Higgins and his entourage, a teenage girl in a red football jersey walked up the aisle onto the stage and, unaccompanied, sang the National Anthem in Irish, Amhrán na bhFiann. She sang it extremely well, but just as she came to the final high notes she started to cough blood, and we realized she was the consumptive character Mollser (Mahnoor Saad). At that point the curtain lifted, and Mollser joined all of the other characters who stood there in tableau before the play itself started (Figure 7).

This production, directed by the British theatre director Sean Holmes, was a stripped-down *Plough* with none of the normal representation of the run-down tenement flats so standard in O'Casey productions. Instead, there was a high scaffolding tower that represented the building. The Clitheroes' flat was rendered with mere tokens of furniture: a single bar electric heater at which Uncle Peter (James Hayes) warmed his dress shirt; the flimsiest of cheap modern wardrobes. The costuming (Catherine Fay) was equivalently modern; like Mollser in her football jersey and sneakers, Jack Clitheroe (Ian Lloyd-Anderson) came in as a contemporary construction worker wearing a high-vis jacket, Nora (Kate Stanley Brennan) in a supermarket checkout uniform; Bessie Burgess (Eileen Walsh), when out on the town in act II, appeared in a fake leopardskin coat. But it was not consistently modern; Fluther Good (David Ganley), for instance, had something approximating to period costume with the obligatory bowler of the 1920s.

There was also a sense of ad hoc eclecticism in the way in which modern references were used. For example, in act II, the Voice of the Man, mouthing the

Fig. 7 Mahnoor Saad in the Abbey Theatre production of *The Plough and the Stars*. Photographer Ros Kavanagh. Courtesy of Abbey Theatre.

speeches of Patrick Pearse, came from an unseen TV, hung high on the front of the stage, which the Barman zapped on and off with his remote control. It was a very ingenious and effective way of rendering O'Casey's theatrically awkward device of imagining the Speaker on a long platform behind the bar who only comes into view from time to time. It also provided an added piece of business between the Covey (Ciarán O'Brien) and the prostitute Rosie Redmond (Nyree Yergain-harsian). When she was making her play for him, she switched the channel on the TV to something suitably romantic, whereupon he marked his resistance by switching it back again. But the television appeared to be a flickering black and white machine of a sort that would hardly have been seen in an Irish pub since the 1970s. Rather than an up-to-the-minute contemporary period, the reference point was to some remembered technological modernity of the past.

The production revelled in a full-throated theatricality as far as possible from naturalistic representation. The stand microphone, on stage for most of the action, was used repeatedly to move the action towards music-hall or cabaret: Jack sang most of his song to Nora in act I amplified out to the audience, Rosie Redmond ended act II with a rousing version of her bawdy ballad, while the drunken Fluther in act III belted out his paean to himself, 'For Fluther's a jolly good fellow'. The physical comedy of the fights in act II was heightened up to slapstick level, the Barman tossing the combatants back and forth, ending up carrying a diminutive, purple-suited Covey bodily out the door. At the same time, the non-representational staging was used to heighten the pathos. Throughout act II, when all the others were off in the bar, we saw Nora left alone sitting high up in the scaffolding tower, while Mollser sat on the other side of the stage playing with her mobile phone. The change of scene from act III to act IV was a frenetic disco dance by Mollser centre stage. It could have been seen as a sort of dance of death, given that she was in her coffin by the next scene, but it also suggested the sort of normal contemporary teenage life that a consumptive child of her time like Mollser would never have had.

In the set designed by Jon Bausor, that transition from act III to IV was the most scenically spectacular move in the play because it involved lowering the scaffolding structure onto its side. It thus provided the sense of shut-in space necessary for the final act where the remaining characters take refuge in Bessie's attic flat. The effect of the scaffolding coming down onto the stage also suggested the collapse of the city, echoing the ruined buildings that figured in so many photos of the aftermath of the Rising. The mixed style of the Abbey production of *Plough* worked well because it replicated the mixed style of the play itself. O'Casey poses real problems for a director who tries to render his drama in a homogeneous naturalistic style because it is in fact a hybrid: old-fashioned melodrama cut with broad farcical comedy, realistic dialogue heightened up to ornate rhetoric; a deliberately cacophonous conflict of modes. It is by this unstable theatrical mixture that in *Plough* he challenges the drama of the Rising as the rebels tried to construct it, unifying, sacramental, unequivocally tragic. Many of the 2016 shows, like that of the Abbey *Plough*, gave us tangential perspectives on the Rising, emphasizing the complexity of the contexts of the event, its different effects on bystanders and participants.

Unfinished Business

The Easter Rising constituted year one of the revolution. Several productions in 2016 looked back at the event with a disillusioned sense of the present state of Irish society a hundred years on. *Johnny I Hardly Knew Ye* by Jim Nolan, veteran playwright and founder of the Red Kettle Theatre Company (Garter Lane Arts Centre, Waterford) took a sceptical view of the business of commemoration itself. The play was set in the office of a local newspaper in the fictional small Irish town of Inishannon, the occasion the build-up to the centenary commemoration of 1916. It was absolutely up to the minute, played in February 2016 in the run-up to the Irish general election about the run-up to an Irish general election. The central figure is the veteran journalist who was sacked from his position on a national daily for his uncompromising investigative reporting, now reduced to the position of acting editor of the *Inishannon Chronicle*. His paper has been bought up by a large company, and he is being pressured by the new commercially minded managing director to sensationalize stories and slant the news in favour of the more conservative sitting Fine Gael government, against the upcoming challenge of the left-wing Republican Sinn Féin Party. The big local event is to be the opening of a peace park, commemorating two local men: one who had a (very tenuous) part in the Rising, the other who served in the British army, all part of the careful political balancing act of the Decade of Centenaries. The editor (Garret Keogh) comes up with the explosive discovery that the site of the park was also the burial place of one of the so-called 'disappeared', a murder victim of the paramilitaries from the 1970s Troubles. Will this uncomfortable truth be told, upsetting all the orchestrated and politically advantageous ceremonies around the opening of the peace park? The audience had to wait until the very final moment of the play to find out. It was nicely built up, with all the different personalities of the reporters on the paper sketched in, the set properly shabby and dishevelled. It was, in fact, an old-fashioned well-made play, with the upfront moral issues of an Arthur Miller, if not an Ibsen. There seemed to be no necessary correlation between dramaturgy and political point of view. *Johnny I Hardly Knew Ye* was politically edgy but theatrically extremely old-fashioned.

Fornocht Do Chonac / Naked I Saw You was an Irish-language play adapted from an original text by Eoghan Ó Tuairisc, performed with English-language subtitles, in An Taibhdhearc, Galway's permanent Irish-language theatre. It took its title from a poem by Patrick Pearse in which the poet turns aside from the naked beauty of love to the love of country and revolution for which he will die. Like *Johnny I Hardly Knew Ye* it was set in the contemporary period and focused on the issue of commemoration. It figured a reclusive dropout sculptor living in a caravan who is persuaded out of retirement to create a Pearse memorial for the local town. It used inset video as well as a more or less realistic set and the climax came with the appearance of a little girl as a dream vision of the lost innocence of the revolution. In this, as in the sculptor's renewed inspiration at the idea of Pearse's leadership, there was a sense that the ideals of 1916 might not be quite lost, in spite of the tackiness of the contemporary memories of them.

Only the title of *Sacrifice at Easter* connected it to the Rising. Written by Patrick McCabe, best known as a novelist, it was staged by Corcodorca in the Elizabeth Fort. The site, a very well-preserved fort high on the slopes of Cork City above the river Lee, built by the British in the early seventeenth century and subsequently used as a police barracks, reminded the audience of the much longer colonial history of Ireland. It was played as a promenade performance, consisting of a number of satiric playlets witnessed by audience members mostly standing in the main courtyard, sometimes performed from a central stage, but also from on top of the walls or at the entrances at the rows of houses within the fort where the policemen and their families had lived. There was one very funny piece in which a variety of performing hopefuls auditioned to appear in a 1916 commemorative production, but for the most part the pieces were vignettes lampooning contemporary Ireland, the wholly inadequate result of the rebels' sacrifice at Easter.

Without doubt the most experimental show of the year was *It's Not Over*, staged by THEATREClub. The unfinished business of the title was the revolution started in 1916. The cast played as dissident Republicans still carrying on the struggle, and most of the episodes featured key incidents from the period of the Troubles: Bloody Sunday in 1972, the shooting of three IRA volunteers in Gibraltar in 1988, the lynching of two British soldiers in Belfast in the same year, the Omagh bombing (1998). But there was no clear trajectory of action, no narrative thread. The show, all four and a half hours of it, was free-form, live-directed by Grace Dyas and Barry O'Connor who whispered in the ear of one performer or another what they were to do next. The Samuel Beckett Theatre in Trinity College Dublin, where it was staged, was stripped bare of seating; there were some chairs but for the most part the audience moved around in the same space as the actors. It was multi-media, simultaneous staging. In a corner of the space, one or other of the performers sat at a table before a microphone, reading continuously from a pile of typescript from what sounded like eyewitness accounts of events in Northern Ireland, sometimes audibly, sometimes not. There was a low platform stage behind a red curtain on which act I of *The Plough and the Stars* was performed, lines unchanged but with a balaclava instead of Nora's 'swanky' hat from Arnotts, token of her social aspirations, and Uncle Peter toting an automatic rifle rather than brandishing a dress sword. Above this stage, black and white video of old newsreels played on a loop. Act II of *Plough* was staged in the cash bar at another corner of the space where audience members could buy drinks throughout. Beside that was a stand where three live musicians played and sang.

The show was knowingly metatheatrical. From time to time, one or other of the actors appeared at a stand mic, introduced him- or herself and apologized for the fact that the show had not started giving a series of excuses, rows with the Dublin Theatre Festival management, ideological disputes between the cast members, and so on. Each one ended with the same statement: 'I refuse to commemorate 1916'. So, this was an anti-1916 commemorative show that kept not starting because it was about 1916 not being over. It was impossible to know quite what the political point of view of the play was. The audience was made to feel inside the atmosphere of unreconciled contemporary Republican circles with repeated question and answer sessions for potential recruits, only occasionally ironized. The most pointed protest against the violence was a very real dead fawn which was carried round on the shoulders of a dancer performer, dripping blood: the deer had been identified in one of the speeches as a symbol of freedom and innocence.

This was a show that divided audiences and critics; those who disliked it thought it pretentious, tasteless, and politically unacceptable. For others it had an admirable urgency and energy. The central conceit of the avant-garde theatre makers as dissident Republicans refusing to accept conventional mainstream politics and mainstream theatre was followed through with imagination and wit. It was in its way a striking latter-day tribute to *The Plough and the Stars*. What O'Casey had done in 1926, ten years after the event, was to deconstruct the Rising by showing it up in relation to the messy, complicated human dramas that surrounded it. What *It's Not Over* did was to deconstruct *Plough*, with any or all histories of the Troubles, in similar ways.

Commemorating the Easter Rising in 2016 was a delicate political balancing act as the government sponsored events of the year showed. The preamble to the programme published by the Department of Foreign Affairs is suggestive:

> Ireland 2016 first and foremost marks the centenary of the Easter Rising in 1916, a seminal moment on Ireland's journey to independence. It is also a once-in-a-century invitation to people of all ages, in Ireland and overseas, to shape and actively engage in a diverse range of historical, cultural and artistic activities designed to facilitate reflection, commemoration, debate and analysis and an active re-imagining of our future.[8]

That sense of the significance of the Rising as the originary event of modern independent Ireland complicated by a twenty-first-century need to acknowledge the cultural pluralities of the island was reflected in the year's theatre. In the dramatization of the historical action, the celebration of the heroism of the participants was qualified by a probing of their human weaknesses. Again and again, the costs of the Rising in its impact on individual lives, the destruction and the violence it caused, was brought home to audiences. Whatever about an 'active re-imagining of our future', there was plenty of disenchantment with the state of Ireland in the contemporary period. The ideals for which the leaders of the Rising had died, that 'sacrifice at Easter' with all its redemptive implications, appeared markedly unrealized in 2016, though not necessarily lost to sight.

If politically the plays produced represented a spectrum of varying attitudes towards the Rising a hundred years on, theatrically they showed the multiplicity of co-existing styles and modes. Site-specific immersive shows took audiences inside history, made them feel the original experience, while never losing the sense of where they were in the latter-day twenty-first-century environment. Interdisciplinary mixed-media productions, using dance, song, and video projections, were commonplace. Irish theatre had modernized to the point where a non-naturalistic production of *The Plough and the Stars* at the Abbey could be enthusiastically received. This was in notable contrast to the hostile reception given to the radical

---

[8] https://www.dfa.ie/our-role-policies/our-work/casestudiesarchive/2015/april/ireland-2016-centenary-programme/ (accessed 15 August 2022).

semi-expressionist Abbey staging of the play by Garry Hynes in 1991.[9] It also stood out in comparison with the much more conventional version of the play produced by the London National Theatre in 2016.[10] Yet there was still a heavy reliance on writerly drama, text-based monologues, conventionally plotted narratives. If *It's Not Over* stood for one extreme of self-consciously postmodern experimentalism, *Thomas Kent, Irish Rebel* and *Johnny I Hardly Knew Ye* could both have been written fifty years earlier. To watch all the 1916-related plays was to learn just how differently drama was conceived by theatre makers and received by audiences across Ireland in 2016.

---

[9] For an account of this production and the controversy it stirred up, see James Moran, *The Theatre of Seán O'Casey* (London: Bloomsbury Methuen Drama, 2013), 190, 202–4.
[10] See https://www.nationaltheatre.org.uk/shows/the-plough-and-the-stars (accessed 15 August 2022), for production images.

PART III
THE POLITICS OF GENDER

7
Waking the Feminists

Women's Voices

In October 2015, the Abbey Theatre launched its programme for the year 2016, the centenary of the Easter Rising. The programme was given the overall title of 'Waking the Nation', the two-way-facing pun perhaps inspired by the fact that one of the plays to be staged was a revival of Tom Murphy's *The Wake*. The initial reaction was positive: Arts Minister Heather Humphries said that she was 'confident that the "fantastic programme" of both old and new will leave theatregoers "very excited" and added there was no better way to showcase the best of Irish culture at home and abroad than through the Abbey Theatre'.[1] However, it was quickly noticed that of the ten productions promised only one was by a woman playwright—a restaging of Ali White's monologue *Me, Mollser* to be toured for younger audiences—and there were to be only three women directors. The stage designer and arts manager Lian Bell, picking up on a phrase of director Maeve Stone, used the hashtag #WakingTheFeminists to start off what became a major social media campaign of protest. Within two weeks, on 12 November, the Abbey Theatre itself was the venue for a public event staged by #WakingTheFeminists.[2] The personal testimony of women actors, directors, playwrights, designers, and dramaturgs was heard on their experience of discrimination, their demand for equality of representation in Irish theatre.

The movement produced some effects quite quickly. There were additions to the Abbey programme for 2016, including Carmel Winters' *The Remains of Maisie Duggan* and a stage adaptation of *Anna Karenina* by Marina Carr. The producer Sarah Durcan, one of the leading figures in #WakingTheFeminists, was appointed to the Abbey's Board of Directors and in its annual report for 2016 there was a new commitment to gender equality.[3] A group representing the movement committed to working for a year to achieve their agenda, ending with a second public meeting, #WakingTheFeminists: One More Thing, on 14 November 2016. One of the outcomes was funding from the Arts Council for research on the representation of women in the profession. This was published in 2017 as *Gender Counts*,

---

[1] See 'Abbey Prepares to Wake the Nation in 2016', https://www.rte.ie/entertainment/2015/1028/737979-abbey-theatre-gets-set-to-wake-the-nation-in-2016/ (accessed 25 October 2023).

[2] The two parts of the event can be seen at: https://www.youtube.com/watch?v=7uVwuEuBmn4 and https://www.youtube.com/watch?v=CpNJTvfOWDY (accessed 25 October 2023).

[3] See https://www.abbeytheatre.ie/annual-report-2016/page-2.html#section12 (accessed 25 October 2023).

Irish Theatre in the Twenty-First Century. Nicholas Grene, Oxford University Press.
© Nicholas Grene (2024). DOI: 10.1093/oso/9780198893073.003.0010

providing an 'analysis of gender in Irish theatre 2006–2015'.[4] Across a range of the different roles, authors, actors, directors, designers, there was a striking disparity between the overall level of female participation across the period, from 32% at the Gate Theatre up to 47% for the Ark (the theatre for younger audiences), the Dublin Fringe Festival, and Rough Magic. Startlingly, there was an inverse proportion between the level of public funding and the involvement of women, with the Gate and the Abbey, which received most from the Arts Council, having the lowest percentages of female representation. There was traditional gender skewing in the field of design, with only 9% of women sound designers, as compared to 79% costume designers, the only category in which there was a majority of women employed. Longstanding complaints about the underrepresentation of women playwrights were borne out by the statistic of just 28% of 1,155 productions surveyed.

By 2022 things looked different, if only in so far as five of the most influential positions in Irish theatre were held by women. Selina Cartmell was just completing her six-year term as Artistic Director of the Gate Theatre and Caitríona McLaughlin had taken control at the Abbey in 2021.[5] With Landmark Theatre Productions, which she set up in 2004, Anne Clarke had proved herself Ireland's most successful theatre producer. Garry Hynes continued to lead Druid, which she co-founded in 1975, as did Lynne Parker with Rough Magic which she helped to establish in 1984. For my book, I decided to interview these five, together with Lian Bell and Sarah Durcan, the initial moving spirits of #WakingTheFeminists, to talk about the issues seven years on. What had been the effect of the events of 2015–16 when the movement started? What did they think were the sources of the gender bias in Irish theatre? And how far had it changed? In what follows, I have collated the responses of the interviewees according to the sort of questions asked. Apart from a rough ordering by topic and some light editing for clarity, I have allowed the women to speak for themselves.

Awakening

How did the movement take shape and develop over 2015–16?

Lian Bell. The Abbey programme [for 2016] was announced on a Wednesday and I did a first Facebook post on that Wednesday; the following Thursday, eight days later, we had our first meeting of people in a room together, and the following

---

[4] Brenda Donoghue, Ciara O'Dowd, Tanya Dean, Ciara Murphy, Kathleen Cawley, and Kate Harris, *Gender Counts* (#WakingTheFeminists, 2017).
[5] McLaughlin was appointed artistic director with Mark O'Brien as executive director, a similar pairing to Roisín McBrinn (Cartmell's successor) and Colm O'Callaghan who were appointed at the Gate for a five-year contract in 2022.

Thursday was the Abbey event [public debate 12 November 2015]. There was a sort of confluence of events. It was just the right moment, it was after the theatre festival and the fringe festival, so with the festivals over, people had a bit more time than they normally would, so we were able to pitch in. I had absolutely no idea it was going to strike a chord, I felt I was just rolling my eyes yet again. There was no idea that this would actually do anything, until it did. The title #WakingTheFeminists was pretty much an accident but fortunately it was incredibly apt because it was this sense of waking up and just realising these things that we've never actually looked at, if we look at them and we start to count, then, all of a sudden, we can see things very clearly. Because we've all just gone around with our eyes slightly closed for our lives.

Sarah Durcan. That event was put together in unprecedented time, it was put together in a week—no producer would be comfortable doing that. We had a debrief after the Abbey meeting and we got together, what should we start, what should be stopped, what should be continued, what worked, what didn't work, what should we do next. If you think about how long it takes to create real change, we realised we could be doing this for the rest of our lives. We could all commit to a year. And it made a deadline. I think in retrospect that was one of the smartest things we did. The second smartest thing we did was making it about governance and not just about individual artistic directors, making it something that was embedded into the actual DNA of organizations which would go on from one artistic director to another because we knew it was a structural problem. And the third thing then was the research, having that baseline research: that was really uncomfortable for a lot of organisations.

Anne Clarke. Lian lit the flame, and it just took off. I can absolutely say, it's rare to have a grassroots movement like that which achieves so much in such a short space of time. And it really did. I think that came about for a couple of reasons. First of all, Lian was someone who was clearly motivated by the injustice of it but was capable of gathering lots of people around her as opposed to being in any way polarizing. And Sarah Durcan, who was also really involved, was just a brilliant strategic brain, and very early identified the fact that we needed to have these very clear goals. We all said we would do it for a year because we could throw ourselves at it for a year. And if we hadn't done that, I don't think it would have had nearly the success it had.

Lynne Parker [whose offices in Rough Magic were used for many of the meetings]. I have to say that the experience of it was very cheering because there were maybe twelve or thirteen women in the room upstairs all trying to achieve a consensus on the way forward and they did! And you cannot imagine, if that had been an all-male group, it would have been possible. You know yourself, you have been at meetings where two big egos will clash and everything just sits down for a bit, but the women are really good at keeping it going.

How shocked or surprised were you by the depth of feeling that was expressed in response to #WakingTheFeminsts?

Garry Hynes. I don't think it came out of nothing, but I think my reaction was like a lot of other people's reactions—it was a wake-up call. It was a serious wake-up call. And for that we will always be grateful to Lian and the people who actually made it happen. It was one of those great moments of energy in the Irish theatre: it just woke us up to ask questions, to be more aware, and it did just that. It was a great big shot of energy, what the Americans call a 'teaching moment'. The strength of the whole movement at the time was the majority of people who became aware of it and as a result of that awareness realised that, yes, of course we have to change and we will, rather than it coming down as a series of things that had to happen.

Lynne Parker. I know that some people that had been working very forcefully as feminists for decades before that were irked by the notion that feminists were being woken—'sorry, I have never been asleep, I've been plugging away at this for a long time'. But in terms of the whole profile-raising exercise, it was absolutely essential.

Caitríona McLaughlin. I was in America when I first saw the [Abbey] programme for 2016 and I couldn't believe it. I was really disappointed to see how few women were included. It was just a really visible articulation of what we all kind of knew. I was surprised to be asked to be involved in the #WakingTheFeminists day here [in the Abbey Theatre] because I did not think I, or my work was well enough known to be included, when fifty women spoke here. I remember sitting on that stage and thinking, I've never heard these women speak before. It really struck me I have not really heard from the majority of them. I had no idea what they were interested in specifically, I had no idea what they thought. And I remember thinking this is not just somebody else's fault, I knew myself I avoided events; like I would have felt 'no, I don't want to speak at that, or I don't have an opinion on that'. I would say try x or y or z—they have more to say. So, not only did I think it's shocking how few of these voices I've heard before, I realised there's an element of taking yourself out of the game because you are in a culture where that's easier. You get to a point where you get a certain number of rejections which puts you in a place where you believe you have nothing to say so you start to extract yourself from the conversation. A behaviour that kind of feeds itself. That's what I felt sitting on that stage and I remember making the decision then I have to say yes to things more.

Selina Cartmell. I don't think I was shocked. I felt incredibly empowered by it, as it was much needed. And I had great respect and admiration for everyone involved who kick-started it all off as there were things unlocked, unearthed and discovered that had not been out there before publicly. And that was really important. It gave a lot of artists, both male and female, a real sense that revolutions are possible and voices can be heard. Ultimately of course it's how that actually works in practice. It's great to have these moments of real sea change, and it's so important for them to evolve. But then it's like, okay, how does this actually roll out and make real meaningful steps forward for change? And what are those changes that can be made, those fundamental changes that can be made in order to achieve gender equality?

Gender Bias

Have you experienced obstacles in your own career as a woman in Irish theatre?

Lian Bell. I don't think I am able to put my finger on any particular thing that happened to me. I couldn't say, oh such-and-such got a job instead of me. I felt it more in relation to looking at other areas of the work. Like there weren't so many women directors, for example, in the Theatre Festival. Those kind of things were a little bit more obvious; and then over time, I thought more about the slightly less obvious and more insidious feelings. I was tech manager in [DU] Players [Trinity College student drama society] and for a good chunk of my late teens and early twenties I was a technician or a lighting designer, and just remembering, I had to be quite masculine in my way of being to fit into that. Because there weren't so many women doing that kind of work and all of us had to be sort of tomboyish in order to fit in.

Anne Clarke. There was one moment when I left the Gate to set up as an independent producer, a very senior playwright said to my former boss that I would never make a producer because I didn't have the 'flair'. I don't know if that would have been an opinion shared by other people, which would have been absolutely a barrier, but apart from that the only barrier was—confidence. You need an awful lot of confidence to be a producer, and I honestly don't think men question themselves as much, as I did as a woman at that time.

Selina Cartmell. I find it interesting to think about how these questions are framed. So, what's it like being a female director? Would a man get asked those questions? Probably not. So, yes, at different times of my career, it has been challenging. I have always believed that female directors need to keep proving themselves throughout their career and you're never really allowed to rest on your laurels and reflect on what you've achieved. There has been a constant need to prove yourself, I think, more than other established male directors. There also might be an element in the mix here of female artists constructing their own barriers as well, a kind of hardwiring. I'm not saying there's a wall of blockage everywhere you go. For example, when I was directing Lear at the Abbey [in 2013], I just thought you needed to be a male director of a certain age to fully understand, inhabit and direct, King Lear. So, there is constant questioning—can I? A struggle with your own confidence as a female artist that I don't see as much with male directors. So, it's really about allowing female artists, from whatever social cultural or economic background, to not have to question themselves or their creative journey and to feel fully supported and empowered to accomplish and achieve the stories they are attracted to or wish to aspire and create.

Garry Hynes. It was only four or five years into my professional career that I began to notice that I was being frequently asked the question, 'What is it like being a woman director?' And it was a concept that hadn't even occurred to me until the question was asked. In every respect Druid was a sort of Garden of Eden situation, and it was only gradually as we went along that we realised that we were bucking the trend in a number of ways. So, I would say that I always found it hard to answer that question, and I used to answer it on the basis, well, I have no idea because I am simply a director and that's it. I think, probably, as my career progressed and broadened, particularly when I left Druid and went into the Abbey [as Artistic Director, 1991–4], I would have become aware of the way that things were stacked against women.

Caitríona McLaughlin. Isn't that significant, the only really successful women in theatre in Ireland had to set up their own companies [Druid, Rough Magic]? Neither of them lasted very long in other institutions. They had to set it up in their own terms. I always thought women were second-class citizens in the Irish theatre for a long time. For me, trying to break into it in Ireland was very near impossible in so far as—and this was not just women but being outside Dublin, making work on a small scale, you had to make it yourself—it was very hard to get anybody to come and see your work or to take you seriously as a director I found. I'll tell you where I really noticed it as a freelancer. I would be in competition with other directors and invariably young men with very little experience would talk about how good they were at their job. Women never would do that, even people with ten years' experience, they would never say I'm really good at this. And inevitably you would see the louder voices getting the job. Like, I've even been in positions, like three times before I got this role [at the Abbey], where I was in a process where they hired a man, and then the company came back and apologized to me. Three times in two years, that happened.

What do you see as the source of gender bias in the profession?

Sarah Durcan. Women working in the arts are absolutely familiar with it I'd say, but it's a problem hiding in plain sight. I'd worked in The Corn Exchange, Dublin Theatre Festival, Dublin Fringe Festival, in management before that, and I had always thought really strategically about the management and government of organizations, and the development of things. So, I definitely knew it was a problem. With a lot of women artists, I could see very talented people weren't quite getting there, and I could see their peers who were men getting chances again and again and again, even if they didn't triumph the first time out. It was so much harder for women.

Lynne Parker. When I went into the Royal Shakespeare Company [directing *The Comedy of Errors* in 2000], I realised what a bearpit of machismo it was. I realised that not all conditions are helpful. I remember sitting across the table during a casting session from an Italian director who was also female, and we looked at one another with raised eyebrows. There was just nothing you could do with this animal behaviour—they were so aggressive and they were also so used to the boxing ring, the wrestling ring, that was the casting process in the RSC, and we were external to it.

Historically the reason women have not written for the theatre more is that it takes an awful lot of confidence. Because if you are writing a book, you can write it and all you have to do is get a publisher interested in it and then you have to get someone to read it. If you are writing a play, you have to get a director interested, you have to have a producer, you have to have a cast and a budget, and you have to have a theatre, and all of these things are expensive, and they take a lot of neck to feel that you're entitled to them. So, given that some people are just incredibly driven and bullish and wonderful, and they happen to be female, then they will say why not. But a hell of a lot of us, including some male writers, ask themselves, is anyone going to like this? Jesus, would anyone go to see it? And this is much more likely to be the state of the playwright, whatever their gender, so that's why it needs encouragement, you need to feel that there is a track there. The more women writers get produced, the more women writers will write.

There's also the fact that you're not getting a career path for actresses; you're either a serving maid or you're Hedda Gabler—there isn't enough in between, whereas men get to play all of those different parts.

Anne Clarke. In terms of historical biases, people simply expect the playwright to be male to the extent that you would often read about a female playwright where you would never read about a male playwright because you assumed the standard was male.

Caitríona McLaughlin. I went to London and I remember having a conversation with—I won't say who it was because he was trying to be helpful and he was giving me advice. He said, frankly, Caitríona, you're female, you're Irish, you haven't been to Oxford or Cambridge, you will not be a director.

The thing I always find difficult is that women book most of the tickets for theatres and they tend not to book female playwrights as much as they book male playwrights. We are familiar with a dramaturgy that is from a male perspective, so we know where we are with that. I think women's stories don't have the same traction that men's stories have historically. We have a habit of listening to men's stories and I think women don't feel their stories are valid in the same way. A female dramaturgical thread seems to have a different preoccupation, and so we all have to educate ourselves somehow to read that way of telling a story—and I mean as an audience not just as a reader—to read plays by women.

In Ireland there was also the impact of the de Valera situation and women's place being in the home, the impact that had in my father's generation, the women in their lives, the fact that they thought that was a good thing, the fact that that they believed that was some sort of elevation of women, whereas it was hobbling and gagging them. I feel that has a massive impact on who we are and how we articulate ourselves and therefore has had a massive negative impact on our theatre culture, on arts.

Lian Bell. We've got the male names which are canonical, and therefore they're more attractive for somebody who's a little bit outside of the conversation. So, coming through as a female playwright, your name is generally less known. So, I'd say that already goes against you. Also, in some cases, people feel like the theatre is putting it on—the way things are marketed—they're putting it on because it is worthy, and therefore the potential audience is not so interested.

For me it's not so much about the difference in the stories, like the narrative of the story, because there is the trope that infuriates most female writers by which men write the big important world-describing plays and women write the domestic emotional interpersonal plays, and that's very limiting. I think the difference is the understanding of character. I do think a woman written by a woman, or the viewpoint on a relationship or on the interaction between humans, can have a different tone when seen from a different viewpoint.

There were certain things we didn't even know we were working around, that we didn't know that we had had to spend so much of our energy navigating over the years. And then when it was brought to light, it was actually really hard. As a young student graduate, there are more women taking the courses, but as soon as they leave, all of a sudden it drops away. Having a family is really hard and all of these things that were quote 'just the way they were', and you had to work around them. Once we all shone a light on it, it was like these are actual barriers in our way.

The hard part of all of this is that theatre doesn't work in isolation, it's part of a society that has a huge imbalance. So, when you come down to things like technicians and sound designers being predominantly male and costume designers and costume assistants being predominantly female, or stage managers, which is a very quote 'nurturing' role, being predominantly female, that's a reflection of a much bigger societal issue. So, of course, we cannot just change theatre in itself as its own bubble. But I suppose the thing we always hoped with #WakingTheFeminists, because theatre in Ireland is relatively small, there was a sense that if we could make a significant enough impact here that it might be a role model or just show that things could change.

Selina Cartmell. I think women are not given as much opportunity as men and out of these opportunities grows confidence and belief and changing the system.

It's about female playwrights being commissioned and programmed by producers and institutions, and given the space and support to write full-length plays for small stages, big stages, whatever size stages. There is this perception that female playwrights are not able to write 'state of the nation' plays or plays with large casts and should be only programmed on smaller stages with domestic settings. It's totally false of course but it is a perception. Audiences, too, are hardwired to believe that if they know the playwright (i.e. Miller, Wilde, Friel) then it's 'safe' and they are guaranteed a 'good night out' and producers will also look at this as 'safe' so they will programme this as it's guaranteed an audience. So, a female classic playwright would then be considered more of a 'risk'. It's a very complex weave, I think, of confidence, of opportunity, and in some cases having to be too over-reliant on having to do the box office to make it all work.

Changed Scene?

What has significantly changed since 2015?

Anne Clarke. Before #WakingTheFeminists, I had actually gone on a talk, a chat at NUIG [University of Galway], and during the Q and A afterwards someone asked did I ever take gender into account when deciding what plays to produce, and I said, hand on my heart, no. What was interesting in retrospect is that I didn't think, oh gosh, maybe I should have. I genuinely didn't realise that this is something I should have been doing. And I do think #WakingTheFeminists changed the landscape; it's changed it for everybody working then and working since. I don't think there's a producer in the country, or a director or an artistic director, if they were asked the same question, who would not find it a strange question to be asked, because of course they take gender into account when they're deciding what to do.

There are more opportunities for work by women to be seen on the stage—the sheer number of female playwrights, for example, being produced. People are mindful of not putting them into a silo like having male writers on the main stage, female writers in the studio space. There's been a shift in the culture.

Selina Cartmell. I think after #WakingTheFeminists everything changed. There is now more awareness, dialogue and transparency. Finding balance is key, not shifting from one extreme to the next in order to tell these stories but to create balance and harmony with gender parity.

Lian Bell. I think it's extraordinary how much happened within that year. It really was unprecedented in terms of the speed of change. Going from the moment where people felt fearful talking about it to, a year later, when the Minister for the Arts was getting all the national cultural institutions to put gender policies in place. So, not only had it become acceptable, it was now official that one had to talk about these things. And that is an amazingly fast turnaround. And the nuts and bolts of things like policy going into place and the research—there are those practical things are countable. But the thing that I feel most proud of is just feeling people can talk about it now. It's helped pave the way for the conversation, which now is happening a lot in theatre, around diversity more broadly in terms of minority representation and minority voices having the space to tell their stories.

These things are so deep-rooted and so long-held that the idea that something that happened in a year from 2015 to 2016 is going to make any really deep changes—I don't think that's going to happen. But it is another little step forward in starting to dislodge that.

Garry Hynes. The profession doesn't look at all as male in terms of its leadership as it would have done back in 2005 or 2010. The climate has changed, hasn't it? The weather has changed around women in the theatre and changed fairly quickly.

Lynne Parker. A few years ago, it was very much the case that the big jobs, the decision-making jobs were male. But that has started to change in the last decade. #WakingTheFeminists has contributed to that, but it was happening anyway, the women were just coming up. When I started Rough Magic, all the lighting designers were male, and now they are all female, all the successful ones. The same thing is happening in sound design, and you're now seeing women working in the technological arts entirely comfortably and being very successful. It's a sea-change. So, I think it's just changed in a quite organic way but something like #WakingTheFeminists got the whole conversation going and rightly so.

Sarah Durcan. The numbers are good and they've really improved, and they've improved drastically, better than anyone thought they would in the last six years.

Caitríona McLaughlin. I have seen more women directors here, definitely. I have seen an appetite for more women directors, which is more important even than people actually wanting to do it. But, also, I think there's a kind of awareness that there are really significant talents in terms of women in the technical side of theatre, designers, lighting designers, sound designers particularly. You do see the impact of #WakingTheFeminists because at the senior management level there are a lot more women than there would have been five years ago. Our head of producing is a woman, our director of operations is a woman, our director of finance and governance is a woman, our communications director is a woman. A lot of our senior managers are women so it's not just the arts makers.

That's the big thing with #WakingTheFeminists, you didn't notice because that's how it always was, that's how you behaved and how you were spoken to and how you were treated. But now you notice and therefore you can actually do something. I don't believe I would be here [Artistic Director of the Abbey] without #WakingTheFeminists happening. I don't think I would have felt the obligation to put myself out there.

8
Masculinity and Its Discontents

'What the hell *is* it with men?' exclaims Adele in frustrated indignation in Mark O'Rowe's *Our Few and Evil Days*.[1] The immediate occasion for her outburst is Gary, the lover of her best friend Belinda whose abuse drove her to suicide, and who has tried to justify his behaviour by attributing it to his own insecurity. Adele does not know that her own boyfriend Dennis was only pursuing her as a means of reaching Adele's mother for whom he has an obsessive infatuation. And though Adele is worried by the sporadic violence of her father, she never gets confirmation that it was indeed he who killed her 11-year-old brother, following on the boy's rape of his mother, the terrible secret at the heart of the Gothic family. 'What the hell *is* it with men' is the question O'Rowe and his contemporaries Conor McPherson and Enda Walsh repeatedly put up to their audiences.

All three dramatists had breakthrough plays in the 1990s, considered in the first chapter of this book. The other two playwrights discussed there, Billy Roche and Martin McDonagh, have figured less prominently in twenty-first-century Irish theatre. Roche has written relatively little new work. McDonagh has worked as much in the cinema as the theatre; though his earlier plays are very frequently revived, the plays he has written since 2000 have none of them been set in Ireland and only one of them has belatedly been produced on the Irish stage.[2] However, McPherson, O'Rowe, and Walsh have continued to write prolifically and have been very successful nationally and internationally. From *Dublin Carol* (2000) through *Port Authority* (2001), *Shining City* (2004) and *The Seafarer* (2006) through to *The Night Alive* (2013), McPherson's plays have opened in London before being staged in Dublin and produced in New York to great acclaim. Walsh has been a major figure in European as well as Anglophone theatre, with several of his plays having their premieres in Germany, Switzerland, and Portugal. O'Rowe's *Terminus* (2007) went on to major success at the Edinburgh Festival, several revivals, and a world tour.

These playwrights have worked across different forms—O'Rowe and McPherson in film, Walsh in opera and musical theatre—and have not confined themselves to male-dominated plays. McPherson's *Girl from the North Country* (2017) is based round the songs of Bob Dylan, while O'Rowe's *The Approach* (2018)

---

[1] Mark O'Rowe, *Our Few and Evil Days* (London: Nick Hern Books, 2014), 89.
[2] *Hangmen*, his 2015 play about capital punishment in Britain, was very successfully staged at the Gaiety Theatre in 2023. Neither *A Behanding in Spokane* (2010) nor *A Very Very Very Dark Matter* (2018) has been seen in Ireland.

consists of dialogue between three female characters, and Walsh's most recent work from *Ballyturk* (2016) to *Medicine* (2021) has focused on issues of existential rather than gendered identity. Nevertheless, their plays, particularly those from the first decade of the twenty-first century, are concentrated on the behaviour of men—abusive, destructive, and dysfunctional.

A number of different contexts for this work have been advanced by scholars. Brian Singleton points to the colonial legacy in which the Irish were feminized against the masculine authority of imperial Britain, and argues that the masculinities represented in contemporary Irish theatre challenged the traditional patriarchal discourse that had continued into the postcolonial period.[3] Fintan Walsh posits a broader crisis of masculinity within which the performances of early-twenty-first-century theatre and cinema should be seen.[4] Stephen di Benedetto looks at the shock value of such plays as politically educative: 'McPherson [...], Walsh and O'Rowe are using the male gaze to interrogate the concepts of what it means and feels like to be a male in Irish society today'.[5] Other critics are sceptical of the radical political claims made on behalf of these playwrights. Karen Fricker, looking at McPherson's *Port Authority* and O'Rowe's *Made in China* (both produced in 2001), argues that the playwrights' attempts at a 'critique of traditional definitions of masculinity' are of limited success, ending up implicitly endorsing conventional gender roles.[6] Clare Wallace too is critical of O'Rowe's work. 'If considered as parables of contemporary Ireland, the messages of these plays are bleak in the extreme, leaving audiences feeling perhaps just as gutted as some of their protagonists'.[7]

'If considered ...'. What is striking about the plays of McPherson, O'Rowe, and Walsh is how little they relate directly to the society of their own time. Twentieth-century Irish drama, beginning as it did with the national theatre movement, typically held the 'mirror up to nation' to quote the subtitle of Christopher Murray's book on the subject.[8] These male-dominated, early-twenty-first-century plays all have characters that can be identified as Irish by their language; they are set in Ireland—with the exception of *The Walworth Farce* (2006) with its

---

[3] Brian Singleton, *Masculinities and the Contemporary Irish Theatre* (Basingstoke: Palgrave Macmillan, 2011).
[4] Fintan Walsh, *Male Trouble: Masculinity and the Performance of Crisis* (Basingstoke: Palgrave Macmillan, 2010).
[5] Stephen di Benedetto, 'Shattering Images of Sex Acts and Other Obscene Staged Transgressions in Contemporary Irish Plays by Men', *Australasian Drama Studies*, 43 (2003), 46–65.
[6] Karen Fricker, 'Same Old Show: The Performance of Masculinity in Conor McPherson's *Port Authority* and Mark O'Rowe's *Made in China*', *Irish Review*, 29 (2002), 84–94 [85].
[7] Clare Wallace, 'Irish Drama since the 1990s: Disruptions', in Nicholas Grene and Chris Morash (eds.), *Oxford Handbook of Modern Irish Theatre* (Oxford: Oxford University Press, 2016), 529–44 [549].
[8] Christopher Murray, *Twentieth-Century Irish Drama: Mirror up to Nation* (Manchester: Manchester University Press, 1997).

Irish expats holed up in their London flat, and *Penelope* (2010) which could be anywhere—and in the case of McPherson mostly in a very specific area of north Dublin. Yet their playworlds have strangely little purchase on the extra-theatrical life outside. McPherson's *The Seafarer* is played out in the basement of a house in Baldoyle, with accurate references to all the streets and public-houses that surround it. But the action, in which one of the group of inveterate drunks plays cards for his soul with the devil, is its own purgatorial space. In *Terminus*, we can follow the perambulations of the characters, ending with a high-speed carchase through the streets of Dublin, but what is spun out by the three alternating monologists (only identified in speech prefix as A, B, and C) is a horror phantasmagoria beyond actuality. Most of all, Walsh's sealed-in spaces figure the mental landscapes of their protagonists, in which interior and exterior worlds are entirely self-generated.

The plays, as a result, put on stage male psychopathologies representative of nothing but themselves. Different as the dramatists are in style and technique, they have certain common features in this show of malfunctioning masculinity. Violence is always threatened, sometimes shockingly omnipresent. It has been a staple of O'Rowe's drama, an early fan of horror and martial arts films.[9] 'I don't think I'd ever say I want to deal with violence as a study of violence', he declared in an interview, 'but I know it is what entertains me. [...] I love violence in its literary form, its cinematic form'.[10] True to those tastes, his plays throughout have graphic displays of physical force and degradation, from anal rape through disembowelling. The frenzy of words and imaginings in Walsh's stage spaces typically builds towards acts of murder. There is much less violence in McPherson, but *The Night Alive* does have a fierce beating and a killing onstage. The men in these plays are needy, vulnerable, obsessed. They feed their neediness on drink—alcohol continuing as the substance abuse of choice in Ireland even after the widespread introduction of other drugs. They fantasize about unattainable women, projecting onto them ideals of otherness that may heal their wounded selves. At the same time, they abuse the actual women in their lives, remorse for this mistreatment returning in ghostly form to haunt them. Plays that never settle for merely verisimilar representation open out into surreal forms in which notional images of redemption may appear in the blighted men's lives. To what end are we asked to witness this dramatization of masculinity and its discontents? The aim of this chapter is to analyse the forms that the spectacle takes and how we might be expected to react to it.

---

[9] See Michael Raab, 'Mark O'Rowe', in Martin Middeke and Peter Paul Schnierer (eds.), *The Methuen Drama Guide to Contemporary Irish Playwrights* (London: Methuen Drama, 2010), 345–64 [345].

[10] Quoted by Wallace, 'Irish Drama since the 1990s', 539, from an interview with Mark O'Rowe by Gerry Stembridge.

Violence: *Made in China* and *The Walworth Farce*

Made in China has a similar urban underworld setting to *Howie the Rookie*, but this time we are inside gangland. The Echelon gang, as its name might suggest, is strictly hierarchical. Hughie, in whose flat the play is set, is a regular member of the gang, while Paddy is only a wannabe gopher. The Echelons are controlled by the sinister never-seen Puppacat, whose orders cannot be questioned. At the opening of the action, Hughie is indignant that he has been asked to go and break the legs of Bernie Denk, who has been molesting the one-legged fortuneteller Nancy. He has no objection in principle to this task but feels he should not have been asked when his mother is seriously ill in hospital, and argues that the response is disproportionate: 'I says to Puppacat, Why've I to break *both* of Bernie's pins? Is one not enough?'[11] The mad logic of tit-for-tat violence continues when Hughie goes on his mission, only to discover that it was a surprise present for himself: Bernie and Nancy, actually lovers who merely had a falling out, have captured the driver of the car responsible for Hughie's mother's accident, and Hughie is offered the opportunity to contribute to a vicious revenge beating. When he turns down this treat, he is demoted from the gang and Paddy gets to replace him.

Within the intricate plotting of the play, what the characters wear is of crucial significance. Paddy comes on soaked, complaining that CopperDolan, the corrupt policeman who shares control of the district with Puppacat, has deliberately splashed and ruined his snorkel jacket.[12] Kilby, the third character still higher up the food chain, wears a leather jacket with a Chinese ideogram which he claims reads Dragon Fist, linking him to the school of martial arts he favours. His longstanding grievance is that CopperDolan stole his original handstitched Dragon Fist jacket. However, later in the play Hughie reveals the truth, that Kilby sold the jacket to Dolan, and when the policeman found out that the characters merely read 'Made in China', he publicly brutalized Kilby (with the gang boss Puppacat's assent) by driving a billiard cue up his rectum. It is because Kilby's digestive system is so wrecked by this assault that he has to make the frequent visits to the toilet that we see through the play. In the climax of the action, the three hoods battle it out with one another. The psyched-up Kilby appears to be triumphant, about to demolish Paddy, when Hughie recovers consciousness and manages to fell him. Hughie escapes, leaving Paddy, now helpless with his legs broken, to face the vengeance of Puppacat for what has been done to Kilby.

---

[11] Mark O'Rowe, *Made in China* (London: Nick Hern Books, 2001), 14.
[12] Fashionable from the 1970s, the snorkel jacket is so called because its hood so covers the face as to leave room only for a snorkel.

The godfathers of the work—and it seems the right metaphor—are Harold Pinter and Martin McDonagh. The structure of the play follows the triangulation of *The Caretaker*. Initially it appears as if Hughie offers his patronage to the subordinate Paddy, as Aston does to Davies in Pinter's play. In the middle of the action, Paddy tries to ingratiate himself with the more powerful Kilby, parallelling Davies's overtures to Mick. But in both plays the attempted transfer of allegiance misfires: it is Davies who loses out at the end of *The Caretaker*, as Paddy does in *Made in China*. Both Pinter and O'Rowe regard with cool detachment the catch-as-catch-can dynamics of male power. The trivial occasions of conflict, however, can be traced back to McDonagh. The mother and daughter battle to the death in *The Beauty Queen of Leenane* is fought out over Complan and Kimberley biscuits; an insult to Coleman's hair style in *The Lonesome West* precipitates the murder of his father. In *Made in China* it is the Rib 'n Saucy flavour of Nik Nak crisps that Kilby and Paddy suck delightedly, while they discuss the finer points of physical combat. The fashion statement of the characters' clothes is key to their construction of their masculine identity. Hughie's liking for John Rocha shirts is assumed to indicate that he is gay; revenge on Kilby for his inauthentic Chinese karate jacket takes the form of an appalling homosexual rape. The violent aggressions of hypermasculinity that play out in O'Rowe are made the more grotesque by the absurdly petty material objects that provide the stuff of the drama.

Though O'Rowe was to revert to the diagetic monologue form in *Crestfall* (2003) and *Terminus*, *Made in China* retains a more or less naturalistic setting and a fully representational dramaturgy. In *The Walworth Farce* (2006), Walsh uses metatheatre to bespeak the violent compulsions of the male ego. In other plays of his, games are played with the conventions of the box set. *bedbound* (2000) begins with the literal collapse of a fourth wall, opening to the audience's view the small child's bed occupied by Dad and Daughter as the final stage of Dad's mad immuring of himself and his family. In *Ballyturk*, late on in the action, it is the back wall that comes down leaving the shut-in room, in which the two men, just identified as 1 and 2, have played out their frenetic games, exposed to the incursion of the death-bringing 3. The setting of *The Walworth Farce* is a one-bed council flat on the Walworth Road in south London, stripped down to a skeleton version of a stage set, only the frames remaining of the walls separating living-room from kitchen and bedroom. Two wardrobes at the back are the changing rooms in which the sons Sean and Blake shift costumes to play their many different roles in their father Dinny's Farce.

Dinny, refugee from Cork, is author, director, and star actor in the Farce, a Bottom-like caricature of the narcissist performer. In the very obviously amdram show which he forces his sons to play out with him every day, there is a trophy for best acting which he awards himself each time. It is all absurdly unreal, as Walsh's stage direction indicates: 'The performance style resembles The Three Stooges'.[13] (The Three Stooges, vaudeville comedy act, whose short films were very popular in the 1930s and 1940s, included much slapstick physical comedy.) In Walsh's Farce, however, the cartoon violence is at another level. The ludicrous plot turns on Dinny masquerading as a wealthy brain-surgeon, owner of a splendid house in Montenotte, grand suburb of Cork, to con his impoverished brother Paddy, home from London for their mother's funeral, out of his share of the inheritance. There are casual references to Sean and Blake as the young sons offstage attacking a policeman, setting fire to a nun, torturing a little boy and his dog, all treated indulgently by Dinny as mere childish pranks. The Farce opens with Dinny and Paddy carrying in the cardboard coffin containing the remains of their mother. But a second matching coffin is brought on, by Jack and Eileen, the actual owners of the house in which Dinny is just the painter-decorator. This coffin contains the body of the father of Eileen and her brother Peter, who was killed when the speed-boat he was travelling in hit a seal propelling him into a field where he collided with a horse that was thrown over a hedge to kill the mother of Dinny and Paddy. And if that was not ludicrous enough, the climax of the Farce has multiple poisonings as would-be adulterous lovers and legacy-hunters kill one another off, leaving Dinny (of course) triumphant.

The mad ostentatiously artificial violence of the Farce masks the reality of the past recalled by Sean, who unlike his younger brother Blake, was just old enough to remember what really happened in Cork. Dinny, in a dispute over the mother's will, stabbed to death his brother Paddy and sister-in-law Vera. His wife Maureen urged him to flee to London where he holed up in the Walworth Road flat belonging to Paddy and Vera. Joined by his sons Sean and Blake, he constructed the alternative reality of the Farce to ward off the threat of the outside world of the city which he imagines in a fantasy version of his flight dwarfing him out of existence: 'With each mile I run, higher they climb and smaller the dot. Higher the buildings and smaller me' (Walsh, *Plays: Two*, 31). The unreality of the violence of the Farce conceals the truth of the murders back in Cork. But there is a third level of violent action, much more disquieting as it plays itself out in real stage time.

It begins with Dinny's attack on Sean, when he discovers that Sean has picked up the wrong shopping-bag at the supermarket and brought home Ryvita and salami instead of sliced pan and oven-roasted chicken, the daily props required for the Farce: 'Sean enters and immediately Dinny swings the frying pan across the back of Sean's head. Sean hits the floor fast' (Walsh, *Plays: Two*, 20). As Tanya Dean points out, this is 'the classic slapstick trope beloved of cartoons, the frying pan as

---

[13] Enda Walsh, *Plays: Two* (London: Nick Hern Books, 2014), 7. All quotations from the play and from *Penelope* are from this edition, cited parenthetically in the text.

a weapon'.[14] But this is not an action within the Farce, and it therefore brings home the violence to the audience. It becomes still more frightening with the entrance of Hayley, the Black British Tesco's check-out woman, who wanders innocently into the men's bizarre world. She is locked in the flat, forcibly recruited by Dinny to play a part in the Farce. When she tries to escape, 'Dinny suddenly pounces on her and grabs her by the throat, pinning her to the door' (Walsh, *Plays: Two*, 51). In so far as Hayley as 'normal' outsider is a stand-in for the audience, the attack on her is a genuine moment of terror. As the Farce builds towards its ridiculous climax of cross-killings, there is an equivalent catastrophe in the lives of the actors. The revolt against the tyrannical father, the tension between the siblings results in Blake killing Dinny, to free Sean and himself, and Sean killing Blake to prevent him killing Hayley. It is like the 'murderous masque' of Elizabethan tragedy where the real cataclysm erupts from within the mimic violence of the play within the play.

Patrick Lonergan sees *The Walworth Farce* as a play of emigration, linking it to Tom Murphy's *A Whistle in the Dark* (1961) and *Conversations on a Homecoming* (1983).[15] The mentality of the diasporic London Irish is certainly caught in the contrast between the alienating cityscape of the metropolis and the idealized home town. The peroration of Dinny's paean to Cork wonderfully guys Corkonians' local patriotism, famous in Ireland:

Ah yes, Cork City. You could call it Ireland's jewel but you'd be A FUCKING IDIOT, BOY, FOR IT IS REALLY AND TRULY, IRELAND'S TRUE CAPITAL CITY. (Walsh, *Plays: Two*, 16–17)

But Walsh denied in interview that the work of Irish playwrights was part of his landscape. And unlike English playwrights, he went on to say, he did not write 'kitchen-sink sociological plays about *now* and about *today*'.[16] Similarly, O'Rowe claimed '[m]y plays were never designed to reflect contemporary Irish society' but took place 'in a kind of hyper-real territory'.[17] The violence in *The Walworth Farce* does not reflect the psychopathology of Irish emigrants in London, any more than *Made in China* paints a picture of gangland Dublin. Irishness, its language and culture, provides a local high colour to the action of these two plays, but it is not of the essence. Violence here, as in much of Walsh and O'Rowe's work, is an imaginative given, an explosive energy in a world of conflicted contending men.

---

[14] Tanya Dean, 'Real Versus Illusory in Enda Walsh's *The Walworth Farce* and *The New Electric Ballroom*', in Mary P. Caulfield and Ian R. Walsh (eds.), *The Theatre of Enda Walsh* (Dublin: Carysfort Press, 2015), 119–30 [126].

[15] Patrick Lonergan, *Irish Drama and Theatre since 1950* (London: Methuen Drama, 2019), 172–3.

[16] Ger Fitzgibon and Enda Walsh, 'Enda Walsh, in Conversation with Ger Fitzgibbon', in Anne Etienne and Thierry Dubost (eds.), *Perspectives on Contemporary Irish Theatre: Populating the Stage* (Basingstoke: Palgrave Macmillan, 2017), 174–90 [185].

[17] Thierry Dubost, Anne Etienne, and Mark O'Rowe, 'Interview with Mark O'Rowe', in Etienne and Dubost, *Perspectives on Contemporary Irish Theatre*, 165–73 [167].

Addiction and Obsession: *Dublin Carol* and *Penelope*

These male playwrights stage violently aggressive men but also men with addictions and obsessions. Drink features largely in the work of McPherson, from the weekend long debauch of his early work *Rum and Vodka* (1992) through to the sodden Christmas of *The Seafarer*. Many of his male characters, so far from macho arrogance, are vulnerable, dependent on the women in their lives, both those they live off (and often abuse) and the unattainable ones they adore. Obsessive objects of desire shape the mental projections that Walsh's characters create in *misterman* (1999) and *The New Electric Ballroom* (2008). In the case of O'Rowe's *Our Few and Evil Days*, there is the enforced return to the scene of trauma. In both Walsh and O'Rowe the obsessions can be with fetishized material things, what their characters eat and wear, the music they listen to. These are men not in control of their damaged lives but shaped and driven by compulsive demands.

McPherson's *Dublin Carol* is set in a north Dublin undertaker's office on Christmas Eve, a grim enough scene. John the undertaker comes in from a funeral where he has had to enlist the assistance of Mark, the nephew of Noel, the proprietor of the business, who is sick in hospital. Noel is a 'good man', saving drunks and down-and-outs from themselves by giving them a job: John was one of his rescue men.[18] In the establishing scene of part I, we hear some of the more upsetting experiences of the trade: the funeral they have just come from of a young man who died of a drug overdose, the baby of a teenager, raped by a relative, which she tried to flush down the toilet. In part II, John's daughter Mary, whom he has not seen for ten years, will appear to tell him that his long-estranged wife Helen is dying of cancer. The nod to Dickens in the title is a sardonic one—this is no heartwarming fable like *A Christmas Carol*.

John evokes for Mark his former state as an alcoholic:

> the way I was then. Jaysus you'd wake up in the morning and you'd still be very pissed. But horrible. [...] You'd want to die. All you could do, this'd be the routine, was hang on 'til opening time, in you'd go. One or two lads in the same predicament. The big red faces, and the big swollen fuckin' heads. God the first one or two pints'd knock the fuckin' head off you [...] (McPherson, *Dublin Carol*, 14)

Later in part III he describes the full cycle of a drinking jag from 'day one' when 'for whatever reason, you've started early and basically polluted yourself' to '[d]ay three' when '[y]ou've got the screaming paranoid shits' (McPherson, *Dublin Carol*, 48–9). Noel's intervention has rescued him from that. But he is still dependent on drink. He is helping himself to whiskey in the late morning after the

---

[18] Conor McPherson, *Dublin Carol* (London: Nick Hern Books, 2000), 11. All further citations from this edition are given in the text.

funeral, though at this stage he denies a drink to the 20-year-old Mark in protective avuncular fashion. At the beginning of part II in the early afternoon he returns to the office with a fresh bottle of whiskey and 'is dying to get a drink into him' even with the inhibiting presence of Mary (McPherson, *Dublin Carol*, 19). And, in spite of his promise to Mary to stay sober until 5 o'clock, when they will go together to visit Helen in hospital, at the top of part III, '[t]hree quarters of the whiskey is gone' and Mark has to wake him from a drunken stupor (McPherson, *Dublin Carol*, 38). All you can say for John at the time of the play's action is that he is a (more or less) functioning alcoholic instead of an incapable one.

The scene with Mary brings out the consequences of John's addiction for his family. When John asks about his son Paul who now lives in England, Mary replies: 'He's the same as he was. Drifts along. He's getting like you, though, more and more' (McPherson, *Dublin Carol*, 21). Mary herself is lost and unhappy with all too vivid memories of childhood with her impossibly irresponsible father. Yet she has introjected something of his mentality. They laugh together about an ex-girlfriend of Paul's who is now reduced to stalking him. This replicates the attitude John takes towards his former lover Carol, the woman for whom he left Helen. With what limited money she has, she feeds his drink dependency. And yet at some level he despises her for her very neediness as a lonely widow who craves his companionship, contrasting her with the superiority of Helen whom he has left. Reflecting on the relationship of her parents, Mary seems to speak for both herself and John: 'it was sort of a pity or something that you were a man and a woman, you know. Like if you could have both been men, or both been women (McPherson, *Dublin Carol*, 33). Unlike homosocial friendship, heterosexual love is inherently distorting and distorted.

John is full of self-blame and self-loathing: 'I'm sorry about the whole stinking business. I think about it now and I want to puke. I wish I'd never been born. It's all been awful' (McPherson, *Dublin Carol*, 29). He aspires to extinction, non-being, at the end of part I recalling with admiration the Nirvana-like peace of an old man who committed suicide surrounded by statues of Buddha. When he claims to Mary that, if he was terminally ill, as Helen is now, he would not want anyone to come to see him, she insists she would. 'Why?' asks John. 'Because I love you', is the reply, followed by a 'long pause' (McPherson, *Dublin Carol*, 26). Even though she follows it immediately with the statement 'I hate you too', it is a key line. Like the despairing Christian who believes he is beyond the reach of God's grace, John in his extreme abjection cannot believe he can be loved.

And yet, as Mary points out, he is full of excuses for his behaviour, trying to produce justifications for an occasion in Limerick from twenty-five years before when he went on a binge and failed to return to his family. At the root of his helpless sense of guilt, as he explains to Mary, is his memory of having failed to stop his father beating up his mother. So self-convicted of cowardice, he was convinced in advance of his inadequacy as husband and father: 'somewhere in me. I knew ... I'd let you ... and your mammy ... down. That if we were attacked. I knew deep down in me, that I'd run away and leave yous to it' (McPherson, *Dublin Carol*, 35). Whether or not this accounts for or extenuates John's conduct, his long-term addiction has disturbed and disturbing consequences for his mental attitudes. In part I he seeks to build male bonding with Mark and in part III he edges the younger man towards his own misogyny. When Mark tells him of an attempt to break up with his girlfriend which failed because of her distress, John suggests that she was putting on an act to keep Mark. 'I'm telling you. You wouldn't be up to them' (McPherson, *Dublin Carol*, 42). Even with his patron and friend, the idolized Noel, there is an undersong of bile and resentment when he goes to visit him in hospital: 'I felt like I hated him because the poor bastard isn't well' (McPherson, *Dublin Carol*, 33).

There is something like an upbeat ending to the play, as John puts back in place the Christmas decorations he and Mark have just taken down, and prepares to go to see his dying wife, as he has promised Mary he would. It is a positive conclusion that McPherson was to amplify in his later Christmas play *The Seafarer*, as we shall see. In *Dublin Carol*, it is not clear how an audience is expected to react to or judge John. In fiction, the unreliability of the unreliable narrator is clear; the distortions and untruths of his/her storytelling are readily apparent. In the theatre it is different. John holds the centre stage, and actors such as Brian Cox, who created the role in London, John Kavanagh who played it in Dublin, bring to the part their presence and authority. The anguish the character clearly feels, his confessional mode of address, draws an audience into empathy. Critical judgement may be suspended, even as John wriggles between excuse and self-recrimination. Rather than a distanced observation of the masculine psychopathology of addiction, we may be disposed, like Mary in the play, to forgive the unforgivable.

On the cover of the first edition of Enda Walsh's *Penelope*, an image of the title character looks out, sultry and alluring in yellow bathing-cap and bright red lipstick. She is the unattainable object of desire for the four characters in the play—unattainable by definition because they are the four remaining suitors to Penelope, wife of Odysseus, faithfully awaiting his return. The play had its origin in a commission by the German dramaturg Tilman Raabke, a frequent collaborator of Walsh, who asked six European playwrights for their reactions to *The Odyssey*. Walsh's response was 'I absolutely love the suitors!'[19] The result was one of those typical modern reworkings of a classic text in which the orientation is reversed, with antiheroes instead of heroes at the centre, as in Tom Stoppard's *Rosencrantz and Guildenstern Are Dead*. In Homer, the suitors are only there

---

[19] Charlie McBride, 'Enda Walsh from the Odyssey to Penelope', *Galway Advertiser*, 10 June 2010. The play was first staged at Theater Oberhausen in Germany before being produced in English by Druid in Galway in 2010.

to be slaughtered at the climax of the poem, just as Odysseus's companions are only there to be eaten in the Cyclops's cave. In Walsh's play, Penelope herself never speaks, Odysseus never actually appears, and instead we watch her would-be lovers hopelessly compete to win the goal which has been their obsessive object for years.

The situation is wrenched out of context and re-imagined in a modern setting that makes it all but unrecognizable. The four men, in trunks and bathrobes, hang out in a drained swimming pool, with a litter of poolside accompaniments: loungers, drinks table, changing screen, a gleaming never-lit barbecue at the centre. The closed-in space of *The Walworth Farce* was partly naturalized; the equivalent setting of *Penelope* is entirely surreal. 'Outside of here there must be a world', says Burns at the start of the play's last long speech (Walsh, *Plays: Two*, 185). But there is no evidence of it, no character equivalent to Hayley in *The Walworth Farce* entering from an identifiably normal outside reality. This is a play premiered in 2010 and early on there is what seems to be a coded fable about the economic collapse of 2008. The children's story of the Magic Porridge Pot is a book that is taken to speak of 'the fast development of an unstable economy': 'What the pot needed was regulation' (Walsh, *Plays: Two*, 143–4). The suitors are all businessmen and their dog-eat-dog competition for Penelope speaks to the ruthless pursuit of commercial success. Burns, the most clear-sighted of the four, puts it to the narcissist Dunne that it is not Penelope's love that he seeks: 'She's an object to you, an ending, another deal!' (Walsh, *Plays: Two*, 174). There is even a hint of the much more far-reaching coming catastrophe of climate change when the time and temperature are given out; at 11.30 a.m. it's already '[t]hirty-three degrees Celsius'—'That's hot and early' (Walsh, *Plays: Two*, 141). But for all these resonances of real-world disasters, as so often in Walsh, the stage space is its own place, with its own laws.

A minor work of Walsh is called *How These Desperate Men Talk*. The men in *Penelope* are desperate indeed and they certainly talk enough. One reviewer of the play's premiere spoke of it as 'word-drunk', another instance of Walsh's 'lust for language'.[20] The men are desperate because, on the basis of a shared premonitory dream, they know Odysseus is about to return to execute his violent revenge. They decide temporarily to co-operate with one another, allowing each suitor the opportunity to woo Penelope, in the hope that any winner will forestall the annihilation of all of them by the wronged husband. Dunne, the man who so loves himself and his body, gives a ludicrously histrionic version of an erotic seducer's speech, in which he has to be prompted by his rivals. (In the Irish premiere the part was played by Denis Conway, who had played Dinny, the self-appointed actor-manager in *The Walworth Farce*.) Fitz, the burned-out drug-addled older man who sits reading Homer, after a rocky start to his courtship

[20] Michael Billington, 'Penelope', *Guardian*, 26 July 2010.

speech, produces a surprisingly effective offering based on the nothingness of himself and a purely imagined life: 'Place my glorious nothing self in this nothing house and bask in nothing' (Walsh, *Plays Two*, 169). Quinn is the dominant figure in the group, equivalent to Homer's Antinous, brashest of the suitors, the unequivocal spokesman for the *Realpolitik* of unceasing competition. His pitch for Penelope is a virtuoso cabaret in which, with lightning costume changes, he plays all the parts in a succession of famous doomed lovers: Napoleon and Josephine, Rhett Butler and Scarlet O'Hara, Romeo and Juliet, John and Jackie Kennedy. But by this point the other three men are in revolt against Quinn and knife him to death. It is left to the younger Burns, who begins as submissive servant to the others, to mourn the death of Murray, the fifth suitor who has committed suicide the night before, and who stands for an unrealized idea of love and friendship. All this is of no avail. The play ends with the actual staging of the sinister dream as the dormant barbecue bursts into flames and 'Burns, Fitz and Dunne stare over it and into their death' (Walsh, *Plays: Two*, 187).

By the use of a CCTV camera, each of the men's performances is doubled: performed live but silently watched on a television by Penelope who lurks behind a scrim at the back of the stage, curtained off inside the house at a level above the pool. Initially, the audience sees her only through the scrim watching the relayed monologue of Dunne with no indication of reaction. Fitz's speech, however, interests her enough so that she stands up, 'raises the curtain and looks down on Fitz. For the first time we see her true beauty. She hasn't aged. She is a woman in her early twenties' (Walsh, *Plays: Two*, 171). This is a key stage direction, as it makes clear that Penelope is not the grass-widow of Odysseus who has spent twenty years awaiting his return, but a phantasm, a pure projection of the men's desire. Before Quinn's show, she actually comes out of the house and stands beside the pool, looking down at the men: 'There's an intensity to her. She's waiting. Something is going to happen' (Walsh, *Plays: Two*, 181). But it is not clear whether it is Quinn's performance for which she is waiting or the return of Odysseus which the men sense is now imminent. Equally ambiguous are the tears that fill her eyes at the end of the speech of Burns, and the final stage direction in which she 'turns and looks offstage and into her new future ...' (Walsh, *Plays Two*, 187).

Many of the obsessions in the play are those of the playwright with the minutiae of the branding—Speedo swimming trunks, a Taunton Deluxe Barbecue—and the music: the jaunty tune 'Spanish Flea' played by the 1960s band Herb Alpert and the Tijuana Brass is heard on the stereo early on in the play, and a succession of their love songs accompany Quinn's show at the climax. But at the centre of the action is the men's obsession with Penelope. Male erotic desire, if it can be called that, is seen as a surrogate for their competitive need for power, control, and success. It is no surprise, in a Walsh play, that this should erupt into violence with the killing of Quinn. However, the revolt against Quinn is precipitated by an unexpected speech of Dunne in which he remembers a moment of maternal tenderness from his childhood: 'From our little kitchen this love breathes out into the world' (Walsh, *Plays: Two*, 181). And it is in the name of some such emotion that is not self-interested, not just the outgrowth of the male ego drive, that Burns declares in his final speech, 'I can't let love die' (Walsh, *Plays: Two*, 186). But that declaration comes too late, as the men face extinction from the overwhelming violence of the superhero Odysseus.

McPherson and Walsh stage men driven by addiction and obsession, dependent on women whom they abuse or idolize. Homosocial bonding is glimpsed as an alternative to the always unsatisfactory relationship of men to women. In *Dublin Carol* there is John's hero-worship of Noel, the 'good man' who rescues him and returns him to something like a normal life. Burns pines for Murray in *Penelope*, maintaining that it is 'possible for a platonic love to exist between two men' (Walsh, *Plays: Two*, 164). But Murray is dead, having killed himself out of despair, and Noel is terminally ill in hospital. The concentration of both playwrights is on the psychopathological behaviour of the men, lives distorted by need, incapable of actual relationship. As audiences we are drawn into the imaginative spaces that such men occupy without a secure perspective from which to judge or diagnose them. These are not suitable cases for treatment, just men in their own ineluctably knotted masculine condition.

Supernatural Stories: *The Seafarer* and *Terminus*

The supernatural has always been a part of McPherson's theatrical vocabulary. As far back as *St Nicholas* (1997) there was the theatre critic and his encounters with the vampires, and *The Weir*, of course, was an aggregation of ghost stories. Both *Shining City* and *The Night Alive* end with surprise apparitions, in one case the dead wife that has haunted her guilty husband appearing to the therapist that has been treating him, in the other the junkie prostitute Aimee showing herself to Tommy as the beautiful vision he wants her to be. So, the devil playing cards for Sharky's soul in *The Seafarer* is not so uncharacteristic of the playwright, improbable as it may seem in an otherwise naturalistic play. For O'Rowe, however, *Terminus* appears to have been a venture into quite new territory. The use of narrated rather than staged action had been a preferred mode in *Howie the Rookie* and in *Crestfall*, graphic violence a feature of all his work. But the demon with a body all composed of worms who comes out of nowhere to save narrator B's life—this is something different for the playwright, like the stylized rhythmic rhyming of the narration.[21] Both plays move the drama beyond psychology on to a metaphysical plane.

---

[21] O'Rowe rewrote *Crestfall* in a comparable mode for its publication in 2011 but this was not the style of the original Gate production of 2003: see Lonergan, *Irish Drama and Theatre Since 1950*, 93.

The Seafarer takes its title and epigraph from the Old English poem, in which the lonely seafarer laments his lot 'in the paths of exile/ Lacking dear friends'.[22] McPherson's central character Sharky has worked on boats, jobs he can no longer get because of his drunken aggression, but the dear friends from which he is isolated are very different from those imagined in the original. In the Anglo-Saxon culture within which the poem was written, the greatest tragedy was to be excluded from the hall, the companionship of the *comitatus*, and the bounty of your lord. The all-male group that features in the play are the men who congregate in the house of Sharky's blind brother Richard; Sharky is physically there with them but feels himself to be apart. Far from the attractions of the Old English hall, where men are honoured among men by their 'ring-giver', McPherson evokes his setting of '[t]he grim living area of a house in Baldoyle. [...] The place lacks a woman's touch. It has morphed into a kind of bar in its appearance' (McPherson, *Seafarer*, 3). If it was a bar, however, it would certainly lose its licence. Graphic noises off suggest the appalling state of the bathroom. Ivan looking to fill Richard's cup with whiskey, empties out the tea then 'rubs the steaming carpet with his foot' (McPherson, *Seafarer*, 21). One of the running gags of the play is the war the outraged householder Richard wages with the 'winos', the group of homeless people who camp in the backyard, the downmarket counterparts of the drinkers inside. It is in vain that Sharky, temporarily off the drink, tries to bring some order to things—tidying up, lighting fires, preparing food; he is mercilessly berated by his brother as a party pooper for his pains.

In *Dublin Carol* McPherson had represented the solitary alcoholic. In *The Seafarer* we meet a group of drunks, each with their distinctive form of alcoholism. This is brought out at the start of act II, where they are in the midst of a card game, a drab Dublin counterpart to the colourful poker night of Tennessee Williams's *Streetcar*. 'Ivan's intoxication is constant, he coasts along, veering neither up into euphoria nor down into depression. It is his efficient life-state, removed, yet heavily present'. Nicky, by contrast, the man who is now living with Sharky's estranged wife, 'is a euphoric drunk. His genuine love for friends and comrades is freed'. Richard 'can lurch from sentimentality to vicious insults within seconds', while Lockhart 'is a philosophical drunk, yet prone to deeper maudlin feelings' (McPherson, *Seafarer*, 52). With the exception of Lockhart, all of these men know one another well, have a shared history going back years. They exist within a completely identifiable social space; a whole series of actual public-houses are mentioned, plausibly within the vicinity of Baldoyle, in the pub-crawl Nicky describes.[23] It is an offstage world populated by the sleazy sounding figures of Big Bernard, Steady Eddie, and Mungo Mickey.

---

[22] Conor McPherson, *The Seafarer* (London: Nick Hern Books, 2006), 1, quoting from Richard Hamer's translation.
[23] See my 'Urban Alienation in McPherson's Dublin', *Hungarian Journal of English and American Studies*, 20.2 (2015), 51–8.

The plot of *The Seafarer* is based on one of the stories associated with the notorious eighteenth-century Hellfire Club in which a stranger joins a card game, only to be detected as the devil by his cloven hooves.[24] But there is no smell of sulphur off Mr Lockhart who 'looks like a wealthy businessman and bon viveur' (McPherson, *Seafarer*, 36), deferred to by the others on the basis of his class superiority; he is fully naturalized within the situation. No-one except Sharky, with whom he has his Faustian pact, ever discerns who he is. Readers of the play text, where act I is headed as 'The Devil at Binn Eadair' (Irish for nearby Howth), will be alerted to what is to come, but audiences watching the Christmas drinking session get under way can have little idea. Lockhart is fluent in the language of his fellow drinkers: 'Sure I might as well be shit-faced as the way I am', he shrugs, accepting a glass of poteen (McPherson, *Seafarer*, 55). It is only when alone with Sharky that he finally identifies himself: 'I'm the son of the morning, Sharky. I'm the snake in the garden' (McPherson, *Seafarer*, 47). Twenty-five years before, when Sharky had been locked up for killing a vagrant in a fight, Lockhart/Satan secured his release, having lost to Sharky at cards. But the deal was that he should have his revenge twenty-five years on, and if Sharky loses, his soul is forfeit.

In *Dublin Carol*, McPherson evoked the state of self-destructive desolation of the alcoholic. Here he equates it with damnation. The representation of the devil is theologically quite orthodox. The otherwise clubbable Lockhart surprises the men by saying he does not like music—'any music' (McPherson, *Seafarer*, 71). When alone with Sharky, he explains why. In heaven, '[a]t a certain point each day, music plays. It seems to emanate from the very sun itself. Not so much a tune as a heartbreakingly beautiful vibration in the sunlight shining down on and through all the souls' (McPherson, *Seafarer*, 78). It is of this celestial harmony of the spheres that he is forever deprived. Lockhart conjures up Hell for Sharky by reminding him of what it was like as an alcoholic wandering the streets alone:

> You're on your own and no-one knows who you are. And you don't know anyone and you're trying not to hassle people or beg, because you're trying not to drink, and you're hoping you won't meet anyone you know because of the blistering shame that rises up in your face and you have to turn away because you know you can't even deal with the thought that someone might love you, because of all the pain you always cause.
>
> Well, that's a fraction of the self-loathing you feel in Hell, except it's worse. Because there truly is no one to love you. Not even Him. (McPherson, *Seafarer*, 77)

To be damned is to have lost God's love and grace forever.

---

[24] See Patrick Lonergan, '"I Do Repent and Yet I Do Despair": Beckettian and Faustian Allusions in Conor McPherson's *The Seafarer* and Mark O'Rowe's *Terminus*', *ANQ*, 25.1 (2012), 24–30 [29 n. 2].

The play builds to the card game in which Lockhart will play for Sharky's soul. Up until near the end, Sharky has managed to stay sober in spite of the taunts of his brother for his lack of sociability. But he is so driven to despair by Lockhart's merciless attack that he starts to drink again. Immediately, we see the violent aggression that alcohol triggers in him, as he quarrels with Richard over the inheritance of the house, with Nicky over Eileen, his estranged wife, and challenges Lockhart to a fist fight outside. Soothed down by the men into embarrassed apologies, he prepares for the last hand of poker in which he knows he will lose. Sure enough, Ivan's four fours, topped by Sharky's four eights, are beaten by Lockhart's triumphant four tens. Sharky is doomed and will have to go with Lockhart to disappear into 'the hole in the wall': the ATM is the ironically appropriate way down to hell in this 2006 play just before the collapse of the Celtic Tiger.

However, a final twist of the plot saves Sharky at the last minute. The very short-sighted Ivan, who mislaid his glasses some time in the course of the drinking session of the night before, at last refinds them and discovers that what he thought was a hand of four fours was actually four aces, the highest poker of all. So, Lockhart has not won after all, and Sharky is spared. Act II, entitled 'Music in the Sun', concludes with an amplified happy Christmas ending. As Lockhart leaves—the devil is excluded on the morning of Christ's nativity—the light under the Sacred Heart, which has failed repeatedly through the action, 'blinks on. The first rays of dawn are seeping into the room' (McPherson, *Seafarer*, 102). The men will go off to attend an early Mass at the Friary. Wrapped under the Christmas tree are presents from Richard to Sharky and Ivan—new mobile phones, symbols of the connectedness from which the isolated seafarer is excluded. It is left to Richard to point up the lesson to Sharky with characteristic abrasiveness: 'We all know you're an alcoholic and your life is in tatters and you're an awful fucking gobshite. We all know that. But you know what? You're alive, aren't you?' (McPherson, *Seafarer*, 103).

The Seafarer plays extremely well and won enthusiastic reviews when it opened at the National Theatre in London in 2006, transferred to New York in 2007, and was finally seen at the Abbey in Dublin in 2008. But there are troubling features to its handling of the subject. The appalling conditions in which the men live and drink attracts a sort of scandalized laughter in the audience; there is a carnivalesque enjoyment of the extremity of the squalor. Sharky might possibly be redeemed by the love of a good woman, the wife of his current employer with whom he has fallen in love, and who has given him the CD of John Martyn singing 'Sweet Little Mystery' on which the play ends. But, given his past record, the chances are not good. Otherwise, women are only represented in the angry offstage wives, the nagging voices of the reality principle that the men evade. Tellingly, Lockhart imagines the feelings of the streetwalking, seafarer-like Sharky in his loneliness: 'you see all the people who seem to live in another world all snuggled up together in the warmth of a tavern or a cosy little house' (McPherson, *Seafarer*, 77).

The companionship of the tavern comes before the domesticity of the house. For all the damnable state of alcoholism—and it seems Ivan is another of Lockhart's victims—it is still the all-male camaraderie of the drinking buddies that provides the play's soft landing.

Without the disguised devil playing cards for Sharky's soul, *The Seafarer* would be just a realistic version of a Christmas drinking session. The three intercut narratives of *Terminus* constitute a radically surreal fantasia. The demon with a body made up of worms who miraculously intervenes to stop B falling from a crane is only the beginning. The demon identifies himself as the soul of C who has been traded to the devil for the gift of singing and who is out to revenge himself on C for this betrayal. There is an interlude in which B and the demon make passionate love. The demon, however, is being pursued by a group of angels, also formed out of worms, because he has improperly stopped B from dying as she is fated to do. A violent combat between angels and demon ensues, with worms flying on all sides, until B persuades her defender that the case is hopeless, and she accepts her death. The demon finally catches up with C, hanging him up by his disemboweled entrails on the arm of the crane. This is not your average night and morning in Dublin.

Violence was a feature of O'Rowe's work from the start but the body count in *Terminus* is well up on anything earlier: five murders, two suicides, and a fatal car crash. By way of gender equity, there is plenty of woman-on-woman aggression. When A, the older woman working for the Samaritans, sets out to help Helen, a former student, who is about to abort her near-term baby, she has to encounter Celine, Helen's vicious lesbian lover. A is twice brutalized by Celine before she finally manages to stop the abortion going ahead by gouging out Celine's eyes and beating her to death with a hurling stick. The male narrator C, however, stands out even in this catalogue of horror. In his first monologue we learn of his 'severe affliction: an overpowering fear of women, all my life, my propensity, when in their company, to flee for fear of getting sick; and at nearly thirty-six years old, my longing to hold or even kiss one'.[25] He makes his pact with the devil for the power of singing which, he hopes, will allow him sufficiently to impress women to overcome his pathological desire for / terror of them. Like all deals with the devil, though, it does not work: he finds he is too shy to ever sing in company. He takes out his frustration instead in serial killing. We see him first at a country dancehall, picking out the least attractive woman present, going back to her house, and in the midst of anal sex ripping her body open with his knife.

The brutal violation of the body is a recurrent feature of the play. It is with a sharpened stick that Celine and her mates plan to penetrate Helen's womb, impaling the unborn baby. In the play's climax, the demon drives his tail through C's

---

[25] Mark O'Rowe, *Terminus* (London: Nick Hern Books, 2007), 16. All further quotations are taken from this text.

rectum right up into his body. We are reminded repeatedly of the fragility of the human body and its mortal corruptibility. The demon is a soul escaped out of hell who explains why he appears made up of worms 'to make the ethereal corporeal' (O'Rowe, *Terminus*, 25). In scholastic doctrine, angels are only visible when embodied in forms of air; in O'Rowe's play they, like the demon, are composed of worms. Living flesh is always potential wormsmeat. C controls a premature erection when dancing with his chosen partner/victim: 'I imagine, as I always do, a crew of woodlice; loathesome, heinous; crawling from the tip of my penis. And like that, it wanes and wizens until it isn't a problem any more' (O'Rowe, *Terminus*, 14).

There is a jauntiness in C's narrative, enforced by the rhyming, that anaesthetizes the moral sense. After his bloody murder of the woman, he 'headed for the latrine, keen to clean myself of the blood and the gore. Sure, isn't that what a shower is for?' (O'Rowe, *Terminus*, 17). Where the hoods of *Made in China* share the delights of Nik Naks, it is Lockets that C sucks, savouring their taste as accompaniment to his murderous pleasure. As a supreme act of charity, he gives his packet of Lockets to the hitchhiker Shane, dying after C has crashed the car: 'I sit beside him, hold his hand, say, "Munch away, my friend, I understand"' (O'Rowe, *Terminus*, 31). The grotesquerie of the play is always on the cusp of comedy. The demon, C's soul, suffers from a similar craving to his host. He escaped from hell, he explains to B, because '[w]hatever the price, I had to touch a woman'. But, where with C this need is turned to sadistic violence, the demon is a touchingly shy lover before B, as he fumbles for speech: 'There's a gap as he stares at his lap and squirms and a hundred thousand worms turn red in a blush' (*Terminus*, 28). *Paradise Lost* seems an unlikely intertext for O'Rowe's play, but there might be an echo here of the passage where Raphael, asked by Adam about whether angels have sex, replies 'with a smile that glowd/ Celestial rosie red, Loves proper hue' (VIII, 617–19).

Terminus is O'Rowe's most ambitious and original play and his most successful to date. It is cleverly constructed, as the monologues, which appear initially disparate, gradually come together, with light bulb moments when we realize the demon is C's soul, B is A's long alienated daughter, and the movie which A and B remember watching together years before was the 1988 comedy drama *Beaches*, with its hit song 'Wind Beneath My Wings' which C will sing in his death throes. What, though, are we to make of that ending? Patrick Lonergan notes the influence of Tom Murphy's *The Gigli Concert* with its Faustian theme and its conclusion in song.[26] Yet there is a difference. In Murphy, JPW King, the quack therapist, takes over the Irishman's longing to sing like Gigli at the end of an intensive co-dependent relationship that makes up the action of the play. The singing of the final lamenting aria from Donizetti's *Lucia di Lammermoor* is a hardwon triumph. By comparison, the emotion generated by C's singing before the crowd of

[26] Lonergan, "'I Do Repent and Yet I Do Despair'", 25, 29.

Dubliners gathered below where he hangs on the crane seems unearned. In the conclusion of the final monologue, C glories in his performance:

> I'm overwhelmed with exultation, but also stunned by the realisation that what I've just done is, without question, worth what's to come, and in addition to this, that its bliss-inducing memory will do more for me to ease whatever suffering is in store for me when I enter into Hell ... (O'Rowe, *Terminus*, 48)

Are we supposed to go along with this emotion, to forget C's vicious misogyny and his psychopathic killings by imagining him singing a sentimental pop song? In *The Seafarer* McPherson founds his concept of damnation in the recognizable experience of the self-hating alcoholic and (whether plausibly or not) reverts to conventional Christian iconography for his happy ending. In choosing a cartoonish unreality of demons and angels, O'Rowe moves *Terminus* beyond any emotional actuality.

So, what *is* it with men? Whether we attribute it or not to some wider global crisis of representation, toxic masculinity is on display in McPherson, O'Rowe, and Walsh in a variety of forms. All these plays are more or less contemporary with the period of their production, the first decade of the twenty-first century, but none of them appear to relate in obvious ways to the social conditions of the time.[27] The diasporic Irish mentality anatomized in *The Walworth Farce* is generic rather than historically specific, a metatheatrical pastiche of emigrant plays like Jimmy Murphy's *The Kings of the Kilburn High Road* (2000). The epic source of *Penelope* dislocates it from any definite context. The spaces in which the male characters live and operate, even when identifiably urban and suburban Dublin as in McPherson and O'Rowe, do not significantly condition their lives. Psychological origins are sometimes offered for the behaviour of the men: John in *Dublin Carol*, with his abusive father, C with his pathological fear of women in *Terminus*. There is perhaps overcompensation for underlying insecurities in the macho violence in which they indulge. Their dependence on drink, their relationship with women, bespeak radical failures in self-esteem. The dysfunctional features of their lives are even raised into a Manichaean conflict of good against evil in *The Seafarer* and *Terminus*.

McPherson spoke in interview about his attempt to capture 'the delusional quality of male reality' in his plays.[28] But how far is it placed as delusional in his work or that of O'Rowe and Walsh? There is bound to be a tendency with plays about men written by men to identify the mentality of the characters with that of the

---

[27] I remain unconvinced by Lonergan's main argument that the Faustian pact of *The Seafarer* and *Terminus* relates to the banking crisis about to hit Ireland shortly after the plays' first production in 2006–7, ingenious though it is, in his '"I Do Repent and Yet I Do Despair"'.

[28] Quoted in Christopher A. Grobe, 'Love and Loneliness: Secular Morality in the Plays of Conor McPherson', *Princeton University Library Chronicle*, 68.1–2 (2006–7), 684–704 [690].

playwrights, all the more since all three of these writers have taken to directing their own plays, moving from author to *auteur*.[29] O'Rowe felt the need to rewrite parts of *Howie the Rookie* 'to make clear that he does not personally share his characters' view of women'.[30] Of course, it is naive to see dramatic fictions as voices for their creators. Yet the very fact that male characters so dominate the stage in these plays is suggestive. Veteran reviewer Michael Billington, in an admiring review of *The Night Alive*, remarked 'I'd like to see a McPherson play in which the woman is not a singular and extraordinary presence'.[31] In almost all these plays we do see women only through the eyes of men as objects of uncomprehending adoration or victims of abuse. For all the frequently appalling actions of the male characters, an audience may be drawn into empathy with them for want of another theatrical vantage point. There is at times an indulgence of, even a complicity with, their self-preoccupations. It is in part in reaction against such plays where men are allowed to strut their stuff, whine about their discontents, that the theatre of women writing about women was conceived, the subject of the next chapter.

---

[29] McPherson has directed his own plays from *Shining City* in 2004, O'Rowe from *Terminus* in 2007, and Walsh from *The New Electric Ballroom* (2008).

[30] Lonergan, *Irish Drama and Theatre Since 1950*, 193, quoting a personal interview with the author.

[31] Michael Billington, 'The Night Alive', *Guardian*, 20 June 2013, https://www.theguardian.com/stage/2013/jun/20/the-night-alive-review (accessed 22 December 2023).

9
Women Writing Women

In her 'Author's Note' to *The Wheelchair on My Face* (2011), her one-act play about getting glasses for the first time as a child, Sonya Kelly describes the context:

> a pre-perestroika 1980s Ireland that was essentially the eastern Europe of western Europe, wriggling free of its theocratic vice grip, the ritualised hyper-feminisation of girls in the guise of purity rituals like the first holy communion, the fear of not complying, growing up a gay child, the fear of not being beautiful and the intoxicating first brush with counter-cultural ideology.[1]

The 'theocratic vice grip' was still very much there in 1980s Ireland. This was the period of the Eighth Amendment which enshrined in the Constitution the right to life of the unborn child, effectively making any form of termination of pregnancy legally impossible; in the 1983 referendum, it was passed with a 66% majority.[2] A second referendum in 1986 to remove the constitutional ban on divorce, even though backed by the then Fine Gael / Labour Party coalition government, was rejected by an almost equally strong majority. But the references to eastern Europe and *perestroika* in Kelly's description, writing in 2017, implies the changes that were to come. After the long period of Soviet-like control when the so-called Marriage Bar forced women to give up their jobs in the public service on marriage, when the Catholic-influenced 1937 Constitution seemed to restrict women to work within the home, the wall was about to fall. A second referendum in 1995 legalized divorce (if by the slimmest of margins), the 2015 referendum gave same sex couples equal rights to marriage, and in 2018 the Eighth Amendment, prohibiting abortion, was repealed by almost exactly the same majority that had enacted it thirty-five years before.

Women playwrights in the twenty-first century sought to represent women's experience in Ireland's repressive past and its changing present, while also exploring the legacy of centuries of patriarchal dominance: 'It's not a good time to be a woman right now', says Woman in Marina Carr's *The Cordelia Dream*. 'It hasn't been a good time to be a woman since the Bronze Age.'[3] And there has been no

---

[1] Sonya Kelly, *The Wheelchair on My Face*; Noni Stapleton, *Charolais*; Margaret McAuliffe, *The Humours of Bandon* (London: Methuen Drama, 2017). This is the edition used for quotations from *The Humours of Bandon*, discussed below.

[2] For the context here, see Fintan O'Toole, *We Don't Know Ourselves* (London: Head of Zeus, 2021), 336–50.

[3] Marina Carr, *Plays: 2* (London: Faber, 2009), 246.

shortage of women playwrights to represent their experience. One of the startling features of the male-dominated Abbey programme for 2016, which started off the #WakingTheFeminists movement, is just how many female dramatists were working at the time, several of whom had been staged by the Abbey itself. So, for example, Nancy Harris's *No Romance*, a series of three interlinked one-act plays, had been produced in the Peacock in 2011. Following the 2009 success of Elaine Murphy's *Little Gem*, her play *Shush*, featuring an all-female cast of five, was commissioned and staged by the Abbey in 2013. Stacey Gregg had her first full-length play *Perve* produced by the Abbey and, at the very time of #WakingTheFeminists in the autumn of 2015, *Shibboleth* (discussed in an earlier chapter) had just finished its run in the Peacock. Other companies had also contributed to the emergence of women playwrights. Druid, in their series of 'Druid Debuts', gave a rehearsed reading to Abbie Spallen's first play *Abeyance* in 2001. Rough Magic provided a platform for a number of female dramatists, including Morna Regan (*Midden*, 2001), Hilary Fannin (*Phaedra*, 2010), and Kelly (*How to Keep an Alien*, 2014). The Fishamble 'Show in a Bag' series represented an opportunity for writer performers to showcase their work in a low-budget portable form and, as in the case of Kelly's *Wheelchair* and Margaret McAuliffe's *The Humours of Bandon* (2016), this was to lead on to highly successful national and international tours.

Rape and sexual assault did not feature in many Irish plays before 2000 but playwrights since then have confronted the violence against women so long a more or less taboo subject.[4] A stage adaptation of Louise O'Neill's novel *Asking for It* (2018) dramatized the way the rape victim is blamed for what has been done to her; two plays in the 2021 Dublin Theatre Festival, Caitríona Daly's *Goose Goose Duck* and Geoff Power's *Stronger*, in very different ways, followed through the consequences of sexual violence. In 2022, Deirdre Kinahan in *Outrage* and ANU in *The Wakefires* exposed the assaults suffered by women in the revolutionary period. In this chapter, I want to focus on three earlier plays that centre on sexual abuse: Marina Carr, *On Raftery's Hill* (2000); Abbie Spallen, *Pumpgirl* (2006); and Deirdre Kinahan, *Rathmines Road* (2018).

Even when not subject to violence, Irish women have lived within the constraints of traditional patriarchal gender roles. One way to challenge such constraints has been through defiantly mocking performance. As playwright/performers, Kelly with *How to Keep an Alien*, McAuliffe in *The Humours of Bandon*, and Sarah Hanly with *Purple Snowflakes and Titty Wanks* (2021) achieve liberation by satirically subverting the expectations laid upon them. Those gender roles, however, remain deeply problematic, particularly for those like the transgender protagonist of Gregg's *Scorch* (2015) prosecuted for gender fraud, or the central character in Harris's *Somewhere Out There You* (2023) who is driven to create a romcom narrative for herself. Women playwrights in the twenty-first century

---

[4] One exception is Graham Reid's *Dorothy* (1980).

have shown what Irish women have endured in the past and its psychological consequences; they have mocked the absurdities, indignities, and distortions imposed upon them; and they have dramatized the continuing difficulties created by fixed gender boundaries.

Confronting Violence

In May 2000, I was in Washington for the two-week festival 'Island: Arts from Ireland'. It was an initiative of Jean Kennedy Smith, former US Ambassador to Ireland, designed to showcase the best in Irish music, literature, theatre, and film. One of the plays chosen was Marina Carr's *On Raftery's Hill*, which came to Washington just after its premiere in Galway in a co-production by Druid and the London Royal Court. I was there at the opening night in the resplendent 1,100 seat Eisenhower Theater in the Kennedy Center. The great and the good of Washington were assembled, no doubt many of them friends of Smith herself. Act I ended with the all-but onstage rape of a daughter by her father. Eighteen-year-old Sorrel had her clothes ripped from her by Red Raftery, and she is pushed down on to a table: 'Now, this is how ya gut a hare. (*Stabs knife in table.*) Blackout'.[5] I have never heard such stunned silence from an audience before finally there was a nervous spatter of applause.[6] Whatever ideas of Ireland they might have had, from *The Quiet Man*, *Ryan's Daughter*, or even *Dancing at Lughnasa*, nothing could have prepared them for this.

On Raftery's Hill followed immediately after the Midlands Trilogy, *The Mai* (1994), *Portia Coughlan* (1996), and *By the Bog of Cats …* (1998), which had made Carr's name. In the new play she retained the very rough Midlands accent, spelled out on the page: terminal 'g's omitted, 'a' for 'of', 'thah' for 'that'. But the lyricism that had added grace to the language in the earlier work had all but disappeared, and so had the folklore which gave the Trilogy its mythic dimensions. As one reviewer of the 2018 revival of *Raftery's Hill* put it, 'unlike most of Carr's other original works, there's nothing otherworldly in this depiction of suffocation, sexual violence and complicity in ugly secrets'.[7] This was an unrelieved picture of a grimly dysfunctional rural family. The three previous plays had women protagonists, unhappy, disturbed women, all of whom end up killing themselves in despairing protest at a world in which they could never feel at home. *On Raftery's Hill* was Carr's first play to be dominated by a brutally tyrannical patriarch from

---

[5] Carr, *Plays: 2*, 35. All further quotations from the play are from this edition.
[6] Apparently, 'many audience members left at the interval, or indeed walked out', according to Melissa Sihra, 'New Stages of Performing Carr', in Cathy Leeney and Anna McMullan (eds.), *The Theatre of Marina Carr: 'Before Rules Was Made'* (Dublin: Carysfort Press, 2003), 92–103 [97].
[7] Peter Crawley, 'On Raftery's Hill Review: A Striking and Pummelling Production', *Irish Times*, 2 May 2018, https://www.irishtimes.com/culture/stage/theatre/on-raftery-s-hill-review-a-striking-and-pummelling-production-1.3481560 (accessed 17 November 2023).

whom there is no escape, not even into death. The traumatized Raftery women are trapped by the law of the father and its warped mentality. It is a tragedy in which there is certainly fear, and some pity, but hardly the possibility of classical catharsis.

I coined the term 'black pastoral' to describe those texts of the 1990s that sardonically subverted traditional idylls of Ireland—Patrick McCabe's *The Butcher Boy*, Martin McDonagh's *The Beauty Queen of Leenane*, Frank McCourt's *Angela's Ashes*.[8] *On Raftery's Hill* is the blackest pastoral of them all. Carr here draws on predecessors within the Irish dramatic tradition. So, for example, the demented grandmother Shalome echoes Mommo in Tom Murphy's *Bailegangaire*, both stuck in the past. Shalome is always setting off to return to her long dead father in Kinnegar, like Mommo, who also wants to go home and is waiting for her father with his 'big stick'.[9] Carr channels Synge in florid execration, as with Dinah's curse on her mother: 'May she roast like a boar on a spih in the courtyards a Hell' (Carr, *Plays: 2*, 28). But the grotesquerie of *Raftery's Hill*, like the other black pastorals, goes beyond realistic representation in its all-out assault on any remaining pieties about rural Ireland.[10] Raftery's farm, '[t]hree hundred acre a the finest land this side a the Shannon and west a the Pale' (Carr, *Plays: 2*, 17), is littered with the unburied bodies of dead animals, stinking up the whole valley around. (One reviewer was reminded of Stella Gibbons's satiric novel *Cold Comfort Farm*).[11] There are, no doubt, neglectful farmers in Ireland who do not take adequate care of their livestock. But Red Raftery who cuts the udders off a cow, shoots her, and tips her in the river is hardly representative. The symbolic nature of the action is emphasized by Dara Mood, Sorrel's young suitor, when describing the incident: 'Cows is the most beauhiful creatures, gentle and trustin and curious, and they've these greah long eyelashes' (Carr, *Plays: 2*, 32). Raftery is driven by misogynistic hatred of the female in any species.

The stunned audience at the interval in the Kennedy Center had not yet heard the revelation of act 2: the daughter that Red rapes at the end of act 1 is also his granddaughter, product of his relationship with his older daughter Dinah, which is ongoing. If rape is a crime that goes regularly underreported, for obvious reasons incest is likely to be even less often prosecuted. In Carr's play, a parallel case in the neighbourhood of a daughter impregnated by her father is introduced early on. That one ends tragically, with the girl dying while she nurses her stillborn baby. What is significant here is Raftery's reaction to being told the story of the incest: 'Don't belave ud. Don't believe wan word of ud. Sarah Brophy goh whah

---

[8] Nicholas Grene, 'Black Pastoral: 1990s Images of Ireland', *Litteraria Pragensia*, 10.20 (2000), 67–75.
[9] See Tom Murphy, *Plays: Two* (London: Methuen Drama, 1993), 124.
[10] Eamonn Jordan comments on how the set of the Druid production emphasized this non-naturalistic dimension in *Dissident Dramaturgies* (Dublin: Irish Academic Press, 2010), 86–7.
[11] Michael Billington, 'On Raftery's Hill', *Guardian*, 5 July 2000, https://www.theguardian.com/stage/2000/jul/05/theatre.artsfeatures (accessed 16 November 2023).

was comin to her' (Carr, *Plays: 2*, 19). The denial of the facts and the blaming of the woman are characteristic. When later told that the father has killed himself by drinking weedkiller, he does not see incest as an occasion for suicide: 'Sure, even if he done to Sarah what they're all sayin he done, what did he have to go and down a mug a weedkiller for?' (Carr, *Plays: 2*, 42). Isaac, Raftery's hunting companion, though himself a semi-comic figure with his obsessive devotion to his cat, supplies a normative view here: 'I can't imagine how any father could do thah to hees daugher' (Carr, *Plays: 2*, 43). The play dramatizes the psychopathological case of Red Raftery and his family where incestuous rape is more or less accepted.

Raftery's highly toxic masculinity is related to his fear of losing authority and control. His relations with women he sees as an unending war between the sexes: 'give em an inch next thing you're wearin a bra' (Carr, *Plays: 2*, 21). His rape of Sorrel is triggered by overhearing her and Dara talking about their life together on the farm after he is dead. When Sorrel continues for weeks traumatized after the rape, her father urges reconciliation: 'We'll let bygones be bygones young wan. Just apologise to me and we'll say no more abouh ud'. Well indeed might Sorrel exclaim, 'Apologise to you!' (Carr, *Plays: 2*, 46). His son Ded is so terrorized by his father that he lives in the cowshed on a diet of calf food and sweets, playing his violin to himself, only venturing into the house when he is reassured that Raftery is absent. Yet Raftery wants a son instead of this wreckage of a man that his bullying has produced, and, in exasperation, is prepared to offer him anything: 'Ya want a new fiddle? The farm? Ud's yours if ya want? Jaysus, whah do ya want?' (Carr, *Plays: 2*, 25). Raftery oscillates between blustering denial—'No wan harmed anywan. No wan!' (Carr, *Plays: 2*, 49)—and efforts to bribe and placate those he will not acknowledge he harmed. At different times, each of his children is promised the farm, or a share in the farm; it will be part of the advantageous marriage settlement for Dara and Sorrel that Red proposes, which will allow him to go on pretending that nothing happened.

On Raftery's Hill is so devastating, however, in that it not only exposes the psychology of Raftery, but its roots and its consequences for the family. The women of past generations are associated with a gracious culture degraded by the men of the farm. Shalome, the only character who does not speak in dialect, remembers Dinah and Sorrel's mother: 'She was a lady. When she first came to the Hill we had musical evenings, card parties, dancing, always dancing, sandwiches and port wine and fruitcake all laid out in the parlour. But your father put a stop to all of that' (Carr, *Plays: 2*, 11). The strains of Ded playing his mother's violin in the cowshed is all that is left of this vision. But we can see the element of nostalgic fantasy in Shalome's genteel memories, like her recollection of her life with her mother in India. A tender femininity is always elusively elsewhere, barred from expression by the patriarchy. And within the Raftery family the women themselves are made complicit with the tyranny of the father. It was Dinah's own mother, she of the musical evenings, that first sent her to sleep with her father. Shalome stands accused by Ded of having failed to intervene when he dragged Dinah to be raped by Raftery. Although Dinah urges her father to spare Sorrel, she blames her sister/daughter for the violation when it has happened: 'For eighteen years I watched thah wan like a hawk, protected her from you, and what does the stupid little bitch go and do? Gives ouh abouh you under your own roof' (Carr, *Plays: 2*, 45). It is Dinah who voices the conventional male belief in sublimating sexuality in outdoor work: 'We should be allas workin the farm and there'd be none a this, everythin goes bockety when we don't be ouh workin the fields and the cattle and the pigs' (Carr, *Plays: 2*, 47). Sorrel herself is drawn into the distorted culture of the family, breaking with Dara over his criticism of her father: 'He's good at the back of ud all' (Carr, *Plays: 2*, 54). And she will not report the rape: 'she's a Raftery, a double Raftery, well versed in subterfuge' (Carr, *Plays: 2*, 47).

The audience at the Kennedy Center was right to be shocked; *On Raftery's Hill* is a shocking play. All through, there are references to humans behaving like animals, recalling Victorian simian caricatures of the Irish. 'We're a band a gorillas swingin from the trees' (Carr, *Plays: 2*, 58) concludes the disillusioned Sorrel. The inturned terrible world of the Raftery family may not be representative of Irish rural life as a whole. Yet Carr felt the need to put a graphic image of rape at the centre of the culture that produced it: a culture of ignorance, sexual repression, and silence. We get a glimpse of one sort of dysfunctional Irish marriage in Dara's vignette: 'My father's wan sad picnic in the rain. He never speaks to me mother, just kind a grunts and pints and sits in the corner drinkin cans a condensed milk and sighin to heeself' (Carr, *Plays: 2*, 32). It is an indictment of patriarchy—'Daddies never die' (Carr, *Plays: 2*, 59)—but it is an indictment also of the psychological and emotional poverties of an Ireland too long unexposed.

With their 300 acres, the Rafterys are 'strong farmers', looking down from their Hill in typical agrarian class consciousness on the 'scrubbers from the Valley' like Dara Mood (Carr, *Plays: 2*, 54). It is set somewhere unidentified in the Midlands, 'this side a the Shannon and west a the Pale', and in no particular time period. Spallen's *Pumpgirl*, by contrast, is quite precisely located in time and place. Though at the head of the text readers are only told, 'The play is set in a petrol station in present-day Ireland', it is clear that this is south Armagh, close to the Border.[12] And, with a reference to the birth of Geri Halliwell's daughter, the time can be pinpointed to May 2006, not long before the play opened at the Edinburgh Festival in August. This is a depressed area, economically and in every other way. The petrol station is doing almost no business: 'Surprised we get anyone in here these days. Diesel's cheaper in the South so the cars just fly on past' (Spallen, *Pumpgirl*, 12). Hammy McAlinden 'works in the local chicken hatcheries but the dole don't know' (Spallen, *Pumpgirl*, 16). He and the other two speaking characters live in

---

[12] Abbie Spallen, *Pumpgirl* (London: Faber, 2006), 9. This is the text used for all later quotations from the play.

a housing estate, like the one in Newry where Spallen herself grew up. These are people well down the social food chain and Pumpgirl (known only as that, even though her name Sandra is mentioned twice) is at the abject bottom.

Just eight years after the Good Friday Agreement, the play is set in one of the areas of Northern Ireland most affected by the Troubles, brought out in casual references in the text. There is 'the new hotel that got bombed in '94' (Spallen, *Pumpgirl*, 16), and 'that oul' burnt out library van [...] where two Prods were took and killed about fifteen years ago. Their families have stuck wreaths and things onto the trees. It looks well' (Spallen, *Pumpgirl*, 20). But this is not like the other post-Troubles plays discussed in Chapter 5; it is not centrally focused on the fall-out from the violence—the continuing nightmare of the 'disappeared', the failure to deal with legacy issues, the remaining animus within divided communities. It dramatizes instead the politics of gender, the relations between men and women in this dead-end social landscape. The play's form of three braided monologues by Hammy, his wife Sinead, and Pumpgirl continues a tradition initiated by Brian Friel with *Faith Healer* and continued by Conor McPherson and Mark O'Rowe, something commented on by many of the reviewers.[13] Spallen uses the divided narrative to bring us into the inner lives of the speakers, alienated from one another and from the impoverished world in which they live.

We meet Hammy first in the exhilaration of a stock-car race, his macho bravado enhanced by his soubriquet of No-Helmet, whatever the cost in bangs on the head: 'No-Helmet Hammy McAlinden cuttin' up the track. The pain, the ecstasy and mc' (Spallen, *Pumpgirl*, 13). Yet even he can see the tackiness of the winner's podium and the plastic trophy, with an announcer who does not even get his name right. He consoles himself by having sex with a woman he picks up in the pub, in spite of an initial brush-off that has him commenting vengefully: 'The ice bitch. The stuck-up cow. I'll bet she's not a real blonde. Look at her. Marilyn from the back, Manson from the front' (Spallen, *Pumpgirl*, 19). We see the other side of his non-relationship with Sinead in her monologue, describing how she lies in bed every night waiting for the same routine of his return from the pub, pretending to be asleep, 'with my hand stuffed in my mouth. I used to put it there to stop my crying, in the days when I gave a shite, but now it's only to stop up the laughin' (Spallen, *Pumpgirl*, 15). The deadly state of their marriage is rendered vividly in a later speech: 'the silence that's there between me and Hammy. The one with swearwords full of hate hangin' in the air makin' a smell like mould, like washin' left too long in the machine then hung out to dry' (Spallen, *Pumpgirl*, 31).

---

[13] See Carole Quigley, 'Living in a Rape Culture: Gang Rape and "Toxic Masculinity" in Abbie Spallen's *Pumpgirl*', in David Clare, Fiona McDonagh, and Justine Nakase (eds.), *The Golden Thread: Irish Women Playwrights 1716–2018*, Vol. 2: *1992–2016* (Liverpool: Liverpool University Press, 2021), 99–108.

In this situation where no-one has much occasion for pride or self-worth, Pumpgirl is the butt of everyone's jokes, an object of universal contempt. Dressing mannishly in reversed baseball cap and combats, she has introjected conventional male attitudes: 'I can't stand the women drivers' (Spallen, *Pumpgirl*, 12). Her lack of femininity attracts the derision of both sexes. The giggling girls in the car ask 'Well, we were just wondering like, if you were, like, a *man* or a *woman*?' (Spallen, *Pumpgirl*, 13); McCabe describes her as the 'one who walks like John Wayne and looks like his horse' (Spallen, *Pumpgirl*, 25). She is well aware of his predatory attitude, the 'oul' coyote face that's not for good-lookin' girls' (Spallen, *Pumpgirl*, 23). Rape here is an assertion of male power rather than an expression of desire.[14] The turns of the narrative bring a sickening realization that McCabe, who leads the gang rape of Pumpgirl, Hammy's lover, is the man who has just seduced his wife Sinead on the very same evening. Pumpgirl is only an instrumental object in the men's humiliation of Hammy. And yet, as she endures the male violence, half numbed with drink and drugs, it is herself she accuses: 'I can't help feeling I've done something wrong' (Spallen, *Pumpgirl*, 34). She even tries to console Hammy, the last of the four men to take her: 'he looks so sad I whisper in his ear, "It's okay"' (Spallen, *Pumpgirl*, 35).

In *Pumpgirl*, as in *On Raftery's Hill*, the rape happens at the end of the first act. But the sequel in the second act is very different. Pumpgirl seems to block out what has happened to her and reverts to her deluded belief that Hammy loves her, only staying with his wife 'because of the kids'. 'He's my friend. I'm glad he's my friend. There's no one in the world like Hammy. Me and Hammy talk for hours. We do' (Spallen, *Pumpgirl*, 44). Sinead, left pregnant by McCabe, is beaten up when she approaches him. He is terrified that the paramilitaries are after him and looks at Sinead as if 'I'm an almighty punishment squad, and isn't he the IRA punishee about to find himself up a ditch somewhere lookin' at his nuts in a black plastic bag' (Spallen, *Pumpgirl*, 47). As a released former inmate of Maghaberry where many political prisoners were held—hence his sardonic nickname of Shawshank—with a very well-appointed house south of the Border, he has no doubt good reason to be afraid. However, when he is told of Sinead's pregnancy, he only chuckles with relief and abandons her bleeding on the side of the road. The most remarkable change takes place in Hammy. Ashamed of his part in the rape, he takes revenge by burning McCabe's truck, but he is so overcome by guilt and remorse that he commits suicide. The master image of the play is the story Pumpgirl relates:

> this car that had gone into the bog up round Camlough. The people had been trapped inside. The car sank with them in it and they were there for ages, stuck, air running out, but no one could see it from the road except maybe the number

---

[14] For an overview of feminist theories of rape, see Lisa Fitzpatrick, *Rape on the Modern Stage* (Cham: Palgrave Macmillan, 2018), 3–11.

plate and only if you were lookin'. And when the car was dragged out they found marks in the ceiling, like animal scratches, and bits of the beigy white roof-plastic under the fingernails of the people inside. They'd tried to claw their way out of the car while they were dying in the dark. (Spallen, *Pumpgirl*, 20)

It is of this that Pumpgirl thinks as she is raped, and it sums up the claustrophobic despair of these people's lives.

It is a grim play indeed, which would be all but intolerable if it were not for the leavening of the writing: precise on detail, sharply observed on sights and smells, close up and impersonal, even funny by times. Together with her later plays, *Strandline* (2009) and *Lally the Scut* (2015), both of them exploring similar territory, *Pumpgirl* helped her to win the 2016 Wyndham-Campbell Prize worth $165,000—a prize Marina Carr was to win the following year. Having opened at the Edinburgh Festival in 2006, it went on to be staged at the Bush Theatre in London later that year, and had its Irish premiere at the Lyric Theatre, Belfast, in 2008. When it was revived for an Irish national tour in 2019, Spallen wrote about what she hoped would be its impact in terms of increased empowerment of women victims of rape. She had attended a Finnish production and the 'day before the play opened I read an article where a spokesperson from the local Rape Crisis Centre said they were expecting a rise in calls after the production. If one young girl can watch this play and dial that number then I have done something useful'.[15] *Pumpgirl*, however, is less directly didactic and monitory than this makes it sound. It is a vivid dramatization of the psychological and emotional dynamics that produce the rape at its centre.

Those who attended the production of *On Raftery's Hill* in Washington, those who saw *Pumpgirl* in Edinburgh or in Shepherd's Bush in London, were watching the lives of others, rural or working-class Irish. By contrast, for the audience at the Peacock Theatre in Dublin where *Rathmines Road* was staged as part of the 2017 Dublin Theatre Festival, the characters were people like themselves. Sandra and Ray are middle-class professionals in their 30s, who work in television in London. Their two children are being looked after by a grandmother while they return to Ireland to sell Sandra's old-fashioned house in the Wicklow village of Glenealy. They do not speak in Carr's heavy Midlands accent, nor yet in Spallen's sharp Armagh demotic. Theirs is the standard English of educated Irish people of the time. Dairne, a school friend of Sandra, who joins them, has transitioned from her former self as David, a further sign of twenty-first-century Ireland. At times it seems as if the play is to be a farcical sitcom where everything goes hilariously wrong: Ray tries to light a fire, but the long-disused chimney belches smoke; Eddie, husband of the estate agent Linda (another school fellow of Sandra and Dairne),

---

[15] Abbie Spallen, 'On Touring Pumpgirl', http://decadenttheatrecompany.ie/playwrights/abbie-spallen/ (accessed 20 November 2023).

gets stuck in a low-slung chair, turning over everything in his efforts to free himself; Linda hurts her ankle going to help him. But there is something much more seriously the matter: Sandra has recognized Eddie as one of the men who raped her in a student flat on Rathmines Road twenty-odd years ago.

Rathmines Road appears to be a conventionally naturalistic play told through realistic dialogue. There are no monologues here, as in *Pumpgirl*, giving us access to the inner thoughts and feelings of the characters. Sandra tells Dairne of the rape when the others are out of the room, looking over the house. But what we see, after an initial morning after scene, is the night before—as it might have played out. So, in scene 2 we have the set-up, Dairne and Sandra's awkward catching up conversation, the introduction of Ray, Sandra, and Eddie, all the mishaps over the fire and the chair, Sandra's odd behaviour. But then in the extended scene 3, alternative versions of what might have happened are offered. Sandra relives the event in nightmarish detail: how a group had gone to a flat after a drunken night in a club, she had been dancing and having sex with one man, who then held her down as she was assaulted by two others, including Eddie, who raped her from behind, smashing her nose against a wall. Hearing all this, Ray attacks Eddie, who denies the charge; Eddie and Linda storm out, indignantly threatening to go to the police to report the false accusation. But there is another sequel, in which Linda and Eddie come back, pleading with Sandra not to tell her story. Eddie is now headmaster of a school, and the accusation of the rape will ruin him and destroy their family. He is finally brought to confess, reluctantly and ashamedly, that what Sandra says is true.

The play exposes the context of the rape. There is the appalling men's conspiracy, which was not just a one-off event; it was some 'sort of student game they used to play'.[16] As Eddie later says: 'I knew they did this ... They bragged about it. They said that girls loved it ... They said that girls agreed ...' (Kinahan, *Rathmines Road*, 86–7). There is the trauma experienced by Sandra, with two years' breakdown in London after the experience, and continuing panic attacks. Linda makes a vehement speech protesting at the sexist attitudes towards all women, while Dairne talks of the persecution she experienced as a boy who felt herself to be female. But, most damagingly, we see the distrust that the revelation causes in Ray, Sandra's loving husband, whom she credits with having rescued her from the deep self-loathing caused by the rape. At first, he is inclined not to believe her: 'Rape!', he says to Dairne. 'That would affect everything? You couldn't keep it ... you couldn't just keep that down could you?' (Kinahan, *Rathmines Road*, 60). Later, even after he accepts that it is true, their relationship is shadowed by the fact of the rape that she has kept from him. 'Now everything ... everything is starting to feel like a lie' (Kinahan, *Rathmines Road*, 96). And this is what decides Sandra not to expose

---

[16] Deirdre Kinahan, *Rathmines Road* (London: Nick Hern Books, 2018), 55. All other quotations from the play are taken from this text.

what has happened to her: 'I can't do it. I can't. I will destroy everything' (Kinahan, *Rathmines Road*, 98). So, the play ends with a repeat of the opening scene, with Ray and Sandra having just made love on the couch in the sitting-room, Ray knowing nothing except that Sandra behaved rather oddly the night before, sending Linda and Eddie away, and deciding not to sell the house.

Deirdre Kinahan is a prolific playwright with a range of different sorts of work including the gentle *Halcyon Days* (2013) about the relationship of two people in an old people's home, and *An Old Song, Half Forgotten* (2023), a moving play built around an actor suffering from Alzheimer's. *Rathmines Road*, however, is designed as a case study showing all the reasons Sandra can*not* confront her rapist, can*not* tell her husband what has happened to her, can*not* and could *not* go to the police. This is the deliberate intention of the play, as Kinahan makes clear in her preface to the text, headed 'A Reckoning'. She comments on the 'reckoning' represented by referenda and tribunals in which contemporary Ireland has been coming to terms with its past. 'Unfortunately there are many areas in which we still fail and fail spectacularly. In *Rathmines Road*, I want to explore our collective response to accusations of rape and sexual assault, and our complete failure judicially, socially and culturally, to negotiate the dreadful consequences of these crimes' (Kinahan, *Rathmines Road*, iv). Though the play was quite powerful in performance, with Karen Ardiff in the lead, its weakness was in the very programmatic nature of its subject and structure. Neither *On Raftery's Hill* nor *Pumpgirl* suffer from this sort of palpable polemic design. What the three plays share, however, is a confrontation with the sexual violence inflicted on women through so much of Ireland's history, the need to show on stage in all its ugliness the truths that a patriarchal culture sought to deny, conceal, and repress.

Performing Freedom

In 2009 Abbie Spallen remarked, '[t]here are so many actors writing these days, and if they are mostly women, it's about women wanting to write good parts for women'.[17] This was certainly true of Margaret McAuliffe, Sonya Kelly, and Sarah Hanly, all of whom wrote plays that offered them the chance to show their talents as performers. *The Humours of Bandon*, *How to Keep an Alien*, and *Purple Snowflakes and Titty Wanks* were more or less autobiographical, on the principle that you should write what you know. McAuliffe was remembering her own time in traditional Irish dance competitions; Kelly created a comic version of the efforts to allow her Australian partner to stay with her in Ireland; like the character in her

---

[17] Abbie Spallen, quoted in Sara Keating, 'Lines in the Strand', *Irish Times*, 18 November 2009, https://www.irishtimes.com/culture/stage/lines-in-the-strand-1.773843 (accessed 23 November 2023).

one-woman show, Hanly had moved from Ireland to London to train in musical theatre. The plays provided arresting parts for the writer/performers. More than that, though, both in their narratives and in the performances themselves, they claimed a freedom from the restrictions imposed upon them by their gender.

Humours was an extraordinary tour de force in performance, with McAuliffe not only playing all the parts with their different voices—the young dancer Annie O'Loughlin-Harte, her long-suffering Cork-accented mother, her Dublin dance teacher Assumpta, and rivals from the North—but dancing to illustrate the dialogue. It has been a huge popular success from its first showing in Dublin in 2016 with national and international tours continuing to May 2023 in Washington, DC. The social context is deftly sketched in: the mother from middle-class Sutton, bewildered at the prospect of trekking right across the city to the Basketball Arena in working-class Tallaght where the dancing competition is held, on the phone to a friend after a whole day in the packed stadium—'tis like being in steerage on the *Titanic*'.[18] The politics of the competition is dramatized, the deadly rivalry masked by reciprocal compliments and obligatory sporting smiles by the losers.

From the beginning we are made aware of the pain inflicted on the dancer's body, with the tying of the curlers in Annie's hair overnight. 'Are they very sore?', asks the mother. 'Yeah', comes the reply, 'and wherever I put my head down, s'gonna kill me but I wanted them tight, they have to be tight' (McAuliffe, *Humours*, 75–6). The appearance of the girls was all-important in traditional Irish dancing, but (before *Riverdance*) it was strictly not sensual. As McAuliffe explained in interview: 'All of the dancing takes place really using the bottom half of your body. The upper half of your body is very straight, and your hands are down by your sides'.[19] To avoid any suggestion of the erotic, the girls' costume has to change when they are adults, as Annie remarks: 'Once ye turn eighteen, you've to start wearing black tights. (*Shrugs shoulders.*) Something about indecency? Or that it's inappropriate?' (McAuliffe, *Humours*, 86). The arc of the first parts of the narrative is fairly predictable: Annie comes third in the under-17s and is heartbroken; in the open competition the next year she wins and becomes national champion. But when it comes to the time to 'defend her title', as her teacher Assmpta puts it, she has become disillusioned, and in an act of complete defiance she dances not to the traditional 'Napoleon's Retreat' but vigorously, with full physicality, to Michael Jackson's 'Smooth Criminal'. It is a dance that outrages all present but represents her act of independent liberation: 'I have a skill. I have a niche skill and I can use it any way I like. I don't have to stay here and defend anything, but myself' (McAuliffe, *Humours*, 100).

[18] Kelly, *Wheelchair*, Stapleton, *Charolais*, McAuliffe, *Humours*, 80.
[19] Celia Wren, 'Irish Arts Group Solas Nua Brings "The Humours of Bandon" to D.C.', *The Washington Post*, 22 May 2023, https://www.washingtonpost.com/theater-dance/2023/05/22/solas-nua-the-humours-of-bandon/ (accessed 23 November 2023).

If *Humours* showcased McAuliffe's dancing skills, *How to Keep an Alien* makes comic capital out of Kelly's ineptitude, cast as an actor in a play where she is supposed to be able to dance. It is here that she meets Kate, the assistant stage manager who shares her satiric impatience with the production, and they fall in love. Kate, however, is about to be deported to Australia, having come to the end of her temporary visa in Ireland. This, as the play's subtitle has it, is 'a story about falling in love and proving it to the government'.[20] If Sonya and Kate can show that they have been living together for two years and are in a permanent relationship, then Kate can be granted a *de facto* visa. There are all the ups and downs of their love, when they are separated, get together again temporarily when Kate lands a job in Scotland. The play comically sends up the bureaucratic procedures that they have to go through to 'prove' they are together, with echoes of the film *Green Card*, when Sonya has to coach herself through the details of Kate's life. Sound effects, supporting dialogue from Justin Murphy playing the stage manager of the show, fill out the sense of contemporary life with its absurdities from the inadequacies of Skype-speak through the background music of Ryanair flights.

But Kelly shows her awareness that the lovers' difficulties are First-World problems, with the intercut letters from Ann Flanagan, Irish ancestor of Kate, and the terrible hardships of nineteenth-century emigration to Australia. And throughout the play there is a dog that doesn't bark: at no point is there any comment on the fact that this is a gay rather than straight relationship. A turning-point for Sonya, nervous about going to Australia to meet Kate's family, is the whole-hearted letter of support for the visa application from Mary-Anne, Kate's mother: 'Despite the fact that I have never met Sonya, I know that if Kate travelled to the other side of the world to be with her, she must be a truly special person' (Kelly, *Alien*, 280). The happy ending comes with the arrival of the visa, affirming a situation where, for all the formal obstacles, the love of a same sex couple is generally accepted.

Purple Snowflakes and Titty Wanks—the very title is designed to be provocative. The protagonist Saoirse calls herself a 'purple' because she dislikes the word 'lesbian'; she overdoses on snowflakes of cocaine when performing in a pantomime in Dagenhan; Jack O'Quiffe looks for a 'titty wank' from Saoirse in the church car park, jerking off between her undeveloped 16-year-old breasts. The play begins as it means to go on. Saoirse tells her friend Aisling that 'I'm just veryvery horny', and she has 'learnt how to make my own orgasms' with the aid of anal beads.[21] She goes to the nun Sister Patricia in her convent school for instructions on how to give a satisfactory handjob or blowjob: 'how do you pleasure a man without knowing how to?' (Hanly, *Snowflakes*, 19). You would suppose that a

---

[20] Sonya Kelly, *How to Keep an Alien*, in Patrick Lonergan (ed.), *Rough Magic Theatre Company: New Irish Plays and Adaptations, 2010–2018* (London: Methuen Drama, 2020), 253. All further quotations are from this edition.

[21] Sarah Hanly, *Purple Snowflakes and Titty Wanks* (London: Faber, 2021), 11. This is the edition used for all further quotations from the play.

play concerned with anorexia and bulimia, featuring bondage sadomasochism, in which the central character has a near-suicidal breakdown, might be fairly sombre stuff. But in Hanly's one-woman performance it was made often hilariously funny. It is a very angry play, but the anger is turned into shamelessly satiric laughter.

The first target of satire is the Irish Catholic Church, a church that has lost virtually all its authority in the twenty-first century and maintains only the thinnest hypocritical façade. Brenda, Saoirse's mother, lives with a priest, Father Mick, after her husband has disappeared—off to join an order of monks in Rome, as it later comes out—and they have to pretend he is dead to cover the scandal of his disappearance. Mrs O'Heffer, the school principal as St Maria's Enniskerry, is on easy first name terms with Brenda, asking casually after Father Mick when she rings up to report that Saoirse has been 'speaking sexu-ally' about 'cunnilingus'—'it's oral sex, I believe'; Saoirse's punishment is to be taken out of normal classes and put into a drama club where she can exercise her talents playing Creon in the school production of *Antigone* (Hanly, *Snowflakes*, 21–2). On her last day in school after she has been expelled, Saoirse has full sex for the first time with her friend Orla (who gave her the anal beads) in the 'holy room', the convent oratory. Interrupted by Sister Patricia, the two appear before Mrs O'Heffer. Saoirse is leaving, so beyond punishment, but Orla who is remaining in the school is warned: 'Be aware who you talk to. Or—Do. That—not on our premises' (Hanly, *Snowflakes*, 38). In other words, do whatever you like, but do not give scandal to the Church.

Inadequate sex education is the least of the shortcomings of life as a teenage girl in *Purple Snowflakes*. 'Women', Saoirse protests to Sister Patricia, 'are conditioned to do what they're told—We are not Taught how to say: No' (Hanly, *Snowflakes*, 19–20). That is what leaves Saoirse at the mercy of boys like Cónal Flynn and Jack O'Quiffe. Both Saoirse and Aisling suffer from eating disorders. The tragic turn in the narrative comes late on in the play when we realize that Aisling has died from anorexia at the age of 20, and the conversations that Saoirse has with her for much of the action are all in her head. It is the news of Aisling's death, we learn retrospectively, that has brought Saoirse close to killing herself in the earlier scene on Southend Pier. Saoirse suffers from bulimia, with the effects of vomiting different foods spelled out in appallingly funny detail: 'I fucking love chocolate, the thing about chocolate is it tastes just as good coming back up as it does going down' whereas cornflakes 'scratch my oesophagus on the way back up' (Hanly, *Snowflakes*, 24). Though Saoirse leaves for England to escape her Irish conditioning, training in musical theatre school is just another form of body dysmorphia, as the women obsess about their bodies: 'they're all measuring each other's waists with tapes and eating lettuce' (Hanly, *Snowflakes*, 45). In fact, it is a vicious circle of self-loathing that drives her to need to act, as she tells the silent psychiatrist: 'You play other people because you have idea who you really are. Your body is a constant reminder you are not worthy to live in it because you don't take yourself seriously so nobody else does too' (Hanly, *Snowflakes*, 62).

Hanly says that she used Elaine Aston's *Feminist Theatre Practice* as her theoretical framework for the play when it was being developed during her time as a student at the Mountview Academy of Theatre Arts.[22] The play as a whole is a strong feminist protest against what Saoirse calls 'the paternal law' (Hanly, *Snowflakes*, 14). She desperately does not want always to be given the male role in the school plays but is forced to take on Creon. At the performance, she guys the part with a pair of fake testicles (which she takes out of her bum bag like all the portable props she needs), and, holding them aloft, shouts out 'Do you have any idea what you have done to our women?' (Hanly, *Snowflakes*, 31). Challenging her set role in the script here is like Annie's dancing to Michael Jackson in *Humours*, a public act of dissent. In the published text of the play, there is a figure of a Giant who voices conventional sexist attitudes, explained by Saoirse when she revolts against him: 'I am so fed up of this giant fucking voice, hardwired in my head so that a world based on balls-only constructs, led by *just* men, can remain enforcing rules, on the body, basic human rights' (Hanly, *Snowflakes*, 72). Giant was omitted from the play in performance, probably for good reason: the allegory based on Jack the Giant Killer, the pantomime in which Saoirse plays Jack, was one level too many in a complex play. But the vehement rejection of the 'paternal law' is fundamental.

In an earlier draft, Hanly gave the central character her own name Sarah and it was her anorexic friend who was Saoirse.[23] Both Saoirse and Aisling are common Irish names, but their meaning in Irish—Saoirse = freedom, Aisling = dream vision—is given significance when Saoirse imagines herself buying the family home, and turning it into a 'sisterhood', a 'gal pad': 'A freedom dream. Saoirse Aisling' (Hanly, *Snowflakes*, 89). The upbeat ending to the play seems somewhat forced. Saoirse returns home for the First Communion of her niece Gabriella who, already at 7, represents a next generation feminist complaining about differential rates of communion presents: 'Tom made more money off his and that's not fair' (Hanly, *Snowflakes*, 90).

Purple Snowflakes has many of the characteristics of a first play; it is a bit showy, a bit self-indulgent, even self-congratulatory. But Hanly has a good deal to congratulate herself about. The triumph of the play came in the writing and the performance. As Hanly said in interview, 'giving the woman the agency in the storytelling, allowing her to stand on stage telling stories that are obviously creations of a world that encapsulates an imbalance of power: that in itself is an affirmative

---

[22] Tamara A. Orlova, 'Theatre Review: Purple Snowflakes and Titty Wanks', *Ikon: London Magazine*, 6 February 2018, https://www.ikonlondonmagazine.com/Theatre-Review-Purple-Snowflakes-and-Titty-Wanks (accessed 25 November 2023).
[23] See Orlova, 'Theatre Review'.

action, an empowering thing'.[24] The female-authored play takes back control from the (usually male) playwright. But the sheer level of energy, skill, and control of the performer is also a declaration of mastery. And this is true of all three of the texts considered in this section. The plays allow the writer/performers to mock themselves, expose their weaknesses and their messed-up states of mind and body, while the theatrical performances tell a different story. McAuliffe can make fun of her obsession with winning in the absurd traditional Irish dance competitions, and then shows just what she can do in her own terms with the skills she has acquired. Kelly can afford to betray her lack of dancing skills, her apparent failure as a stand-up comedian, because the whole show, with its quicksilver jokes and its virtuoso acting, contradicts that image of the loser. Hanly represents the suffering body of a deeply disturbed young woman, yet she is so physically fit, so technically skilled, that, alone on stage, she can completely command an audience for an hour. These are women who show what women can do as theatre makers in spite of all the sexist prescriptions laid upon them.

Other Selves

'You play other people because you have no real idea who you really are'. Acting for Saoirse may be a way of masking confusion but in *Snowflakes*, as in *Humours* and *Alien*, the performance is an affirmation of the performer herself. Theatre, however, can tell other stories of other selves. Stacey Gregg's *Scorch* centres on Kes, born female who identifies as male and, having had sex with his girlfriend, is tried and convicted of gender fraud. The first face-to-face encounter with his girlfriend Jules, playing the part of a boy constructed online is for him '[m]ore real than real life'.[25] Similarly, Casey, the protagonist in Nancy Harris's *Somewhere Out There You*, refuses to accept the part assigned her by her family as the plain, patronized sibling, disabled by mental illness, always contrasted with her successful sister. Both plays, in their different ways, challenge the narratives of boy-meets-girl romantic comedy, dramatizing instead the shifting nature of the performed self.

Scorch opens with Kes telling stories of his childhood, an 8-year-old girl who likes waistcoats rather than dresses and wants to pee standing up, the shock he feels when boobs '[j]ust pop up overnight', his addiction to game shows where he always plays the 'dude', his first meeting up with Jules online. Then there is the stage direction: 'Full house lights. We are a support group' (Greg, *Scorch*, 14, 16).

---

[24] Sara Keating, 'An Irish Catholic Fleabag? This One-Woman Show Is Darker and More Disturbing', *Irish Times*, 29 September 2021, https://www.irishtimes.com/culture/stage/an-irish-catholic-fleabag-this-one-woman-show-is-darker-and-more-disturbing-1.4682043 (accessed 25 November 2023).

[25] Stacey Gregg, *Scorch* (London: Nick Hern Books, 2016), 21. All other quotations from the play are from this edition.

From this point on the play, staged in the round, becomes a play within a play, as the audience sees Kes emerge, listens to his narrative, as though in a LGBTQ+ encounter meeting. Given that the play was first staged at the Outburst Queer Arts Festival in Belfast in 2015, it was likely that the spectators would have been quite comfortable in that role. Kes certainly senses sympathy and is exhilarated by the opportunity to tell his story: 'Circle's nodding, listening. First time I'm saying any of this. Out loud. To you. Now. Voluntarily'. He has just been telling about the joy of first sex with Jules, and the ecstasy he feels here is a compound of postcoital elation and the liberation of being able to speak of himself: 'Want to kiss kiss SNOG everyone in the circle, not in a sexy way, just. Drunk on freedom. I'm Kes. Birds spring from my heart feel I feel alive' (Greg, *Scorch*, 24).

Gregg comes from Northern Ireland and makes use of a Belfast background in *Shibboleth* and her earlier play *Lagan* (2011). But she has also used non-specific settings in *Perve* (2011) and *Override* (2013). While *Scorch* might possibly be set in Belfast—in the original Belfast production Gregg used local young people for the voiceover section of comments on Kes's conviction—it exists primarily in a virtual online world of gaming, video, and film.[26] One film in particular obsesses Kes: 'there's this movie—watch it a zillion times—this guy dresses as a girl to get the girl. I *love* that movie' (Gregg, *Scorch*, 17). This is probably *Anything for Love* (1993), a romcom in which a bullied boy dresses as a girl and wins the love of both the bully and his sister. The Shakespearean situation sorts itself out eventually and boy, revealed as such, duly gets girl.[27] The images and references that Jules and Kes share are all taken from popular movies; they can recite together whole lines from *Terminator 2*. Kes tells himself that Jules is more or less aware of his biological gender: 'Guess, she knows, or. Prefers not asking. An understanding. You know?' (Gregg, *Scorch*, 23). He thinks of himself as a 'lead in a crazy romcom', and when all is revealed, his family will happily accept the situation: 'Kind of think it'll be like the movies. In the movie it'd all be over and there'd be tears but they'll hug me and say (*Recorded movie voice.*) "we love you just the way you are"'. But he discovers, '[i]t isn't like the movies' (Gregg, *Scorch*, 20, 28).

The build-up of the love affair feels very like a romantic comedy: from the initial encounter online, first Skype meeting, to full consummation; even the breakup with Jules when she discovers the truth about Kes feels a part of a standard story. But then comes the court summons and the trial. He is initially convinced that the jury will understand: 'I know, once the jury hears my story, once they ask Jules what really happened [...] I know they'll see I've been the perfect boyfriend, respectful. That I love Jules. And she loved me' (Gregg, *Scorch*, 29). Kes cannot

[26] In the Drama Online text, the setting is given as Northern Ireland: https://www-dramaonlinelibrary-com.elib.tcd.ie/playtext-detail?docid=do-9,781,784,604,011&tocid=do-9,781,784,604,011-div-00000002&actid=do-9,781,784,604,011-div-00000015 (accessed 30 November 2023).
[27] See https://en.wikipedia.org/wiki/Anything_for_Love (accessed 28 November 2023).

associate his relationship with Jules with the crimes of which he is accused: 'sexual assault by penetration', 'fraud', 'abuse'. But, under the force of those accusations, he 'glitches and disintegrates', being made to feel that his 'body is this weird black hole I drag round' (Gregg, *Scorch*, 29–30). And he is duly sentenced to three years in prison, with his name placed on the sex offenders' register. The play had its origins in similar cases for gender fraud in the UK, discussed in a preface to the published text, and it in part works as a protest against the injustice of such prosecutions (Gregg, *Scorch*, 3–9). But its power lies in the touchingly ordinary feelings of a teenager in love that Kes shows, and the way in which the self he creates in that experience is destroyed.

More than most playwrights, Nancy Harris likes to keep her audience guessing. In *No Romance*, the first two one-act plays feature apparently unrelated situations: a needy woman goes to have her photo taken in absurdly mythological costume; a husband and wife quarrel beside the laid-out corpse of his mother. It is only in the final play that we discover that the pornographic materials, mentioned in the first two episodes, are created by an aged woman, with her own unhappy history, about to be moved into an old people's home by her harassed son. In *The Beacon* (2019) there is the mystery of the long-ago disappearance at sea of Michael, husband of Beiv, the woman artist suspected of his murder, not least by her aggressively hostile son Colm; but then there is a second unexplained disappearance of Colm's recently married American wife. In the play's final scenes, the wife reappears and Beiv throws completely unexpected light on the death of her husband. In both plays, Harris uses the technique of uncertainty and mystification to explore the complexities of sexual identity and the shifting dynamics of surface stories.

Somewhere Out There You starts with a disconcerting jump from a prologue, featuring a headmaster interviewing a mother about her son who has come to school dressed as Cleopatra, to the start of the main play, where Casey has invited her family to meet her new boyfriend Brett. Her parents Alan and Pauline, her sister Cynthia, and brother-in-law Eric are sceptical of the love at first sight narrative that Casey and Brett gushingly retell, and frankly incredulous when told that the couple are getting married. But the experience of marriage of both the couples is not likely to make them take the romantic view. Pauline and Alan are divorced; Cynthia, discontented in her marriage, is constantly sniping at Eric. And there is indeed something forced sounding about the Casey/Brett relationship. One explanation is offered when we see both of them, separately, discussing their psychological problems with what appear to be therapists. But it is not until act 2 that we discover that the supposed therapists, Sebastian and Tess, in fact run a theatrical agency that supplies actors to provide boyfriends, girlfriends, and even marriage partners (so-called 'lifers'), to meet the specs of their paying customers. Brett is in fact performing in Casey's script. And only in the epilogue are we given confirmation that Brett is the adult version of the little cross-dressing boy of the prologue.

Somewhere sends up the conventions of romantic comedy and has great fun doing it. There are speeded up cameos of Brett and Casey's romantic walk round Dublin, 'like an old-fashioned Hollywood silent movie', and their weekend in Paris 'as seen in a Hollywood movie from the 1940s'.[28] As Casey enthuses about the visit to Paris, the artificiality of the narrative is pointed up by Cynthia: 'Everything can't be so wonderful and so great and so perfect all the time. This is real life' (Harris, *Somewhere*, 64). The romance of first meetings is particularly exposed to cynicism, and Cynthia sneers at Eric's version of their own story: 'It's basically a romcom— we get married in the end'. As she now sees it, his accosting her in the supermarket and offering her an opening in television was just a pick-up—'[h]e gave me the job so he could get in my pants' (Harris, *Somewhere*, 80). Cynthia is the antagonist of the play, and the scenario seems to be going along predictable lines when she and Brett become attracted to one another and fall into one another's arms. But there are more twists and turns along the way to the final big discovery scene, the wedding rehearsal dinner that goes disastrously awry.

'Somewhere out there you': the title with its implied ellipsis dots seems to point towards the romantic concept of the true love waiting to be discovered on some enchanted evening. But that is just the stereotype that the play systematically deconstructs; the 'you' that is 'somewhere out there' is the elusive self not the complementary other. Within this context there can be no assured opposition between illusory role-playing and true reality. On the face of it, Casey's story of her love affair is just an attempt to offset her depressed conviction that she is always, inevitably, a failure; as she says herself to her assembled family in the last scene: 'I wanted you to see me as someone different. Someone who could go for romantic walks in a city, or take a trip to Paris and buy scarves. I wanted you to see me as someone who a person like Brett might fall in love with' (Harris, *Somewhere*, 138–9). For Cynthia, of course, this represents a satisfactory admission of defeat by her sister: 'You can't buy love, Casey. It has to come *naturally*. Be natural. That's the only way to know if it's true' (Harris, *Somewhere*, 139). Cynthia is convinced that the feeling she now has for Brett is true because it is natural and spontaneous. But the play as a whole casts doubt on the very category of the 'natural' when it comes to social behaviour. Cynthia is living out the role of the sexy successful sister—now gripped with jealousy—just as her mother continues to cling to the self-deceiving belief that she is the one true love of Alan's life, and he will return to her.

Somewhere gives the audience what they want from a romcom, the happy ending where Casey and Brett come together in a passionate embrace, but not in the form that they might expect. Brett has been shown up as an actor engaged in several contracts, as the gay Italian partner of the writer of detective stories from down the country (a bit implausibly introduced in the last scene), as well as Casey's

---

[28] Nancy Harris, *Somewhere Out There You* (London: Nick Hern Books, 2023), 47, 63. This is the text from which all other quotations from the play are taken.

fiancé. Casey gives up: 'I'm terminating the contract as of this minute', she tells Sebastian, who has appeared as the prospective celebrant of the wedding (Harris, *Somewhere*, 140). However, Brett declares his desire to continue: 'I want to stay with you, Casey, if you'll let me', not as the happy ever after monogamous husband but in the three days a week relationship they have had, which might include going on working as partner to other people the rest of the time. 'The only thing I've ever wanted in life is be someone else' exclaims Brett. 'And no one would ever let me be it' (Harris, *Somewhere*, 141). *Somewhere* not only plays games with the clichés of film and theatre. Like *Scorch*, it radically dismantles the concept of stable identity and affirms the validity of constructed selves.

Both the Abbey and the Gate now have women artistic directors, Caitríona McLaughlin and Róisín McBrinn, and, for the first time ever in 2023, the two theatres produced plays by women as their main Dublin Theatre Festival offerings: *Somewhere* at the Abbey, and Erica Murray's *The Loved Ones* at the Gate. For its Christmas show the Abbey revived Behan's *The Quare Fellow* with its cast of twenty-two male characters played by fifteen women and non-binary actors. The theatre has announced the Gregory Project for 2024: to commemorate 120 years since its establishment, it is to honour Lady Gregory, one of its co-founders, with productions of seven plays by women (though Gregory is not among them).[29] There are to be two premieres of work by Marina Carr, an original play *Audrey or Sorrow*, and *The Boy*, an adaptation of the Oedipus plays, planned for 2020 but deferred because of Covid. Mary Manning's *Youth's the Season—?*, first produced at the Gate in the 1930s, will be revived, as will Elizabeth Kuti's *The Sugar Wife* (2004). *Dublin Gothic*, a new play by Barbara Bergin, will be staged, and two more adaptations, Hilary Fannin's version of Gorky's *Children of the Son* and Nuala Ní Dhomhnall's Irish language translation of Aeschylus's *The Persians*. Retrospective compensation is being made for that almost all-male 2016 programme that provoked the #WakingTheFeminists movement. There are now more opportunities for women theatre makers as actors, directors, and designers. And women playwrights over the last twenty years have shown how women have suffered as victims of sexual assault, what they can achieve as writer/performers, and the restricted and distorting gender roles that they are called upon to play. This is now a central part of what constitutes Irish theatre.

---

[29] See https://www.abbeytheatre.ie/whats-on/the-gregory-project/ (accessed 29 November 2023).

State of Play 3

2020–2

The year 2020 started normally. January and February are always slack months, with the Christmas shows and the pantos running on, but there were some twenty new productions, mostly small scale. Then in mid-March, in Ireland as across the world, everything stopped. The Druid production of *The Cherry Orchard* in Tom Murphy's version, which had opened in Galway, did not make it into Dublin as planned. *The Fall of the Third Republic*, Michael West's most ambitious political play (the Corn Exchange), with its large cast on the Abbey main stage, was cancelled mid-run and the company given six hours to leave the theatre. There were then no live performances for six months. In September 2020, I queued to have my temperature taken and, masked up, I entered the Watergate Theatre in Kilkenny to see the Rough Magic adaptation of Mike McCormack's novel *Solar Bones*. Stanley Townsend gave a superb performance in the one-man show, and at the end the audience of some fifty socially distanced people in the 328-seat theatre tried to give it the ovation it deserved. (Happily, it was revived for a national tour in 2022.)

The industry responded quickly to the crisis. The Abbey mounted an online series called *Dear Ireland*, in which fifty dramatists, fifty performers, were commissioned to deliver brief pieces as postcards to the nation.[1] The Irish National Opera put up *Twenty Shots of Opera*, giving a range of composers, singers, and directors an opportunity to experiment with a form normally confined to full-scale productions.[2] As live performance began to be possible again in 2020 and 2021, outdoor sites were favoured. In October 2020, a dramatization of Patrick Kavanagh's *The Great Hunger* was given a peripatetic staging in the grounds of the Irish Museum of Modern Art, Kilmainhan (Abbey/IMMA), and in the same month Druid produced DruidGregory, a composite of five of Lady Gregory's short plays, in a tour starting in the gardens of Coole Park. Bewley's Café Theatre, normally confined to the tiny space at the top of the Grafton Street café, in the spring of 2021 staged a Walkabout Theatre series of one-act plays in Phoenix Park and Stephen's Green. Theatre happened in unlikely places: an adaptation of a Mary Lavin short story *In the Middle of the Fields* (Lime Tree Theatre) was played outside the medieval walls of Kilmallock, Co. Limerick in July 2021; the following year, *Disapppearing*

---

[1] See https://www.abbeytheatre.ie/dear-ireland/ (accessed 2 December 2022).
[2] See https://www.irishnationalopera.ie/20-shots-of-opera/operas (accessed 2 December 2023).

Islands (Performance Corporation) was staged on a pier in Belmullet, looking out across the Atlantic.

Through the latter part of 2021, however, and 2022, there was a damburst of deferred shows. This included many revivals of plays by modern Irish playwrights that had achieved classic status: Sebastian Barry's *The Steward of Christendom* (Gate), Marina Carr's *Portia Coughlan*, Brian Friel's *Translations*, and Tom Murphy's *A Whistle in the Dark*, all in the Abbey in 2022. There were no less than three productions of Beckett's *Happy Days*, by Landmark as an online show in 2021, a staging by Blue Raincoat in 2022, and (outstandingly in 2021) a Company SJ and Abbey Theatre Irish-language version, *Laethanta Sona*, on Inis Oirr in the Aran Islands where Winnie (Bríd Ní Neachtaín) faced the audience in a mound clad in limestone flags matching the gray of sky and sea behind her. As the Decade of Centenaries continued, so did the commemorative shows. To mark the centenary of the 1920 Bloody Sunday shootings, *14 Voices from the Bloodied Field*, a series of playlets about the victims, was filmed by the Abbey in the Croke Park scene of the event, while ANU's *The Secret Space* and *The Book of Names* in 2021 both similarly related to the period of the War of Independence. ANU also had two shows, *All Hardest of Women* and *Lolling*, that took off from episodes in *Ulysses*, as the centenary of the publication of the novel was celebrated in 2022 in a multi-disciplinary project Ulysses 2.2., in which ANU partnered with Landmark and the Museum of Literature of Ireland (MoLI).

In many ways, therefore, after the hiatus of the Covid lockdown, it was business as usual in the Irish theatre. But the period 2020–2 also saw various sorts of increasing diversification: diversity in the media used for theatrical shows, diversity in the representation of sexuality, and racial diversity. It is on these three that I want to concentrate in this final report on the state of play in Irish theatre.

Media

Video projections have long been a part of live theatre in Ireland, used particularly effectively, for example, as the point of view of the dying A in Michael West's *Freefall*, discussed in Chapter 2. Lockdown, however, forced companies to put performances online and to think creatively about the uses that could be made of virtual technologies. So, for example, Frank McGuinness's *The Visiting Hour* (2022) was transmitted online from inside the empty Gate Theatre as the meeting of a daughter separated by a pane of glass from her demented father in a geriatric hospital, representing the conditions of lockdown. In 2021 Pan Pan produced a four-part film, *Mespil in the Dark*, about the artistic community in the Dublin Mespil flats, before staging a live (and largely unrelated) play of the same title in 2022. During the 2020 lockdown, a striking experiment in what constituted live theatre came with *To Be a Machine (Version 1.0)*, credited to the company

Dead Centre and Mark O'Connell, whose book on robotics provided the basis for the show. Jack Gleeson, who had become famous as the evil King Joffrey in *Game of Thrones*, was performing live in the Project Theatre Upstairs, but the seats were not filled with actual audience members but with the screened images that all of those 'attending' the show had created as videos. Those of us watching on our laptops at home saw individuals in the theatre laugh, or the whole audience nod off. At one point, all the seats were filled with replicas of the one 'person' the actor was addressing. The book, which investigated the issue of transhumanism, became a dramatization of mind and body, technically fascinating, at times beautiful (Figure 8).

Go to Blazes, one of the last of the Ulysses 2.2 project from 2022, was created by David Bolger as a combination of live performance and virtual reality. It was staged in the studio space of Bolger's Coiscéim Dance Theatre as a response to 'Calypso', the fourth episode of *Ulysses*, in which readers meet Bloom for the first time. The famous opening line, 'Mr Leopold Bloom ate with relish the inner organs of beasts and fowls', and his particular enjoyment of kidneys, with their 'fine tang of faintly scented urine', was the cue for the first section where the dancer Justine Cooper spoke of the science of smell, passing round samples for the audience to sniff (urine and excrement among them). These were then illustrated by notes on the piano, bringing together smell and sound, before we moved into the virtual reality (VR) part of the show concerned with sight. Initially, all we saw when we put on our headsets was the figure of Bloom waiting for the lights to cross in an entirely contemporary Dublin—it was a feature of all the *Ulysses 2.2.* shows not to attempt any sort of re-creation of the Edwardian setting. But as he moved out of sight on his way to the pork butchers, the dancing began. Rosie Stebbing danced alone in a white costume, echoed in billowing white drapes behind, expressing the theme of metempsychosis expounded to her by Bloom in this episode, the words displayed on a screen above. Next there was a *pas de deux* between Jonathan Dowdall and Justine Cooper, using just a sheet and a table as props to represent the complex dynamics of Bloom and Molly. Finally, we saw Dowdall ascending a staircase to deliver Molly her breakfast in bed. What was so very striking was not only the translation of the various motifs of Joyce's text into another art form, but the use of the tiny bare brick studio, in which we sat, for dances that could not possibly have been staged there live while leaving any room for an audience.

Opera is included in the Awards scheme along with theatre, with an award going for Best Opera each year, and the operatic productions considered in the direction and design categories. For the most part, the Irish National Opera stages works from the canon, Mozart, Donizetti, Verdi, Puccini, and Strauss, while the Wexford Festival Opera produces more obscure works from the same historical repertoire. There were some original operas in 2022, however, such as *The First Child* (Irish National Opera (INO)/Landmark) a collaboration between Enda Walsh and composer Donnacha Dennehy; and Michael Gallen's *Elsewhere* (Straymaker / Abbey

Fig. 8 Jack Gleeson with virtual audience member in the Dead Centre production of *To Be a Machine (Version 1.0)*. Photographer Ste Murray. Courtesy of Dead Centre.

/ Miroirs Étendus / Once Off Productions), based on the strange episode of the Monaghan Asylum Soviet of 1919. Conor Mitchell's *Propaganda* (Lyric), staged in the same month as *Elsewhere*, was described as a 'new musical' rather than an opera. Based around the 1948 Soviet blockade of Berlin it used the full resources of the theatre—three-level set with walkways, video projections, jazzy period singing.

This full-works treatment could not have been less like the rough and ready production of *Oliver Cromwell Is Really Very Sorry* by Xnthony, stage name of Anthony Feigher, in the 2022 Dublin Fringe Festival. (The title is surely the funniest of any play I saw in my three terms as an Awards judge.) Acted by a company of five actors, each taking on multiple parts in a series of quick costume changes, it was a wildly satirical version of Cromwell (played by Xnthony himself), the most execrated figure in Irish history. Oliver was initially seen as a pretty-faced gay student, a wannabe actor whose only aspiration was to play Henry V. Forced to come home on the death of his father and made to marry Puritan Elizabeth (played by drag artist Lórcan Strain), he was then called to service by a Welsh-accented God (Iestyn Arwel) and given his mission to Ireland. The multiple songs that interspersed and interrupted the action (composed by Ódú) were raucous, the acting vignettes were caricatured throughout. Though the whole thing was tongue-in-cheek quickfire parody, Cromwell was not by any means exculpated. At the point of his invasion of Ireland he appeared in a white robe with the cross of St George, the white just barely blood spotted. In an extended version of this same robe, as he almost takes the crown, the blood spattering was everywhere. This camped-up show, produced on a shoestring, represented a pungent commentary on history as seen from Ireland and England.

The cross-over between dance and theatre was a notable feature of this period. Michael Keegan-Dolan, whose *Swan Lake* was one of the highlights of 2016, wrote and choreographed *How to be a Dancer in Seven-Two Thousand Easy Lessons* (Teać Daṁsa), a semi-autobiographical show at the Gate Theatre in 2022, part narrated, part danced with Rachel Poirier. There was an autobiographical dimension also to Jean Butler's *What We Hold* (Our Steps and Lovano) danced as a promenade show through the various rooms of the Dublin City Assembly House. The dancer Kévin Coquelard appeared in *birdboy* (United Fall), a remarkable solo performance for children, in a one-day re-opening of lockdown in October 2020, and again in the multi-disciplinary *Tin Soldier*, Louis Lovett's virtuoso adaptation of the Hans Christian Anderson tale at the Gate in 2022. One of the major achievements of this period, winning a whole series of awards in the 2021 *Irish Times* Theatre Awards was *Volcano* by Luke Murphy Attic Projects (Figure 9).

It was played in four episodes, which could be seen either on successive days or in a single continuous session. Just four audience members at a time were placed, each in a separate booth off a dark corridor, with a window looking into the long narrow enclosed space of Nun's Island Theatre, a converted church in Galway. The individual experience of the isolated spectator in his/her cell spoke to the

Fig. 9 Will Thompson and Luke Murphy with audience member in the Luke Murphy Attic Projects production of *Volcano*. Photographer Emilija Jefremova. Courtesy of Luke Murphy Attic Projects.

play's story, the space odyssey of two men on the Amber Project, a futuristic enterprise for volunteers to be sent out beyond the solar system to represent life on our planet. It was only in the final episode that this framing narrative became clear. For the first three sections, we watched bewildered as the two figures, X (Luke Murphy) and Y (Will Thompson), were jolted through a number of disjointed incidents, representing memories of their own past lives and that of other interrupting consciousnesses. This was, in fact, a mission that had gone disastrously wrong, and we kept hearing the announcement that the decision has been taken to 'decommission Pod 261' in which the men were immured.[3] Both Murphy and Thompson are dancers, and the play was a showcase of their extraordinary talents in a huge variety of styles of movement. But their equally remarkable acting, as they attempted to while away the time and stave off panic with games and performances, was enhanced by the technology of inset television clips, the decomposing set (Alyson Cummings and Pai Rathaya), and the constantly changing costumes (Pai Rathaya). As Sara Keating put it, reviewing a 2023 revival: 'Tense, troubling and touching, Volcano [...] interrogates representational practices within its highly artificial constructed reality, offering a new kind of storytelling in theatre to rival

---

[3] I am very grateful to the producer Gwen Van Spijk who gave me access to the unpublished script of the play.

any other modern medium. It is not an overstatement to say that you will not have seen anything like this before'.[4]

Sexualities

thisispopbaby has probably done more than any other company to enlarge the range of Irish theatre and challenge its norms. Set up in 2007, led by Phillip McMahon and Jennifer Jennings, it describes itself as 'a theatre and events production company that rips up the space between popular culture, counter culture, queer culture and high art—providing both a vehicle for our associate artists' dreams and an electrifying access point to the arts'.[5] Their 2016 show, *RIOT* played in a large tent in Merrion Square established a cabaret format hosted by drag artist Panti Bliss, combining spoken rap, acrobatics, dance, song (both rock and traditional Irish ballads), interaction with the audience, who were encouraged to get up and buy drinks at the bar during the show. Their comparable show in 2022, which unfortunately I did not get to see, was *WAKE* which played in the National Stadium, described in a five-star review as 'a celebration of live performance and of being alive', the choreography 'Riverdance for the club queens'.[6] Though these sorts of big mixed-media events are part of their repertoire, they have also staged (relatively) straight drama. So, for instance, there was their production of *Shit*, by the Australian playwright Patricia Cornelius, revoiced in fierce Dublin demotic, featuring three abused and abusive women, opening with an assault of obscene language, and maintaining a high energy level of aggression throughout.[7] Much quieter, dealing with female trauma from a different point of view, was Mark O'Halloran's *Conversations after Sex*, winner of Best New Play in the 2021 Awards. This consisted in a year's worth of casual pick-ups by the protagonist with a variety of men after the suicide of her partner, a tour de force by Kate Stanley Brennan and Fionn Ó Loinsigh who played all her very different lovers (without any costume changes as neither actor wore much in the way of clothes).

When *Conversations after Sex* went on tour, it was published in a single volume with *Trade*, O'Halloran's two-hander on the encounter between a middle-aged man and a rent-boy, played as a site-specific show in a Dublin guesthouse

---

[4] Sara Keating, 'Volcano Review: Edge-of-Your-Seat Entertainment—You Won't Have Seen Anything Like This Before', *Irish Times*, 23 July 2023, https://www.irishtimes.com/culture/stage/review/2023/07/23/volcano-review-edge-of-your-seat-entertainment-you-wont-have-seen-anything-like-this-before/ (accessed 4 December 2023).
[5] See https://www.irishtheatre.ie/company-page.aspx?companyid=30365 (accessed 5 December 2023).
[6] Sara Keating, 'Wake Review: thisispopbaby's New Show Is Like Riverdance for Club Queens', *Irish Times*, 12 September 2022, https://www.irishtimes.com/culture/stage/2022/09/12/wake-review-thisispopbabys-brilliant-new-show-is-like-riverdance-for-club-queens/ (accessed 5 December 2023).
[7] I saw this production on opening night in March 2020, after which it was closed by Covid, and only returned in 2022.

in 2011.[8] Homosexuality, only decriminalized in the Republic of Ireland in 1993, highly controversial on stage before that, had become mainstream by the twenty-first century. So, for example, Aisling O'Meara's charming *Next Please*, part of the Bewley's 2021 Walkabout Theatre, staged the emotional switchbacks of a female couple meeting for a first date. Eugene O'Brien's *Heaven*, produced by Fishamble, winner of the 2022 Best New Play award, was a sensitive study of a woman married to a repressed gay man. Paul McVeigh's *Big Man*, produced in the same month by the Lyric Theatre in Belfast, was a moving one-man show dramatizing the failure of a gay love affair. Two other 2022 Belfast plays emphasized the consequences of years of repression and the ongoing assaults of homophobia. Dominic Montague's *Callings* (Kabosh) was built around Cara-Friend, an actual call centre for gay people set up in the 1970s, combating the deep prejudices of Northern Ireland of the time. It had a relatively upbeat ending celebrating the rights achieved for the LGBTQ+ community. By contrast, Amanda Verlaque's one-woman coming out play, *This Sh*t Happens All the Time* (Lyric), by its very title, rammed home the point that the problem had by no means gone away.

Shows in this period brought out the terrors and the dangers of gay sex, past and present. *Party Scene* by Philip Connaughton and Phillip McMahon (thisispopbaby 2022) was a play for four male dancers that suggested a contemporary scene of drugs and promiscuity—one character repeatedly trying to establish whether he had had sex with anyone on Saturday night. The choice of Phillip McMahon's *Once Before I Go* as the Gate's 2021 Dublin Theatre Festival production, directed by then Artistic Director Selina Cartmell, was a measure of how high profile the subject had become. The play had a split time action: part one was in 2019, the date picked out in stage-high letters in rainbow colours—the set by Francis O'Connor and lighting by James Ingalls, were spectacularly camp throughout. A latter-day Dave, formerly Daithí (Seán Campion) meets up with Lynn (Aisling O'Sullivan), both in late middle age, long estranged though both living in London. They catch up on one another's lives: Daithí, financially broke after a period of drug addiction, planning to move back to Ireland with his young trans lover Jase; Lynn now separated from her long-term Black lesbian partner, with whom she has two children. Part two then switched to 1987, when Daithí and Lynn (played by Desmond Eastwood and Martha Breen) were young activists in the Dublin gay liberation movement. At the centre of the action is Bernard, Lynn's brother and in due course Daithí's lover, flamboyantly gay, who, in a scene in Paris celebrating his 30th birthday, is revealed to be infected with AIDS. The plot was somewhat creaky, Lynn accusing Daithí of having deserted Bernard when he was dying, not knowing this was by Bernard's own wish; the parts of young Daithí and young Lynn were underwritten. But the play was made by the performance of a pink-haired Matthew Malone as Bernard. He did not steal the show—he *was* the show. His final singing of the

---

[8] Mark O'Halloran, *Conversations After Sex, Trade* (London: Methuen Drama, 2023).

Fig. 10 Matthew Malone in the Gate Theatre production of *Once Before I Go*. Photographer Ros Kavanagh. Courtesy of Gate Theatre.

1983 Peter Allen song, 'Once Before I Go', was simultaneously bravely defiant and plangently elegiac (Figure 10).

Tara Flynn in *Haunted* told of the several occasions when her father 'cheated death'. Each time he was going, there came the repeated gag line: 'AND THEN HE DIDN'T FECKING DIE'.[9] The father who refuses to die has a long history in Irish theatre going back to Old Mahon in the last scene of *The Playboy*. 'Are you coming to be killed a third time or what ails you now?' exclaims Christy, looking at the undead man he has just murdered for a second time.[10] Flynn's cruel father who refused to understand her is a well recognizable type. *Haunted* was staged with Panti Bliss's *If These Wigs Could Talk*, in a double bill by the Abbey and thisispopbaby in 2022. It made for a moment of relieved comic laughter when Panti's Mayo man father up from the country, looked at the Caravaggio painting of *Boy Bitten by a Lizard*, said loudly: 'Caravaggio ... Definitely one of your lot! He'd be drinking in your place alright'.[11] *If These Wigs Could Talk* made its own polemic case for the continuing need to fight for LGBTQ+ rights, but the father's casual acceptance of 'your lot' created a significant moment of *détente*.

The figure of the father takes on a different significance in a time when gender roles are much more openly questioned. In Amy Conroy's *Luck Just Kissed You Hello*, the title taken from David Bowie's ironic song 'Boys Keep Swinging', three

---

[9] Tara Flynn, *Haunted*; Panti Bliss, *If These Wigs Could Talk* (London: Methuen Drama, 2022), 8.
[10] J. M. Synge, *Collected Works*, Vol. IV: *Plays 2*, ed. Ann Saddlemyer (London: Oxford University Press, 1968), 171.
[11] Flynn, *Haunted*; Panti, *Wigs*, 67.

sons come together as their paralysed father Ted inches towards death. Mark, a trans man who grew up as Laura, and Gary, his gay twin brother, both loathed Ted, and remembered with horror holidays by the sea with him, when he tried to toughen them up. Sullivan, their straight foster-brother, in contrast, keeps trying to recall the love which Ted inspired in him. In the original 2015 staging, Conroy herself played Mark—extremely convincingly. For the 2022 revival at the Abbey, Riley Carter, a trans actor from England, was cast for the role and was an excellent foil for Ross O'Donnellan as Gary and Jamie O'Neill as Sullivan, though his undisguised English accent sounded a bit anomalous in the reunion of the three Irish brothers. The play exposed a whole series of life-lies: the sordid reality of Gary's supposedly smoothly successful life as a businessman; the affair that Mark, when still Laura, had with Jenny, Sullivan's now pregnant wife; Sullivan's fears about becoming a father. At times, there seemed too many twists and turns of the plot. But the play impressively dramatized what the director Wayne Jordan described as Conroy's 'cubist approach to Irish masculinities'.[12] And the emotional dynamics by which Mark was enabled finally to speak the eulogy for his father's funeral, ended the play as something of a liberated peace-making gesture towards the traditional Irish patriarch and his legacy.

Race

In the treatment of sexuality, Irish theatre has had some catching up to do. Issues that were long ago central elsewhere—think of Tony Kushner's *Angels in America* (1991–3) on the AIDS crisis—were long suppressed in the conservative Ireland of the twentieth century. This is even more true of matters of race. Up until the beginning of the twenty-first century Ireland was overwhelmingly monocultural, all but all white, all but all Christian, in the Republic nearly uniformly Catholic. By the 2022 Census that situation had changed radically. Of those normally resident in the Republic 20% were not born in Ireland, most of them originating elsewhere in Europe, Polish being the most commonly spoken language other than English.[13] Still relatively small numbers of people were Asian (3.7%) and Black (1.5%), but it was now identifiably a multi-ethnic, multi-racial society.[14]

---

[12] *Luck Just Kissed You Hello*, 'Director's Note' in Abbey Theatre programme, 2022.
[13] See Central Statistics Office, *Census of Population 2022: Summary Results*, https://www.cso.ie/en/releasesandpublications/ep/p-cpsr/censusofpopulation2022-summaryresults/migrationanddiversity/ (accessed 12 December 2023).
[14] See Wikepedia, 'Demographics of the Republic of Ireland', https://www.google.com/search?q=What+proportion+of+the+population+of+the+Republic+came+from+Asia+or+Aftirca&rlz=1C1GCEU_enIE1073IE1076&oq=What+proportion+of+the+population+of+the+Republic+came+from+Asia+or+Aftirca&gs_lcrp=EgZjaHJvbWUyBggAEEUYOTIGCAEQ IRgK0gEJMzE3NDNqMGo0qAIAsAIA&sourceid=chrome&ie=UTF-8 (accessed 12 December 2023).

The first play on the Irish stage with an African as central protagonist was Donal O'Kelly's *Asylum! Asylum!* (Abbey, 1994) about the legal predicament of a Ugandan immigrant who arrives in Ireland without a visa. Roddy Doyle created *Guess Who's Coming for the Dinner* (Calypso 2001) as an Irish version of the 1967 Sydney Poitier film about an interracial relationship. Elizabeth Kuti's *The Sugar Wife* (Rough Magic, 2005), dramatized the visit of a formerly enslaved African-American woman, visiting Dublin as part of the abolitionist movement in 1850. In 2006, the Abbey produced *Blue/Orange*, the Britiah playwright Joe Penhall's play about mental illness, with a Black protagonist. But in each of these cases the part of the Black character was cast with a British actor. It was not until well into the second decade of the twenty-first century that issues of racial diversity began to be prominent in Irish theatre, and colourblind casting started to be a common practice.[15]

So, for example, in Eoghan Quinn's play *Colic*, staged in the 2022 Dublin Theatre Festival, set in contemporary Dublin, the Black British actor Ekow Quartey was cast as the husband of Kate Stanley Brennan, without any comment on the fact that this was an interracial marriage. Earlier that year, Annie Ryan and Michael West's adaptation of Joyce's *Dubliners*, with its set and costuming suggested a Dublin of urban dereliction, matching the original paralysed Edwardian milieu. In a production where each of the eight performers took on multiple roles, Gabriel Adewusi, the Nigerian-Irish actor who trained in Dublin, reappeared across the show in parts as different as Corley, one of the 'Two Gallants', and the elderly Protestant Mr Browne in 'The Dead'. No less than seven of the ten-member cast of *Absent the Wrong* (Abbey 2022), Dylan Coburn Gray's 2022 response to the Mother and Baby Homes Report, were Irish-based or Irish-trained actors of different ethnicities.[16] One of these, Jolly Abraham, originally from New York but now working in Dublin, appeared in several other 2022 shows. She played a number of parts in *An Octoroon* and was one of the pairs of actors who were cast in *Good Sex*, by Dead Centre and Emilie Pine, walking in unrehearsed to a script they had never seen, speaking lines fed to them from a glassed-in sound booth under the instructions of an intimacy director. It took only a slight adjustment of Conor McPherson's *The Weir* for Abraham to play Valerie in the Abbey revival of the play—a Valerie with an American rather than a Dublin background. For most of the shows in which non-white actors were cast, however, there was not even that gesture towards verisimilitude. Whatever parts

---

[15] A comic anecdote is told of Yeats's enthusiastic reception of the idea of an Abbey production of Marc Connelly's 1930 Broadway hit *The Green Pastures*, leaving director Lennox Robinson puzzling over where he would find sixty Black actors. See R. F. Foster, *W.B. Yeats: A Life*, Vol. II: *The Arch-Poet 1915–1939* (Oxford: Oxford University Press, 2003), 392–3.

[16] For details, see https://www.abbeytheatre.ie/whats-on/absentthewrong/ (accessed 23 December 2023). I did not see this show because the playwright decided, as a protest against the *Irish Times* on a matter of political principle, that the Theatre Awards judges were not welcome to attend.

they played, these were simply performers who happened to be Black or Asian or mixed race.

Window a World, staged as part of the 2022 Dublin Theatre Festival, could be seen as a significant sign of the shifting nature of Irish theatre. Its creator Choy-Ping-Clarke-Ng is 'a Hong Kong-Irish theatre maker and designer of set, costume and video', according to the programme. All these skills were on display in the show watched standing in the street in Temple Bar, with visual projections and sound heard on headphones. The first image was of a young woman taking off wig and make-up to be revealed as a man, listening to an extended voiceover message in Chinese, a message from his aunt in Hong Kong (as we found out when it was subsequently translated). The performer was identified as having a Hong Kong father and Irish mother, and the personal and professional problems of such a person in a globalized world were highlighted when we saw the performer, talking to a friend in California, worrying that he only got parts as a 'diversity hire', and having to get help with his limited Cantonese from a waitress in a Chinese restaurant. The show ended with a switch from street scenes in Hong Kong projected on the wall to live performance by the drag artist on the top of the building above.

The two 2022 productions that made race most central were Sonya Kelly's *The Last Return* (Druid) and Branden Jacobs-Jenkins' *An Octoroon* (Abbey). *The Last Return* looked initially like a throwback to Ionesco's theatre of the absurd. None of the characters had individual names: Ticket Person (Anna Healey), completely uninterested, sat in the box-office of the theatre foyer, repeating the one monotone message: 'The Oppenheimer *Return to Hindenberg* is sold out. If there are any returns, they will be distributed ten minutes before the performance begins'. Each of those waiting for such a return ticket, the Newspaper Man (Bosco Hogan), the Umbrella Woman (Fiona Bell), and Military Man (Fionn Ó Loinsigh), had an equally ridiculous reason for being desperate to see the show. They all regarded with suspicion a colourful backpack, which sat on a chair at the head of the queue for returns, marking the place of a young woman who had gone to the café. The Woman in Pink (Naima Swaleh) who joined them was a Somali migrant who initially seemed to speak no English, communications being painstakingly made to her through Google Translate. However, it subsequently appeared that she was fluent in five different languages, and, if granted the last return, will sell it for six times its value as a lesson in the capitalist ethics under which she, like so many other Africans, have suffered. The play had a violent climax brought on by a security alert, in which all the characters die, apart from Woman in Pink and Ticket Person. When the young woman reappeared from the café in the final moments, she turned out to be the daughter of the Woman in Pink, long sought after through Europe after being separated from her mother in their migration into Italy. The bizarre situation, the growing hysteria of the characters, fine ensemble playing, all made it a powerful production. However, while the absurdist comedy skewered satirically the ludicrousness of First-World values, the political tendentiousness of the speeches by the Woman in Pink, the sentimentally contrived happy ending, felt like a heavy-handed switch in theatrical mode.

An Octoroon is an American play originally staged in New York in 2014 and given its European premiere in London in 2017. However, its production at the Abbey, Ireland's National Theatre, was particularly significant because the play was described in the programme as 'a radical reboot of Dion Boucicault's play, *The Octoroon*'. Boucicault's 1859 original, written when he was managing a theatre in New York just before the Civil War, cashed in on the then urgent issue of slavery with its melodrama about Zoe, the octoroon of the title who is believed to be free and passes for white, the beloved of the white owner of the estate, but who, because of her parentage, stands liable to be sold at auction to the villainous neighbouring landowner M'Closkey. Though Boucicault opposed slavery, his play was cannily constructed to offend neither South nor North in a deeply divided New York, but based its appeal instead on two theatrical sensation scenes that were his trademark: the onstage burning of a Mississippi riverboat, and the then new and dramatic use of a photograph as evidence of a murder.[17]

Jacobs-Jenkins had the greatest fun sending all of this up, starting with a Black playwright (identified by his own initials as BJJ), frustrated by the unwillingness of white actors to play the slave-owners in his adaptation of *The Octoroon*, deciding to play the parts himself. In the opening prologue, accordingly, we saw Patrick Martins as BJJ, putting on whiteface and an impossible blonde wig, while on the other side of the stage, Boucicault himself (Rory Nolan), identified only as Playwright, grumbling that no-one remembered him anymore, made up as Indian chief Wahnotee, the wordless role that Boucicault played in the original. To complete the metatheatrical set-up, the light-skilled Jolly Abraham, who came on as Boucicault's harried assistant, put on heavy black make-up to appear as the loyal estate overseer Pete, as well as his own grandson Paul. Nothing could have more effectively mocked the lamentable tradition of theatrical blackface, while deconstructing the idea of race itself.

The success of the production and the play was to allow an audience to enjoy the melodrama—the encumbered estate under threat by the villain M'Closkey, the self-sacrifice of the white heiress Dora (Maeve O'Mahony) in offering her fortune to buy Zoe (Umi Myers) at auction and allow her to marry George— and to laugh at it throughout. There were incidental tributes to Boucicault: the safety curtain (Boucicault's theatrical innovation) which rose after the prologue, Martins as BJJ, playing both George and McCloskey fighting with himself, as Boucicault in *The Corsican Brothers* had famously taken on the parts of the twin antagonists. An interstitial dialogue between BJJ and Playwright explained how

---

[17] See Richard Fawkes, *Dion Boucicault: A Biography* (London: Quartet Books, 1979), 106–11. On the controversial reception of the play in New York, see Deirdre McFeely, *Dion Boucicault: Irish Identity on Stage* (Cambridge: Cambridge University Press, 2012), 9–12.

they would *not* represent the burning boat scene. Boucicault's piously sentimental house slaves Dido and Minnie were turned into a comic chorus talking in Black English, spattered with the n-word so unspeakable by white people. Their role throughout was to subvert the Boucicauldian melodramatics. *The Octoroon* ended in tragic pathos as Zoe poisons herself to avoid being sold into slavery, thus freeing George to marry Dora: there was no way in 1859 Boucicault was going to risk a (then illegal) interracial marriage on the New York stage. Jacobs-Jenkins had Minnie (Leah Walker) shruggingly accept Zoe's offstage death. She urged Dido (Mara Allen): 'If Zoe's lightskinned ass wanna [...] go poison herself over some white man, then you need to let her do that and move on'.[18] Most of the Black cast of *An Octoroon* were from Britain, like the director Anthony Simpson-Pike, but three of them were trained in Ireland: Martins, Jeanne Nicole Ní Ainnle (Grace), and Loré Adewusi (Bre'er Rabbit / Captain Ratts). The production in the Abbey of a modern play about race, ricocheting off Boucicault, was a landmark event in the history of Irish theatre (Figure 11).[19]

Fig. 11 Maeve O'Mahony, Patrick Martins, Jolly Abraham, and Mara Allen in the Abbey Theatre production of *An Octoroon*. Photographer Ros Kavanagh. Courtesy of Abbey Theatre.

---

[18] Branden Jacobs-Jenkins, *An Octoroon* (London: Nick Hern Books, 2017), 76–7.
[19] *An Octoroon*, though nominated for Best Production in the Awards, provoked controversy in the media because of the nomination of two white actors for supporting roles, the controversy itself a sign of the emerging issue of diversity.

The Covid lockdown, though catastrophic for Irish theatre makers at the time, brought positive changes, accelerating the development of technological innovation. When live performance returned, it was richer and more various than ever. The year 2021–2 was an outstanding time for theatre goers—and Awards judges. There were exciting revivals, like *The Steward of Christendom*, with Owen Roe triumphantly making his own the part created in 1995 by the great actor Donal McCann. There was the outstanding originality in form and execution of the multi-part dance drama *Volcano*. All the resources of theatre—music, dance, video projections, virtual reality—were combined to (at best) magnificently coherent effect. Mainstream plays such as *Heaven, Conversations After Sex*, and *Once Before I Go* showed how far Irish theatre had travelled from its traditionally timid representation of sex. *Good Sex* dramatized that very representation and the naturalistic conventions that supported it, while everywhere there was a new awareness of the fluidity of gender and sexual roles. As Ireland became a modern, multi-cultural, multi-ethnic society, diversity in theatre, so long an issue in other countries, began to be a pressing concern for Irish theatre makers also. It is still, relatively speaking, a small community, with Black Irish actors only beginning to come through professional training in numbers. But the impact is already to be seen in colourblind casting and a changed understanding of race. Irish theatre in 2022 was thriving, modernizing, coming into its own in a global world.

Conclusion

Irish Theatre in the Twenty-First Century—there is no way of future-proofing a book with such a title. As I write, less than a quarter of the century has passed, and by 2050, much less 2100, Irish theatre will no doubt look very different. In fact, one of the aims of this book has been to represent what is necessarily transient and ephemeral, theatre as it happened in Ireland in a given year or sequence of years. My 'State of Play' sections were intended to provide snapshots of moments in time with a range of shows that were acted across the island. Many of these were never revived or even designed to be revived. I wanted to give some sense of what it felt like to be a theatregoer—even if an unusually assiduous theatregoer—in 2006, 2016, 2020–2. Whatever trends might or might not be discernible, whatever current preoccupations of the theatre makers, this is what it felt like to be there.

Art forms do not change neatly as one century turns into another. So, much that has been characteristic of twenty-first-century Irish theatre was already under way in the 1990s, as I tried to show in my first chapter. A principal impulse has been to work against the Irish theatrical traditions that were so dominant through the twentieth century. National exceptionalism in the late colonial and postcolonial periods had favoured self-consciously Irish subjects and a conservative dramaturgy. Experimental styles of theatre that had flourished in Europe and the US were avoided, in part because, when more adventurous staging was attempted, it received a cool reception abroad. There was a niche market in London and New York for plays identifiably 'Irish' by their richly colloquial language and real-seeming representations of an imagined Ireland. As Irish playwrights revolted against the expectation that their characters should speak in a lyrical style, making drama out of the broken speech of the inarticulate, directors reached for the non-naturalistic forms which had largely been excluded from Irish theatre. Traditions that went back to the beginnings of the national theatre movement, in which play and play text had been sovereign, were exchanged for a theatre of physicality, of stylized acting, and of anti-illusionist discontinuity.

As Ireland rapidly modernized as a society, Irish theatre sought to catch up with modern styles already well established elsewhere. However, many of the plays exploiting this (for Ireland) new dramaturgy, applied it to the work of the past. Text might be decentred within the experimental companies, but frequently they showed how plays from the classic Irish repertoire could be seen differently, reproduced in changed styles. Though theatre makers in the twenty-first century responded to the conditions of the time—the hectic conditions of the economic boom and its catastrophic collapse—many were still very much concerned with the ways the Irish present remained so much entangled with its own past history. That history itself was represented in fashions that challenged orthodox national narratives, and occluded and suppressed parts of the past were given dramatized expression. In spite of the landmark Good Friday Agreement in 1998, the legacy of years of political violence in the divided community of Northern Ireland was an ongoing concern of Irish playwrights. Adaptations of classical plays had long been a part of Irish theatre, but in this period they were given a self-consciously contemporary relevance. The dominance of men in Irish theatre, reflecting the patriarchal cast of twentieth-century Irish society, produced the 2015 reaction of #WakingTheFeminists and a changed scene in the years that followed, with women in many more leadership roles and an evolving awareness of the multiplicities of gender and sexuality.

Ireland in the twenty-first century has continued to be known for its playwrights; Martin McDonagh, Marina Carr, Conor McPherson, and Enda Walsh all have major international reputations. But it has been the acting companies and their productions, as much as the new plays that have been produced, that have been most striking in this period. Although the Abbey and the Gate have both had their vicissitudes, they have mounted important work throughout. And the independent theatre sector has been outstanding in its energy richness, and variety. Inevitably, some of the smaller companies have come and gone. On the whole, though, there has been good support from the Arts Council / An Chomhairle Ealaoín in the Republic and the Arts Council of Northern Ireland. The institution of the Basic Income for the Arts in 2022 as a pilot scheme by the government was particularly to be welcomed in a situation where theatre makers still live so very precariously.[1] With the increasing professionalization of theatrical training, there is now a growing pool of very talented, highly skilled theatre artists working in the field. And in researching this book, I have found that it was interviews with company directors and producers that were most illuminating.

The two most long-lasting theatre companies have made a major contribution to Irish theatre in the period. In 2024 it is forty years since the establishment of Rough Magic, in 2025 it will be fifty years after the foundation of Druid. For most of their history, they have each had a single artistic director, Garry Hynes and Lynne Parker. Druid made the name of Martin McDonagh with *The Leenane Trilogy* (1997), which won a Tony Award for Hynes as Best Director when it transferred to New York. The company has staged a number of other original plays, notably those of Sonya Kelly—*Furniture* (2018) and *The Last Return* (2022). But Druid is best known for its marathon productions of plays from the past. After DruidSynge,

---

[1] See https://www.gov.ie/en/campaigns/09cf6-basic-income-for-the-arts-pilot-scheme/ (accessed 19 December 2023).

discussed in Chapter 3, there came DruidMurphy (2012), three plays by Tom Murphy concerned with emigration, DruidShakespeare (2015), an adaptation of four of the history plays, DruidGregory, and DruidO'Casey (2023), a staging of the Dublin plays covering the revolutionary period. For most of these Hynes has worked with designer Francis O'Connor and choreographer David Bolger, and has used many of the same actors, since 2013 listed as the company's 'ensemble'. They include Druid's co-founder Marie Mullen, and four younger actors, Marty Rea, Garrett Lombard, Aaron Monaghan, and Rory Nolan. It is these last four who acted in Druid's exceptionally fine production of *Waiting for Godot* in 2016. A key to the success of Druid has been the teamwork of the same performers and designers, collaborating over years with Hynes as director.

Rough Magic has won more awards for Best Production in the *Irish Times* Theatre Awards than any other company, beating Druid by just one. It began in the 1980s by staging contemporary British and American political plays but was soon producing new work by Irish playwrights: Declan Hughes and Arthur Riordan (both founding members of the company), Donal O'Kelly, and Gina Moxley. Some of the outstanding works staged by Rough Magic, *Improbable Frequency*, *Phaedra*, and *Hecuba*, have been discussed earlier in the book. Parker, though she has often cast the same actors, has not worked with a single core group of performers, as Druid has. However, one of the most important initiatives of Rough Magic has been SEEDS, set up in 2001 as a 'structured development programme for emerging theatre practitioners across all disciplines'.[2] This apprenticeship and mentoring scheme was particularly important before the establishment of The Lir in 2011, and has contributed to the emergence of some of the most gifted Irish theatre makers. Like Druid, Rough Magic has been known as much for its revivals of classic plays as for its original works, with notable Shakespeare productions from *The Taming of the Shrew* through to *A Midsummer Night's Dream* (2018)—providing Paul Mescal with his first award as part of the Best Ensemble of that year—and *The Tempest* (2022). Both Druid and Rough Magic have remained faithful to play texts, however imaginative and innovative their staging. It has been the quality of such work, together with watching the development of new forms of theatre in a modernizing and secularizing Ireland, that has given interest and excitement to me over the course of the twenty-first century so far. And it is in the hope of sharing such interest and excitement with readers that this book has been written.

---

[2] See https://www.roughmagic.ie/seeds-history/ (accessed 20 December 2023).

Bibliography

Abbey Theatre, 'Absent the Wrong', https://www.abbeytheatre.ie/whats-on/absentthewrong/
Abbey Theatre, 'Annual Report', https://www.abbeytheatre.ie/annual-report-2016/page-2.html#section12
Abbey Theatre, 'Dear Ireland', https://www.abbeytheatre.ie/dear-ireland/
Abbey Theatre, 'The Gregory Project', https://www.abbeytheatre.ie/whats-on/the-gregory-project/
Amos, Keith, *The Fenians in Australia 1865–1880* (Kensington, NSW: New South Wales University Press, 1988).
https://en.wikipedia.org/wiki/Anything_for_Love
https://www.gov.ie/en/campaigns/09cf6-basic-income-for-the-arts-pilot-scheme/
Barry, Sebastian, *Plays 1* (London: Methuen Drama, 1997).
Beckett, Samuel, *Complete Dramatic Works* (London: Faber, 1986).
Billington, Michael, 'On Raftery's Hill', *Guardian*, 5 July 2000, https://www.theguardian.com/stage/2000/jul/05/theatre.artsfeatures
Billington, Michael, 'Penelope', *Guardian*, 26 July 2010.
Billington, Michael, 'Dublin Theatre Festival Takes the Recession Seriously', *Guardian*, 11 October 2010.
Billington, Michael, 'The Night Alive', *Guardian*, 20 June 2013, https://www.theguardian.com/stage/2013/jun/20/the-night-alive-review
Billington, Michael, 'Cyprus Avenue: The Most Shocking Play on the London Stage', *Guardian*, 11 April 2016, https://www.theguardian.com/stage/theatreblog/2016/apr/11/cyprus-avenue-david-ireland-belfast-play-royal-court-theatre-upstairs
https://www.blueraincoat.com/about
Bolger, Dermot, *The Townlands of Brazil* (Dublin: New Island, 2007).
Bourke, Angela, 'Keening as Theatre', in Nicholas Grene (ed.), *Interpreting Synge: Essays from the Synge Summer School 1991–2000* (Dublin: Lilliput Press, 2000), 67–79.
Brantley, Ben, 'From Thebes to Suburbia: In Dire Need of Therapy', *New York Times*, 24 May 2008.
Brecht, Bertolt, 'The Street Scene: A Basic Model for an Epic Theatre', in John Willett (ed. and trans.), *Brecht on Theatre* (London: Methuen, 1964), 121–9.
Caldwell, Lucy, *Three Sisters* (London: Faber, 2016).
Caldwell, Lucy, 'On Writing *Three Sisters*', in Linda Anderson and Dawn Miranda Sherratt-Bado (eds.), *Female Lines: New Writing by Women from Northern Ireland* (Dublin: New Island, 2017), 117–18.
Carr, Marina, *Plays: 1* (London: Faber, 1999).
Carr, Marina, *Plays 2* (London: Faber, 2009).
Carr, Marina, *Plays: 3* (London: Faber, 2013).
Central Statistics Office, *Census of Population 2022: Summary Results*, https://www.cso.ie/en/releasesandpublications/ep/p-cpsr/censusofpopulation2022-summaryresults/migrationanddiversity/
Chambers, Lilian, Ger FitzGibbon, and Eamonn Jordan (eds.), *Theatre Talk: Voices of Irish Theatre Practitioners* (Dublin: Carysfort Press, 2001).
Chekhov, Anton, *Plays*, trans. Michael Frayn (London: Methuen Drama, 1998).
Connolly, Sean, 'Dreaming History', *Theatre Ireland*, 13 (1987), 42–4.
Conroy, Amy, *Luck Just Kissed You Hello*, Abbey Theatre programme (Dublin: Abbey Theatre, 2022).

Coonan, Clifford, 'Playboy Comes Home', *Irish Times*, 13 December 2006, https://www.proquest.com/docview/308913761/A868D81EAFB4EEAPQ/1?accountid=14404

https://theconversation.com/northern-ireland-census-shows-more-catholics-than-protestants-a-political-scientiston-what-this-really-means-191273

Coupe, Alexander, 'Defiantly Mercurial: An Interview with Stacey Gregg', *The Honest Ulsterman*, February 2021, https://humag.co/features/defiantly-mercurial

Crawley, Peter, 'The Grown-Ups', *Irish Times*, 16 February 2006, https://www.irishtimes.com/culture/review-1.1016232

Crawley, Peter, 'Dublin Theatre Festival Review: *The Playboy of the Western World*', *Irish Times*, 5 October 2007.

Crawley, Peter, 'Phaedra', *Irish Times*, 5 October 2010.

Crawley, Peter, 'Improbable Frequency', *Irish Times*, 22 March 2012, https://www.irishtimes.com/culture/music/classical/improbable-frequency-1.486463

Crawley, Peter, 'Viewed from Afar: Contemporary Irish Theatre on the World's Stages', in Fintan Walsh, *'That Was Us': Contemporary Irish Theatre and Performance* (London: Oberon, 2013), 211–28.

Crawley, Peter, 'Monto Is Back: The Sex Trade and the Business of Hope', *Irish Times*, 24 September 2014, https://www.irishtimes.com/culture/stage/monto-is-back-the-sex-trade-and-the-business-of-hope-1.1938979

Crawley, Peter, 'On Raftery's Hill Review: A Striking and Pummelling Production', *Irish Times*, 2 May 2018, https://www.irishtimes.com/culture/stage/theatre/on-raftery-s-hill-review-a-striking-and-pummelling-production-1.3481560

Curtis, Maurice, *To Hell or Monto: The Story of Dublin's Most Notorious Districts* (Dublin: The History Press, 2015).

Dean, Tanya, 'Phaedra Backwards', *irish theatre magazine*, October 2011, http://itmarchive.ie/web/Reviews/Current/Phaedra-Backwards.aspx.html#:~:text=But%20the%20real%20loss%20in,is%20unfocussed%20and%20emotionally%20d

Dean, Tanya, 'Druid Cycles: The Rewards of Marathon Productions', in Fintan Walsh, *'That Was Us': Contemporary Irish Theatre and Performance* (London: Oberon, 2013), 181–95.

Dean, Tanya, 'Real Versus Illusory in Enda Walsh's *The Walworth Farce* and *The New Electric Ballroom*', in Mary P. Caulfield and Ian R. Walsh (eds.), T*he Theatre of Enda Walsh* (Dublin: Carysfort Press, 2015), 119–30.

https://www.decadeofcentenaries.com/

https://www.dfa.ie/our-role-policies/ourwork/casestudiesarchive/2015/april/ireland-2016-centenary-programme/

di Benedetto, Stephen, 'Shattering Images of Sex Acts and Other Obscene Staged Transgressions in Contemporary Irish Plays by Men', *Australasian Drama Studies*, 43 (2003), 46–65.

Dixon, Ros, and Irina Ruppo Malone (eds.), *Ibsen and Chekhov on the Irish Stage* (Dublin: Carysfort Press, 2012).

Donoghue, Brenda, Ciara O'Dowd, Tanya Dean, Ciara Murphy, Kathleen Cawley, and Kate Harris, *Gender Counts* (#WakingTheFeminists, 2017).

Donoghue, Emma, Marina Carr, Joseph O'Connor, Frank McGuinness, Thomas Kilroy, Éilis Ní Duibhne, Hugo Hamilton, and Rachel Feehily, *Signatories* (Dublin: UCD Press, 2016).

Doyle, Roddy, 'Wild and Perfect: Teaching *The Playboy of the Western World*', in Colm Toíbín (ed.), *Synge: A Celebration* (Dublin: Carysfort Press, 2005), 139–44.

http://www.druidsynge.com/

http://archive.druid.ie/websites/2009-2017/about/nationaltouring

Dubost, Thierry, Anne Etienne, and Mark O'Rowe, 'Interview with Mark O'Rowe', in Anne Etienne and Thierry Dubost (eds.), *Perspectives on Contemporary Irish Theatre: Populating the Stage* (Basingstoke: Palgrave Macmillan, 2017), 165–73.

Eldridge, David, *Festen* (London: Methuen Drama, 2004).

Ervine, St John, *Some Impressions of My Elders* (London: Allen and Unwin, 1922).

Etienne, Anne, and Thierry Dubost (eds.), *Perspectives on Contemporary Irish Theatre: Populating the Stage* (Basingstoke: Palgrave Macmillan, 2017).
Euripides, *The Medea*, trans. Rex Warner, in David Grene and Richmond Lattimore (eds.), *The Complete Greek Tragedies*, Vol. III: *Euripides* (Chicago: University of Chicago Press, 1959).
Fannin, Hilary, and Ellen Cranitch, *Phaedra*, in Patrick Lonergan (ed.), *Rough Magic Theatre Company: New Irish Plays and Adaptations, 2010–2018* (London: Methuen Drama, 2020).
Fawkes, Richard, *Dion Boucicault: A Biography* (London: Quartet Books, 1979).
Feeny SJ, Joseph, 'Martin McDonagh: Dramatist of the West', *Studies*, 87 (1998), 24–32.
https://fieldday.ie/about/
Fitzgibon, Ger, and Enda Walsh, 'Enda Walsh, in Conversation with Ger Fitzgibbon', in Anne Etienne and Thierry Dubost (eds.), *Perspectives on Contemporary Irish Theatre: Populating the Stage* (Basingstoke: Palgrave Macmillan, 2017), 174–90.
Fitzpatrick, Lisa, *Rape on the Modern Stage* (Cham: Palgrave Macmillan, 2018).
Flanagan, Eimear, 'Stormont without NI Leadership for a Third of Its Lifespan', *BBC News*, 14 February 2022, https://www.bbc.com/news/uk-northern-ireland-60249249
Flynn, Tara, *Haunted*; Panti Bliss, *If These Wigs Could Talk* (London: Methuen Drama, 2022).
Foster, R. F., *W.B. Yeats: A Life*, Vol. II: *The Arch-Poet 1915–1939* (Oxford: Oxford University Press, 2003).
Foster, R. F., *Vivid Faces: The Revolutionary Generation in Ireland 1890–1923* (London: Allen Lane, 2014).
Fricker, Karen, 'Same Old Show: The Performance of Masculinity in Conor McPherson's *Port Authority* and Mark O'Rowe's *Made in China*', *Irish Review*, 29 (2002), 84–94.
Fricker, Karen, 'The Bacchae of Baghdad', *Guardian*, 15 March 2006, https://www.theguardian.com/stage/2006/mar/15/theatre2
Fricker, Karen, 'The Playboy of the Western World', *Variety*, 15–21 October 2007.
Fricker, Karen, 'Theater: An Energetic Irish Troupe That Keeps on the Move', *New York Times*, 3 October 1999, https://www.nytimes.com/1999/10/03/theater/theater-an-energetic-irish-troupe-that-keeps-on-the-move.html
Friel, Brian, *Selected Plays* (London: Faber, 1984).
Friel, Brian, *Making History* (London: Faber, 1988).
Frost, Robert, *The Complete Poems* (London: Jonathan Cape, 1951).
Gallagher, Conor, 'North Should Prepare for United Ireland Possibility—Ex-DUP Leader', *Irish Times*, 28 July 2018, https://www.irishtimes.com/news/ireland/irish-news/north-should-prepare-for-united-ireland-possibility-ex-dup-leader-1.3578620.
Gregg, Stacey, *Shibboleth* (London: Nick Hern Books, 2015).
Gregg, Stacey, *Scorch* (London: Nick Hern Books, 2016).
Gregory, Lady, *Our Irish Theatre* (New York: G. P. Putnam's Sons, 1913).
Grene, Nicholas, 'Two London Playboys: Before and after Druid', in Adrian Frazier (ed.), *Playboys of the Western World* (Dublin: Carysfort Press, 2004), 80–2.
Grene, Nicholas, 'Black Pastoral: 1990s Images of Ireland', in Martin Prochazka (ed.), *After History* (Prague: Litteraria Pragensia, 2006), 243–55.
Grene, Nicholas, 'Chekhov and the Irish Big House', in Ros Dixon and Irina Ruppo Malone (eds.), *Ibsen and Chekhov on the Irish Stage* (Dublin: Carysfort Press, 2012), 139–48.
Grene, Nicholas, 'An Interview with Garry Hynes', *Irish University Review*, 45.1 (2015), 117–25.
Grene, Nicholas, 'Urban Alienation in McPherson's Dublin', *Hungarian Journal of English and American Studies*, 20:2 (2015), 51–58.
Grene, Nicholas, and Patrick Lonergan (eds.), *Irish Theatre Local and Global* (Dublin: Carysfort Press, 2012).
Grene, Nicholas, and Chris Morash (eds.), *The Oxford Handbook of Modern Irish Theatre* (Oxford: Oxford University Press, 2016).
Grobe, Christopher A., 'Love and Loneliness: Secular Morality in the Plays of Conor McPherson', *Princeton University Library Chronicle*, 68.1–2 (2006–7), 684–704.

Gussow, Mel, 'Review/Theater; "The Great Hunger", A Dearth of Words', *New York Times*, 18 March 1988, https://www.nytimes.com/1988/03/18/theater/review-theater-great-hunger-a-dearth-of-words.html

Hanly, Sarah, *Purple Snowflakes and Titty Wanks* (London: Faber, 2021).

Harris, Nancy, *Somewhere Out There You* (London: Nick Hern Books, 2023).

Heaney, Mick, 'Cheap Talk from a Grubby Playboy', *Sunday Times*, 14 October 2007.

Heaney, Seamus, *The Burial at Thebes* (London: Faber, 1990).

https://www.failteireland.ie/IrelandsHiddenHeartlands.aspx

Howard, Jane, 'All That Fall Pan Pan Theatre—Review', *Guardian* 15 January 2014, https://www.theguardian.com/culture/australia-culture-blog/2014/jan/15/all-that-fall-pan-pan-theatre-review

Huber, Werner, '"What's the News from Kilcrobally?" Notes on the Reception of Contemporary Irish Theatre in German-Speaking Countries', in Nicholas Grene and Patrick Lonergan (eds.), *Irish Theatre Local and Global* (Dublin: Carysfort Press, 2012), 81–91.

Hunt, Hugh, *The Abbey: Ireland's National Theatre 1904–1978* (New York: Columbia University Press, 1979).

Ireland, David, *Cyprus Avenue* (London: Bloomsbury Methuen Drama, 2016).

Ireland, David, *Everything between Us* (London: Bloomsbury Methuen Drama, 2017).

Ireland, David, 'Interview: *Cyprus Avenue*', https://www.youtube.com/watch?v=oeDidHSC7_A

Irish National Opera, https://www.irishnationalopera.ie/20-shots-of-opera/operas

Irishplayography.com, https://www.irishplayography.com/

Irish Theatre, https://www.irishtheatre.ie/company-page.aspx?companyid=30365

Irish Theatre, https://irishtheatre.ie/resources-page.aspx?contentid=148#:~:text=Categories%3A%20Best%20Actor%2C%20Best%20Actress,Special%20Award%2C%pecial%20Tribute%20Award

Irish Times, 'Trimble Says Great "Opportunity" to Start Healing Process Promises Stable Future for All in Northern Ireland', 11 April 1998.

Jacobs-Jenkins, Branden, *An Octoroon* (London: Nick Hern Books, 2017).

Jenkinson, Rosemary, *The Bonefire* (London: Methuen Drama, 2006).

Jordan, Eamonn, *Dissident Dramaturgies* (Dublin: Irish Academic Press, 2010).

Jordan, Eamonn, 'Unmasking the Myth: Marina Carr's *By the Bog of Cats ...* and *On Raftery's Hill*', in Michael Walton and Marianne McDonald (eds.), *Amid Our Troubles: Irish Versions of Greek Tragedy* (London: Methuen, 2002), 245–62.

Jordan, Eamonn, and Eric Weitz (eds.), *The Palgrave Handbook of Contemporary Irish Theatre and Performance* (London: Palgrave Macmillan, 2018).

Kavanagh, Patrick, *Collected Poems*, ed. Antoinette Quinn (London: Penguin, 2004).

Keating, Sara, 'Lines in the Strand', *Irish Times*, 18 November 2009, https://www.irishtimes.com/culture/stage/lines-in-the-strand-1.773843

Keating, Sara, '*Laundry*', *Irish Theatre Magazine*, 29 September 2011, http://itmarchive.ie/web/Reviews/Ulster-Bank-Dublin-Theatre-Festival-2011/Laundry.aspx.html#:~:text=Laundry%20is%20shocking%20and%20difficult,our%20culture%20for%20so%20long

Keating, Sara, 'An Irish Catholic Fleabag? This One-Woman Show Is Darker and More Disturbing', *Irish Times*, 29 September 2021, https://www.irishtimes.com/culture/stage/an-irish-catholic-fleabag-this-one-woman-show-is-darker-and-more-disturbing-1.4682043#:~:text=Sarah%20Hanly's%20debut%20play%20is,skewed%20psychology%20thrust%20upon%20women&text=At%20the%20beginning%20of%20Sarah,of%20the%20Greek%20tragedy%2C%20Antigone

Keating, Sara, 'Wake Review: Thisispopbaby's New Show Is Like Riverdance for Club Queens', *Irish Times*, 12 September 2022, https://www.irishtimes.com/culture/stage/2022/09/12/wake-review-thisispopbabys-brilliant-new-show-is-like-riverdance-for-club-queens/

Keating, Sara, 'Volcano Review: Edge-of-Your-Seat Entertainment—You Won't Have Seen Anything Like This Before', *Irish Times*, 23 July 2023, https://www.irishtimes.com/culture/

stage/review/2023/07/23/volcano-review-edge-of-your-seat-entertainment-you-wont-have-seen-anything-like-this-before/
Kelly, Nicholas, *The Grown-Ups* (London: Methuen Drama, 2006).
Kelly, Sonya, *The Wheelchair on My Face*; Noni Stapleton, *Charolais*; Margaret McAuliffe, *The Humours of Bandon* (London: Methuen Drama, 2017).
Kelly, Sonya, *How to Keep an Alien*, in Patrick Lonergan (ed.), *Rough Magic Theatre Company: New Irish Plays and Adaptations, 2010–2018* (London: Methuen Drama, 2020), 253–85.
Kilroy, Ian, 'Greek Tragedy, Midlands Style', *Irish Times*, 20 September 2002.
Kilroy, Thomas, *Double Cross* (Oldcastle: The Gallery Press, 1994).
Kinahan, Deirdre, *Wild Sky* (Navan: Meath County Council Arts Office, 2016).
Kinahan, Deirdre, *Rathmines Road* (London: Nick Hern Books, 2018).
Lanters, José, '"We'll Be the Judges of That": The Critical Reception of *DruidSynge* in the USA', in Nicholas Grene and Patrick Lonergan (eds.), *Irish Theatre Local and Global* (Dublin: Carysfort Press, 2012), 35–47.
Lehmann, Hans-Thies, *Postdramatic Theatre*, trans. Karen Jürs-Munby (London: Routledge, 2006).
Lonergan, Patrick, Review of *All that Fall*, *irish theatre magazine*, https://aran.library.nuigalway.ie/bitstream/handle/10379/6663/All_That_Fall_Irish_Theatre_Magazine_%7C_Reviews_%7C_Current_%7c_All_That_Fall.pdf?sequence=1&isAllowed=y
Lonergan, Patrick, *Theatre and Globalization: Irish Drama in the Celtic Tiger Era* (London: Palgrave Macmillan, 2009).
Lonergan, Patrick, 'Donal O'Kelly', in Martin Middeke and Peter Paul Schnierer (eds.), *Methuen Drama Guide to Contemporary Irish Playwrights* (London: Methuen Drama, 2010), 328–44.
Lonergan, Patrick, '"I Do Repent and Yet I Do Despair": Beckettian and Faustian Allusions in Conor McPherson's *The Seafarer* and Mark O'Rowe's *Terminus*', *ANQ*, 25.1 (2012), 24–30.
Lonergan, Patrick, '"Feast and Celebration": The Theatre Festival and Modern Irish Theatre', in Nicholas Grene and Chris Morash (eds.), *The Oxford Handbook of Modern Irish Theatre* (Oxford: Oxford University Press, 2016), 637–53.
Lonergan, Patrick, *Irish Drama and Theatre since 1950* (London: Methuen Drama, 2019).
Lonergan, Patrick (ed.), *Rough Magic Theatre Company: New Irish Plays and Adaptations, 2010–2018* (London: Methuen Drama, 2020).
Lowe, Louise, *The Boys of Foley Street*, in Patrick Lonergan (ed.), *Contemporary Irish Plays* (London: Bloomsbury Methuen Drama, 2015), 359–75.
McBride, Charlie, 'Enda Walsh from the Odyssey to Penelope', *Galway Advertiser*, 10 June 2010.
McBride, Ian, 'The Truth about the Troubles', in Jim Smyth (ed.), *Remembering the Troubles* (Notre Dame: University of Notre Dame Press, 2017), 9–43.
McCafferty, Owen, *Plays: 1* (London: Faber, 2013).
McCafferty, Owen, *Plays: 2* (London: Faber, 2016).
McDiarmid, Lucy, *The Irish Art of Controversy* (Dublin: Lilliput Press, 2005).
McDiarmid, Lucy, *At Home in the Revolution: What Women Said and Did in 1916* (Dublin: Royal Irish Academy, 2015).
McDonagh, Martin, *Plays: 1* (London: Methuen, 1999).
McDonald, Henry, 'Belfast Pub Wrecked as Violence Flares before World Cup Qualifier', *The Observer*, 29 March 2009.
McDonald, Marianne, 'The Irish and Greek Tragedy', in Michael Walton and Marianne McDonald (eds.), *Amid Our Troubles: Irish Versions of Greek Tragedy* (London: Methuen, 2002), 37–82.
McDonald, Marianne, 'Marina Carr's *Ariel*', *Didaskalia*, https://www.didaskalia.net/reviews/2002_10_02_01.html.
McFeely, Deirdre, *Dion Boucicault: Irish Identity on Stage* (Cambridge: Cambridge University Press, 2012).
McGee, Lisa, *Girls and Dolls* (London: Nick Hern Books, 2006).
McGuinness, Frank, *Observe the Sons of Ulster Marching towards the Somme* (London: Faber, 2016 [1986]).

McKay, Susan, *Northern Protestants on Shifting Ground* (Belfast: Blackstaff Press, 2021).
McKay, Susan, *Northern Protestants: An Unsettled People* (Belfast: Blackstaff Press, 2021 [2000]).
McPherson, Conor, *The Weir* (London: Nick Hern Books, 1998).
McPherson, Conor, 'If You're a Young Irish Playwright, Come to London', *New Statesman*, 20 February 1998.
McPherson, Conor, *Dublin Carol* (London: Nick Hern Books, 2000).
McPherson, Conor, *The Seafarer* (London: Nick Hern Books, 2006).
Meredith, Finola, 'Van Morrison's Belfast: From Cyprus Avenue to Hyndford Street', *Irish Times*, 29 August 2015, https://www.irishtimes.com/culture/music/van/van-morrison-s-belfast-from-cyprus-avenue-to-hyndford-street-1.2332247
Merriman, Vic '"As We Must": Growth and Diversification in Ireland's Theatre Culture 1977-2000', in Nicholas Grene and Chris Morash (eds.), *The Oxford Handbook of Modern Irish Theatre* (Oxford: Oxford University Press, 2016), 389-403.
Middeke, Martin, and Peter Paul Schnierer (eds.), *Methuen Drama Guide to Contemporary Irish Playwrights* (London: Methuen Drama, 2010).
Mitchell, David, 'Cooking the Fudge: Constructive Ambiguity and the Implementation of the Northern Ireland Agreement, 1998-2007', *Irish Political Studies*, 24.3 (2009), 321-36.
Moffatt, Alex 'Spruced-Up Playboy's Bursting with Comic Life', *Daily Mail*, 5 October 2007.
Moore, Walter, *Schrödinger: Life and Thought* (Cambridge: Cambridge University Press, 1989).
Moran, James, *The Theatre of Seán O'Casey* (London: Bloomsbury Methuen Drama, 2013).
Moran, James, 'Irish Theatre in Britain', in Nicholas Grene and Chris Morash (eds.), *The Oxford Handbook of Modern Irish Theatre* (Oxford: Oxford University Press, 2016), 607-22.
Morash, Chris, 'Places of Performance', in Nicholas Grene and Chris Morash (eds.), *The Oxford Handbook of Modern Irish Theatre* (Oxford: Oxford University Press, 2016), 425-42.
Morash, Chris, *Yeats on Theatre* (Cambridge: Cambridge University Press, 2022).
Moriarty, Gerry, 'Robinson and McGuinness Want "Peace Walls" Down within Ten Years', *Irish Times*, 10 May 2013.
Murphy, Tom, *Plays: Two* (London: Methuen Drama, 1993).
Murray, Christopher, *Twentieth-Century Irish Drama: Mirror Up to Nation* (Manchester: Manchester University Press, 1997).
Murray, Christopher, 'The Adigun-Doyle *Playboy* and Multiculturalism', in Nicholas Grene and Patrick Lonergan (eds.), *Irish Drama: Local and Global Perspectives* (Dublin: Carysfort Press, 2012), 109-20.
Murray, Simon, and John Keefe, *Physical Theatres* (London: Routledge, 2007).
https://www.nationaltheatre.org.uk/shows/the-plough-and-the-stars
https://www.northernireland.gov.uk/publications/haass-report-proposed-agreement
Norway, Mrs Hamilton, *The Sinn Fein Rebellion as I Saw It* (London: Smith Elder, 1916).
Ó Conchubhair, Brian, 'Twisting in the Wind: Irish-Language Stage Theatre 1884-2014', in Nicholas Grene and Chris Morash (eds.), *The Oxford Handbook of Modern Irish Theatre* (Oxford: Oxford University Press, 2016), 251-68.
O'Brien, Harvey, 'Improbable Frequency', *irish theatre magazine*, 15 March 2012, http://itmarchive.ie/web/Reviews/Current/Improbable-Frequency.aspx.html.
O'Halloran, Mark, *Conversations After Sex, Trade* (London: Methuen Drama, 2023).
O'Halpin, Eunan, *Spying in Ireland: British Intelligence and Irish Neutrality During the Second World War* (Oxford: Oxford University Press, 2008).
O'Kane, Eamonn, *The Northern Ireland Peace Process from Armed Conflict to Brexit* (Manchester: Manchester University Press, 2021).
O'Kelly, Donal, *Catalpa* (Dublin: New Island Books, 1997).
O'Kelly, Donal, *Bat the Father Rabbit the Son*, in John Fairleigh (ed.), *Far from the Land: New Irish Plays* (London: Methuen Drama, 1998), 191-234.
O'Kelly, Emer, 'Playboy of the Badlands: A Riot', *Sunday Independent*, 7 October 2007.
Orlova, Tamara A., 'Theatre Review: Purple Snowflakes and Titty Wanks', *Ikon: London Magazine*, 6 February 2018, https://www.ikonlondonmagazine.com/Theatre-Review-Purple-Snowflakes-and-Titty-Wanks

O'Rowe, Mark, *Howie the Rookie* (London: Nick Hern Books, 1999).
O'Rowe, Mark, *Made in China* (London: Nick Hern Books, 2001).
O'Rowe, Mark, *Terminus* (London: Nick Hern Books, 2007).
O'Rowe, Mark, *Our Few and Evil Days* (London: Nick Hern Books, 2014).
O'Sullivan, Michael, *Brendan Behan: A Life* (Dublin: Blackwater Press, 1997).
O'Toole, Fintan, 'Nowhere Man', *Irish Times*, 26 April 1997.
O'Toole, Fintan, *We Don't Know Ourselves* (London: Head of Zeus, 2021).
https://www.panpantheatre.com/shows/freehouse
https://www.panpantheatre.com/shows/the-rehearsalplaying-the-dane
Parker, Stewart, *Three Plays for Ireland: Northern Star, Heavenly Bodies, Pentecost* (London: Oberon Books, 1989).
Parr, Connal, 'Something Happening Quietly: Owen McCafferty's Theatre of Truth and Reconciliation', *Irish University Review*, 47 (2017), 531–48.
Patrick, Michael, and Oisín Kearney, *The Border Game* (London: Samuel French, 2021).
Paulin, Tom, *The Riot Act* (London: Faber, 1985).
https://www.peacewall-archive.net/peacewalls-50
Pease, Zeph W., *The Catalpa Expedition* (New Bedford, MA: George S. Anthony, 1897).
Pašeta, Senia, *Irish Nationalist Women, 1900–1918* (Cambridge: Cambridge University Press, 2013).
Phelan, Mark, 'From Troubles to Post-Conflict Theatre in Northern Ireland', in Nicholas Grene and Chris Morash (eds.), *The Oxford Handbook of Modern Irish Theatre* (Oxford: Oxford University Press, 2016), 372–88.
https://www.piventheatre.org/our-story/ourhistory/
https://planningtribunal.ie/wp-content/uploads/2019/04/sitecontent_1257.pdf
Quigley, Carole, 'Living in a Rape Culture: Gang Rape and "Toxic Masculinity" in Abbie Spallen's *Pumpgirl*', in David Clare, Fiona McDonagh, and Justine Nakase, *The Golden Thread: Irish Women Playwrights 1716–2018*, Vol. 2: *1992–2016* (Liverpool: Liverpool University Press, 2021), 99–108.
Raab, Michael, 'Mark O'Rowe', in Martin Middeke and Peter Paul Schnierer (eds.), *Methuen Drama Guide to Contemporary Irish Playwrights* (London: Methuen Drama, 2010), 345–64.
Ramsden, Timothy, *Oedipus Loves You* Review, 14 February 2008, https://reviewsgate.com/oedipus-loves-you-to-23-february/
Reid, Christina, *Plays: 1* (London: Methuen Drama, 1997).
Richards, Shaun '"The Outpouring of a Morbid Unhealthy Mind": The Critical Condition of Synge and McDonagh', *Irish University Review*, 33.1 (2003), 201–14.
Richtarik, Marilynn, *Getting to Good Friday* (Oxford: Oxford University Press, 2023).
Riordan, Arthur, and Bell Helicopter, *Improbable Frequency* (London: Nick Hern Book, 2005).
Robinson, Lennox, *Selected Plays*, ed. Christopher Murray (Gerrards Cross: Colin Smythe, 1982).
Roche, Anthony, *Contemporary Irish Drama*, 2nd ed. (London: Palgrave Macmillan, 2009).
Roche, Billy, *The Wexford Trilogy* (London: Nick Hern Books, 1992).
https://www.roughmagic.ie/seeds-history/
https://www.rte.ie/archives/2021/1021/1255124-border-customs-postsbombed/
RTÉ, *DruidSynge*, three-DVD set (Dublin: Wildfire Films/Druid, 2007).
RTÉ, 'Abbey Prepares to Wake the Nation in 2016' https://www.rte.ie/entertainment/2015/1028/737979-abbey-theatre-gets-set-to-wake-the-nation-in-2016/
Ruiz, Noelia, 'Scenic Transitions: From Drama to Experimental Practices in Irish Theatre', in Eamonn Jordan and Eric Weitz (eds.), *The Palgrave Handbook of Contemporary Irish Theatre and Performance* (London: Palgrave Macmillan, 2018), 293–308.
Ryan, Annie, and Michael West, 'Annie Ryan and Michael West in Conversation with Luke Clancy', in Lilian Chambers, Ger FitzGibbon, and Eamonn Jordan (eds.), *Theatre Talk: Voices of Irish Theatre Practitioners* (Dublin: Carysfort Press, 2001), 424–31.
Share, Bernard, *Slanguage—A Dictionary of Slang and Colloquial English in Ireland* (Dublin: Gill and Macmillan, 1997).

Shuttleworth, Ian, 'Oedipus Loves You / Oedipus', *Financial Times*, 18 February 2008, https://www.ft.com/content/e31fc274-de4a-11dc-9de3-0000779fd2ac

Sihra, Melissa, 'New Stages of Performing Carr', in Cathy Leeney and Anna McMullan (eds.), *The Theatre of Marina Carr: 'Before Rules Was Made'* (Dublin: Carysfort Press, 2003), 92–103.

Sihra, Melissa, *Marina Carr: Pastures of the Unknown* (Cham: Palgrave Macmillan, 2018).

Singleton, Brian, *Masculinities and the Contemporary Irish Theatre* (Basingstoke: Palgrave Macmillan, 2011).

Singleton, Brian, 'ANU Productions and Site-Specific Performance: The Politics of Space and Place', in Fintan Walsh (ed.), *'That Was Us': Contemporary Irish Theatre and Performance* (London: Oberon, 2013), 21–36.

Singleton, Brian, *ANU Productions: The Monto Cycle* (London: Palgrave Macmillan, 2016).

Spallen, Abbie, 'On Touring Pumpgirl', http://decadenttheatrecompany.ie/playwrights/abbie-spallen/

Spallen, Abbie, *Pumpgirl* (London: Faber, 2006).

Sun, The, 'Peking at Your Knickers', 24 March 2006.

Sweeney, Joanne, 'Sister Act—Lucy Caldwell Takes on Her Biggest Literary Challenge Yet', *Irish News*, 27 October 2016.

Synge, J. M., *Collected Works*, 4 vols, ed. Robin Skelton (London: Oxford University Press, 1962–8).

Synge, J. M., and W. B. Yeats, *Shadows: A Trinity of Plays by J.M. Synge and W.B. Yeats. Riders to the Sea, The Shadow of the Glen, Purgatory* (London: Oberon, 1998).

Szabo, Carmel, *The Story of Barabbas, the Company* (Dublin: Carysfort Press, 2012).

Tatlow, Antony, 'The Chinese Playboy', *Dublin Review of Books*, June 2008, https://drb.ie/articles/the-chinese-playboy/

Taylor, Cliff, 'Ireland Ranked as the Most Globalised of 62 States Due to Exports', *Irish Times*, 8 January 2003, https://www.irishtimes.com/news/ireland-ranked-as-the-most-globalised-of-62-states-due-to-exports-1.344603

Tracy, Robert, 'Rehearsing the 1916 Rising: Theatre Politics and Political Theatre', in Ros Dixon and Irina Ruppo Malone (eds.), *Ibsen and Chekhov on the Irish Stage* (Dublin: Carysfort Press, 2012), 127–38.

Trench, Rhona, *Blue Raincoat Theatre Company* (Dublin: Carysfort Press, 2015).

Trimble, David, 'Nobel Lecture', https://www.nobelprize.org/prizes/peace/1998/trimble/lecture/

Trotter, Mary, *Ireland's National Theaters: Political Performance and the Origins of the Irish Dramatic Movement* (Syracuse: Syracuse University Press, 2001).

https://twitter.com/shanehoranpr1/status/1356249383625494532

Venuti, Lawrence, *The Translator's Invisibility: A History of Translation* (London: Routledge, 2018 [1995]).

Verçosa, Fernanda, 'Interview with Owen McCafferty Scenes from the Big Picture', *ABEI*, 15 (2013), 65–76.

Wallace, Clare, 'Irish Drama since the 1990s: Disruptions', Nicholas Grene and Chris Morash (eds.), *The Oxford Handbook of Modern Irish Theatre* (Oxford: Oxford University Press, 2016), 529–44.

Walsh, Enda, 'The Best Performance I've Ever Seen', *Guardian*, 22 August 2010, https://www.theguardian.com/stage/2010/aug/22/enda-walsh-penelope-traverse-hampstead

Walsh, Enda, *Plays: One* (London: Nick Hern Books, 2011).

Walsh, Enda, *Plays: Two* (London: Nick Hern Books, 2014).

Walsh, Fintan, *Male Trouble: Masculinity and the Performance of Crisis* (Basingstoke: Palgrave Macmillan, 2010).

Walsh, Fintan, *'That Was Us': Contemporary Irish Theatre and Performance* (London: Oberon, 2013).

Walsh, Ian R., 'Embers', *irish theatre magazine*, 12 August 2011, http://itmarchive.ie/web/Reviews/Current/Embers.aspx.html

Walton, Michael, and Marianne McDonald (eds.), *Amid Our Troubles: Irish Versions of Greek Tragedy* (London: Methuen, 2002).
https://web.archive.org/web/20091031053514/http://www.thecboi.org/about/
West, Michael, in association with the Corn Exchange, *Freefall* (London: Methuen Drama, 2010).
West, Michael, in association with the Corn Exchange, *Dublin by Lamplight* (London: Bloomsbury Methuen Drama, 2017).
Wikipedia, 'Demographics of the Republic of Ireland', https://www.google.com/search?q=What+proportion+of+the+population+of+the+Republic+came+from+Asia+or+Aftirca&rlz=1C1GCEU_enIE1073IE1076&oq=What+proportion+of+the+population+of+the+Republic+came+from+Asia+or+Aftirca&gs_lcrp=EgZjaHJvbWUyBggAEEUYOTIGCAEQIRgK0gEJMzE3NDNqMGo0qAIAsAIA&sourceid=chrome&ie=UTF-8
Wills, Clair, *That Neutral Island* (London: Faber, 2007).
Wren, Celia, 'Irish Arts Group Solas Nua Brings "The Humours of Bandon" to D.C.', *The Washington Post*, 22 May 2023, https://www.washingtonpost.com/theater-dance/2023/05/22/solas-nua-the-humours-of-bandon/
Yeats, W. B., *Explorations* (London: Macmillan, 1961), https://www.youtube.com/watch?v=7uVwuEuBmn4 https://www.youtube.com/watch?v=CpNJTvfOWDY
YouTube, 'President Obama Speaks to the People of Northern Ireland', https://www.youtube.com/watch?v=sc9gupTbsIo

Index

For the benefit of digital users, indexed terms that span two pages (e.g., 52–53) may, on occasion, appear on only one of those pages.

Abbey Theatre, 3, 8, 23, 26, 32–33, 36–37, 44–46, 48, 55–58, 60, 65, 70, 87–88, 108, 125, 137, 142, 146–148, 151–152, 155–160, 164, 185–186, 204, 205–206, 215–218, 221
   Dear Ireland, 205–206
   14 Voices from the Bloodied Field, 206
   Gregory Project, 204
   An Octoroon, 218f
   The Plough and the Stars, 147f
   Waking the Nation, 142, 155
Abbey School of Acting, 23–24
Abraham, Jolly, 215–217, 218f
Adaptation, 119–136
Adewusi, Gabriel, 215–216
Adewusi, Loré, 217–218
Adigun, Bisi, 2, 45, 53–57
Aeschylus, 120–121
   Oresteia, 120–121, 125
   The Persians, 204
Allen, Mara, 217–218, 218f
Allen, Peter, 212–213
   'Once Before I Go', 212–213
Amos, Keith, 82–84
   The Fenians in Australia, 82–83
Anderson, 209
   The Tin Soldier, 209
ANU Productions, 24–25, 73, 80–81, 90–95, 145–146, 206
   All Hardest of Women, 206
   The Book of Names, 206
   Lolling, 206
   Monto Cycle, 2–3, 80–81, 90–95
      The Boys of Foley Streets, 90, 92–95
      Laundry, 90–94
      Vardo, 90, 93–95
      World's End Lane, 90–94
   The 1916 Tour: Beyond the Barricades; 145–146
   The Secret Space, 206
   Sunder, 145–146
   These Rooms, 145–146

Ulysses 2.2 project, 206–207
   The Wakefires, 186
Arambe Productions, 53–54
Aran Islands, 23, 58–59
   Inis Oírr, 206
Ardiff, Karen, 140–141, 195
Ark, The, Dublin, 155–156
Arts Council/An Chomhairle Ealaoín, 25–26, 28–29, 36–37, 155–156, 221
   Basic Income for the Arts, 221
Arts Council of Northern Ireland, 221
Arwel, Iestyn, 209
Asmus, Walter, 60–61
Aston, Elaine, 199
   Feminist Theatre Practice, 199
Avant-garde theatre, 2, 23–43
axis, Ballymun, 58–59, 72–73

The Bacchae of Baghdad, 60
Ball, Angeline, 55
Bao Gang, 52–53
Bao Shuo, 52
Barabbas, 2, 24–28, 31, 33, 36–37, 42–43
   Come Down from the Mountain, John Clown, John Clown, 25–26
   Half Eight Mass of a Tuesday, 25–26
   Macbeth, 25–26, 42–43
   The Whiteheaded Boy, 25–28, 33, 42–43, 50
Barker, Howard, 65
Barnes, Ben, 48
Barnstorm Theatre Company, 160
Barry, Sebastian, 8–10, 80–81, 206, 219
   Boss Grady's Boys, 8, 10
   Our Lady of Sligo, 80–81
   Prayers of Sherkin, 80–81
   The Steward of Christendom, 8–10, 206, 219
Bates, Michael, 141–142
Battle of the Somme, 137–140
Bausor, Jon, 148
Beckett, Samuel, 7, 28–9, 41, 60–1, 79, 206
   Act Without Words II, 28
   All That Fall, 41
   Breath, 60–61

INDEX 233

Cascando, 41–42
Eh Joe, 60–62
Embers, 41–42
Endgame, 29, 40–41, 60–61
Happy Days, 60–61, 206
Krapp's Last Tape, 29, 60–61
Laethanta Sona (*Happy Days*), 28, 206
Not I, 60–61
Ohio Impromptu, 60–61
A Piece of Monologue, 60–61
Play, 29
Rockaby, 60–61
Rough for Theatre II, 29
That Time, 60–61
Waiting for Godot, 29, 60–61, 137, 221–222
Bedrock, 24–25, 28, 60–61
Beckett's Ghosts, 60–61
Behan, Brendan, 10, 17–18, 23, 122–123, 204
The Quare Fellow, 10, 204
Beijing, 50–52, 56–57
Belfast, 2–3, 67–68, 99–103
Bell, Fiona, 216–217
Bell, Lian, 155–164
Bell Helicopter, 2–3, 80–81, 86–90, 95
Improbable Frequency, 2–3, 80–81, 86–90, 95
Beltable Theatre, Limerick, 65
Belton, Cathy, 49, 66
Bennett, Andrew, 35–37, 40–42, 71f
Berger, Glen, 65
Underneath the Lintel, 65
Bergin, Barbara, 204
Dublin Gothic, 204
b∗spoke Theatre Company, 65
Betjeman, John, 87
Bewley's Café Theatre, 145, 205–206, 211–212
Walkabout Theatre, 205–206, 211–212
Bigot, Georges, 32
Billington, Michael, 131, 183–184
Black Box Mime Theatre Company, Sligo, 25
Black pastoral, 13, 188
Blakeney, Jean, 113–114
Bliss, Panti, 211, 213
If These Wigs Could Talk, 213
Blue Raincoat, Sligo, 2, 24–25, 28–31, 42–43, 48, 49–50, 58, 65–66, 138, 206
Alice in Wonderland, 29, 48
The Chairs, 29–30, 42–43, 65–66
Happy Days, 206
Hunting Darwin, 31
The Last Pearl, 31
The Poor Mouth, 29
Shackleton, 30–31, 138, 139f
At Swim Two Birds, 29
The Third Policeman, 29

Bolger, David, 138, 207, 221–222
Bolger, Dermot, 72–73
The Townlands of Brazil, 72–73
Border, 107–113
Boss, Owen, 90–91
Tumbledowntown, 90–91
Boucicault, Dion, 217–218
The Corsican Brothers, 217–218
The Octoroon, 217
Bowie, David, 213–214
'Boys Keep Swinging', 213–214
Branar, 144
Maloney's Dream/Brionglóid Maloney, 144, 144f
Brantley, Ben, 39
Breen, Martha, 212–213
Brennan, Kate Stanley, 146, 211, 215–216
Brecht, Bertolt, 44
Señora Carrar's Rifles, 44
Breslin, John, 81–82
Brexit, 97–98
Brokentalkers, 24–25
Silver Stars, 24
Burke, Dee, 91–93
Bush Theatre, London, 8–9, 193
Butler, Jean, 209
What We Hold, 209

Cabaret, 87–88
Cadle, Giles, 66
Caldwell, Lucy, 2–3, 120–121, 132–136
Three Sisters, 2–3, 120–121, 132–136
Calipo, Drogheda, 58
Calypso, 58, 81, 85
Campion, Seán, 212–213
Carney, Liam, 70
Carr, Marina, 2–3, 8–10, 17, 22, 120–129, 136, 142, 155, 185–190, 204, 206, 221
Anna Karenina, 121, 155–156
Ariel, 120–121, 125, 126, 128
Audrey, or Sorrow, 204
Blood Wedding, 121
By the Bog of Cats, 2–3, 9, 120–125, 128, 135–136, 187–188
The Boy, 204
The Cordelia Dream, 121, 185–186
Girl on an Altar, 120–121
Hecuba, 2–3, 120–121, 125–128, 135–136, 222
To the Lighthouse, 121
The Mai, 8, 122–123, 187–188
Phaedra Backwards, 120–121, 125, 129
Portia Coughlan, 9, 122–123, 187–188, 206
On Raftery's Hill, 10, 186, 187–195

Carr, Marina (*Continued*)
  Signatories, 142
  16 Possible Glimpses, 121
Carson, Molly, 113–114
Carter, Riley, 213–214
Cartmell, Selina, 156–164, 212–213
Carty, John, 30–31, 139f
Casement, Roger, 141–142
Catalpa, The, 81–82
Catholics, 96, 99, 105, 107–108
Celtic Tiger, 2–3, 58–59, 69–70, 129
Chekhov, Anton, 2–3, 65–66, 119
  The Cherry Orchard, 119–120, 205
  'The Lady with the Dog', 119
  The Seagull, 32, 36–37, 119, 120
  Three Sisters, 2–3, 119, 120, 132–136
  Uncle Vanya, 119–120
Churchill, Caryl, 65
Churchill, Winston, 86–87
Civic, Tallaght, 58–59
Civil War, 1922-3, 107–108
Clancy, Andrew, 41–42
Clan-na-Gael, 81–82
Clarke, Anne, 156–164
Clarke, Jocelyn, 28–29
Clarke-Ng, Choy-Ping, 216
  Window a World, 216
Classic Stage Ireland, 62–63
  As You Like It, 62–63
Coburn, Veronica, 25–28, 31
CoisCéim Dance Theatre, 138
  Go to Blazes, 207
  Invitation to a Journey, 138
Commedia del' arte, 32–35, 71, 87–88
Company SJ, 206
  Laethanta Sona, 206
Connaughton, Philip, 212–213
  Party Scene, 212–213
Conroy, Amy, 213–214
  Luck Just Kissed You Hello, 213–214
Conway, Denis, 175–176
Cooper, Justine, 207
Copeau, Jacques, 25
Coquelard, Kévin, 209
Corcadorca, Cork, 58, 67–68
  The Tempest, 67–68
Cork, 17–18, 67–68, 143–144
Corn Exchange, The, 2, 24–25, 31–37, 42, 58, 71, 87–88, 160–161, 205
  Dublin by Lamplight, 32–34, 87–88
  Dubliners, 36–37
  Everyday, 34–35, 71, 71f
  The Fall of the Second Republic, 36–37, 205
  Foley, 32

Freefall, 34–37
A Girl is a Half-formed Thing, 36–37
Man of Valour, 36–37
A Play on Two Chairs, 32
The Seagull, 36–37, 42–43
Cornelius, Patricia, 211
  Shit, 211
Cosgrove, Aedín, 37, 40–41, 51
Covid, 36–37, 206, 219
Cox, Brian, 174
Cox, Jane, 71
Craig, William, 105
Cranitch, Ellen, 2–3, 120–121, 128–131, 135–136
  Phaedra, 2–3, 120–121, 128–131, 135–136
Crash Ensemble, 138
  Invitation to a Journey, 138
Crawley, Peter, 55, 89–90
Crean, Tom, 31
Crotty, Derbhle, 71f
Cullen, Barry, 30–31, 139f
Culleton, Jim, 140
Cummings, Alyson, 209–211

Daly, Caitríona, 186
  Goose Goose Duck, 186
Daly, Peter, 64f
Daly, P.T., 90–91
David Teevan, Ten42 Productions, 145
Dead Centre, 24–25, 38, 206–207, 219
  Good Sex, 215–216, 219
  To Be a Machine (Version 1.0), 206–207, 208f
Dean, Tanya, 56–57, 170–171
Decade of Centenaries, 3, 137, 138–140, 206
Decadent Theatre Company; 137
Decroux, Etienne, 25
Democratic Unionist Party, 96–97, 113–114
Dennehy, Donnacha, 207–209
  The First Child, 207–209
Dennehy, Ned, 38
Department of Foreign Affairs, 151
de Valera, Eamon, 87
Devaney, Brian F., 30–31, 139f
Devlin (McAliskey), Bernadette, 119–120
Devoy, John, 81–82
di Benedetto, Stephen, 166
Dickens, Charles, 172
  A Christmas Carol, 172
Dineen, Ferghal, 143–144
  Thomas Kent, Irish Rebel, 143–144, 151–152
Diss, Eileen, 61
dlr Mill Theatre, Dundrum, 58–59
Dongbei province, 51–52

Donoghue, Emma, 142
  Signatories, 142
Dowdall, Jonathan, 207
Doyle, Roddy, 2, 45, 53–57, 81, 215
  Barrytown Trilogy, 54–55
  The Commitments, 54–55
  Guess Who's Coming for the Dinner, 215
  The Van, 81
Doyle, Simon, 38
  Oedipus Loves You, 37–40
Draoicht, Blanchardstown, 58–59
Druid Theatre Company, Galway, 8–9, 45–48, 58, 137, 156, 160, 185–187, 205–206, 221–222
  DruidGregory, 205–206, 221–222
  DruidMurphy, 221–222
  DruidO'Casey, 221–222
  DruidShakespeare, 221–222
  DruidSynge, 2, 45–48, 56–57
  Waiting for Godot, 137, 221–222
Dubbeljoint, 72
Dublin, 2–3, 17–18, 45, 53–54, 58–59, 68–70
Dublin City Assembly House, 209
Dublin Fringe Festival, 65, 137–138, 155–156, 160–161
Dublin Institute of Advanced Studies, 87
Dublin International Theatre Symposium, 37
Dublin lockout, 1913, 138–140
Dublin Theatre Festival, 7–8, 66, 160–161, 186, 193–194, 204, 212–213
Durcan, Sarah, 155–164
Dyas, Grace, 150
Dylan, Bob, 165–166

Easter Rising, 3, 137–152
Eastwood, Desmond, 212–213
Edinburgh Festival, 190–191, 193
Edmundson, Helen, 65
  Mother Teresa is Dead, 65
Edward VII, 33–34
Edwards, Hilton, 23
Egoyan, Atom, 60–61
Eighth Amendment, Irish Constitution, 185
Eisenhower Theater, Kennedy Center, Washington, 187–190
Eldridge, David, 66–67
  Festen, 66–67
Elizabeth, Fort, Cork, 149–150
Ellis, Brendan, 49–50
Ennis, Caitríona, 92–93
'Emergency' (Second World War), 86
Emergency Powers Act, 86–87
Ervine, St John, 44
Euripides, 2–3, 119, 120–124

The Bacchae, 60, 119
Hecuba, 2–3, 120–121, 126–127
Hippolytus, 121, 129, 131
Iphigenia in Aulis, 125
Medea, 2–3, 119, 120–124, 128
European theatre, 23–31, 42, 120–121
Everyman Theatre, Cork, 143

Fabulous Beast Dance Theatre, 24–25
Factory Space, 28–29
Fannin, Hilary, 2–3, 120–121, 128–131, 135–136
  Children of the Sun, 204
  Doldrum Bay, 129
  Phaedra, 2–3, 120–121, 128–131, 135–136, 185–186, 222
Fanning, Arnold Thomas, 141–142
  McKenna's Fort, 141–142
Farrell, Elizabeth, 142
Fay, Catherine, 146
Fay, Frank, 32–33
Fay, William, 32–33
Feehily, Rachel, 142
  Signatories, 142
Felloni, Tony, 92–93
Field Day Theatre Company, Derry, 58, 77
Fire and Ice Theatre Company, 141–142
Fishamble: the New Play Company (Pigsback), 58, 68–70, 137–138, 140, 145
  Inside the GPO, 140f
  Show in a Bag, 137–138, 185–186
  Whereabouts, 68–70
    Carr, Shane, 68–69
      Mean Sweeps I and II, 68–69
    Cronin, John, 69
      Twenty-Two, 69
    Grogan, John, 69
      Blind Spot, 69
    Lowe, Louise, 69
      Eclipsed I and II, 69
    McKeon, Belinda, 69
      Drapes, 68–69
    Murphy, Colin, 68–69
      Dublin Noir, 68–69
    Newell, Anna, 68–69
      My Brother Is Disappearing, 69
    Olohan, Jack, 69
      Bernard Opens Up, 69
    O'Neill, Jody, 69
      Lament for Joseph, 69
    Strawbridge, Jacqueline, 69
      Eggshell, 69

Fiishamble: the New Play Company (Pigsback) (*Continued*)
   Swift, Tom, 68–69
      The Other Woman, 68–69
Fitzgerald, Barry, 23–24
Fitzgerald, Liz, 140*f*
Flynn, Tara, 213
   Haunted, 213
Focus Theatre, 65
Fosse, Jan, 65–66
   A Dream of Autumn, 65–66
Foster, R. F., 142
   Vivid Faces, 142
Fouéré, Olwen, 49
Frawley, Monica, 64
Frazer, Willie, 113–114
Frears, Stephen, 81
Fricker, Karen, 55, 166
Friel, Brian, 7–10, 17–18, 77, 79–80, 119, 120, 191
   Faith Healer, 9–10, 191
   Making History, 77, 79–80
   Philadelphia Here I Come!, 7–9
   Three Plays After, 119
   Three Sisters, 119–120
   Translations, 58, 77, 79–80, 206
   Uncle Vanya, 119
   The Yalta Game, 119
Frost, Robert, 113
   'Mending Wall', 113

Gaiety School of Acting, 23–24
Gallen, Michael, 207–209
   Elsewhere, 207–209
Galloglass, Clonmel, 58, 65–66
Galway Arts Festival, 138
Gambon, Michael, 61–62, 62*f*
Ganley, David, 146
Garter Lane Arts Centre, Waterford, 148–149
Gate Theatre, 23, 58, 60–61, 66, 137, 155–156, 159, 204, 209, 212–213, 221
   Beckett on Stage, 60–61
   Eh Joe, 62*f*
   Once Before I Go, 213*f*
General Post Office, Dublin, 140
Gleeson, Jack, 206–207, 208*f*
Gonne, Maud, 32–33
Good Friday Agreement, 2–3, 22, 72, 96–98, 100, 107–108, 191, 220–221
Gordon, Sylvia, 109–110
Gorky, Maxim, 204
   Children of the Sun, 204
Gray, Dylan Coburn, 215–216
   Absent the Wrong, 215–216

Greek tragedy, 2–3, 119–128
Gregg, Stacey, 2–3, 98, 107–111, 185–186, 200–202
   Lagan, 108, 201
   Override, 201
   Perve, 108, 185–186, 201
   Scorch, 108, 186–187, 200–202, 204
   Shibboleth, 98, 107–111, 117–118, 185–186
Gregory, Augusta, 23, 33–34, 60, 204
Greig, David, 65, 137
   Outlying Islands, 65
   Pyrenees, 65
Grene, Nicholas, 1
   The Politics of Irish Drama, 1
Grianan, An, Letterkenny, 58–59
Groundwork NI, 109–110
Guardian, 60
Gunning, Jonathan, 144, 144*f*
Gussow, Mel, 24

Haass Report, 103
Halligan, Manus, 140*f*, 141
Hamilton, Hugo, 142–143
   Signatories, 142–143
Hamilton, Malcolm, 25, 29
Hanly, Peter, 87–88
Hanly, Sarah, 3, 186–187, 195–200
   Purple Snowflakes and Titty Wanks, 186–187, 195–200
Hardy, Thomas, 123
   The Mayor of Casterbridge, 123
Harris, Nancy, 3, 185–187, 200, 202–204
   The Beacon, 202
   No Romance, 185–186, 202
   Somewhere Out There You, 186–187, 200, 202–204
Hastings, Michael, 65
Hatch Theatre Company, 65
Hayes, James, 146
Hayes, Michael, 49
Healey, Anna, 216–217
Heaney, Mick, 55
Heaney, Seamus, 60, 119–120
   The Burial at Thebes, 60, 119–120
   The Cure at Troy, 60
Henry, Niall, 2, 25, 28–31, 42, 45, 48–50, 56–57
Hickey, Tom, 24
Higgins, Michael D., 146
Hillen, Sean, 26–27
Hogan, Bosco, 216–217
Holmes, Sean, 146
Home Rule, 138–140

Homer, 174–175
  The Odyssey, 174–175
Horniman, A.E., 32–33
Hughes, Declan, 222
Humphries, Heather, 155
Hurley, Frank, 30
Hynes, Garry, 2, 45–48, 56–57, 151–152, 156–164, 221–222

Ibsen, Henrik, 65–66, 148–149
Industrial Schools, 123
Ingalls, James, 212–213
Ionesco, Eugene, 29
  The Bald Prima Donna, 29
  The Chairs, 29–30
  Rhinoceros, 29
Ireland, David, 2–3, 98, 103–105, 113–118
  Cyprus Avenue, 98, 103–105, 113–118
  Everything Between Us, 98, 102, 103–105
Irish Constitution, 1937, 86–87
Irish Literary Revival, 9
Irish Museum of Modern Art, Kilmainhan, 205–206
Irish National Opera, 205–209
  Twenty Shots of Opera, 205–206
Irish Playography, 1 n.2
Irish Theatre Institute, 137–138
Irish Times, 89–90
  Irish Times Irish Theatre Awards, 1, 36–37, 58–59, 137, 138, 209, 211–212, 222
Isherwood, Christopher, 87–88
  Goodbye to Berlin, 87–88
'Island: Arts from Ireland', Arts festival, Washington DC, 187
Island Theatre Company, 65

Jacobs-Jenkins, Branden, 215–218
  An Octoroon, 215–218
Jenkinson, Rosemary, 72
  The Bonefire, 72
Jennings, Jennifer, 211
Johnson, Terry, 65
  Hysteria, 65
Johnston, Denis, 23
  The Moon in the Yellow River, 23
  The Old Lady Says No!, 23
Jones, Marie, 8–10
  A Night in November, 8
  Stones in his Pockets, 9–10
Jordan, Wayne, 213–214
Joyce, James, 17–18, 32–33, 206, 207, 215–216
  Dubliners, 32–33, 215–216
  Finnegans Wake, 17–18
  Ulysses, 32–33, 206, 207

Kabosh, Belfast, 67–68, 211–212
  The Waiting Room, 67–68
Kavanagh, John, 174
Kavanagh, Patrick, 15–16, 24, 86–87, 205–206
  The Great Hunger, 24, 205–206
  'Inniskeen Road: July Evening', 15–16
  'Lough Derg', 86–87 n.27
Kavanagh, Una, 91–92
Keegan-Dolan, Michael, 138, 209
  How to be a Dancer in Seven-Two Thousand Easy Lessons, 209
  Swan Lake/Loch na hEala, 138, 209
Keane, John B., 7
  The Field, 7
Keane, Raymond, 25–28, 31
Kearney, Oisin, 2–3, 98, 111–113, 117–118
  The Alternative, 111
  The Border Game, 98, 107–108, 111–113, 117–118
  My Left Nut, 111
Keating, Sara, 92–93, 209–211
Keenan, Rory, 63–64, 64f, 66
Kelly, Aidan, 141
Kelly, Conor, see Bell Helicopter
Kelly, Darragh, 63, 89
Kelly, Nicholas, 70
  The Grown-Ups, 70
Kelly, Sonya, 3, 185–187, 195–197, 199–200, 216–217, 221–222
  Furniture, 221–222
  How to Keep an Alien, 185–187, 195–197, 200
  The Last Return, 216–217
  The Wheelchair on My Face, 185–186
Kennelly, Brendan, 119–121
  Antigone, 119
  Medea, 119
  The Trojan Women, 119
Kenny, Enda, 92–93
Kenny, Mike, 144–145
  The Messenger, 144–145
Kenny, Pat, 92–93
Kent, Thomas, 143–144
Keogh, Garret, 148–149
Kilbarrack, 53–54, 56–57
Kilmainham prison, 142–143
Kilroy, Thomas, 7–8, 77, 119–120, 142–143
  The Death and Resurrection of Mr Roche, 7–8
  Double Cross, 29, 77, 78
  The Seagull, 119–120
  Signatories, 142–143
Kinahan, Deirdre, 3, 145, 186, 193–195
  Halcyon Days, 195

INDEX

Kinahan, Deirdr (*Continued*)
   An Old Song, Half Forgotten, 195
   Outrage, 186
   Rathmines Road, 186, 193–195
   Wild Sky, 145
Kirby, Simone, 63, 66
Knight, Trevor, 82
Kushner, Tony, 214
   Angels in America, 214
Kuti Elizabeth, 65–66 n.8, 80–81, 204, 215
   The Sugar Wife, 80–81, 204, 215
   Treehouses, 65–66 n.8

LAB Gallery, The, 91
Lally, Mick, 46
Lambe, Lisa, 88
Landmark Theatre Productions, 138, 156, 206–209
   Ulysses 2.2 project, 206–207
Lantern Productions, 143
Lao Wei, 52–53
Lavin, Mary, 205–206
   In the Middle of the Fields, 205–206
Lawrence, D. H., 44
   The Widowing of Mrs Holroyd, 44
Leahy, Ronan, 66, 141
Lecoq, Jacques, 25, 29–30, 49–50
Lee, 93–94
Lehane, Ruth, 29–30
Lehmann, Hans-Thies, 37–38, 41
Leonard, Hugh, 7–8
   Stephen D, 7–8
Lewis, Louise, 71*f*
Lime Tree Theatre, 205–206
Lir, The, 23–24, 137–138, 222
Livin' Dred Theatre Company, 137
Lloyd-Anderson, Ian, 146
Lombard, Garrett, 221–222
Lonergan, Patrick, 7, 41–42, 171, 182–183
Loose Canon, 24–25, 28
Lovett, Louis, 27, 36–37, 209
Lowe, Louise, 2–3, 69, 90–91
   The Boys of Foley Street, 91 n.41
   Tumbledowntown, 90–91
Lowell, Robert, 128–129
Luke Murphy Attic Projects, 209–211, 219
   Volcano, 209–211, 210*f*, 219
Lyon International Student Festival, 37
Lyric Theatre, Belfast, 137, 193, 207–209, 211–212

McAnally, Aonghus Og, 145
Mac Anna, Tomás, 7–8
McAuley, Ciaran, 49–50

McAuliffe, Margaret, 3, 137–138, 185–187, 195–197, 199–200
   The Humours of Bandon, 137–138, 185–187, 195–197, 200
McBride, Eimear, 36–37
   A Girl is a Half-formed Thing, 36–37
McBrinn, Róisín, 204
McCabe, Eugene, 7–8
   King of the Castle, 7–8
McCabe, Patrick, 149–150, 188
   The Butcher Boy, 188
   Sacrifice at Easter, 149–150
McCafferty, Owen, 2–3, 98, 99–103, 105–109, 117–118
   Closing Time, 102
   Mojo Mickeybo, 99
   Quietly, 98, 102, 105–109, 117–118
   Scenes from the Big Picture, 98–103, 117–118
   The Waiting List, 99
McCann, Donal, 219
McCartney, Robert, 96–97
McCormack, Mike, 205
   Solar Bones, 205
McCormick, F.J., 23–24
McCormick, John, 37
McCourt, Frank, 188
   Angela's Ashes, 188
McDiarmid, Lucy, 142
   At Home in the Revolution, 142
McDonagh, Martin, 2, 8–13, 21–22, 165, 169, 221–222
   The Beauty Queen of Leenane, 8–9, 11–13, 169, 188
   A Behanding in Spokane, 165 n.2
   Hangmen, 165 n.2
   The Leenane Triilogy, 8–9, 46, 221–222
   The Lonesome West, 169
   A Very Very Very Dark Matter, 165 n.2
McGee, Lisa, 72–73
   Derry Girls, 72
   Girls and Dolls, 72–73
McGovern, Barry, 63, 64*f*
McGuinness, Frank, 8, 77, 78–79, 119, 137–138
   Donegal, 138
   Observe the Sons of Ulster Marching Towards the Somme, 8, 77, 78–79, 137
   Uncle Vanya, 119–120
   The Visiting Hour, 206
McIntyre, Tom, 24, 80–81
   Good Evening, Mr Collins, 80–81
   The Great Hunger, 24
McKay, Susan, 97, 113–114
   Northern Protestants on Shifting Ground, 113–114

McLaughlin, Caitríona, 156–164, 204
Mac Liammóir, Micheál, 23
Mac Lochlainn, Marc, 144
   Maloney's Dream/Brionglóid Maloney, 144
McLynn, Pauline, 63–64
McMahon, Phillip, 211–213, 219
   Once Before I Go, 212–213, 219
   Party Scene, 212–213
McPherson, Conor, 2–3, 8–10, 15–17, 22, 138,
      165–167, 172–174, 177–181, 183–184,
      191, 215, 221
   Dublin Carol, 165, 172–174, 178, 179, 183
   Girl from the North Country, 165–166
   The Night Alive, 165, 167, 177, 183–184
   Port Authority, 165–166
   Rum and Vodka, 172
   The Seafarer, 165–167, 172, 174, 177–181,
      183
   Shining City, 165, 177
   St Nicholas, 8–9, 177
   The Weir, 8–9, 15–17, 137, 215–216
McVeigh, Paul, 211–212
   Big Man, 211–212
Maffey, Sir John, 87
Magdalene homes, 34, 92–93
Mahon, Derek, 119, 128–129
   The Bacchae, 119
   King Oedipus, 119
   Phaedra, 119, 128–129
Mahon Tribunal, 69–70
Malone, Matthew, 212–213, 213*f*
Manning, Mary, *Youth's the Season–?*, 204
Marceau, Marcel, 25
Martins, Patrick, 217–218, 218*f*
Martyn, Edward, 32–33
Mason, Patrick, 24
Matthews, Aidan Carl, 119
   Antigone, 119
Maugham, Somerset, 137
   The Constant Wife, 137
Mayorga, Juan, 65–66
   Way to Heaven, 65–66
Meaney, Colm, 81
Meath County Council, 145
Mercier, Paul, 70
   Homeland, 70
Mescal, Paul, 222
Midlands, Irish, 122–123
Miller, Arthur, 65, 148–149
Milton, John, 182
   Paradise Lost, 182
Miroirs Étendus, 207–209
Mitchell, Conor, 207–209
   Propaganda, 207–209

Mitchell, Gary, 72
   Remnants of Fear, 72
Mnouchkine, Ariane, 32
   Théâtre du Soleil, 32
Monaghan, Aaron, 221–222
Monaghan, Zita, 144*f*
Montague, Dominic, 211–212
   Callings, 211–212
Moran, Janet, 36–37, 71*f*
Morash, Chris, 23, 58
Morrison, Conall, 60
Mother and Baby Homes Report, 215–216
Moukarzel, Bush, 38
Moxley, Gina, 38, 40–42, 222
Mullen, Marie, 46–47, 221–222
Murfi, Mikel, 25–28, 31, 45, 49–50
Murphy, Colin, 140, 142–143, 146
   Inside the GPO, 140*f*, 142-3, 146
Murphy, Elaine, 185–186
   Little Gem, 185–186
   Shush, 185–186
Murphy, Jimmy, 53–54, 137, 183
   The Kings of the Kilburn High Road, 53–54,
      183
Murphy, Luke, 209–211, 210*f*
Murphy, Tadhg, 63, 64*f*, 68
Murphy, Tom, 7–8, 16, 29, 119, 120, 205
   Bailegangaire, 16, 137
   The Cherry Orchard, 119–120, 205
   Conversations on a Homecoming, 171
   A Crucial Week in the Life of a Grocer's
      Assistant, 7–8
   Famine, 7–8
   The Gigli Concert, 182–183
   The Morning After Optimism, 7–8
   The Wake, 137, 155
   A Whistle in the Dark, 7–8, 29, 171, 206
Murphy, Tom, 71*f*
Murray, Christopher, 166–167
Murray, Erica, 204
   The Loved Ones, 204
Murray, Jed, 92–93
Murray, Peta, 65
   Wallflowering, 65
Museum of Literature of Ireland
      (MoLI), 206
   Ulysses 2.2 project, 206–207
Myers, Umi, 217–218

Nabokov, Vladimir, 32
   Lolita, 32
National Stadium, 211
National Theatre, London, 151–152, 180–181
National theatre movement, 2–3, 23

Nassau Hotel, 33–34
Negga, Ruth, 32, 38, 60
Nevin, Catherine, 54
New Statesman, 8–9
New York Times, 24, 39
Ní Ainnle, Jeanne Nicole, 217–218
Ní Chaoimh, Bairbre, 85
Ni Dhomhnall, Nuala, 204
   The Persians, 204
Ní Dhuibhne, Éilís, 142–143
   Signatories, 142–143
Ní Ghráda, Máiréad, 7–8
   An Triail, 7–8
Ní Neachtaín, Bríd, 206
Nolan, Jim, 148–149, 151–152
   Johnny I Hardly Knew Ye, 148–149, 151–152
Nolan, Rory, 63, 64*f*, 87–88, 217, 221–222
Northern Bank robbery, 96–97
North of Ireland/Northern Ireland, 2–3, 96–118, 191
   Census, 2021, 113–114
Northern Ireland (NI) Executive, 78
Norton, Helen, 137–138
   To Hell in a Handbag, 137–138
Nun's Island Theatre, Galway, 209–211

O'Brien, Ciarán, 146–147
O'Brien, Eugene, 211–212, 219
   Heaven, 211–212, 219
O'Brien, Flann (Brian O'Nolan), 29, 87
   At-Swim-Two-Birds, 29, 87
   An Beal Bocht/The Poor Mouth, 29, 87
   The Third Policeman, 29, 87
O'Casey, Sean, 10, 17–18, 23, 122–123, 145–148, 151–152
   The Plough and the Stars, 146–148, 151–152
O'Connell, Mark, 206–207
   To Be a Machine (Version 1.0), 206–207
O'Connor, Barry, 150
O'Connor, Francis, 46–47, 212–213, 221–222
O'Connor, Robbie, 145
   Rebel Rebel, 145
O'Donnellan, Ross, 213–214
Ódú, 209
O'Halloran, Mark, 36–37, 71*f*, 211, 219
   Conversations after Sex, 211, 219
   Trade, 211–212
Ó hAnnarracháin, Eoin, 143–144
   Thomas Kent, Irish Rebel, 143–144, 151–152
O'Kane, Eamonn, 97–98
O'Kelly, Donal, 2–3, 9–10, 80–86, 95
   Asylum! Asylum!, 81, 215
   Bat the Father Rabbit the Son, 81–82
   Catalpa, 2–3, 9–10, 80–86, 95

Farawayan, 81
O'Kelly, Emer, 55
Ó Loinsigh, Fionn, 211, 216–217
Omagh bombing, 96–97
O'Mahony, Maeve, 217–218, 218*f*
O'Malley, Sandra, 30–31, 139*f*
O'Meara, Aisling, 145, 211–212
   Next Please, 211–212
   Rebel Rebel, 145
Once Off Productions, 207–209
O'Neill, Eugene, 65
O'Neill, Jamie, 213–214
O'Neill, Louise, 186
   Asking for It, 186
O'Neill, Michelle, 113–114
O'Reilly Theatre, Belvedere School, 87–88
Oriental Pioneer Theatre, Beijing, 50–51
Ormsby, Frank, 98
O'Rowe, Mark, 2–3, 8–10, 20–22, 165–169, 171, 177, 181–184, 191
   The Approach, 165–166
   Crestfall, 169, 177
   Howie the Rookie, 8–9, 20–22, 177, 183–184
   Made in China, 166, 168–169, 171, 182
   Our Few and Evil Days, 165, 172
   Terminus, 165–167, 169, 177, 181–183
O'Sheil, Conal, 144–145
O'Sullivan, Aisling, 212–213
Ó Tuairisc, Eoghan, 149
   Fornocht Do Chonac/Naked I Saw You, 149
Our Steps and Lovano, 209
Outburst Queer Arts Festival, Belfast, 200–201

Paisley, Ian, 119–120
Pankhurst, Dale, 97
Pan Pan, 2, 24–25, 37–43, 45, 50–54, 56–57
   A Doll House, 39–40
   All That Fall, 41
   Cascando, 41–42
   Embers, 41–42
   Freehouse, 42–43
   Macbeth 7, 39–40, 42–43
   Mespil in the Dark, 206–207
   Oedipus Loves You, 37–40
   The Playboy of the Western World, 37, 50–57
   The Rehearsal: Playing the Dane, 39–41
   The Seagull and Other Birds, 39–40, 42–43
Park, Simon, see Bell Helicopter
Parker, Lynne, 62–64, 156–164, 221–222
Parker, Stewart, 77, 79–80, 137
   Heavenly Bodies, 77 n.1
   Northern Star, 77, 79–80, 137
   Pentecost, 77 n.1
Patrick, Michael, 2–3, 98, 111–113

The Alternative, 111
The Border Game, 98, 107–108, 111–113, 117–118
My Left Nut, 111
Pašeta, Senia, 142
  Irish Nationalist Women, 142
Passion Machine, 58
Paulin, Tom, 60
  The Riot Act, 60, 119–120
Pavilion Theatre, Dun Laoghaire, 58–59
Peace walls, Belfast, 97–98, 107–108
Peacock Theatre, 45, 48, 50, 70, 81, 108, 185–186, 193–194
Pease, Zeph, 82–83
  The Catalpa Expedition, 82–83
Penhall, Joe, 65, 215
  Blue/Orange, 65, 215
Performance Corporation, 68, 205–206
  Disappearing Islands, 205–206
Phelan, Jack, 36
Physical theatre, 25–31
Piesse, Amanda, 39–40
Pine, Emilie, 215–216, 219
  Good Sex, 215–216, 219
Pinget, Robert, 60–61
  The Old Tune, 60–61
Pinter, Harold, 169
  The Caretaker, 169
Pirie, Hamish, 110
Piven, Byrne, 31–32
Piven, Jeremy, 32
Piven, Joyce, 31–32
Piven Theatre Workshop, 31–32
Playhouse, Derry, 58–59
Poirier, Rachel, 209
Postdramatic theatre, 37–38, 41
Power, Geoff, 186
  Stronger, 186
Prime Cut, Belfast, 60–61, 65
  Endgame, 60–61
Project Arts Theatre, 50–52, 58–59, 63, 65, 141–142, 206–207
Protestants, 77, 95, 96–97, 99, 104–105, 107–109, 113–114, 132

Quartey, Ekow, 215–216
Quinn, Eoghan, 215–216
  Colic, 215–216
Quinn, Gavin, 2, 37–43, 45, 50–53
  Negative Act, 37
  Oedipus Loves You, 37–40

Race, 214–219
Racine, Jean, 2–3, 120–121, 128–131

Phaedra, 2–3, 120–121, 128–131
RADA, 23–24
Rameau, Jean-Philippe, 120–121, 129, 131
  Hippolyte et Aricie, 120–121, 129, 131
Raabke, Tilman, 174–175
Rathaya, Pai, 209–211
RAW Productions, 65–66
Rea, Marty, 221–222
Rea, Stephen, 77
Reardon, Daniel, 40, 42
Red Kettle Theatre Company, Waterford, 2–3, 58, 85, 148–149
Regan, Morna, 185–186
  Midden, 185–186
Reid, Christina, 77–79, 95
  Tea in a China Cup, 77–79, 95
Reid, Paul, 36–37
Reidy, Gabrielle, 70
Reilly, Thomas, 92–93
Republic of Ireland, Census 2022, 214
Republicans, 96, 107–108, 113–114, 141–142
Rice, Simon, 71f
Richter, Falk, 65–66
  The System Parts I and II, 65–66
Riordan, Arthur, 2–3, 80–81, 86–90, 95, 222
  Improbable Frequency, 2–3, 80–81, 86–90, 95, 222
  Peer Gynt, 86
  The Train, 86
Robinson, Lennox, 25–27
  The Whiteheaded Boy, 25–28
Robinson, Peter, 113–114
Roche, Billy, 2, 8–10, 13–18, 165
  A Handful of Stars, 8
  Poor Beast in the Rain, 8, 13–15
  Wexford Trilogy, 8–9
Roe, Owen, 63–64, 66–67, 219
Rose and Crown pub bombing, 105
Rough Magic, 2–3, 58, 62–63, 65–66, 72, 81, 86, 87–90, 137, 155–156, 160, 164, 185–186, 205, 215, 221–222
  SEEDS programme, 222
  A Midsummer Night's Dream, 222
  The Taming of the Shrew, 62–64, 64f, 222
  The Tempest, 222
Royal Court Theatre, 8–9, 16, 187
Royal Shakespeare Company, 128, 161
RTÉ, 92–93
Ryan, Annie, 31–37, 87–88, 215–216
Ryan Report, 66

Saad, Mahnoor, 146, 147f
Sadler's Wells, 138

Scaife, Sarah-Jane, 28
Schrödinger, Erwin, 87
Second Age, 62–63
   Macbeth, 62–63
Semper Fi, 67–68
Sexualities, 22, 211–214
Shackleton, Ernest, 30
Shaffer, Peter, 29
   Equus, 29
Shakespeare, William
   As You Like It, 62–63
   Hamlet, 39–41, 137
   King Lear, 159–160
   Macbeth, 62–63
   A Midsummer Night's Dream, 222
   Othello, 137
   The Taming of the Shrew, 62–64
   The Tempest, 222
Shanley, John Patrick, 65
   Doubt, 65
Shaw, Bernard, 137
   Saint Joan, 137
Shaw, Niamh, 91–92
Shepard, Sam, 65
   True West, 65
Sick and Indigent Roomkeepers, Dublin, 67–68
Simpson, Christopher, 60
Simpson-Pike, Anthony, 217–218
Singleton, Brian, 166
Sinn Féin, 96–97, 113–114
Sligo, 25, 28–29
Smith, Jean Kennedy, 187
Solstice Arts Centre, Navan, 58–59
Sophocles, 38, 60, 119
   Antigone, 38, 60, 119–120
   Oedipus at Colonus, 38, 60
   Oedipus the King, 38, 41, 60, 119
   Philoctetes, 60, 119
Spallen, Abbie, 185–186, 190–196
   Abeyance, 185–186
   Lally the Scut, 193
   Pumpgirl, 186, 190–195
   Strandline, 193
Stebbing, Rosie, 207
Stembridge, Gerry, 25–26
Stone, Maeve, 155
Stoppard, Tom, 87
   Rosencrantz and Guildenstern Are Dead, 174–175
   Travesties, 87
Storytellers Theatre Company, 58
Strachan, Kathy, 47
Strain, Lórcan, 209
Stratiev, Stanislav, 65–66

It's a Short Life, 65–66
Straymaker, 207–209
Strindberg, August, 137
   Creditors, 137
Sunningdale Agreement, 105
Swaleh, Naima, 216–217
Sweeny, Conan, 49
Swift, Tom, 68–69
   Drive-by, 68
Symons, Ailish, 68
Synge, J.M., 2, 9, 10–13, 23, 42–57, 122–123, 213
   Le baladin du monde occidentale (Playboy), 48
   Deirdre of the Sorrows, 44, 47–48
   The Playboy of the Western World, 2, 9, 11–13, 15, 37, 44–57, 213
   Riders to the Sea, 44–48
   The Shadow of the Glen, 44, 47
   The Tinker's Wedding, 44, 46–47
   The Well of the Saints, 44, 46, 47

Taibhdhearc, An, Galway, 149
Talbot St bombing, 92–93
Tall Tales, 65
   Women Writing Worldwide, 65
Taylor, Jill Bolte, 35–36
Teać Daṁsa, 138, 209
Terrera, Giles, 55
THEATREClub, 150–151
   It's Not Over, 150–152
thisispopbaby, 211–213
   RIOT, 211
   WAKE, 211
Thompson, Will, 209–211, 210f
Three Stooges, The, 169–170
Tighe, Dylan, 38
Tondut, Mary, 83
Town Hall Theatre, Galway, 58–59, 144
Townsend, Stanley, 205
Trimble, David, 96
Trinity College Dublin, 37, 56–57, 137–138, 150
   D.U. Players, 159
   Samuel Beckett Theatre, 42–43, 150
Troubles, Northern Ireland, 89, 96–118, 191
   'disappeared, the', 73, 89, 97, 149, 191
Truth and Reconciliation Commission, South Africa, 97
Turner, Aidan, 68
Tynan, Kenneth, 10

Ulster Covenant, 138–140
Ulster Division, British Army, 138–140
Ulster Unionist Party, 96

Ulster Workers Council strike, 105
Unionists, 96–97
United Fall, 209
  birdboy, 209
University College Dublin, 142
University of Galway, 163

Vanguard, 105
Vartan, Jamie, 28–31, 49
Venuti, Lawrence, 119–120
Verdant Productions, 142
Verlaque, Amanda, 211–212
  *This Sh*t Happens All the Time*, 211–212

#WakingTheFeminists, 3, 142, 155–164, 185–186, 204, 220–221
  Gender Counts, 155–156
Walker, Paul and Eugene O'Brien, 67–68
  God's Grace, 67–68
Wallace, Clare, 166
Wallace, Naomi, 65
  The Trestle at Pope Lick Creek, 65
Walsh, Catherine, 47
Walsh, Eileen, 55, 146
Walsh, Enda, 2–3, 8, 10, 17–20, 22, 85, 138, 165–167, 169–171, 174–177, 183–184, 207, 221
  Arlington, 138
  Ballyturk, 165–166
  bedbound, 169
  Disco Pigs, 8, 17–20, 22
  The First Child, 207–209
  The Ginger Ale Boy, 20
  How These Desperate Men Talk, 175–176
  Medicine, 165–166
  misterman, 172
  The New Electric Ballroom, 172
  Penelope, 166–167, 174–177
  The Walworth Farce, 166–167, 169–171, 175–176
Walsh, Fintan, 166
Wang Zhuo, 52–53
Warner, Rebecca, 93–94
Watergate Theatre, Kilkenny, 58–61, 144–145, 205

Watkins, Neil, 69
West, Michael, 31–37, 71, 119, 205, 215–216
  Dublin by Lamplight, 32–34
  Everyday, 34–35, 71
  The Fall of the Second Republic, 36–37, 205
  Foley, 32
  Freefall, 34–37, 206–207
  A Play on Two Chairs, 32
West, Rachel, 65–66
White, Ali, 155
  Me, Mollser, 155
White, Jonathan, 137–138
  To Hell in a Handbag, 137–138
Wilde, Oscar, 32–33
Wilder, Thornton, 28
  The Long Christmas Dinner, 28
Williams, Ralph Vaughan, 44
  Riders to the Sea, 44
Williams, Tennessee, 32, 65
  A Streetcar Named Desire, 32
Wilton, Penelope, 62
Winters, Carmel, 155–156
  The Remains of Maisie Duggan, 155–156
Wooster Group, 39
World War I, 138–140
Worsley, Henry, 31
Wycherley, Don, 141
Wyndham-Campbell Prize, 193

Xia Zi Xin, 52–53
Xinjiang province, 50–52
Xnthony (Anthony Feigher), 209
  Oliver Cromwell Is Really Very Sorry, 209
Yeats, W.B., 23, 30, 32–34
  At the Hawk's Well, 30
  The Cat and the Moon, 30
  Oedipus at Colonus, 60
  Oedipus the King, 60
  On Baile's Strand, 30
Yergainharsian, Nyree, 146–147
Yue Sun, 50–51

Zhang Wan Kun, 52–53